Between Contacts and Colonies

Between Contacts and Colonies

Archaeological Perspectives on the Protohistoric Southeast

Edited by
Cameron B. Wesson and Mark A. Rees

THE UNIVERSITY OF ALABAMA PRESS
Tuscaloosa

Copyright © 2002
The University of Alabama Press
Tuscaloosa, Alabama 35487-0380
All rights reserved

Typeface: Goudy and Goudy Sans

Library of Congress Cataloging-in-Publication Data

Southeastern Archaeological Conference (54th : 1997 : Baton Rouge, La.)
  Between contacts and colonies : archaeological perspectives on the protohistoric period Southeast / edited by Cameron B. Wesson and Mark A. Rees.
     p. cm.
Papers presented at a symposium held in 1997 during the 54th annual Southeastern Archaeological Conference, Baton Rouge, La.
Includes bibliographical references and index.
  ISBN 0-8173-1167-X (pbk. : alk. paper) — ISBN 0-8173-1253-6 (cloth : alk. paper)
  1. Indians of North America—Southern States—Antiquities—Congresses. 2. Indians of North America—Southern States—History—Congresses. 3. Southern States—Antiquities—Congresses.
I. Wesson, Cameron B., 1968–   II. Rees, Mark A. III. Title.
E78.S65 S653 1997
975'.01—dc21

2002005416

ISBN 978-0-8173-1167-4 (pbk. : alk. paper) — ISBN 978-0-8173-1253-4 (cloth : alk. paper)
ISBN 978-0-8173-8474-6 (electronic)

The University of Nebraska Press has generously granted permission for the use of extended quotations from *William Bartram on the Southeastern Indians,* edited and annotated by Gregory A. Waselkov and Kathryn E. Holland Braund. © 1995 by the University of Nebraska Press.

Contents

List of Illustrations   vii

Acknowledgments   ix

1. Protohistory and Archaeology: An Overview
   Cameron B. Wesson and Mark A. Rees   1

2. Human Ecology at the Edge of History
   Kristen J. Gremillion   12

3. Seasonality, Sedentism, Subsistence, and Disease in the Protohistoric: Archaeological versus Ethnohistoric Data along the Lower Atlantic Coast
   Rebecca Saunders   32

4. Caddoan Area Protohistory and Archaeology
   Timothy K. Perttula   49

5. William Bartram and the Archaeology of the Appalachian Summit
   Christopher B. Rodning   67

6. "As caves beneath the ground": Making Sense of Aboriginal House Form in the Protohistoric and Historic Southeast
   David J. Hally   90

7. Prestige Goods, Symbolic Capital, and Social Power in the Protohistoric Southeast
   Cameron B. Wesson   110

8. Warfare in the Protohistoric Southeast: 1500–1700
   David H. Dye   126

9. Elite Actors in the Protohistoric: Elite Identities and Interaction with Europeans in the Apalachee and Powhatan Chiefdoms
   John F. Scarry and Mintcy D. Maxham   142

10. Subsistence Economy and Political Culture in the
    Protohistoric Central Mississippi Valley
    Mark A. Rees   170

    References   199

    Contributors   261

    Index   263

Illustrations

3.1 Location of early historic peoples 34
4.1 Redrawn version of the "De Soto Map," ca. 1550 50
4.2 The distribution of Caddoan archaeological phases at initial contact 51
4.3 Early Caddoan structures near mound A at the George C. Davis site 55
4.4 Map of a Caddo village on the Red River 56
4.5 Redrawn version of Guillaume Delisle Map, 1972 64
5.1 Cherokee towns and the route of William Bartram 68
5.2 Archaeology in the upper Little Tennessee Valley, North Carolina 69
6.1 Post hole and feature map of King site winter house (structure 4) 93
6.2 Location of known late prehistoric and protohistoric sites with square, semi-subterranean structures 94
6.3 Atasi phase winter house at Fusihatchee site 95
6.4 Dallas phase winter house at Toqua site 96
6.5 Pisgah phase winter house at Warren Wilson site 97
6.6 Rembert phase winter house at Rucker's Bottom site 98
6.7 Irene phase winter house at Irene site 99
6.8 Rectangular summer house at King site 100
6.9 Circular house and rectangular summer house at the Sugar Creek site, central Georgia 101

6.10 Atasi phase summer house at Fusihatchee site   102

6.11 Late eighteenth-century Tallapoosa phase rectangular summer house at Fusihatchee site   104

6.12 Summer and winter/hot house structures at Chota-Tenasee site   106

7.1 Location of the Creeks during the Historic period   118

7.2 Central Alabama cultural chronology   119

7.3 Changes in burial goods distribution from Creek sites   120

7.4 Changes in Creek domestic architecture   121

7.5 Changes in Creek domestic storage features   122

9.1 Apalachee chiefdom and settlement distribution   146

9.2 Powhatan and neighboring Virginia chiefdoms   154

10.1 Locations of sites mentioned in the text   183

10.2 Map of the Upper Nodena site   184

10.3 Plan view of the Block B excavations at the Upper Nodena site   185

10.4 Percent NISP for faunal classes from various Mississippian sites   188

10.5 Percent NISP for major faunal classes from sites in the Central Mississippi Valley   189

10.6 Percent NISP for major faunal classes from four Caddo sites   191

10.7 Percent NISP for major faunal classes from Hayti bypass and Cahokia sites   193

Acknowledgments

The contributions to this volume were originally presented in 1997 in a symposium, Protohistory and Archaeology: Advances in Interdisciplinary Research, at the 54th Annual Meeting of the Southeastern Archaeological Conference, Baton Rouge, Louisiana. Although several participants in the symposium were unable to take part in this volume, the editors and contributors wish to acknowledge their valuable role in stimulating debate on the archaeology of the protohistoric Southeast. In addition, we would like to acknowledge the insightful remarks of the symposium discussants, Jerald T. Milanich and Tristram R. Kidder.

Moreover, we would like to acknowledge the kind assistance of Shannon Freeman and James Wall, who reviewed selected portions of the volume and offered perceptive comments on its structure and direction. Many thanks are also extended to Ross Hassig and Paul Minnis for their helpful suggestions regarding the editorial process. Maria Aviles and Johanna Rees are to be lauded for their unwavering personal support during the many stages of this book's production.

We would also like to thank two anonymous reviewers for providing comments that helped clarify the general focus of the volume and its constituent chapters. Many thanks are due as well to the staff of the University of Alabama Press and to Sandra Williamson. Finally, we want to thank the individual authors who contributed to this volume. Their endurance during the numerous professional changes and temporal delays experienced by the editors during the production of this volume is greatly appreciated.

1 / Protohistory and Archaeology
An Overview

Cameron B. Wesson and Mark A. Rees

Initial contacts between Native Americans and Europeans set in motion a process of acute cultural transformation for indigenous peoples. These contacts were followed by widespread death from European-introduced diseases, displacement of local populations, reorganization of existing political economies, introduction of new material goods and technologies, and the emergence of political confederacies and ethnic identities. Although these events were profound and widespread, scholars interested in documenting the nature of post-contact Native American culture change are faced with several daunting research challenges. One of the principal impediments is a paucity of historic documents relating to the period immediately after initial Native American-European contacts. For most Native American peoples of the Southeast, almost two centuries passed between their first interactions with Europeans in the sixteenth century and the production of detailed historical documents in the eighteenth century (a temporal span commonly referred to as the Protohistoric period). Some accounts date from the opening moments of contact, others from almost two hundred years later, and there is little in the way of historical documentation to connect these disparate depictions of Native American cultures.

In addition to troublesome gaps in the historical record, the archaeological record presents its own difficulties with regard to protohistoric culture change. Chief among these impediments are divisions within the discipline of archaeology that have marginalized protohistoric studies. Theoretical and methodological boundaries between prehistoric and historic archaeologies have made studies of protohistoric phenomena problematic. Prehistoric archaeology has a traditional bias toward "untainted" pre-contact cultures, while historic archaeology has been biased toward indigenous cultures with suitable historical records (Beaudry 1988; Deagan 1988; Euler 1972:202; Galloway 1993:101; C. Hudson and Tesser 1994a; Lightfoot 1995; Trigger 1982:13, 1985:118; W. R. Wood 1990). Such disciplinary divisions, coupled with other research obstacles, have limited archaeological and historical inquiry into protohistoric culture change, resulting in a protohistoric Southeast which was, until recently, a liminal terra incognita. As C. Hudson and Tesser (1994a:2) point out, the Protohistoric period represents "the forgotten centuries" of southeastern studies, lying somewhere between contact and colonization.

Research addressing the cultural dynamics of the Protohistoric period has accelerated dramatically with the intense scholarly attention directed at the recent quincentennial anniversary of Columbus's first voyage to the Americas. Growing in number particularly over the past decade, archaeological studies of the Protohistoric period are now at the forefront of the field (Galloway 1993, 1997a; C. Hudson 1997; C. Hudson and Tesser 1994b; Lightfoot 1995; Lightfoot et al. 1998; Rogers and Wilson 1993; B. D. Smith 1990; D. H. Thomas 1990, 1991; Trigger 1985:116; Wilcox and Massey 1981; W. R. Wood 1990). Archaeologists are now focusing on the Protohistoric period throughout the Southeast, armed with an improved understanding of the complexity of culture contact situations and important new theoretical paradigms that attempt to reveal Native American perspectives on protohistoric culture change.

This volume presents current research examining protohistoric Native American culture change across the Southeast. Each contribution presents a unique perspective on protohistoric culture change, revealing how the knowledgeable use of historical documents, innovative archaeological research, and emerging theoretical perspectives in anthropology can be combined to better understand this crucial period. The remainder of this chapter examines the theoretical and methodological factors that have led to the present state of protohistoric studies in southeastern archaeology and places the individual contributions to this volume within this framework. In conclusion, we propose an approach to protohistoric culture change built on the analysis of indigenous political dynamics that synthesizes culture historical and processual explanations.

Archaeology, Ethnohistory, and Protohistory

Archaeologists and historians have long acknowledged that European contact acutely affected Native American cultures (Brasser 1978; Crane 1981; Hickerson 1997; Phillips et al. 1951:419–421). However, two diametrically opposed interpretations of these effects have permeated anthropological research for the majority of this century. An earlier generation of scholars downplayed the disruption European contacts represented to native cultures, while a later generation has exaggerated these same impacts. These differences in interpretation appear to be based more on the theoretical approaches and a priori assumptions of individual researchers than on discernable differences in the archaeological or historical records.

Observing these changes from the theoretical perspective of acculturation that dominated their era, earlier scholars viewed Native American culture change as the shift from indigenous practices to the adoption of Euroamerican cultural practices.

Studying protohistoric culture change was limited to charting the decline of indigenous practices and the rise of European-introduced customs (Corkran 1967; Crane 1981; Swanton 1928, 1946). Native American cultures of the eighteenth and nineteenth centuries were thus seen as perfect and unbroken analogs of their prehistoric ancestors. Based partly on the nineteenth-century notion that native cultures were static prior to European contact, this view suggests a lack of creative intellect among native peoples and denies them an active, causal role in the process of culture change (Cusick 1998:134–139; Trigger 1982:11). Archaeological evidence was used to support these views by demonstrating that native cultures had changed very little over millennia. The changes that were observed in the archaeological record were usually attributed to migration, diffusion, or adaptation rather than to internal sociopolitical dynamics (Galloway 1993:89–92; Trigger 1982:11)

A contrasting view to that of the acculturationists is found in the work of scholars who view the Protohistoric period as an era of cultural collapse (Dunnell 1991; Ramenofsky 1987, 1990; Sheldon 1974; M. T. Smith 1987, 1994b). This collapse is thought to have been so profound as to make comparisons between prehistoric and historic southeastern cultures impossible (Dobyns 1983, 1991; Dunnell 1991). Scholars who take this position propose instead that we treat prehistoric and historic Native Americans as distinct (and disparate) cultures. As Dunnell (1991:573) contends, "modern Indians, both biologically and culturally, are very much a phenomenon of contact and derive from only a small fraction of peoples and cultural variability of the early sixteenth century." Thus, historic Native Americans are seen as fundamentally different and culturally distinct from their predecessors (Lightfoot 1995:202). From this perspective, stark divisions between pre-contact and post-contact cultures make the diachronic analysis of protohistoric culture change virtually impossible.

Dramatic changes most certainly occurred during the Protohistoric period, but these changes (like those for other non-Western cultures contacted by Europeans) did not completely sever native peoples from their pre-contact cultural predecessors (Deagan 1988; Dirks 1992; Wolf 1982). Views of essential continuity have also been exposed as naïve, unrealistic, and essentially ethnocentric (Galloway 1993). Trigger (1985:117) argues that "gratuitous revisionism is no less misleading than the discredited assumption of cultural immutability that it seeks to replace." In the end, both approaches inhibit our understanding of indigenous social and political change and disenfranchise Native Americans from their own histories.

Much of the confusion in these approaches stems from the improper use of historical documents. Unfamiliarity with the complexities of textual analysis and unwillingness to question textual authority have plagued the use of historical documents in protohistoric research (Galloway 1993, 1997a; Greenblatt 1993:xvii). As W. R. Wood (1990:101–102) notes, "too many archaeologists use historical records as they would . . . modern monographs—except that they tend . . . to be more critical of the modern data than of the older materials." Greenblatt (1993:viii) contends that traditional interpretations of Native Americans formulated on the basis of early historical documents render these peoples "either as Hobbesian pagans in a state of nature, condemned to lives that are solitary, nasty, brutish, and short, or as mute, naive, miserable victims, condemned only to deception and enslavement." Colonial encounters and Native American cultures were often misrepresented in European writing, resulting in static depictions of native peoples assimilated within local landscapes (Dirks 1992). As Dirks (1992:2–3) asserts, "Claims about nationality necessitated notions of culture that marked groups off from one another in essential ways, uniting language, race, geography, and history in a single concept. Colonialism encouraged and facilitated new claims of this kind, re-creating Europe and its others through its histories of conquest and rule." In either case, the end result is a misuse of historical documents, together with a further distancing of Native Americans from a history of sociopolitical process (Sahlins 1993).

Historical documents have traditionally been employed in archaeological research through use of the direct historical approach (Heizer 1941; Steward 1940, 1942; Strong 1935, 1940; VanStone 1970; W. R. Wedel 1938, 1940). Research based on this approach has often resulted in the application of a timeless, antihistorical ethnographic present onto Native American cultures, a continuation of earlier flawed attempts to understand the prehistoric-historic transition (Galloway 1993). Although the use of historical documents presents a significant challenge to archaeologists, appropriate techniques for using these sources may be effectively wedded to archaeological research (Galloway 1993, 1997a; Stahl 1993; Trigger 1982, 1985, 1986; H. R. Wood 1990). Written documents may provide a wealth of information that can be employed in the critical analysis of protohistoric phenomena.

In truth, Native American societies experienced dramatic political and economic changes prior to the arrival of the first Europeans. Before European contacts, Native American societies were not stable exemplars of evolutionary types existing in states of perpetual sociocultural stasis, as theorists traditionally maintained. Native cultural practices were indeed radically transformed by social actions throughout the Prehistoric, Protohistoric, and Historic periods (Trigger 1985). However, the nature of these changes cannot be inferred from general ethnological principles alone (Trigger 1982:13). In addition, although historical documents may reveal the effects of many of these changes, they do not allow for an unambiguous understanding of these societies prior to contact with Europeans. The study of Native American societies prior to and during initial contacts is primarily an archaeological rather than an ethnographic problem (Trigger 1982, 1985, 1986), and archaeologists play an indispensable role in understanding the nature of protohistoric Native American culture change.

Although the impact of acculturationist approaches to Native American culture change has been profound, anthropologists working within theoretical traditions rooted in more historical perspectives have also had an impact (Linton 1940; Redfield et al. 1936; Spicer 1962; Trigger 1982:4). Their interest in interdisciplinary approaches to Native American history ultimately led to the development of the field of ethnohistory (Brain et al. 1974; C. Hudson 1973; Sturtevant 1966). As a result of increased interest in anthropological histories, ethnohistorical research has grown in importance, and the willingness to use historical documents has intensified (e.g., essays in C. Hudson and Tesser 1994b; Rogers and Wilson 1993; D. H. Thomas 1990, 1991).

There is much to be learned about Native American protohistory, and it is only with a more detailed understanding of this period of transition that we can begin to examine indigenous sociopolitical processes within specific cultural contexts. Despite these limitations, Trigger (1985:118) states that "archaeology offers the only hope for defining a substantial baseline for studying the initial changes brought about by European contact. In eastern North America, archaeological data from the sixteenth century are vital for understanding the nature of native cultures prior to the arrival of the Europeans and of the changes that followed." Whatever reservations archaeologists have concerning the incorporation of historical documents into their studies, it is apparent that the Protohistoric period is crucial to achieving an anthropological understanding of the Native American past. By uniting archaeological data and historical documents the borders of a historically relevant, archaeological anthropology can be expanded.

Prehistoric and Historic Archaeologies

Although the separation of prehistoric and historic archaeologies compromises the study of sociopolitical processes and long-term social change, this division has a long history in North American archaeology and is rooted in a segregated view of humanity (Lightfoot 1995:200; Trigger 1982, 1985, 1986). Native Americans and their villages were considered separate and distinct entities from Europeans and Euroamerican settlements, and their study seemed to require very different methodological and theoretical approaches (Lightfoot 1995:202). While prehistoric archaeologists were developing methods and theories appropriate for the investigation of Native Americans, historical archaeologists began to study colonial European material culture (I. W. Brown 1994:59–62; Ferguson and Whitehead 1992:5; Watson 1990:46). Although the availability or absence of historical documents entails distinct methodologies, the epistemological detachment of prehistory from history has had adverse consequences, not the least of which has been the distancing of archaeological theory from historical anthropology.

Paralleling the fragmentation of anthropology into a four-field discipline, arguments for maintaining distinct archaeological divisions have continued. Historical archaeologists have argued that their subject matter is a separate intellectual field from prehistoric archaeology since historical archaeology has not benefited from the application of the methodological and theoretical approaches of prehistorians (Beaudry 1988:1; Deagan 1988; Lightfoot 1995; Mrozowski 1993:107–109). Prehistoric archaeologists who have been critical of ethnographic analogy and the use of the direct historical approach represent an intellectual tradition that relegates history and historical inquiry to "mere chronicle" and overly particularistic research (see Dunnell 1991:573; Leonard 1993; Ramenofsky 1991a, 1991b; Taylor 1983 [1948]). Following the incisive theoretical critique of Walter Taylor (1983 [1948]), the "New Archaeology" of the 1960s unjustly caricatured historical studies as exclusively event-oriented, preoccupied with "inadequate propositions" about the past, and generally lacking in anthropological significance (Binford 1968). Advocates of the new archaeology pursued the goals of evolutionary anthropology through the methodology of a positivist science (Binford 1962; Watson et al., 1971). A central focus of this research was cultural process, a synchronic concept independent of ethnographic context and divorced from long-term historical development (Brumfiel 1992).

This normative, homogenizing culture concept has had a profound impact on interpretations of prehistory, most notably in neo-evolutionary typologies of Native American societies. It has also produced a rampant misunderstanding of historical perspectives in archaeology (Trigger 1978:2–36). James Deetz, whose dissertation is often regarded as an early example of processualism, has been critical of the New Archaeology for its failure to address the simultaneously material and ideological nature of cultural processes through time (see Deetz 1960, 1988; Willey and Sabloff 1993:234–35). Deetz (1988:19) suggests that culture history and culture process approaches are similar in that both use material culture as a basis to learn about the past. A culture history that moves beyond chronology and diffusion to the interpretation of cultural production and sociopolitical process is clearly more anthropologically and historically relevant than a perspective that posits the "adaptive context" of a "total cultural system" (e.g., Sahlins 1985; cf. Binford 1962). In this light, according to Deetz (1988:20), "the distinction between prehistory and history fades into insignificance; it all deals with the past, and only the methods used on different data bases show a difference."

In some ways, southeastern archaeology was sheltered from this theoretical divisiveness through its contributions and adherence to culture history approach (Dunnell 1990). Despite recent criticisms of this approach (Dunnell 1990; Lyman et al. 1997; O'Brien et al. 1998), culture history has in fact recently enjoyed a resurgence, in part because of the production of more refined regional chronologies (see Barker and Pauketat 1992b; Knight and Steponaitis 1998). At the same time, cultural anthropologists studying political and social processes have returned to an earlier emphasis on the importance of history and historical development (Comaroff and Comaroff 1991, 1992; Friedman 1989, 1992; Gellner 1995; Roseberry 1989; Sahlins 1985; Wolf 1982; essays in Dirks 1992).

Within the last decade, southeasternists have made significant contributions to "substantive issues" in North American archaeology (cf. Dunnell 1990:17), most notably with regard to the origins of agriculture and the rise and fall of social complexity (Anderson 1990, 1994a, 1996a, 1996b; Fritz 1992; Fritz and Kidder 1993; Kidder 1992; Knight and Steponaitis 1998; Pauketat 1994; Pauketat and Emerson 1997b; C. M. Scarry 1993a, 1993b; Steponaitis 1991; articles in J. F. Scarry 1996d;). It is no coincidence that many of these theoretical advances have been made not from a stance of culture-process as law-like generalizations, but from improved knowledge of regional culture historical development. Indigenous political dynamics during various periods of European contact, the production of new ethnic identities, resistance to colonialism and missionization, and articulation with the capitalist political economy are issues relevant not only to southeastern archaeology but to the further advancement of anthropology as a social science (e.g., Barker 1992; Deagan 1990; DePratter 1991, 1994; Dye 1990, 1994, 1995; Galloway 1994, 1995; Knight 1994b; Milanich 1994b, 1995; J. F. Scarry 1994b).

Perhaps it is time, then, to rethink the culture historical approach in southeastern archaeology in a framework free from the earlier constraints of hyper-diffusionism, direct historical analogy, and historical particularism. This will obviate both the chronological preoccupation of pre-1960s culture history and the overly relativistic tendencies of some post-processualists. A synthesis of political process, social dynamics, and historical development holds the potential to reassert the relevance of southeastern archaeology within American archaeology and anthropology, as well as broaden the concept of Americanist culture history (Barker and Pauketat 1992a; Pauketat and Emerson 1997a:278). In short, a culture historical approach is alive and well in southeastern archaeology, although it is undergoing substantial transformation and is still in need of cohesive theoretical integration (cf. Lyman et al. 1997).

Instead of focusing on particular historical events, this new culture history is concerned with indigenous social dynamics and political process. This approach is informed by comparative data and theory from historical anthropology that place human agency and power relations at the forefront of analyses (Lightfoot 1995). Some proponents of this approach suggest the use of the temporal scales of long-term and medium-term historical processes as a heuristic device for in understanding political dynamics, social reproduction, and cultural transformation (Cobb 1991; Galloway 1997a; Hodder 1987; essays in Bintliff 1991; articles in Knapp 1992). Rather than advocating historical particularism or structuralist historiography, these studies situate social change within different historical contexts and temporal scales, effectively drawing together the concerns of processualism for external constraints and post-processual attention to internal sociological variables (Kosso 1991; Preucel 1991; Trigger 1991; Whitley 1992).

Such studies need not cede to evolutionism or eco-functionalism a determinative role in social change. Instead, the collective agency of individuals should be examined as an intrinsic factor in historical development. McGuire (1992a:118–119) argues that such an approach allows "a discussion of the relative importance of human agency, structure, and culture in making human history," and that "a true dialectical understanding of the process of change is best achieved when investigators start by examining power (the universal ability of all humans to act) and ask how power shapes all social relations." Through an examination of the changing contexts of power in native societies it is possible for archaeologists to begin to examine the role of human agency, sociopolitical process, and ideology in protohistory.

Lying at the epistemological boundaries of history and prehistory, protohistoric studies are an ideal launching pad for this brand of processual culture history. Referred to as "ethnohistoric archaeology" by Brain (1988:8–11), the study of protohistory involves multiple lines of inquiry at the juncture of archaeology, historiography, and ethnography (see also Brain et al. 1974). An interdisciplinary perspective is thus crucial in bridging the temporal and theoretical constraints imposed by different intellectual traditions. The potential for protohistoric research to mend the rift between prehistoric and historical archaeologies ultimately lies in the transitional, syncretic nature of its subject matter.

The relevance of protohistoric archaeology to an anthropological understanding of Native American pasts is clear. With the implementation of the Native American Graves Protection and Repatriation Act of 1990, archaeologists have had to answer directly to a Native American constituency for the first time (Deloria 1995). The same social and political issues that led to the present state of relations between archaeologists and Native Americans also impose a collective ethical responsibility to address the protohistoric transition more fully (Trigger 1982:9). Without this ethical basis, American archaeology runs the risk of alienating its potentially most important audience. Both archaeologists and Native Americans stand to benefit from a more detailed and socially relevant knowledge of culture history.

Organization of the Volume

These theoretical developments represent a challenge to archaeologists engaged in examining the historical diversity of southeastern North America. By pursuing multiple lines of inquiry, new interpretive frameworks can be developed that will begin to address the paradigmatic divisions between traditional archaeological models of European and Native American cultures. History is no longer reserved for literate European societies but should be seen as an undeniable aspect of all cultural traditions (i.e., Wolf 1982). Thus individual chapters in this volume are organized around different thematic concerns, including cultural ecology, warfare, architecture, subsistence, disease, trade, the construction of social identities, and political economy. Numerous sites from across the southeast are discussed, with individual chapters assessing archaeological data from Alabama, Arkansas, Georgia, Florida, North Carolina, Tennessee, Texas, and Virginia.

In chapter 2, Kristen Gremillion examines ecological changes among indigenous populations during the initial and indirect phases of European contact, showing that these changes are best examined using a multidisciplinary research strategy. She contends that archaeological, environmental, and historic records of ecological relationships differ in regard to processes of creation and epistemological significance, and that each requires a distinct interpretive approach. By assuring that evidence is rigorously evaluated and explicitly linked to hypothetical explanations, Gremillion demonstrates that archaeologists can synthesize disparate sources of information about human ecology and history. She uses paleoethnobotanical studies of protohistoric populations in the Southeast to illustrate the potential of this approach.

In chapter 3, Rebecca Saunders looks at the effects of contact between Europeans and Native Americans along the lower Atlantic coast. Although her case draws more heavily on the Historic period than other contributions to this volume, her research demonstrates the difficulties of bridging the protohistoric-historic transition. Saunders contends that the archaeological applicability of historical documents describing these contacts can be frustrating, given their biases and frequent discrepancies. She considers four specific research questions regarding European–Native American relations: site seasonality, sedentism, subsistence strategies, and the timing and effects of epidemics. Reviewing archaeological and documentary evidence, and considering the epistemological biases of each as she evaluates these issues, Saunders concludes that combined use of the archaeological and historical records can provide critical new insight into the Protohistoric period.

In chapter 4, Timothy Perttula considers Caddoan protohistory. The Caddo experienced a wide range of cultural changes during protohistory, yet many areas of their culture appear to have remained essentially unaltered. Perttula compares documentary evidence of Caddoan communities throughout protohistory, demonstrating the nature of cultural continuities, discontinuities, and sociopolitical relationships. He presents a complex picture of protohistoric Caddoan cultural traditions in which political leaders played decisive roles.

Christopher Rodning explores, in chapter 5, the contributions of the eighteenth-century travel journal of William Bartram to studies in southern Appalachian archaeology. He traces Bartram's travels through the historic Cherokee homelands in the southern Appalachians and considers how Bartram's writing complements the archaeology of the Little Tennessee River Valley and surrounding areas. Drawing upon Bartram's vivid descriptions of the Cherokee countryside, Rodning develops a strategy for blending archaeological and written evidence in anthropological studies of native peoples. He proposes an enriched perspective on local cultural landscapes that expands previous archaeological and ethnohistorical interpretations.

In chapter 6, David Hally examines diversity in late prehistoric and protohistoric domestic architecture. Euroamerican descriptions of Native American domestic structures in the eastern portion of the Southeast from the sixteenth to the nineteenth centuries present a confusing and inconsistent picture of what these structures were like. Archaeological evidence from the sixteenth century indicates that this confusion and inconsistency is partly the result of regional diversity in aboriginal house form and partly the result of changes in house form during the nearly 300-year period of protohistory. Hally demonstrates how archaeological and documentary evidence can be synthesized to explain the changes.

Cameron Wesson examines sociopolitical change in chapter 7, challenging the idea that indigenous people were powerless to shape protohistoric culture change. Rather than viewing the Protohistoric period as an era of collapse, Wesson advocates the view that protohistoric sociopolitical change is best characterized as an intensification of competition between social segments for sociopolitical power. He contends that the changes taking place in protohistoric southeastern societies were more internally driven than previous research has considered.

In chapter 8, David Dye discusses dramatic trends in protohistoric Mississippian warfare, emphasizing its different manifestations in the early Protohistoric period and the late Protohistoric. He specifically examines changes and continuities in warfare and military strategies as they relate to local and regional political dynamics, and outlines the military roles of chiefly elites in terms of changing power and shifting cultural contexts. Dye's analysis demonstrates the capacity of warfare as a major transformative element in Native American sociopolitical institutions.

John Scarry and Mintcy Maxham consider the creation of elite social identities and interaction with Europeans in chapter 9. European exploration and colonization had a profound impact on the native peoples of the Eastern Woodlands, but European-native interactions and their consequences were also strongly influenced by native activity. Native elites maintained or enhanced their social and political positions by negotiating social identities, and throughout the Protohistoric and Historic periods their efforts affected the nature of interactions with Europeans and ultimately the fate of elite identities and native societies. Scarry and Maxham contrast the Powhatan and Apalachee, focusing on the nature of elite identities, elite political strategies, European responses to those strategies, and their immediate and long-term consequences in protohistory.

In chapter 10, Mark Rees examines native polities in the protohistoric Central Mississippi Valley. Noting that sociopolitical complexity in the Central Mississippi

Valley during the late prehistoric-protohistoric transition has traditionally been interpreted as a terminal Mississippian florescence at the onset of European exploration and subsequent demographic upheaval, he suggests that overemphasis of neo-evolutionary types and earlier culture historical concepts obstructs further understanding of regional political dynamics. Rees's analysis of subsistence economy based on evidence from the Upper Nodena site substantiates limited documentary evidence of regional political culture. His integration of historical and processual approaches sheds light on native political development and decline, and provides an anthropological perspective widely applicable to the archaeological study of protohistory.

Rather than demonstrating a coherent paradigmatic approach to the study of protohistory, the studies in this volume represent a variety of approaches to the study of the protohistoric Southeast. What unites these very different essays is a concern with broadening our interpretation of Native American culture change during the centuries between the first contacts and the appearance of detailed descriptions of indigenous peoples. Moreover, all the contributors focus on protohistoric culture change from a perspective based on the experience of Native American communities and social actors. The results transcend earlier approaches to post-contact culture change, illustrating the variable protohistoric experiences of individual Native American peoples in the Southeast. As C. Hudson and Tesser (1994a:13) contend, "Historians, archaeologists, and anthropologists are beginning to see the need for a more interdisciplinary approach in research on these forgotten centuries. Debate will continue for some time. But once the dust has settled, and once enough progress has been made in working out the details of the vast changes that occurred during this time, a new synthesis of the social history of the Southeast will be written." It is hoped that the present volume will help advance southeastern archaeology toward this laudable goal.

2 / Human Ecology at the Edge of History

Kristen J. Gremillion

The body of literature on the archaeology and ethnohistory of the Protohistoric period in the Southeast has received some important additions in recent years (Clayton et al. 1993; Dye 1989; Dye and Brister 1986; M. T. Smith 1987; Waselkov 1989a). Relatively few of these studies, however, examine in detail the ecological aspects of indirect contact between European and Native American populations, nor do they specifically address the potential role of documentary evidence in the reconstruction of prehistoric human ecology. The intense level of interest among archaeologists in the economic and sociopolitical role of maize agriculture in the development and decline of Mississippian polities (Anderson et al. 1995; Muller 1997; Muller and Stephens 1991; Rindos and Johannessen 1991; C. M. Scarry 1986, 1993a, 1993b; C. M. Scarry and Steponaitis 1997) has not been matched by a comparable drive to understand the ecological impact of European contact on these same societies or their immediate descendants. Certainly there have been some important advances in this area of investigation (Gremillion 1989, 1993a, 1995; Gremillion and Reitz 1997; Hammett 1992; Ruhl 1993; J. F. Scarry 1991; Waselkov 1997), but most of these studies address the dietary and economic consequences of direct and sustained interaction between Native Americans and Europeans.

However, greater attention to the Protohistoric period in this regard is warranted given its unique vantage point for the study of the dynamics of ecological change in the past. In the interior Southeast, the period from the de Soto *entrada* to the encroachment of European settlers as far as the Appalachian foothills (ca. 1529 to 1750) was one in which native societies were exposed to novel influences yet were somewhat buffered from the full force of contact with colonial systems (Waselkov 1989a). This situation represents a natural experiment of the sort not usually available to historians or archaeologists. An extended Protohistoric period offers the opportunity to compare the behavioral responses of southeastern groups to a varied array of environmental changes.

During the period of indirect contact, the European presence was felt primarily through the impact of epidemic diseases and new connections to a complex market economy. Plants and animals that came to the attention of the indigenous peoples were merely a subset of those that actually came ashore on the North American continent, and the influence of European populations on the distribution of local resources was geographically limited and for the most part of small magnitude. Subsistence change was selective rather than systemic (Gremillion 1993a). In contrast, two centuries later, the environment had altered radically with the incursion of white settlers and overt competition for land and other resources. European agricultural and stock raising practices caused widespread land clearance and facilitated the spread of introduced weeds and crops. With ecological relationships so modified by rapid and uncontrollable events, options became limited. Successful subsistence adaptations required systemic changes.

The Protohistoric period also offers an unusually well documented glimpse of the economic and ecological processes by which Old World plants and animals colonized the Southeast. Some species proved to be so well adapted to the southeastern landscape that they established natural populations well in advance of European settlement. Of those that were dependent on human care, only a limited suite of Old World domesticates found lasting niches within indigenous subsistence systems.

These observations raise important questions about processes of cultural change: How readily are foods and dietary habits transmitted between populations in the absence of direct contact and the cultural information that goes along with it? What economic and ecological characteristics seem to have influenced decisions to accept or reject novel plants and animals? To what degree is apparent conservatism in subsistence patterns simply a function of patterns of local availability governed by the geography of trade routes and mechanisms of exchange?

No study of change can afford to ignore the initial state against which later conditions are to be measured. The protohistoric interval helps in establishing such a baseline by supplementing the archaeological record with written documentation of traditional subsistence practices, vegetation, and fauna. Unlike other periods, it offers a twofold advantage with respect to indigenous ecological dynamics: the ability to exploit ethnohistorical as well as archaeological sources of evidence, and an environmental situation as yet only lightly impacted by the European presence.

Integration of Archaeological and Historical Data

Although the application of both documentary and archaeological data to environmental research is essential for addressing a number of important research questions, the potential of such an approach remains incompletely realized (Deagan 1996:363). Perhaps historians and archaeologists alike feel somewhat uncomfortable outside their own research territories (Galloway 1986). Certainly there are many opportunities on both sides for uncritical use of data and theories, as is always the case when disciplinary boundaries are crossed. The contrasts between research strategies striving for verification and those emphasizing interpretation may interfere with collaboration between specialists in the two fields, as it does among historians (Iggers 1997). In practical terms, the Protohistoric raises particularly troublesome methodological issues, such as the validity of extrapolation from non-contemporary written source material (thereby raising the specter of the myth of the "ethnographic present" and its illusion that non-Western societies have no history; see Wolf 1982). Researchers may also have been discouraged by the fact that there is relatively little documentation of botanical and zoological specifics for the Protohistoric proper, and that which does exist is frustratingly vague and uneven, reflecting the preoccupations of economic opportunists rather than naturalists. This situation adds to the appeal of the much richer records of later periods, when botanically knowledgeable travelers and naturalists made numerous forays into the southeastern interior.

Despite the very different methodological requirements of artifact-based as compared to text-based research, both archaeologists and historians must contend with the problem of using present-day phenomena to reconstruct past behavior. The researcher using multiple lines of evidence must apply the same level of rigor to evaluating the context of both sorts of records, even though the problems of interpretation and analytic techniques are specific to each field. The information contained in the documentary record is a secondhand (at best) report; similarly, the data generated by material assemblages offers an imperfect record of the phenomena of interest.

Although texts, unlike artifacts, do in a sense "speak for themselves," they may lie. The archaeological record is unintended and therefore not capable of "lying," yet it is removed from past reality by other biases, such as differential preservation. Historical "facts," like archaeological artifacts, have "proveniences" that give them meaning. They cannot be, nor can artifacts be, simply "dug up" (P. E. Hoffman 1993:13).

The problem of observer bias, a historiographic universal with special implications for ethnohistory (Brettell 1986), demands the critical evaluation of source material. Archaeologists have come under fire by historians for neglecting this essential task (Galloway 1986; P. E. Hoffman 1993), which is no less important for investigating ecological change and subsistence behavior than it is for compiling information on ritual life and ideology—aspects of culture that are more likely to trigger an observer's cultural biases. In fact, the record of vegetation and plant use for the protohistoric Southeast is anything but straightforward and should not be taken at face value, although much useful information exists.

In this paper, I explore some of the methodological issues that face archaeologists who wish to incorporate historical data sources into their investigations of changing relationships between human groups and the natural environment in the protohistoric Southeast. I first discuss the nature of the historical and archaeological data relevant to the human ecology of the protohistoric Southeast, with particular attention to documentary sources, some of which may be unfamiliar to archaeologists. I then illustrate the application of this approach to documenting the introduction of Old World crops and weeds and explaining their ecological and cultural consequences. Throughout I try to show how documentary evidence can be integrated into the type of scientific format of explanation favored by Americanist archaeologists.

Historical Documentation of Human Ecology in the Southeast

The following discussion highlights documentary sources that are particularly useful for the reconstruction of ecological conditions in the Southeast during the period of initial and indirect contact between Native Americans and Europeans. It is selective in being restricted to documents that were originally written in or that have been translated into English. However, it should convey some sense of their relative strengths and weaknesses as sources of ecological information and of the diversity of perspectives from which Europeans wrote about the human landscape of the Southeast.

Documents in Context

Spanish Exploration of the Interior (1529-1540)

The earliest explorations into the southeastern interior were sponsored by the Spanish crown and reflect the expansionist and economic goals of that polity. Although colonization and missionization of the natives provided ultimate justification for such ventures, their immediate objectives were to control and subdue native populations and obtain wealth. Accounts of the first expeditions, such as de Soto's in 1529–1540, reflect these concerns in the form of "explorer's rhetoric"; only later reports of missions of colonization, such as that of Tristan de Luna in 1559, are significantly colored by "settlers' rhetoric" (P. E. Hoffman 1993:12). Yet whether distorted or not, firsthand accounts of interest to the ecologist are few; as conquerors, Spanish explorers had little interest in collecting ethnographic tidbits or botanizing along their swath of destruction through the Southeast (Elliott 1970:18–19).

Descriptions of local landscapes that do survive in early accounts of Spanish exploration tend to be sketchy at best, in contrast to their rather detailed accounts of native peoples. This bias reflects both the comparatively slow development of scholarly interest in natural history in Spain (K. Thomas 1983:281) and the demands of a literary tradition that typically celebrated the heroic deeds of individuals (Elliott 1970:20). Elements of the natural environment through which the invaders moved were reduced to their pragmatic implications: land was poor or fertile, riv-

16 / Kristen J. Gremillion

ers navigable or crossable (or not), and territory was populated or conveniently uninhabited. In contrast, some understanding or at least knowledge of the social forms and political dynamics of native southeasterners would have been a critical component of any effective strategy of conquest.

Despite this bias, accounts such as that of the Gentleman of Elvas, who accompanied de Soto, are rich in descriptions of certain anthropogenic components of southeastern landscapes. The Spaniards were continually preoccupied with the question of supplying a large military force with food, so they were especially attentive to the status of agricultural fields and storage facilities. Thus it is possible to glean some important details from Elvas regarding agricultural economy, such as the use of small outbuildings to store maize (Elvas 1993:87[1557]) and the fact that in December, maize was still standing in the snow-covered fields near one village. Elvas's description of productive stands of fruit and nut trees in open fields (1993:93 [1557]) includes specific types of plants that were used for food. Furthermore, the combination of an obviously nonnatural setting (economic trees grouped together in an anthropogenic habitat) and Elvas's assessment that the trees were wild suggests a relatively casual form of management, one that would have been unfamiliar to Europeans accustomed to a landscape that had been thoroughly transformed by millennia of human activity.

Thomas Harriot and John White at Roanoke (1585-1587)

The earliest detailed English sources are associated with the short-lived Roanoke colony of 1585–1587. Thomas Harriot's *Briefe and True Account* (1972 [1590]) was based on his 1585–1586 reconnaissance mission and was intended to persuade skeptical would-be colonists in the wake of the failure of the first Roanoke colony of 1585. Despite the propagandistic elements of the text, Harriot's descriptions and John White's drawings of people working at subsistence tasks are honestly rendered and meticulously detailed. Harriot was one of the foremost scholars of his day and took seriously the responsibility of making observations in accordance with scientific method and providing accurate descriptions (Hulton 1972). Harriot's interests in the Algonkian language and the economic possibilities of the prospective colony converged to produce unusually detailed descriptions of local plants, their Algonkian names, and their uses. John White's watercolors, translated more or less faithfully into engravings by Theodor de Bry, capture the variety of habitats in and around native settlements, illustrating the broad spectrum of ecological relationships that connected human groups to the natural environment in which they lived. For example, the illustration of the "Towne of Secota" shows separate plots for maize and pumpkins, dooryard gardens containing tobacco plants and sunflowers, a hunting party pursuing deer amidst a grove of fruit trees, and the village water source (a nearby stream). The questions that arise about the accuracy of such depictions need not be used simply to winnow out unreliable data; instead, they can be used to direct further research. Were Algonkian maize fields really so near the village, or has the artist collapsed the scale in order to include all the items of interest on a single page? To what extent do the orderly, rectangular garden plots shown in the picture reflect the English aesthetic preference during this period for straight rows and geometric shapes in cultivated landscapes (K. Thomas 1983:256)? Although they require careful evaluation, such depictions add much to our understanding of pre-contact land use by indigenous populations.

English Travelers, 1670-1728

Most of the English accounts of the interior postdate the first Spanish explorations by approximately a century and provide a valuable counterpoint to them in both content and motive. Sources that predate 1670 (the establishment of Charles Town as the primary source of English goods for interior native communities) reflect a protohistoric situation of cultural contact in which interior groups had some access to European goods. These goods came primarily from Spanish sources by way of Native American trade intermediaries (Waselkov 1989a) and may have included some introduced plants and animals. Sources dating to between 1670 and about the mid-eighteenth century report on societies that had experienced an influx of trade goods and variable levels of direct contact with Europeans but did not yet have Euroamerican colonists as neighbors.

Because they are later in time than the initial Spanish texts, English accounts sometimes include descriptions of the distribution of introduced plants and the attitudes of native people toward them. These can be quite valuable for documenting the spread of exotics, particularly if used in conjunction with archaeological evidence. Narratives by travelers such as John Lawson, who visited the Coastal Plain and Piedmont of the Carolinas in 1701 (Lawson 1967 [1709]), are more likely than early Spanish sources to reflect some botanical knowledge and the keen interest of the naturalist (whether professional or amateur) in unfamiliar plants and animals. The descriptions and illustrations of trained naturalists such as Mark Catesby, who recorded the flora and fauna of South Carolina and Florida during the 1720s, are particularly valuable for their accuracy, though they may not deal specifically with the ethnobiology of local groups (Catesby 1771).

Some expeditions from the English colonies, though not planned with natural history in mind, nevertheless lent themselves to the collection of ecological information. For example, William Byrd's task of surveying the disputed boundary line between Virginia and North Carolina in 1728 required careful attention to the distribution of trees (which were used as reference points by surveyors) and other landscape features. The progress of Byrd's surveying party was interrupted by fires that had been set by natives (W. Byrd 1967:228, 284 [1929]), a widespread practice that served to increase the productivity of natural habitats (Day 1953; Hammett 1992). Because such travels into frontier territory were obliged to rely for their provisions on native guides and their hunting skills, expedition members sometimes made note of the types of game they encountered and the methods used to procure and prepare them (e.g., W. Byrd 1967:150, 178, 196 [1929]).

In contrast to the Spanish, the Englishmen who described ecological features of the region were guided by a variety of motives that were most often related to enterprises of colonization and trade. John Lawson, like many other travel writers of the European expansionist period, wrote as a propagandist for settlement as well as to enlighten and to entertain (Adams 1980). This fact probably explains the apparently inflated yield figures reported in the *New Voyage* (Lindgren 1972). However, despite the biases of their authors, many early observations of interior southeastern groups by English travelers are recognized as largely accurate depictions (for example, the works of Lederer, Byrd, and William Beverley) (Randolph 1973). Many subjects of ecological significance that were deemed of sufficient interest to be recorded, such as food storage and preparation practices or anthropogenic landscape features, had little propagandistic potential. Even the most blatantly self-promoting narratives, such as that of John Smith (Hawke 1970), are likely to contain reasonably accurate descriptions of Native American subsistence practices, which were quite irrelevant to the writer's prestige.

A comparison of two English accounts will serve to illustrate how the purpose of reconnaissance missions into the southeastern interior shaped the resulting documents and affect their relevance for the ecologist. John Lederer, a German, made his first journey into the hinterlands of Virginia in 1669; later trips took him as far as the Catawba River in South Carolina and the Shenandoah Valley (both in 1670). Lederer hoped to locate a pass through the Appalachians, and he produced a record of his journey as an aid to future explorers. His account was published by William Talbot of London, who translated it into English from the original Latin. Talbot comments in his preface that he has checked Lederer's descriptions against others then extant of Native Americans, and has found them in agreement (which could of course simply mean that the authors had plagiarized each other). In keeping with his objectives, Lederer provides descriptions of physiography and vegetation that contain much informative detail about the anthropogenic characteristics of this still largely indigenous landscape. Describing his trek through the Piedmont and Coastal Plain, he frequently alludes to making a path through tangles of bushes and vines, a situation that generally indicates interruption of the forest canopy (either through natural or cultural means) (Lederer 1966: 2, 7 [1672]). Whereas Native American settlements were open and cleared of vegetation, tracts of forest in the mountains offered little hindrance to travel on horseback, suggesting a closed canopy that prevented the development of a thick understory (Lederer 1966:24 [1672]). Lederer also describes the storage of maize and other foods (p. 15), the processing of mast (p. 15), cultivation practices (p. 15), and the implementation of a botanical snakebite remedy (p. 22). His goal of assisting future explorers would have put accuracy of environmental description at a premium. Furthermore, Lederer is faithful to the empiricist tradition; though he speculates briefly about mineral wealth, he quickly admonishes himself with a reminder that he has sworn to report "things onely that I have seen in my Travels, I will deliver no Conjectures" (Lederer 1966:16 [1672]).

In contrast to Lederer, Edward Bland published parts of his travel journal in order to attract settlers to Virginia (Bland 1966 [1651]). His account of travels in the Coastal Plain in 1650 includes reports of flora, fauna, and topography that are clearly designed for practical application to economic ventures. Bland was attentive to the productive potential of the land, transportation logistics, and economic opportunities rather than to the inherent interest of features of natural history. In the course of advertising for prospective colonists, he does mention features of the landscape that reveal much about the human impact on it, such as the existence of abandoned Native American fields (Bland 1966:7 [1651]). However, Bland's account is less useful than that of Lederer for ecological research, both because of the scarcity of pertinent information and the greater likelihood of intentional distortion.

The French in the Lower Mississippi Valley, 1698–1734

The struggle for control of the Gulf Coast and lower Mississippi Valley being waged between major colonial powers during the early eighteenth century is a key contextual feature of French accounts of that period. Perhaps the best known of these is Le Page du Pratz's *Histoire de la Louisiane* (published in French in 1758 and in English as *The History of Louisiana* in 1763 and 1774), which has long been an important source of ethnographic information on the Natchez. Despite its flaws as a chronicle of early European settlement and the editorial liberties taken by the English edition of 1774 (Tregle 1975), much can be learned from Le Page's *History* about local ecological conditions and the subsistence practices of indigenous groups at a time when European settlement of the Gulf Coast was still tentative and contested. This situation is illustrated by the fact that on Le Page's arrival there in 1718, New Orleans consisted of a single palmetto-leaf hut marking the location for the new capital (Le Page du Pratz 1975:21 [1774]). By the time he began publishing his accounts, Le Page was much concerned with encouraging French colonization (Tregle 1975:xxv) and in that sense spoke as a propagandist. If his motives as a frontier opportunist and champion of French colonialism justify some scholarly concern about accuracy, these same motives also gave Le Page an especially sharp eye for details of landscape such as soils, vegetation, and animal life.

The journals of Iberville likewise pertain to France's initial settlement of the lower Mississippi Valley, but otherwise are very different in scope and intent from Le Page's *History*. Pierre Le Moyne d'Iberville was on a mission to locate the mouth of the Mississippi River and to establish fortifications that would secure it against

20 / Kristen J. Gremillion

incursions by the English or the Spanish (McWilliams 1981). The English were especially threatening as competitors, for by this time they had established a thriving peltry trade that reached well into the interior (Braund 1993; Usner 1992). These concerns are reflected in Iberville's terse descriptions of pertinent landscape features such as channel depth, soil drainage, and vegetation. Because such information was part of an official report on local conditions and colonization potential, there is reason to have confidence in its basic truthfulness even if some details (such as identifications of flora and fauna) may not be entirely accurate. Iberville's report also contains many scattered but informative details regarding Native American land use practices and the spread of introduced plants and animals.

Nomenclature in Historical Perspective

In exploring historical texts for reports of plant and animal life, inconsistent use of plant names is often a problem. Observers varied greatly in their knowledge of plant and animal terms (whether folk or scientific). It was not uncommon for the untrained observer to apply an existing name on the basis of superficial morphological similarity to some European species, which might or might not be taxonomically related. Reporting of names in indigenous languages (e.g., by Harriot) is quite valuable linguistically but often leaves us in the dark botanically (depending on the current status of the language) unless a thorough description is given. These issues are perhaps less troublesome where European observers are reporting familiar plants that had come into use among Native American groups, particularly when they have some botanical training. The widespread adoption of the Linnean taxonomic system during the 1750s and 1760s (K. Thomas 1983:85) resulted in greater consistency in the naming of plants observed by travelers. However, even scientific names have often been changed as a result of taxonomic revision following the strict rules of botanical and zoological nomenclature. The researcher must be familiar enough with these rules to search lists of synonyms in order to translate older Linnean species names into their current correct equivalents.

Colloquial names given by the less botanically knowledgeable chroniclers are helpful but frequently ambiguous. For example, Iberville recounts in his first journal the vegetation of a wooded island, which included "horse-beans like those of St. Domingue" (1981:39). In English, "horse-bean" is used for both *Canavalia* and *Vicia faba* (Vaughn and Geissler 1997). *Vicia* has been reported from a house structure at the original site of Mobile (Gremillion 1996b), a settlement that was not established until Iberville's third voyage in 1702. *Canavalia* beans are commonly grown in the West Indies, which might explain the reference to St. Domingue. Both are cultivated, so the appearance of either plant outside a garden would indicate some ability to naturalize and thus considerable ecological flexibility. There is also the possibility that Iberville made a mistake and was actually looking at a native wild legume with large pods. Unfortunately, we shall probably never know.

The need for a thorough analysis of historical context of scientific names is illustrated quite clearly in reports by Bernard Romans and William Bartram that *Dolichos* was an important food crop among the Creeks and Cherokees in the late eighteenth century (Swanton 1946:285–286). A search of taxonomic databases (International Association for Plant Taxonomy 1998; USDA Agricultural Research Service 1998) reveals that *Dolichos unguiculatus* L. (1753) and *Dolichos sinensis* L. (1754) are names that were used by Linnaeus to refer to the plant known today as *Vigna unguiculata* ssp. *unguiculata* (the cowpea or black-eyed pea). It seems likely that this is the plant Bartram refers to, in light of the success of the cowpea as a southern crop and its archaeological occurrence in a Creek village (Gremillion 1993a, 1995). However, Linnaeus's *Dolichos* also included *Dolichos lablab* L. (1753) and *Dolichospurpureus* L. (1763), which are today recognized as *Lablab purpureus* L. and known colloquially as the hyacinth bean or bonavist. Although this species seems less likely as a candidate for the crop grown by Creeks and Cherokees in the eighteenth century, the hyacinth bean is cultivated today in the United States and is naturalized in the southern states (Delorit and Gunn 1986). Lawson mentions the "Bonavis" as one of the legumes cultivated in Carolina (though not necessarily by natives) (Lawson 1967:82 [1709]).

Terms used for landscape features may also have changed in their usage over the centuries. While *savanna* and *marsh* (or the archaic *marish*) retain their meanings today (as grassland with sparse trees and wet grassland, respectively), *desert* does not. The frequent mention of deserts in travelers' accounts of the seventeenth and eighteenth centuries does not imply aridity or sparse vegetation as it does today. According to the Oxford English Dictionary, a now obsolete usage of *desert* is as "an uninhabited and uncultivated tract of country; a wilderness" and was once applied to any wild region, including forested ones. This definition is more economic than ecological, lumping together lands that have not been subjected to human modification and control irrespective of other characteristics.

The Archaeological Record of Human Ecology in the Southeast

The archaeological record of human ecology in the protohistoric Southeast consists largely of macrobotanical and macrofaunal remains from refuse deposits on archaeological sites. Often these collections are large and diverse, both because of the relatively sedentary settlement habits of most of the indigenous communities represented and the short time that has elapsed since deposition. The various issues involved in analyzing remains of this kind and interpreting the resulting data as evidence for subsistence and diet have been thoroughly reviewed elsewhere (e.g.,

Grayson 1984; Hastorf and Popper 1988; Hudson 1993; Lyman 1982; Pearsall 1989; Yarnell 1982) and pertain to prehistoric and historic sites alike.

Among introduced plants, the peach (*Prunus persica*) is surely the best represented, relative to its actual use, because of the durability of its seeds and tendency to carbonize well. In contrast, seeds of watermelon (*Citrullus lanatus*) (Blake 1981) and of legumes are less likely to be preserved through charring, being less dense and seldom prepared in a manner conducive to deposition in a hearth (Yarnell 1982). Such biases are generally less extreme in the case of animal bones. However, livestock species should be better represented than many of the commensal animals that entered North America with Europeans, such as rodents.

Archaeobiological coverage of the protohistoric and early historic Southeast is geographically uneven due to historical factors, such as the growth of regional research programs, funding opportunities, and scholarly research interests (Gremillion 1993a). Collections excavated prior to the mid-1970s are more likely to contain faunal than floral remains, and some are valuable sources of data. However, they suffer from comparison with more modern collections simply because of the many improvements in recovery and sampling techniques that have been made since then. Quantitative analyses of such materials need to be conducted with extra caution, but they often provide information on the presence of introduced animals and plants.

Archaeobotanical data from the sixteenth century are sparse, with the exception of the Spanish mission sites (Reitz and C. M. Scarry 1985; Ruhl 1993; J. F. Scarry 1991), which represent a colonial situation rather than a protohistoric one. For the interior Southeast, not all investigated sixteenth-century aboriginal occupations have been adequately sampled for plant remains. However, there are good records for the lower Little Tennessee River Valley (J. Chapman and Shea 1981; J. Chapman et al. 1982) and the North Carolina and Virginia Piedmont (Gremillion 1989, 1993b) that span the sixteenth and seventeenth centuries. Substantial archaeobotanical data sets also exist for scattered individual sites, for example the Graham-White site in Virginia (Gremillion 1995) and the Creek village of Fusihatchee in central Alabama (Gremillion 1995; Gremillion and Reitz 1997).

Wood charcoal, which is generally quite abundant on protohistoric sites in the Southeast, has considerable potential for reconstructing woody vegetation. Although perhaps not entirely free of biases introduced by firewood selectivity (Smart and Hoffman 1988), wood charcoal profiles can be quite useful for tracking long-term changes in forest composition. Woody species introduced by way of European contact are likely to be represented by their wood as well as reproductive parts. To date, wood identification has been neglected in many archaeobotanical reports for the protohistoric Southeast, which tend to focus instead on plant food remains (e.g., Gremillion 1989, 1995).

Other indicators of ecological dynamics include pollen and phytoliths, both of which can provide either environmental or economic data, depending on variables such as context and abundance. Because of the brief span of time involved, it may be difficult to differentiate protohistoric deposits of these microremains from modern ones in non-archaeological settings, depending on rates of sediment deposition. Pollen cores often produce a single recent layer that represents the last several centuries (see, for example, Delcourt et al. 1986). Preservation of pollen tends to be poor on open archaeological sites in the Southeast, so palynology is unlikely to yield much information about the use of economic plants during the Protohistoric period. Phytolith studies have as yet received little attention in the Southeast.

In summary, protohistoric sites in the Southeast contain a rich record of subsistence activities in the form of plant and animal remains, most of which represent refuse. The relatively young age of these deposits increases the likelihood that preserved remains will be in good condition and thus identifiable as compared to those derived from older sites. On the other hand, non-archaeological pollen cores (which often come from bogs or ponds) may not permit time periods as brief as two centuries to be singled out for analysis, and pollen on open archaeological sites is seldom preserved well enough to permit quantitative analysis.

Dispersal of Old World Plants in the Southeast

The introduction of nonnative crops and weeds is a topic that lends itself particularly well to the combined investigation of documentary and archaeological sources, which complement each other in many respects. The archaeobotanical data can be relied on to inform about plant use and ecological relationships in particular communities for which no written information exists, and they have the potential to reveal much about the mundane details of diet and subsistence that often went unremarked upon by European observers. Conversely, certain features of the documentary record, such as attitudes and beliefs about particular plants, ritual use, and specific ways of modifying the environment (to name a few) are archaeologically invisible or extremely difficult to document with any confidence. The two data sources also overlap in key areas in such a way as to permit cross-verification. The spread of a particular species can sometimes be documented with a fairly high degree of precision by combining written reports and archaeological instances in this fashion.

Glimpses of Traditional Plant Use

Assessment of change requires some knowledge of an initial state—in this case the ecological relationships between human groups and plants prior to European contact. For this purpose, only the archaeological record prior to ca. 1492 is uncompromised by the possibility of European influence. That record indicates, first, that only a small percentage of the total available plant species were associated closely enough with humans to be incorporated into archaeological deposits. For example, of 3,250 species of angiosperms documented in Radford et al.'s flora (1968), only 39 are represented on the 12 North Carolina Piedmont sites reported in Gremillion (1989). Even taking into account preservation biases and the restricted geographical area represented by these sites, the degree of emphasis on a few economic plants and weeds is striking. Archaeobotanical evidence from throughout the Southeast, especially the interior portions, indicates a widespread general pattern of plant use in which agriculture played a central role (Gremillion 1989, 1995; C. M. Scarry 1986; Yarnell and Black 1985). Maize was the chief crop, accompanied by cucurbits (squashes and gourds), legumes, and various minor crops. Mast, especially hickory nuts and acorns, was also an important source of carbohydrates and fats. A varied array of fleshy fruits, such as grape and persimmon, contributed a diverse mix of micronutrients. Seed assemblages indicate considerable anthropogenic disturbance of vegetation near settlements, producing a mosaic of plant community types (Gremillion 1989).

Documentary accounts from the Protohistoric and early Historic periods suggest a similar roster of plant foods, with the addition of introduced species (Gremillion 1989:172). Such accounts also shed some light on ecological details that are less accessible archaeologically. For example, responses to seasonality included periodic dispersal for hunting, storage of plant foods, and an annual cycle of agricultural activities (Gremillion 1989:75 ff.). Maintenance of both dooryard gardens and more distant (perhaps communal) agricultural fields was a common pattern throughout the Southeast into colonial times (Bartram 1955:251, 284 [1791]; Gremillion 1989:143–4; Waselkov 1997). Fruit and nut trees were managed in orchard-like settings (Bartram 1955:57 [1791]; W. Byrd 1967:208 [1929]), a practice which was observed by the earliest European visitors (Elvas 1993: 93 [1557]).

Indigenous groups modified the landscape through agricultural clearing and the use of intentionally set fires, producing a mosaic of plant communities, including scrub and parklands as well as mature forest and both active and abandoned agricultural fields (Bland 1966 [1651]; W. Byrd 1967 [1929]; Day 1953; Gremillion 1989:135 ff.; Lawson 1967 [1709]:52, 57; Lederer 1966 [1672]:15). At least five sources spanning most of the eighteenth century and representing coastal and interior locations report the abundance of strawberries on Native American old fields (Adair 1930:49 [1775]; Bartram 1955:288 [1791]; Beverley 1947:141 [1705]; Lawson 1967:38 [1709]; Le Page du Pratz 1975:153 [1774]). Le Page du Pratz (1975:131, 134, 158 [1774]) saw many examples of grasslands that were produced and maintained by frequent controlled burning in order to attract game. Fire management increased the production of certain types of vegetation favored by deer and other game species, and improved the productivity of edible seeds and fruits (Hammett 1992).

Weeds and Landscape Change

Although the landscape encountered by the first European explorers was already an anthropogenic one that had been shaped and modified by millennia of human occupation, the environmental disturbance that followed European colonization occurred on a much greater scale. Further, such large-scale ecological changes can often be traced to the inadvertent introduction of alien plant species either directly from Europe or from its New World colonies. Eurasian weeds were often able to compete successfully with native weeds; in some cases the invaders possessed a distinct advantage in the form of longstanding coevolutionary relationships with domestic herd animals (Crosby 1986:157). It is possible that Eurasian weeds were closely tied to Euroamerican settlement and relied on the complex of farming and pastoralism to expand their geographic range into the interior Southeast. In this case, we would not expect to find seeds of these taxa in protohistoric archaeological contexts. An alternative hypothesis is that at least some of the exotic weeds established a foothold in the region by colonizing other types of disturbed habitats, such as those created by Native American settlement and land management.

Archaeological evidence favors the hypothesis that major population advances of introduced weeds were tied to European settlement. Archaeobotanical assemblages reveal no unambiguous examples of Eurasian weeds in the southeastern interior prior to the late seventeenth century. Prickly mallow (*Sida spinosa*), a weed of fields and waste ground that has been naturalized from the tropics (Strausbaugh and Core 1978:634), was present as early as the mid-seventeenth century in southeastern Virginia, as evidenced from the recovery of a single seed from the Graham-White site (Gremillion 1995). Also represented at Graham-White were one seed each of *Eragrostis* (lovegrass) and *Digitaria* (crabgrass). The latter is well-known today as a particularly noxious weed introduced from the American tropics. However, these archaeological specimens may represent either Eurasian or American species (Radford et al. 1968:138; Strausbaugh and Core 1978:126). A somewhat later example is a single seed of *Eleusine indica* (goosegrass) from mid- to late eighteenth-century context at the Creek village of Fusihatchee (Gremillion 1995). Exotic weeds are represented archaeobotanically on the coast as early as the sixteenth century, but there they are associated with Spanish settlements. Goosegrass and prickly mallow, for example, have both been identified at sixteenth-century mission sites (Ruhl 1993).

Few documents tell us much about whether introduced weeds spread in advance of Euroamerican settlement during the two centuries between initial Spanish exploration of the southeastern interior and its permanent settlement by Euroamericans. Although Byrd's *Histories* were written by a botanically knowledgeable traveler in the Carolina hinterland, his mentions of individual plants are few and almost exclusively of useful plants, especially medicinals (Adams 1967 [1929]). This preoccupation with economic plants is characteristic of the early development of European botany, although by Byrd's time plants were studied for their inherent interest as well (K. Thomas 1983:27). Lawson's account is more detailed than Byrd's, but it reflects the great diversity of useful herbs, both native and introduced, that occupied English homesteads in the colonies (Lawson 1967:84 [1709]) and thus are not indicative of presettlement dispersal. The same is true of John Josselyn's list of introduced weeds found in New England in the mid-seventeenth century, which includes such common and successful taxa as dandelion (*Taraxacum officinale*), shepherd's purse (*Capsella bursa-pastoris*, a member of the Mustard family), and plantain (*Plantago major*). Plantain, claims Josselyn, was known as "Englishman's foot" to native people because it was said to spring up only where the English had passed (Josselyn 1972 [1672]), and the same observation seems to have been made as far south as Virginia (Crosby 1986:156). Interestingly, both Lawson and Josselyn connect the spread of these plants with cattle; according to Lawson (1967:83 [1709]), the larger sort of purslane (*Portulaca oleracea*) "is never met withal in the Indian Plantations, and is, therefore, suppos'd to proceed from Cow Dung, which Beast they keep not."

Both archaeological and documentary sources indicate that the spread of exotic weeds in the interior Southeast was closely tied to the migration of the Euroamerican settlers and livestock with which they were ecologically linked. This finding suggests that the composition of plant communities, even those representing some degree of anthropogenic disturbance, was not radically altered during the Protohistoric despite the establishment of populations of introduced weeds in colonized areas along the Atlantic and Gulf coasts.

The Introduction of Economic Plants

With food plants, especially those that were managed in some way, the record is somewhat clearer. Food plants have many more opportunities to enter the archaeological record than those that are otherwise associated with humans, and they are more likely to attract the notice of foreign observers. Furthermore, such economic plants had the potential to catalyze far-reaching changes in patterns of subsistence. In order to accurately describe and explain the impact of introduced crops, it is necessary to document the chronology of their introduction and spread with special attention to the mechanisms of dispersal and the type of contact involved. Doing so helps to avoid the error of attributing absence to decision-making rather than simple unavailability. The ecological impact and subsistence role of introduced plants are often difficult to assess, but they can be addressed for the Protohistoric using documentary as well as archaeological evidence. Finally, empirical generalizations must be converted into testable hypotheses, using some body of theory as a framework.

Earliest evidence for introduced crops in the Southeast comes from the Spanish missions of the Gulf and Atlantic coasts. These settlements were planned communities in which clergy were supported largely by Native American labor, and consequently their success depended upon an aggressive program of acculturation that included conversion both to Catholicism and sedentism (Deagan 1985; Milanich 1994a). In this context, colonists attempted to replicate Iberian culinary and subsistence traditions by importing and experimenting with a variety of familiar food plants. The archaeological and documentary records for sixteenth-century mission sites report the introduction of such exotics as watermelon, melon, fig, pea, olive, peach, and wheat (Hendry 1934; Ruhl 1993). Of course, not all of these introductions "took"; often they were unsuited to the southeastern coastal climate. Interpretation of the causes of their adoption by native peoples is complicated by the element of coercion central to the Spanish mission system.

The archaeological record for the seventeenth and early eighteenth centuries includes some evidence from native communities of the southeastern interior that were receiving trade goods from European sources, but indirectly, by way of Native American intermediaries (Waselkov 1989a). These records indicate that native peoples were growing, or at least importing, exotic plants for their own use and in the absence of coercive pressure from colonial institutions. For example, cowpeas were recovered from mid- to late-seventeenth-century context at the Creek village of Fusihatchee (Gremillion 1995; Waselkov 1989a). This legume, native to Africa, was known to Le Page du Pratz as the "Apalachean bean," hinting at Apalachee middleman traders of the Gulf Coast as a likely source (Waselkov 1989a). Watermelon, another African crop, was quite popular in the historic Southeast, although its remains are seldom preserved archaeologically (Blake 1981, 1986). Important exceptions are seeds from two late seventeenth-century sites in the North Carolina Piedmont, Upper Saratown and Fredricks (Gremillion 1989). Watermelon was also reported as being grown in inland Georgia by the early seventeenth century (Blake 1986) and by French colonists in Louisiana in the early eighteenth century (Le Page du Pratz 1975:186 [1774]). Several varieties of watermelon are said to have been cultivated in coastal North Carolina in the late seventeenth century (Beverley 1947:141 [1705]; Lawson 1967:83 [1709]). Lawson reports the use of many legumes and cucurbits in native communities of the inner coastal plain of North Carolina, and at least some of these seem to have been of Old World origin. Examples include "melons" and "cucumbers" (both probably *Cucumis melo*) and "Calavancies" (*Vigna unguiculata*, assuming equivalence to Le Page's "Garavanzas" [1975:203 1774]).

Of the Old World crops documented archaeologically in the interior Southeast before the eighteenth century, peach is the most abundant and widespread. This plant, native to Asia, gained wide acceptance among southeastern groups. Brought to the New World as early as Columbus's second voyage, peaches may have been introduced to the coastal Southeast early in the sixteenth century. They became a common component of Spanish mission gardens along the Atlantic and Gulf coasts following the founding of St. Augustine and Santa Elena in the 1560s (Reitz and Scarry 1985; E. S. Sheldon 1978; M. T. Smith 1987:125). After 1620, peaches become increasingly visible archaeologically in the southeastern interior (Gremillion 1989; Knight 1985:79). Unlike many crops introduced by the Spanish, peaches flourished in the climate of the Southeast and spread rapidly (Reitz and Scarry 1985:55; Ruhl 1993).

Both archaeological and documentary evidence indicate that Old World crops had little impact either ecologically or economically in the interior Southeast prior to permanent Euroamerican settlement. However, some plants were used and grown by native people living in traditional settlements, and in some cases (e.g., the peach) they became a consistent part of the diet along with the existing suite of New World food plants. Why were some plants adopted and not others? To answer this question, it is necessary to consider both historical factors (such as availability) and functional issues (such as the economic costs and benefits associated with the new foods). The analysis of economic factors is heuristically useful because it has the potential to permit development of evolutionary explanations for subsistence change. However, this strategy does not preclude consideration of the many other influences on decision-making.

It is difficult to establish which of the many food plants introduced by Europeans were actually available through exchange to southeastern groups. Potentially, all would have been, although in actuality it seems unlikely that plant foods or seeds would have been a valued trade item. During the seventeenth century, the traffic between European sources and interior groups took place through native intermediaries. The ethnic groups that specialized in middleman trade between European coastal settlements and inland communities, such as the Appalachees, sought to profit by transporting items of prestige or functional value that were otherwise unavailable. Foodstuffs have relatively little potential for high returns in this sort of system. However, the contacts between traders and their clients or travelers and their hosts provided a pathway for the diffusion of plants by other means, such as gift giving. Iberville (1981:123) offers a glimpse of this type of transmission when he reports that he distributed seeds of wheat, peas, orange, apple, and cotton to native villagers just south of Natchez. Whether in fact this sort of dispersal occurred cannot be determined for the majority of Old World plants that were established at least temporarily along the coast. However, it seems reasonable to assume that some selectivity was employed by Native Americans and that the plants we know were adopted represent a subset of those that were available in the environment.

Certain plants had ecological characteristics that facilitated their spread. For example, peach trees often germinate spontaneously and require little in the way of husbandry. Le Page du Pratz (1975:22 [1774]) planted a peach stone after he noticed it had already sprouted while lying on the ground. Lawson remarked of eastern North Carolina that "Eating Peaches in our Orchards makes them come up so thick from the Kernel, that we are forced to take a great deal of Care to weed them out; otherwise they make our land a wilderness of Peach-Trees" (Lawson 1967:115 [1709]). Although Lawson's tendency to exaggerate has to be taken into account here, the ability of the peach to become naturalized in suitable habitats is well known. The weediness of the peach tree ensured that it could easily be dispersed with minimal human assistance. This fact may account for the "one sort of this Fruit, which the Indians claim as their own, and affirm, they had it growing amongst them, before any Europeans came to America" (Lawson 1967:115 [1709]). Differences in fruit and seed between native-grown and other sorts of peaches led Lawson to suspect that the peach was "a spontaneous fruit of America" (Lawson 1967:115 [1709]). However, he also observed that peaches did not grow "in the Woods" in areas inhabited by the English (Lawson 1967:116 [1709]), which led him to question their indigenous character. Similarly, Robert Beverley of Virginia believed peaches (and nectarines) to be "Spontaneous some-where or other on that Continent; for the Indians have, and ever had greater variety, and finer sorts of them than the English" (Beverley 1947:315 [1705]). Later in the eighteenth century, Peter Kalm heard from travelers to the Mississippi valley that "the woods there abound with peach trees which bear excellent fruit, and that the Indians of those parts say that the trees have been there since time immemorial" (Benson 1987:416).

Many Old World plants that were adopted during the Protohistoric period share characteristics with specific native crops, a fact that would have made them less costly to produce than unfamiliar plants would have been. Peach, watermelon, and cowpea all had ecological and botanical analogues in traditional agriculture. Management of fruit and nut trees and cultivation of cucurbits and legumes were established systems into which these new plants could be easily inserted. This factor is important because it minimized the loss of productivity expected while learning the requirements of a new crop; it also kept the risk of crop failure to a minimum. In contrast, incorporation of entirely unfamiliar resources would have entailed potentially destabilizing systemic changes that would have required high input of time and labor in exchange for a payoff of unknown magnitude. Risk was also limited by the practice of adding to, rather than replacing, traditional food crops. Having a large number of food items in the diet decreases variability in yields, although it also may be less efficient than producing only a few high-yielding resources (Gremillion 1996a; Winterhalder and Goland 1997). The weedy tendencies of all three of these plants permitted them to grow under a fairly wide range of conditions, a factor that also facilitated their adoption even in the absence of an accompanying body of knowledge about their growth requirements.

These characteristics of introduced plants suggest that low costs in terms of time, energy, and potential risk were important factors influencing their adoption.

But what benefits did they offer, other than possibly lowering the overall variability of yields by increasing the number of items in the diet? A superficial assessment of nutritional content shows that peach compares unfavorably to most other fleshy fruits utilized by southeastern Native Americans prior to European contact (Gremillion 1996a). Watermelon is calorie-poor because of its high water content. Cowpea, however, is comparable in nutritional content to New World legumes that were already in use (Watt and Merrill 1975). Obviously different criteria were at work in decisions to adopt different species. One thing to keep in mind is that any potential material benefits need to be considered relative to costs. Thus, despite being relatively calorie-poor, peach was both cheap to produce and potentially very productive. A grove of peach trees located near a settlement kept travel costs to a minimum while not adding significantly to costs of production; in comparison, scattered plants producing other types of fruit in the wild might have produced lower net returns. Other aspects of the nutrient profile may also have functional significance that contributed to the long-term success of a crop; peach, for example, is extremely rich in Vitamin C compared to native fleshy fruits (Gremillion 1996a).

Of course, economic decisions were not based upon calculation of caloric yields or measurement of vitamins. However, traditional farmers were quite capable of assessing risk and estimating production costs and likely yields associated with novel resources. These considerations guided decisions about which crops to grow and in what quantities. And if micronutrients were not a subject of discussion around the hearth fire, perceived qualities such as flavor strongly influence dietary innovation. For example, peach and watermelon have high sugar content that makes them attractive to the human palate. Both biological features (such as preference for sweet tasting foods and aversion to bitter ones) and cultural traditions that may run counter to such evolved propensities are involved in decisions of this kind. Other biologically based food preferences and aversions are likely evolved traits that discriminate between foods with different nutritional characteristics (Johns 1994; Rozin 1987). Thus we must look both to decision-making criteria and beyond them to their evolutionary causes and consequences. Although there is strong justification for looking first to functional (adaptive) explanations for change and stability in diet and subsistence, the answers may certainly lie elsewhere. Sometimes food fads follow the lead of celebrities or represent status seeking. However, if these factors truly determined human food preferences over the long term, it is unlikely that our species would have survived as long as it has.

Conclusions

Both documentary and archaeological data can be brought to bear on questions of ecological change in the protohistoric Southeast. In fact, neglecting either one would greatly impoverish our understanding of this subject. However, both types of data should be deployed in an appropriately critical manner, using the tools of both historians and archaeologists. Since most of us are not formally trained in both history and archaeology, we need to be alert to the temptation to bypass the methodological drudgery and seize whatever information appeals to us. Such is the case with ethnobiological data as well as any other, even though we tend to think of plants and animals and landscapes as being more empirically accessible than human cultural traditions and behaviors. For the protohistoric Southeast, many published documents are useful sources of ecological details if read with due attention to the authors' biases. Likewise, the archaeological record for this period is quite rich. The case study of the introduction of Old World plants to the Southeast illustrates how both types of data can be examined in light of evolutionary and ecological theory to develop explanations for ecological change in the wake of European contact.

3 / Seasonality, Sedentism, Subsistence, and Disease in the Protohistoric

Archaeological versus Ethnohistoric Data along the Lower Atlantic Coast

Rebecca Saunders

Along the lower Atlantic coast, the period between ca. A.D. 1500 and 1600 was a time of intermittent, sometimes violent, contact between Spanish and French explorers and Native Americans. This relatively brief period nevertheless produced an extensive documentary record. Use of these documents can be frustrating however, as written information is often insufficient or contradicts archaeological data. This holds true for a number of research questions. Four are considered here: site seasonality, sedentism, subsistence strategies, and the timing and effects of epidemics. Archaeological and ethnohistoric evidence are reviewed and the epistemological biases of each are considered in an evaluation of these critical issues.

Archaeology done in conjunction with documentary resources in North America, a.k.a. Historical Archaeology, has been under critical scrutiny since its conception (see, e.g., Cleland 2001a; Deagan 1982 and Little 1996 for reviews). A great deal of paper has been generated as Historical Archaeologists struggled to conceive, communicate, and convince others of the relationship of the components of the discipline. After more than three decades, concerns about what questions are most appropriately addressed with the databases, and how to most effectively integrate archaeological and ethnohistoric information, continue to generate commentary (e.g., Deetz 1988; Knapp 1992; Little 1992, 1996; S. M. Wilson 1993; S. M. Wilson and Rogers 1993; T. C. Young 1988). Though different authors stress different aspects, it seems a consensus has emerged—one that accepts the validity of the distinct kinds of questions generated by descriptive, processual, and post-processual archaeologies, as well as particularistic and Annales-school histories (cf. Cleland 2001b). In addition, most agree that the role of each disciplinary database—whether as supplementation (as handmaiden) or for use in the reconstruction of past lifeways, the determination of general societal or cultural evolutionary trends, testing scientific principles, or studying cognitive patterns in the past (Deagan 1982)—can change as research focuses shift and different aspects of complementarity emerge.

Despite increased terminological sophistication, in practice many studies combining archaeological and documentary evidence exhibit the same problems recognized twenty years ago. Published reports are often "seriously unbalanced—relying largely on either archaeological or historical information—or are frustratingly segregated into separate sets of insights deriving from separate data sets" (Deagan 1997:4). The lopsided quality of these studies is attributable to a number of things. For instance, many archaeologists simply do not have the time to develop the skills to give them access to primary documents or to use these skills if they have them. Recognizing this, many have collaborated with historians studying similar topics. However, with some felicitous exceptions, collaboration with historians has not been intensive enough or comprehensive enough to promote a balanced appraisal of the data of the past. While we have come a long way since arguing with each other over which database was the more "objective," historians and archaeologists have failed to convey to each other an appreciation of the pernicious biases present in their respective databases. To archaeologists, the richness of the ethnohistoric record is seductive, and we want to believe that we can use documentary information to answer important questions (from the particularistic through the cognitive) about material culture, site locations, demographics, sociopolitical systems, and mind-sets of Native Americans. We have known for years that many of these documents cannot be trusted, even at the level of depictions of material culture (e.g., Milbrath 1989; Sturtevant 1977) or physical characteristics of Native Americans (Iscan and Kessel 1997). Yet many historical archaeological studies continue to take documents at face value, a methodological remnant of the Direct Historical Approach (Galloway 1997a:284). Similarly, though we often lament the biases in the archaeological record—for instance, those introduced through poor recovery techniques in early excavations—we still use the data to make statements (of dubious validity) about past lifeways.

To illustrate these points, I will trace the debate concerning the settlement and subsistence systems and the incidence of epidemic disease among two groups living along the lower Atlantic coast at contact: the Guale of the northern Georgia coast and the Timucua of the southern Georgia and Florida coasts (Figure 3.1). The debate deserves a wide audience, because it exemplifies the inevitable frustrations involved in attempting to merge documentary and archaeological information. To anticipate the conclusions: Practically nothing can be taken at face value from either the documentary evidence or the archaeological database amassed to date.

The lower Atlantic coast was a busy place in the early sixteenth century. Both the French and Spanish attempted to establish colonies there between 1526 and 1564. With the massacre of the French colonists at Fort Caroline in 1565, the Spanish were able to establish St. Augustine that same year and Santa Elena in 1566 (Figure 3.1). The Spanish attempted to pacify the coast using missionaries. Spanish Jesuits preached as far north as present-day Virginia, but retreated in 1572.

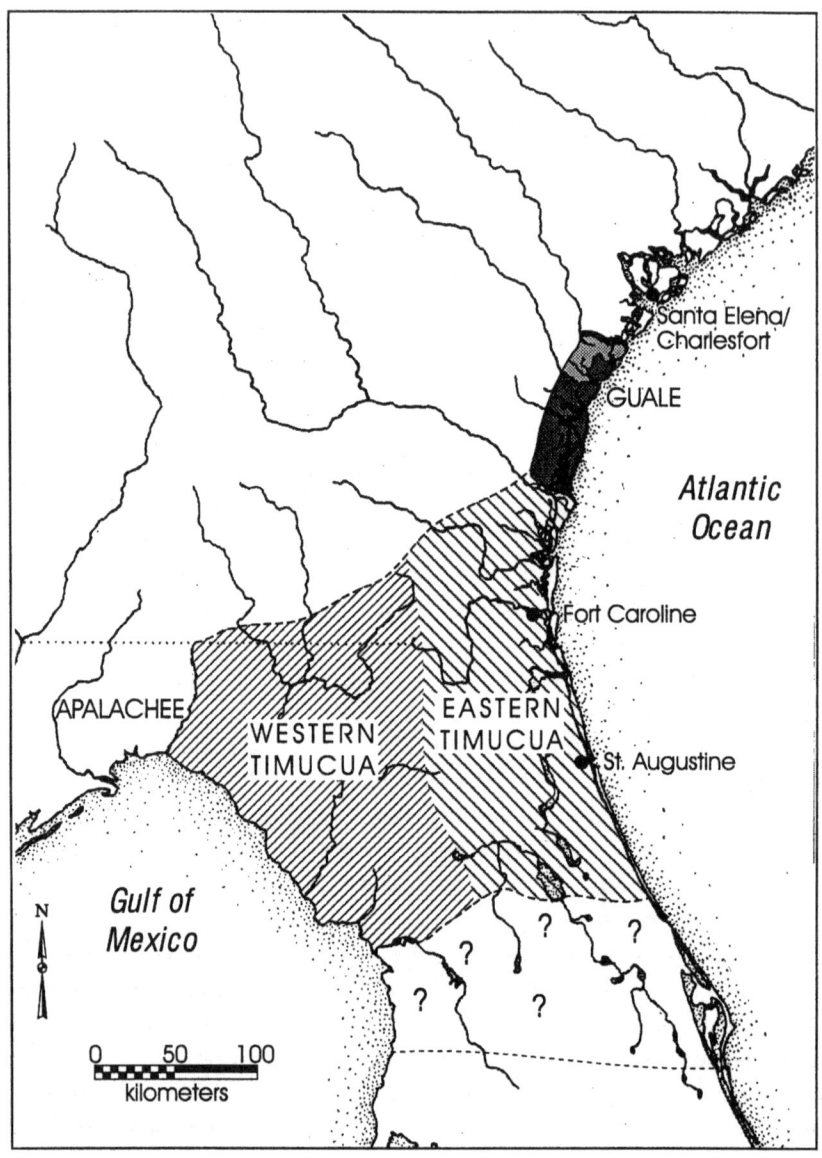

Figure 3.1 Location of early historic peoples.

They were replaced by Franciscans, who confined their activities on the coast to the area between Santa Elena and St. Augustine. The missionaries were to convert the natives and settle them around missions where they would provide the food and labor to sustain both the missions and the Spanish towns. In general, missionization was not successful until after 1600, when there was a mass capitulation on the part of the coastal tribes (Saunders 2000a; Worth 1998).

The years between ca. 1520 and 1600 are of concern here, because descriptions of Native American settlement and subsistence patterns in documents dating to this interval have been used to infer prehistoric lifeways. In addition, comments on the health or morbidity of populations have been construed to indicate massive depopulation prior to 1600. There has also been a good deal of archaeological work done in the areas these groups occupied. As will be seen, however, when used together archaeological and historical databases are contradictory. A resolution of the debate over settlement, seasonality, subsistence, and disease in the late Prehistoric and Protohistoric periods along the lower Atlantic coast is not likely in the near future.

Sedentism, Seasonality, and Subsistence

Questions concerning the degree of sedentism, the intensity of maize agriculture, and seasons of site occupation are intimately linked. The seminal discussion of these issues for the lower Atlantic coast was L. H. Larson's *Aboriginal Subsistence Technology on the Southeastern Coastal Plain during the Late Prehistoric Period* (1980; see also Larson 1978). Larson relied on both archaeological and ethnohistoric data for the reconstruction of Guale and Timucuan subsistence systems. His evidence included "archaeological data from the period immediately preceding the European entry into the region and the ethnohistorical record immediately following this entry [to] define the adaptations for the late [Prehistoric] period. In addition, an examination of the natural environment [permits] us to specify which divisions of the environment evoked particular adaptive responses" (Larson 1980:1).

Curiously, Larson omitted the use of archaeological data from early historic contexts in his stated methodology. In practice, he relied heavily on data from the Pine Harbor site, which had early and late Irene (A.D. 1300–ca. 1580) phase village and mound-mortuary components and a Mission period mortuary component with a *terminus post quem* of A.D. 1620 (Cook 1980; Saunders 1992c). Larson appropriately stressed the need to look at early as opposed to later documents (because of the influence of missions and other colonial enterprises on Native American subsistence practices), although he occasionally used later references (e.g., Bartram and Lawson; Larson 1980:113–114). None of the documents, however, were subjected to a historiographic analysis that might have exposed the hidden agendas of the various European authors.

The Documentary Record

Several primary documents were key in Larson's (and others') assessment of the agricultural potential of coastal Georgia and Florida. Relying on the reports of the expeditions of the Frenchmen Jean Ribault (1562) and René Laudonnière (1564), and letters written between 1566 and 1570 by Spanish Jesuit missionaries, Larson argued that village locations were shifted regularly as the infertile soils of the Gulf Coastal Plain were exhausted. One of the most frequently cited of these Jesuit relations, written by Fray Antonio Sedeño, gives the flavor of the missives (and misgivings) of the time:

> On [the coast] no fruit other than palmettos and wild nuts are found, which are so wretched that there is hardly anyone who takes advantage of them. The animals found are deer, bears, and lions. It is full of large pine forests and unproductive forests; and this is the cause . . . that the few Indians that are there are so scattered; for as they have nothing with which to fell the forests for their plantings, they go where they can find a little land without woods to sow their maize; and as the land is so miserable, they move with their *ranchos* from time to time in search of other lands which can bear fruit (Zubillaga 1946:424, quoted in G. D. Jones 1978:190).

Larson suggested the possibility of seasonal mobility (1980:225–226), but he did not elaborate on this in his conclusions (see also Larson, personal communication, 1987, in D. H. Thomas 1993:49).

Movement into the forest during the winter to collect acorns and oysters, as well as to fish and hunt, was also reported by Laudonnière (1975:15 [1586]) in a preface to *Three Voyages*. This preface, a compendium of information on coastal peoples, may refer to the Orista, the Guale, the Timucua, or to all three. Laudonnière (1975:121 [1586]) reiterated this winter (January, February, March) dispersal pattern in recounting the developments at Fort Caroline on the St. Johns River, that is, specifically with regard to the Timucua.

Larson's ideas were formalized and elaborated by Crook (1978, 1986). Referring principally to the Guale, Crook proposed a sophisticated "Annual Model" of settlement shifts based on "ethnohistoric evidence and modern ecological data" (Crook 1986:17). He suggested that the majority of the Guale engaged in a shifting *seasonal* subsistence round, in which particular sociopolitical units were linked with seasonal subsistence activities. In the early winter, matrilineages lived adjacent to estuaries, where they exploited molluscs, fish, and deer. In the spring, when swidden plots had to be prepared, the population was more dispersed, and one or two nuclear families worked the same plot in the oak forests. Crook hypothesized subsistence stress at this time, when stored foods became exhausted. Molluscan resources and estuarine fish became the principal resources during this period. In June large schools of anadromous fish arrived, and by July the first harvest could be reaped. At this time, matrilineages converged into strategically located, permanent town sites, where the chief and his retinue resided throughout the year. In the fall, the population dispersed again to the oak forests, where deer, and the oak and hickory nuts that attracted them, were available.

Seasonality, Sedentism, Subsistence, and Disease / 37

For his formulation, Crook (1986:17, 19) relied on essentially the same pre-1600 documents cited by Larson, but he fleshed out "Social Group Form" with reference to later observations—for example, of the Creek. All the ethnohistoric data were presented without exegesis. Crook (1986:52) then compared his model with available archaeological evidence and found a dispersed settlement pattern with "increasing archaeological evidence that dispersal was in a seasonal cycle, but that the details of this cycle remain to be adequately documented." He did note that very late prehistoric occupations might have been more nucleated than earlier late Irene phase prehistoric sites (Crook 1986:52).

The Larson/Crook model has been adopted in whole or in part by a number of researchers (D. H. Thomas 1993:49), but some aspects of it have been criticized. G. D. Jones (1978) doubted the mobility involved in the model, arguing that the Jesuit letters must be read in the context of the missionaries' unqualified failure. In addition, he noted the tremendous disparity between the "misery" of the native inhabitants described in Jesuit documents written between 1569 and 1570 and the abundance of agricultural supplies described in early French and Spanish documents written between 1562 and 1566. In short, Jones contended that the model of residential mobility was based on intentional overstatements of the poverty and mobility of the Guale in the primary documents. Letters to their superiors in the Old World had to justify the Jesuit's failures to make a single stable conversion in all of *La Florida*. Jones's (1978:191) summation is worth quoting in full:

> The fact that the Jesuits presented a picture of Guale horticulture and settlement patterns that is unique for over a century of Guale coastal history demands special explanation. I strongly suspect that the Guale inhabitants were scattering in order to avoid contact with the missionaries, whom they refused to listen to or accept. Significant factors in their resistance would have been the practice of forced tribute payment in maize to the Santa Elena garrison and the epidemic of 1569–1570, which was blamed on the priests. Sedeño's letter[s] read as if they were intentionally exaggerating the "misery" of the pagans, perhaps in order to procure a transfer. Rogel's letter is clearly an apology for his abandonment of the mission, placing the blame for his failure on the intransigent natives and the policies of the secular authorities. While it is apparent that the Guale practiced shifting cultivation, the Jesuit portrait of a highly mobile, dispersed population with insufficient maize to last the year and a weakly developed political system does not conform with the earlier French reports or with subsequent documentation. The Jesuit documents, therefore, should be treated with considerable caution.

Indeed, Jones's scenario of mobility as resistance was observed by Ribault in 1562 (1964:82–83 [1563]): "for if any rude and rigorous means shuldbe used towardes this people, they would flye hither and thither through the woodes and forestes and abandon there habitations and cuntrye."

According to Laudonnière's narrative, relations were good between the French inhabitants of Fort Caroline and the Timucua in the winter and spring of 1565—in other words, there should have been no reason for the natives to flee "hither and thither" except as part of their usual custom. However, by late April the French were "in great need of foodstuffs" (Laudonnière 1975:121 [1586]). "Even though the Indians had returned by this time, they could not help us except with some fish, without which we certainly would have died. Before this they had already given us the greater part of their corn for our merchandise" (Laudonnière 1975:122 [1586]). A few pages later, however, Laudonnière notes that meal and fish were available at "very dear prices."

> To make things worse, fearing to be captured by us and seeing that we had spent everything we had, they would not come within gunshot range from our fort. At that distance they brought their fish in their little boats; and there our soldiers were forced to go. Oftentimes I saw our Frenchmen give the very shirts off their backs to obtain one fish. If at any time they remonstrated with the savages about excessive prices, these villains would answer brusquely, "If you value your merchandise so greatly, eat it, and we will eat our fish." Then they would break into laughter and mock us in derision. (Laudonnière 1975:124 [1586])

Reading this account, one is forced to wonder whether the retreat to the forest from February to March was customary or precipitated by the presence of the French. In this respect, it is significant that, for the Gulf coast, Galloway (1995:161) noted that the natives involved with the 1559–1561 Tristán de Luna expedition were "cautiously friendly and willing to trade for food supplies" while their crops ripened. "Once the crop was harvested, it would be carried off and the villages abandoned." Galloway (1995:161) suggested that this represented "a continued Indian use of traditional techniques for dealing with European intruders." Atlantic coast natives may also have taken stored foods with them when they dispersed.

Instead of positing the precarious existence portrayed by the Jesuits, then, G. D. Jones (1978:179) argued that, for the Guale, agricultural production, in combination with other subsistence items, was sufficient to account for the presence of permanent, dispersed towns, a hierarchical chiefdom level of social organization, and long-distance trade networks. As indicated above, information for the Timucua can be similarly interpreted.

Jones's argument has been addressed by Crook (1986:73), who stated that the documents Jones used were written too late to accurately reflect the late Prehistoric period. Though Jones did use documents dating as late as 1670 to flesh out Guale subsistence practices, his summation described above is based on documents dating only as late as 1570. In any event, the French documents are seven to eight long years of contact earlier than those of the Jesuits and, on the basis of Crook's argument, should be the more relevant to a late prehistoric situation.

Relying on independent documentary and archaeological evidence of societies contiguous to the Guale and Timucua, I (Saunders 2000a) have been inclined to agree with Jones's critique of the Jesuit documents and with his reconstruction of a sociopolitically complex, sedentary society (but see below). However, although Jones examined the underlying biases of the Jesuit documents, he interpreted none of the sociopolitical context of the early secular Spanish and colonial French documents. Paul Hoffman (1984, 1990, 1994) has done so for the early Spanish. According to Hoffman, in contrast to the Jesuits' exaggeration of Native American poverty, early Spanish explorers were inclined to exaggerate the natural abundance, agricultural potential, and the adaptability and tractability of the natives they encountered.

This propagandizing can be seen in the 1523 deposition of Lucas Vasquez de Ayllón concerning his slaving voyage to the Atlantic coast in 1521. Hoffman's reading of the record indicated that Ayllón exaggerated the human, sylvan, agricultural, and mineral resources of the region, which he called Chicora, to secure a license for colonization. To bolster his claim, Ayllón appealed to a Ptolemaic geographical concept that assumed similar environmental and geological conditions at similar latitudes. Chicora was the "New Andalucia," comparable in resources to the most productive agricultural region in Spain. To make this claim, Ayllón fudged the location of Chicora north by 2–4 degrees of latitude.

Ayllón established a colony, San Miguel de Gualdape, in 1526, but the luckless venture survived only six weeks before famine, disease, and internal strife led to abandonment. The colony may have been established in the Guale population center around Sapelo Sound (P. E. Hoffman 1990). Sixteenth-century historian Gonzalo Fernández de Oviedo (1959) wrote an account of the voyage of colonization, but Peter Martyr (1964), who wrote extensive accounts of the earlier Ayllón voyages, barely mentioned the colony. Oviedo editorialized his narrative with Puritan critiques of the actions of Ayllón (and others; Avalle-Arce 1997:376). This and other sixteenth-century accounts are "textbook" examples of narrative history imbued with the "philosophy of history" (Galloway 1997a:287; see also Braudel 1980:4) and "the great paradigmatic stories that underlie the culture of the writer" (Galloway 1997a:288). Oviedo's account has not been subjected to serious critique, though Paul Hoffman (1990) has noted some internal discrepancies.

Absent details are as intriguing as present ones. For instance, though Oviedo described in considerable detail the fishes he saw, and mentions other fauna and flora, there is no mention of maize or any other agricultural product, of cleared fields, or of encounters with native populations. According to Oviedo, the Spaniards with Ayllón saw no "*poblaciones*" (populations, also town or village), only some houses or *caserías* (rural farmsteads) "distant from one another." (He did describe one *bujío* [council house] large enough to hold 200 persons [Oviedo 1959: IV:327, 328]).

The absence of Native Americans in the account is remarkable. The 1526 expedition should have targeted areas of dense, agricultural populations for the establishment of the colony; a great deal of ethnographic information (now generally agreed to have described Sioux populations to the north of the colony) is available in Martyr from the 1521 Ayllón expedition. A 1529 version of the Ribeiro map notes one possible reason for the deserted coast. The caption by "The Land of Ayllón" states "the natives fled inland out of fear so that when winter came many persons died from hunger and cold" (P. E. Hoffman 1990:86). The natives' fear is understandable. On the reconnaissance voyage of 1521, 60 Native Americans from the area around Winyah Bay were enticed on board ship and taken as slaves to Santo Domingo.

Despite the failure of Ayllón's colonization attempt, the idea of Chicora, popularized by Oviedo and Martyr, was the impetus for subsequent Spanish, French, and English voyages (P. E. Hoffman 1990:x, 40). However, by the 1540s and 1550s, after considerable expense, loss of life, and continued failure, the Spanish regarded the entire eastern seaboard as *unfrutuosa* (unfruitful) (P. E. Hoffman 1990:101, 119).

By contrast, the French, with access to the popular accounts of most of the Spanish voyages (P. E. Hoffman 1990:207), were not discouraged. Though contradictory, their texts promised riches. In addition, the French believed that colonies "might provide goods the Spanish empire ordinarily supplied France and . . . could serve as bases for attacks on the Spanish in time of war" (P. E. Hoffman 1990:207). Jean Ribault (with René Laudonnière as second in command) explored the coast from the St. Johns River to the South Edisto River, and established Charlesfort among the Orista, the immediate northern neighbors of the Guale, in 1562. In a subsequent voyage, in 1564, Laudonnière established Fort Caroline among the Timucua on the St. Johns River. According to Ribault, the land was "pleasaunt and frutfull, lacking nothing of all that maye seme necessarye for mans food" (Ribault 1964:61–62 [1563]). Ribault (e.g., 1964:62, 73 [1563]) emphasized the mercantilist possibilities of "New France," continually referring to the "commodities" available. Despite these glowing reviews, and help from the local Orista and Guale, Charlesfort was abandoned shortly after it was founded. On the subsequent voyage, Laudonnière and the artist Jacques Le Moyne depicted hierarchical chiefdomships with abundant agricultural produce in the Timucua area.

Ribault's account of his exploration, written in an English prison, piqued English interest in Florida. John Hawkins, the English naval officer and slaver, investigated. When Hawkins was greeted by Laudonnière at Fort Caroline on August 15, 1565, the personnel of the Florida fort were starving and mutinous (cf. Laudonnière

1975:142–143 [1586]). "Hawkins judged that the French would not be able to support themselves in the new land and he was convinced that there were no treasures to be found there.... His report led to the abandonment of English interest in Florida" (Dowd 1964:xxxiv).

The documents left from these expeditions have been widely used by archaeologists for ethnographic reconstructions of coastal peoples. However, Ribault and Laudonnière were under the same sociopolitical pressures as Ayllón. They had to exaggerate the bounty of coastal resources to sanction their colonization attempts; only by establishing colonies could the respective parties legitimize their claims to the riches they had never actually seen. Hoffman (personal communication, 1997) described both the early Spanish and French reports as "pure propaganda."

Certain aspects of the social system were not likely to be consciously misrepresented. In any event, they appear in so many documents through time and in space that they must be taken as indicative of contact period practices. Elite sumptuary rituals and polygamy are two examples. However, many customs could be misunderstood and were reinterpreted by analogy to a European pattern, as some have suggested for the patently medieval aspects of the southeastern Native American political system as represented in contact period documents. Given the purposes for which these narratives were designed, population estimates and—prior to the need to explain failure—evidence of tractability and eventual ability to live *en policia* (in "civilized" society), were likely to have been overemphasized. Agricultural and metallurgical potentials might also be inflated.

None of the early documentary sources, then, can be seen as unbiased. The documentary record presents a miasma of motivations and misunderstandings through which interpretations of protohistoric settlement and subsistence patterns must be made. However, an explosion in the number of primary documents available to researchers means that more cross-checking can be done to search for biases. And a new sophistication is emerging in the use of documents by both historians and archaeologists.

The Archaeological Record

Historiographical analysis is not the only method used to critique the Larson/Crook model. Archaeological data have also been mustered to counter claims of scarcity along the coast. With regard to the constraints of the environment on sedentism, Reitz (1982) argued that the productivity of the estuaries along the lower Atlantic coast was quite high, though resource availability did vary seasonally. She took exception to Crook's use of modern trawl data to retrodict seasonal species availability. In addition to criticizing the representativeness of trawl data, Reitz used zooarchaeological data to demonstrate that availability based on modern trawl data did not correlate with prehistoric exploitation (Reitz 1982:83). In fact, Reitz

(1987) found that highly seasonal resources such as anadromous fish were not substantial parts of aboriginal diets during any time period. Most damaging to settlement models using zooarchaeological data recovered prior to the mid-1980s, Reitz found that almost all those data were highly biased by recovery technique and inadequate to address questions of subsistence strategy and temporal change (Reitz 1982:84). Indeed, with the exception of the zooarchaeological and ethnobotanical evidence from the Kings Bay projects (two of thirteen sites reviewed), none of the seasonality/subsistence data discussed by Crook (1986:34–51) was based on fine-screened or floated samples.

Data produced in the last fifteen years are encouraging, but they still do not fully answer the "paleoethnographic" (D. H. Thomas 1993:46) question of the settlement and subsistence systems of the Guale and Timucua. For the Guale, Thomas (1993:51) provided an overview of late prehistoric and protohistoric sites with maize excavated up to about 1982, noting that "very little maize has actually been recovered, and from only a handful of sites." Ruhl (1993) also discussed protohistoric Guale and Timucua diet; but despite the inclusion of more recent work, she could only note that the degree of sedentism and the role of horticulture in both Guale and Timucuan society were still undetermined (Ruhl 1993:261, 262; see also Milanich 1994a:264). However, the addition of molluscan data for some late prehistoric sites on the coast has prompted Russo (1992a:118, 1992b:172) to posit "a year-round occupation of the coast" for the late prehistoric precursors of the Timucua in the St. Marys region (at the boundary between Florida and Georgia). Analysis of growth rings on *Mercenaria mercenaria* and of size classes in the oyster parasite *Boonea impressa* from the Irene phase Meeting House Fields site (Saunders and Russo 1988; Russo 1991) and mercenaria growth rings from features at the Harris Neck site (Braley et al. 1986) indicate sedentism for the late prehistoric coastal Guale.

Another data set casts doubt on our ability to extend this settlement and subsistence pattern into the Historic period under discussion. In a recent article on drought during the colonial period in Virginia, Stahle et al. (1998:565) presented tree ring data indicating "a prolonged drought from 1562 to 1571 that was most severe from 1565 to 1569." These data apply directly to the Jesuit experience in Virginia and should be applicable south through Guale territory (Stahle, personal communication, 1998; data do not extend to Timucua). If so, then the drought began just as the French were building Charlesfort and reached its peak during the Jesuit occupation. Traditional settlement and subsistence systems may have been affected. I have suggested elsewhere (Saunders 2000b) that during climatic extremes such as those that coincided with the first ethnohistoric accounts, the Guale may have drawn upon a repertoire of cultural responses that included survivals (seasonal transhumance) from earlier subsistence practices. However, in light of data indicating coastal sedentism for millenia, it seems more reasonable to suppose that remaining on the coast would provide the best subsistence recourse when drought destroyed crops.

It might be noted in this context that adherents of the seasonal transhumance model seem to share an unstated unilinear evolutionary bias correlating sedentism with intensive agriculture. Few have given serious attention to the idea that populations along the coast could have been sedentary without much reliance on agriculture. However, such ideas are gaining currency as less biased zooarchaeological studies have become available. These indicate that sedentism occurred along the St. Johns River and adjacent coast as early as the late Archaic (Russo 1992a:121; Russo and Saunders 1999).

The paucity of botanical remains suggests that there was little actual reliance on maize in the late Prehistoric or Historic period on the Atlantic coast. However, though Thomas alludes to "a large number of Irene/Pine Harbor sites tested," the database is actually quite poor. Most of the sites are disturbed to one degree or another; few were systematically excavated; and few were subjected to fine-screen or flotation techniques. (The methodological situation is improved in Ruhle's sample, yet few of the more recently recovered contexts are relevant to the issue of Native American subsistence in the late Prehistoric or Protohistoric period.) Thomas's transect survey of St. Catherines Island remains the only systematic, large-scale regional survey in Guale. And with the exception of work at the Meeting House Fields site (Russo 1991; Saunders 1992a, 1992b, 2000a; Saunders and Russo 1988), there has been no attempt to use the St. Catherines Island data to generate settlement patterns or to do additional excavation at selected sites to recover evidence on settlement/seasonality and subsistence patterns outside the mission context.

One other independent line of evidence is available to address the question of subsistence—that provided by physical anthropology in general and stable isotope analysis in particular. On the basis of carbon and nitrogen stable isotope ratios, Schoeninger et al. (1989:90) observed "a marked difference in both carbon and nitrogen . . . in the Savannah period relative to the preagricultural periods" along the Guale coast. These differences were considered to reflect a decrease in the use of marine foods and "a differential dependence on maize" (Schoeninger et al. 1989:92; the data for the Savannah period comes from the Irene Mound site just north of Savannah). Though highly variable, stable isotope values indicate that the majority of individuals tested relied to some degree on maize (Schoeninger et al. 1989:92). More recently, Hutchinson et al. (1998, 2000) have reported regional variations in maize use on the lower Atlantic coast. Values for ^{13}C and ^{15}N in the Irene phase burials at the Irene site show a decrease in maize consumption and an increase in the exploitation of terrestrial mammals relative to the earlier Savannah phase. Values from barrier island sites, like the early Irene phase Southend Mound I (ca. 1300–1400) on St. Catherines Island, and late Savannah sites (ca. 1300–1500), like Couper Field and Indian Field on St. Simons Island, are more similar to Savannah phase burials at the Irene site. The implication is that there was a serious sociopolitical disjunction between the Savannah and Irene phase occupations at the Irene site. This disjunction reverberated through the subsistence system at Irene (Anderson 1994b:318) but was not as disruptive on the coast. For the coastal eastern Timucua area, data indicate "little evidence of maize consumption before the mission period" (Hutchinson et al. 1998:409). However, none of the nine samples used from the two sites on the northeastern Florida coast can be dated more tightly than A.D. 1200–1600 (Hutchinson et al. 1998:404); the relative amount of maize consumption for Protohistoric period coastal Timucua remains an open question.[1]

Though there are still some problems with determining the contribution of different classes of foods on the basis of the values of stable isotope tests, bone chemistry would seem to offer the least biased and most direct approach to the determination of diet. At the very least, comparison of results on populations from the same environment through time will indicate dietary change, even if the exact nature of the change (not to mention its causes) cannot yet be determined. Comparison of these results with paleopathologies and with changes in the zooarchaeological and paleobotanical record should yield powerful statements on Native American diet. Of course, in the absence of stable isotope analysis, any combination of these other methods will also be suggestive. However, traditional paleopathological indicators of maize consumption, such as an increase in caries and porotic hyperostosis, may, in fact, have other causes. (For caries, see Fritz and Kidder 1993:10; Harmon and Rose 1989; Rose et al. 1991. For porotic hyperostosis, see the review in Holland and O'Brien 1997; Larsen and Sering 2001; Schultz and Larsen 1997.) And zooarchaeological samples are subject to the vagaries of preservation—in terms of incorporation into the archaeological record (e.g., some animals could be cleaned off-site); differential processing for consumption (smoking versus boiling versus roasting); and by contemporary or post-depositional activity at the site. The paleobotanical record is even more fragile. On southeastern terrestrial sites, botanical remains must be carbonized to be preserved. Therefore, food preparation techniques and post-consumption practices (e.g., use of maize cobs in smudge pits) will greatly affect the frequency of remains in the sample. Further, pollen is rarely preserved in sandy, coastal soils.

In sum, the archaeological database is still inadequate to address the complex question of late prehistoric and protohistoric Guale and Timucuan subsistence. However, techniques now available and in development should provide the data necessary to better address these questions. New methods of determining seasonality on oyster (Herbert and Steponaitis 1998) or oyster proxies (Russo 1991) and the use of seasonal growth bands on mercenaria and other bivalves (Quitmyer et al. 1985; Quitmyer and Jones 1997)—bolstered by the use of oxygen isotope ratios (Aharon 1982)—will be indispensable in determining seasonality and degree of sedentism. Continued insistence on the use of fine-screened samples and flotation of food remains will provide a better database in the years to come. Finally, stable isotope analyses from tightly dated contexts, especially those that can be controlled for status and gender, will be crucial independent evidence in the determination of subsistence systems.

Disease

One other aspect of the "paleoethnographic" (D. H. Thomas 1993:50) problem remains to be addressed, and that is the degree to which protohistoric populations were decimated by European diseases. While the question is important in and of itself, it is also germane to the discussion of settlement and subsistence patterns. Virgin soil epidemics, which can have a mortality rate of from 60–90 percent, may have preceded the documentary record. If, as some have suggested, massive depopulation occurred along the lower Atlantic coast prior to the colonization attempts of Ribault and Laudonnière, then both the archaeological and documentary records would be affected. Even the earliest accounts and early protohistoric sites along the coast would reflect considerable deculturation—a loss of societal complexity and traditional lifeways—compared to the late Prehistoric (M. T. Smith 1987). Though historians and archaeologists are skeptical of the dire scenario depicted by Dobyns (1983), most agree that epidemics were present along the lower Atlantic coast at least as early as 1526 (e.g., Galloway 1995; Henige 1986; G. D. Jones 1978:194; Ramenofsky and Galloway 1997; M. T. Smith 1987), when disease was introduced by members of the Ayllón expedition (contra DePratter 1994).

The 1526 watershed date was derived from the documentary record of the de Soto expedition. On the way through Cofitachique, which contained trade goods from the Ayllón colony (M. T. Smith 1994b:200), the Gentleman of Elvas (1993:83 [1557]) recorded that "About the town within the compass of a league and a half league were large uninhabited towns, choked with vegetation, which looked as though no people had inhabited them for some time. The Indians said that two years ago there had been a plague in that land and they had moved to other towns." Cofitachequi itself was said to have escaped the plague. Reference to this plague is also found in Vega (1993), but is absent in Biedma (1993 [1605]) and Rangel (1993).

Ayllón notwithstanding, the conventional wisdom has been that the de Soto *entrada* was the biological wrecking ball of southeastern populations. Lately, however, even this adage has been challenged, and the progress of this debate is illustrative of the reevaluation of the protohistoric documentary record in general. Galloway (1995; Ramenofsky and Galloway 1997) shifted the emphasis away from diseases with human vectors and toward those with animal vectors, particularly pigs (deer and turkey can be reservoirs for several of the diseases carried by pigs). The overall effect of diseases spread by the *entrada*, though uneven, remained devastating. In contrast, P. E. Hoffman (1997) and Ewen (1996) saw no evidence that the expedition introduced epidemic diseases in Coosa and Apalachee, respectively. DePratter (1994:215–217) thought accounts of disease in the Cofitachequi region—the disease episode attributed to the Ayllón colony—were based on misunderstandings between the Spanish and the Native Americans. The aforementioned overgrown towns were not recently deserted because of epidemics, DePratter argued, but were abandoned by A.D. 1450, when the lower Savannah River Valley, from the mouth of the river to the central Piedmont, was vacated (Anderson 1994b:242). In terms of what we know about the mechanics of the spread of disease, it is troublesome that Cofitachequi, the political and ceremonial center, was spared, as DePratter noted. But one also has to ask how or why the natives would have confused or misrepresented events just two years past.

In sum, the documentary evidence has begun to be examined with a more critical eye, but conclusions are far from consistent. The archaeological evidence for devastating epidemics in the Protohistoric along the lower Atlantic coast is almost entirely negative—that is, there are few, if any, sites along the coast dating to between 1500 and 1600 with direct, mortuary evidence of epidemics (for the nature of that evidence, see Milner 1980). Nor is there any indirect evidence, such as smaller and fewer sites, or population increases in adjacent areas, for depopulation or out-migration consequent to disease (e.g., M. T. Smith 1987; provided the A.D. 1450 southward migration of the Guale was indeed fully prehistoric). This negative evidence might suggest that epidemics did not become severe until after more sustained contact. However, factors that Galloway (1995) noted as contributing to the spread of diseases by the de Soto expedition—especially periodic native population nucleation and the probable acquisition of pigs—would have been relevant to the territories Ayllón visited as well. In addition, disease was a problem aboard ship. "Many" of Ayllón's 1526 contingent were ill by the time first landfall was made in the South Santee River or Winyah Bay area; the sick were transported south by ship while the able-bodied men went overland to Sapelo Sound (P. E. Hoffman 1990:71). "Deaths from diseases given their opportunity by hunger and, probably, contaminated water supplies, seem to have mounted rapidly in the weeks following the establishment of the colony" (P. E. Hoffman 1990:75). There is no mention in the documentary records of interactions with Native Americans—and hence no basis to infer the spread of these diseases—until after Ayllón himself died on October 18. At this point the wretched colonists became factionalized and some men moved to an Indian village three leagues from the settlement. The Spaniards were feasted for three or four days, ample time to spread disease, and then slain (P. E. Hoffman 1990:77). Thus disease, and the opportunity for its spread, were present in 1526. In light of these circumstances, and even given relatively conservative population estimates for the lower Atlantic coast, where are the thousands of

Native American dead that should appear within the first couple generations of contact if virgin soil epidemics occurred?

This negative evidence is less than convincing because so few protohistoric sites are known. From Amelia Island, Florida, north to St. Catherines Island, Georgia, a distance of almost 100 miles, only seven or eight sites can even be discussed as *possibly* dating to the Protohistoric period (see review in Saunders 1992c). Of these, only the Pine Harbor site (9MC64) contains evidence of post-contact mass burials, and those interments probably date after A.D. 1620 (Cook 1980; Saunders 1992c). Sites dating to the late sixteenth and early seventeenth century do show other evidence of social upheaval, including vitalization of iconography of the Southeastern Ceremonial Complex (which did not occur on the coast with any frequency until after contact), presumably to ward off the baneful effects of Europeans (Cook 1980; Cook and Pearson 1989; Cook and Snow 1983). This is not necessarily indirect evidence of epidemic disease, however. Thus, on the basis of the archaeological evidence, we would have to say that not only were there no epidemics, but there were virtually no people living along the coast in the Protohistoric period. This, even though there were substantial late prehistoric populations (Cook 1988).

The problem here is that our ability to distinguish late prehistoric from protohistoric sites rests solely on the presence of diagnostic European artifacts. No other appreciable differences in Native American material culture or other archaeologically visible lifeways have been identified for the Protohistoric. And, prior to 1600, European artifacts of metal appear to have been scarce and were rapidly taken out of circulation—"consumed as grave goods" (M. T. Smith 1987:157). Though these artifacts may not be representative, some early documents indicate that Native Americans preferred perishable clothing to more durable items as trade goods (Worth 1998). No doubt many Irene phase, Savannah phase, and St. Johns IIb phase sites along the coast were occupied into the Protohistoric period. However, neither our relative nor our absolute dating methods are precise enough to demonstrate this (Saunders 2000a).

Conclusions

The Protohistoric period of the so-called New World is a fascinating time to study. There are few other instances in human history in which such disparate cultures came into prolonged, enforced contact situations. This occurred at a time when one of the cultures had achieved a degree of literacy and the necessary technology to ensure that both narrative and pictorial descriptions of the New World were widely circulated in the Old.

This situation is both a boon and a bane to those seeking to understand the Protohistoric, as well as its past and its future trajectories. Once received uncritically, the documentary record has come under increasing scrutiny. Even direct commentary on epidemics has been questioned. Other narratives, filled with enticing ethnographic detail, are beginning to be understood as self-promotional vehicles. At present, the archaeological record is not adequate to resolve the contradictions in the documentary record. Most sites excavated prior to the 1980s were not excavated with sufficient controls to address subsistence systems; few protohistoric sites with appropriate contexts have been systematically excavated since that time.

But the situation is improving. Our recognition of the contradictions and biases in the records reflects an increasing understanding of historiography and archaeology in both fields. The dynamic between the archaeological and historical record has exposed deficiencies and biases in both—problems that we can address by continuing to use both disciplines to frame the questions and the answers involved in research in the Protohistoric period.

Notes

1. In addition to the dating problem, the stable isotope data itself may be problematic. All of those reported by Hutchinson et al. were done on bone collagen, which was standard procedure when most of these samples were run. More recently, samples using bone apatite have been incorporated into the procedure (Magoon et al. 2001), and results often differ markedly. For example, 24 samples from prehistoric sites along the Florida Gulf coast yielded 13C collagen values around -8, consistent with reliance on maize, but apatite values indicated no maize consumption (Hutchinson et al. 2000; Norr and Hutchinson 1998; Hutchinson, personal communication, 2002). For a number of reasons, Norr and Hutchinson chose the apatite values as correct (but see Magoon et al. [2001:23] for the interpretation of differences in values between the two data sets). Hutchinson (personal communication, 2002) acknowledges that this may cast doubt on collagen-derived data, but, on the basis of his experience, he suggests that apatite and collagen values were unlikely to be as far apart on the Georgia and north Florida coast as on the Florida Gulf coast, so problems similar to those in the Gulf coast data may not arise.

4 / Caddoan Area Protohistory and Archaeology

Timothy K. Perttula

The de Soto chronicles (Clayton et al. 1993; Hudson 1997) introduce us to the Caddo Indian peoples of the Trans-Mississippi South (Figure 4.1). It was a hard introduction all around (cf. P. E. Hoffman 1993). The Gentleman of Elvas had this to say when the Spaniards reached the Caddo province of Naguatex on the Red River in August of 1542:

> The cacique [of Naguatex], on beholding the damage that his land was receiving [from the Spanish forces], sent six of his principal men and three Indians with them as guides who knew the language of the region ahead where the governor [Luis de Moscoso] was about to go. He immediately left Naguatex and after marching three days reached a town of four or five houses, belonging to the cacique of that miserable province, called Nisohone. It was a poorly populated region and had little maize. Two days later, the guides who were guiding the governor, if they had to go toward the west, guided then toward the east, and sometimes they went through dense forests, wandering off the road. The governor ordered them hanged from a tree, and an Indian woman, who had been captured at Nisohone, guided them, and he went back to look for the road. (Robertson 1993:145; brackets added)

Despite the "miserable" condition of the lands traversed by the Spaniards in Caddo country, the Caddo were successful agriculturists, with a Mississippian societal flavor (cf. J. F. Scarry 1996a:13), as well as bison hunters when they were first described in 1542 by the Spanish expedition. These chronicles provide an initial and rare glimpse of the geographic boundaries, distribution, and social organization of a number of major Native American polities in the Southeast U.S. (Ewen 1997:132–133; C. Hudson et al. 1984). Of particular importance is that the chronicles afford hints about several different aboriginal Caddoan populations, their sociopolitical character, and the social and cultural landscape that existed at that time, as well as of their relationships with other Mississippian chiefdoms, when they

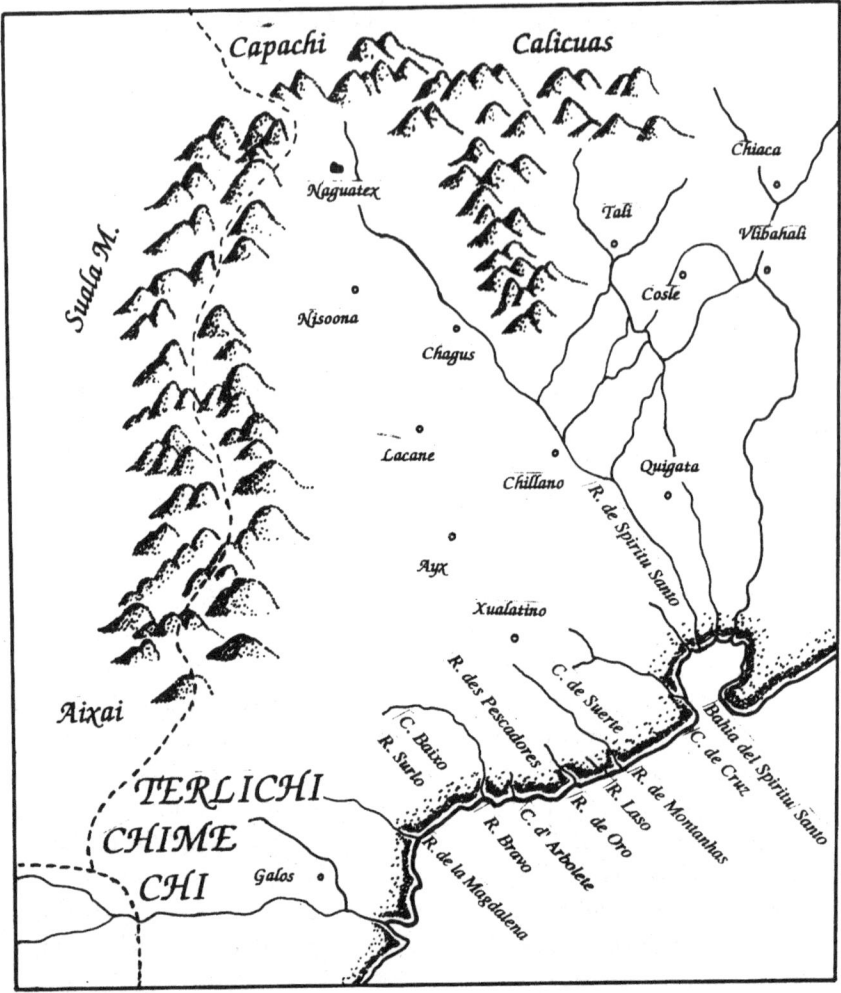

Figure 4.1 Redrawn version of the "De Soto Map," ca. 1550.

were "still in the full state of their indigenous developments" (Brain 1985a:xlviii; see also Ewen 1997:132–133; C. Hudson et al. 1984).

The archaeological record of the Caddo peoples from ca. A.D. 800 indicates that they lived in the Arkansas, Oklahoma, Texas, and Louisiana area, centering on the Red River Valley, but extending from the Arkansas and Red River valleys into the western Ozarks as well as south into deep East Texas and east into central Arkansas (Figure 4.2), in what has been called the Trans-Mississippi South (Schambach 1970; see also Perttula 1997:7). Despite archaeological investigations beginning in the latter years of the nineteenth century, and many major research efforts since

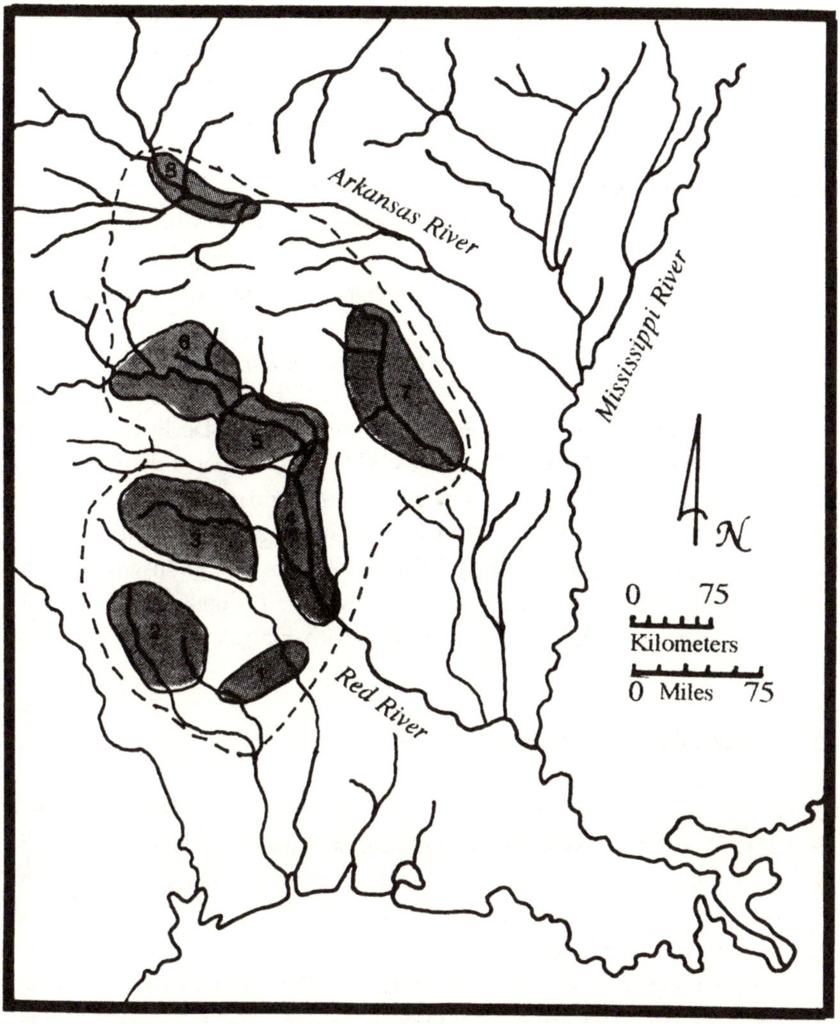

Figure 4.2 The distribution of Caddoan archaeological phases at initial contact. Reprinted from Bulletin of Texas Archaeological Society, by Timothy K. Perttula. © Texas Archaeological Society, 2001. Used by permission.

that time (see compilation in Perttula et al. 1999), current knowledge about the cultural heritage of the Caddo Indian peoples is not widely shared, understood, or appreciated by more than a handful of archaeologists, ethnohistorians, and historians (e.g., Perttula 1996b).

During prehistoric and historic times, however, the Caddo peoples were a powerful group of related theocratic chiefdoms who exercised, through their political and religious elite, great political skill and trading savvy with their southeastern

U.S. Mississippian neighbors (see J. A. Brown 1996; Early 1993; Rogers 1996; Sabo 1995a). Current conceptions of the character of Mississippian societies suggest that the Caddo people shared broad affiliations with them, given that they were maize agriculturists with a hierarchical political organization, and they shared "a set of religious cult institutions and iconographic complexes" (J. F. Scarry 1996a:13). Nevertheless, when boundaries of Mississippian societies are drawn, most of the Caddoan area—other than the Arkansas and Red River basin Caddoan groups (cf. J. F. Scarry 1996b:Figure 1.1)—is excluded from the Mississippian world.

Along with other native populations of the Southeast (Axtell 1997:43–44, 69), the Caddo have withstood—in the face of disease, colonization, and acculturation—the centuries-long and continuing interaction with Europeans (see Avery 1996; Carter 1995a; Perttula 1994, 1996a; Rollings 1995; F. T. Smith 1995). They survived and apparently thrived at critical times amidst the onslaught of European and American empire-building on lands the Caddo had considered their own from time immemorial. In this paper I focus on the Protohistoric period—that period of time between prehistory and history "for which few written records are available, and for which most evidence is derived from archaeology" (Adkins and Adkins 1982:242)—to understand how Caddoan societies began to change and evolve following the initiation of contact and interaction with Europeans in the early sixteenth century.

Caddoan Area Protohistoric Research

Caddoan area Protohistoric period research in recent years has been concerned with the study of initial contacts between Europeans and Caddo peoples, particularly with the effects of that contact on the nature of changes in Caddo societies. I share the views of Trigger and Swagerty (1996:326) that the Protohistoric period "extends from the earliest evidence of European goods or diseases in a region to the start of detailed and continuous written records." In the Caddoan area, the Protohistoric period if tightly defined extends from ca. 1520 to 1685 (Perttula 1997:12), beginning about the time of the earliest contacts between the Caddo and Europeans to the expeditions of La Salle in the late seventeenth century.

The Protohistoric era can be extended into the first several decades of the eighteenth century, prior to the Spanish establishment after 1716 of several permanent missions and the first presidios among the Hasinai Caddo (Hadley et al. 1997:359–364), as this is when detailed, if sometimes complementary or contradictory (cf. Little 1992:4), documentary data are available along with archaeological information. After this time, a relatively voluminous archival and historical record of the Caddo peoples is available (Swanton 1942), but the archaeological record is meager (cf. Girard 1997:19; Kelley 1997; Perttula 1997). Thus, the integration and scrutiny of the body of archaeological, bioarchaeological, and ethnohistoric knowledge of sixteenth- and seventeenth-century Caddo groups has been an approach that has yielded significant insights into Caddo lifeways during this momentous period, most notably giving evidence of their sociopolitical character and ethnic identity, revealing structural relationships as seen through sacred and secular rituals and ceremonies, and documenting changing health conditions.

Protohistoric Archaeological Research

Considerable research attention has been devoted to Caddoan area protohistoric archaeology and native history (e.g., Kelley 1994; Kelley et al. 1996; Perttula 1996b; Perttula and Bruseth 1998; Story 1982, 1995). Certainly the best examples of this work have been Kelley's (1994, 1997) impressive excavations at the 1650–1710 McLelland and Joe Clark sites on the Red River in Northwest Louisiana (probably occupied by the Nakasa Caddo, a little known group) and Story's (1982, 1995) work among the Hainai Caddo at the ca. 1710 Deshazo site in the Angelina River basin in deep East Texas. Caddoan archaeologists, bioarchaeologists, ethnohistorians, and historians, as well as the Caddo peoples themselves (Carter 1995a), have developed a better understanding of the cultural heritage of the Caddo peoples.

Settlements and Communities

When Alonso de Leon came among the Hasinai Caddo in 1690, he described their community along the Neches River as follows: "The principal settlement encompasses fourteen to fifteen leagues, but we were unable to see all of it because of a river [the Neches] that passes through the middle. In the part that we did see there were more than four thousand people" (Hadley et al. 1997:323). He went on to note that there were many other Caddo settlements in the area (according to French testimony, there were nine or more Caddoan communities [Chapa 1997: 138]), as well as "the large settlements of the Cadohadacho [to the north and northeast], whose people plant and store [enough produce] for the year" (Hadley et al. 1997:323).[1]

As in prehistoric times, the Caddoan people during the Protohistoric era lived principally in year-round sedentary, dispersed communities or *rancherías* containing single homesteads and/or farmsteads with one or two structures and small family cemeteries. At the McLelland site on the Red River, the 1650–1710 Nakasa Caddo community consisted of two circular structures (11–12 m in diameter), a possible ramada, several burials, a sheet midden deposit covering ca. 450 m^2, and an assortment of extramural pits and features (Kelley 1997:Figure 15) that likely represent cooking and working areas. Hamlets and/or larger villages with a number of houses, middens, burials and cemeteries, and open plaza areas are also known archaeologically, particularly in areas along the Red River and elsewhere across the Caddoan area that evidently had higher population densities (including the "heavily settled valley" of San Pedro Creek in deep East Texas noted by de Leon in 1689 [Chapa 1997:149; see also Erickson and Corbin 1996]). Occasionally these hamlets or villages had small earthen mounds that capped important public structures (Perttula 1996b:310). Along Big Cypress Bayou in the Pineywoods of Northeast Texas, protohistoric Titus phase communities (see Figure 4.2) also had large community cemeteries, sometimes containing 150–300 burials, in addition to the family cemeteries at the farmsteads and hamlets (Perttula and Nelson 1997:378–380 and Figure 155). The distribution of the large community cemeteries appears to reflect the overall density of Titus phase populations and the overall distribution of Titus phase settlements across the region.

Caddoan settlements and communities in prehistoric and protohistoric times were regularly associated with the important (though usually vacant) centers that had earthen mounds and/or public architecture (Schambach 1996; see Figure 4.3). As Schambach (1996:41) notes, the main mounds dating after ca. A.D. 1300 "contain the remains of important buildings rather than important people," as was not the case among ca. A.D. 900–1300 Caddoan groups whose mounds contained the shaft burials of elite members of Caddoan society.

Archaeological investigations along the major streams and tributaries document the construction and use of earthen mounds among the Caddo in the sixteenth and seventeenth centuries. These mound centers have been categorized as "vacant in the sense that there was no domestic occupation off the mounds, with the population living in small farmsteads scattered around the countryside" (Schambach 1996:41), but some other mound centers occupied about this time along the middle reaches of the Red River (among the McCurtain phase; see Figure 4.2) had dense settlements strung out along the natural levees and alluvial landforms.

One of these dispersed Caddoan communities was mapped in 1691–1692 by Don Domingo Teran de los Rios during his expedition to the Kadohadacho (Hatcher 1932). Teran's map (Figure 4.4) shows that the Caddo village was divided into individual compounds or *ranchitos* containing one to three grass- or cane-covered structures, above-ground granaries, outdoor ramadas or arbors, as well as compound cultivated plots. A *templo* or temple mound was in use at the far western end of the village (see Figure 4.4), seemingly "half buried in the top of the mound" (Schambach 1996:41) from earth placed there to bury the temple after it had been ritually burned and extinguished.

William Stinson Soule's 1874 photograph of a Caddoan village in western Oklahoma (Long Hat's camp) (Nye 1968:400–401) depicts the same relationship of structures, ramadas or arbors, and open plaza-like areas within the compound as Teran's maps did some 180 years earlier. Alonso de Leon was told in 1689 by a Frenchman that each Caddo "has his own house and large garden, enough to plant corn for his use" (Chapa 1997:138). The similarity in Caddoan settlement be-

Figure 4-3 Early Caddoan structures near mound A at the George C. Davis site.

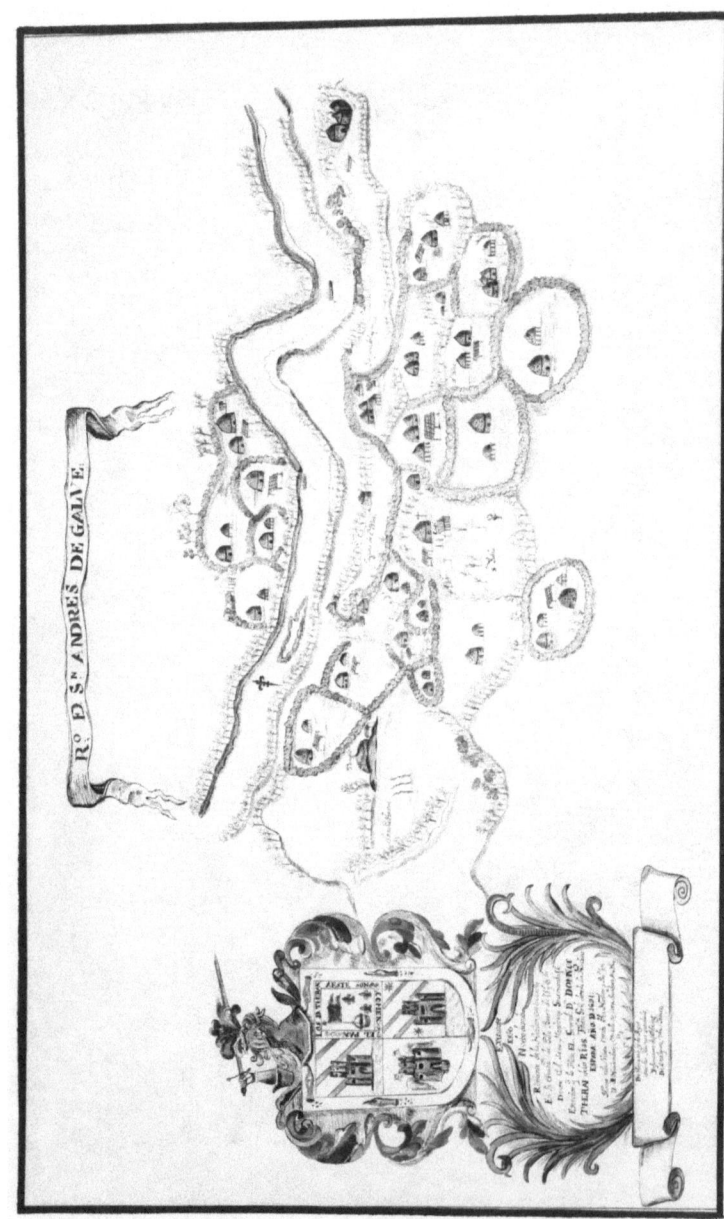

Figure 4.4 Map of a Caddo village on the Red River.

tween these historical sources is the basis for the Teran-Soule settlement model proposed by Schambach (1983:7; see also Schambach et al. 1983), where "the settlement pattern . . . at the time of European contact was the dispersed farmstead, vacant ceremonial center."

The four to nine km long Upper Nasoni community mapped by Teran appears to have been located at the Hatchel-Mitchell-Moores archaeological complex in Bowie County, Texas (see Creel 1996; M. M. Wedel 1978). The archaeological remains at this important Caddoan center comprised at least five mounds, including one platform mound used for several hundred years that contained 16 circular structures, as well as extensive habitation and cemetery areas (Creel 1996). Creel (1996:505) suggests that the complex was continuously occupied from ca. A.D. 1200 to the early nineteenth century. The nearby Upper Kadohadacho village (including sites 3M13/30 and 3M14) described in the seventeenth and eighteenth centuries was apparently as extensive as the Upper Nasoni *rancheria*, with village areas, cemeteries, and seven earthen mounds (Sierzchula et al. 1995).

Mounds and Mortuary Behavior

In protohistoric times, there were considerable differences in the complexity of Caddo mortuary practices that relate to the treatment at death of the social elite. Caddoan groups living along the Red River, the Little River, and the Ouachita River (see Figure 4.2) interred their social elite (usually a paramount male) in shaft/pit tombs in the burial mounds, accompanied by exotic prestige goods as well as large numbers of other kinds of grave goods (see Early 1988; M. P. Hoffman 1983; Webb 1959). Burial mounds do not appear to have been constructed or used by Caddo groups after about A.D. 1650.

The rest of the population of these Caddo groups were buried in family cemeteries near the houses they lived in, possibly with the same rituals and ceremonies as the elite but without many of the exotic grave goods (see Kelley 1997). Among the Titus phase Caddo groups (see below), the social elite and non-elite began to be buried in large community cemeteries. While some elite individuals were treated at death in a manner comparable to elites in Caddoan populations on the major rivers, generally these individuals were buried in the same manner of body preparation, treatment, and position in either family or community cemeteries (Perttula and Nelson 1998:381, 393).

The diversity in mortuary practices and rituals that existed among protohistoric Caddoan groups is well illustrated by an examination of the kinds of grave goods included with the deceased, particularly ceramic vessels. Fray Casanas commented in 1691 that the Caddo buried "their dead with all their arms and utensils which each possess" (Swanton 1942:208), and it is evident that the grave goods represent, in a symbolic and material sense, the items used by that individual in life, as well as goods needed to accompany the deceased on his or her journey to the other world. The archaeological evidence from across the Caddoan area indicates that protohistoric ceramic mortuary assemblages differ from region to region in the composition of jars, bottles, bowls, and carinated bowls (Perttula and Nelson 1998: Table 34). In fact, no two contemporaneous Caddo mortuary vessel assemblages from different groups are similar, and Perttula and Nelson (1998:396) interpret this to "mean that there was a very considerable diversity among Caddoan groups in their cultural practices, beliefs, and world-views about what males and female adults and children needed in life and death and that there were cultural boundaries between Caddoan groups not regularly crossed by networks of personal and group contacts." Inverse relationships in the representation in mortuary contexts of food-serving vessels, cooking and storage jars, and bottles (probably used for holding liquids, corn meal, and offerings) between eastern and western Caddoan groups express a basic dichotomy in belief and cultural practices, one that highlights the existence of well-defined social boundaries in protohistoric times. Interestingly, Derrick and Wilson (1997:Figure 5) note an analogous east-west dichotomy in the styles of cranial modeling used by Caddoan groups, as well as a similarity in cranial modeling styles between most of the Caddoan groups living in Northeast Texas.

Looking in more detail at the mortuary practices of Caddoan groups living in the Pineywoods of Northeast Texas (where information is available on more than 110 cemeteries [Perttula and Nelson 1998:Table 221]), mortuary behavior among the ca. A.D. 1430–1680 Titus phase Caddoan groups suggests that most adults had the same social status. Burial accompaniments followed lines of age and sex, as well as group philosophical and religious precepts and beliefs about the kinds, amounts, and placement of grave offerings that were important to include for the deceased's journey to the next life (e.g., Parsons 1941; Swanton 1942:204–210). Nevertheless, 46 percent of the known community cemeteries and 12 percent of the family or hamlet cemeteries had individuals of apparent high rank or vertical social position (Perttula and Nelson 1998:380). In some of the larger community cemeteries, the social elites appear to have been placed in central burial locations, signifying their central and powerful place in the community, and rows of the non-elite radiated out from the center. The long-term group memory of grave locations suggests that differences in social position of individuals and social groups were as important to maintain after death as they had been expressed among the living.

The mortuary treatment of the Caddo social elite during Titus phase times was quite diversified. The burials of the Titus phase elite included: (a) burial in a shaft tomb; (b) burial in a mound; (c) burials with large chipped bifaces; (d) individual extended supine burials with large quantities of grave goods, especially quivers of arrow points; and (e) double extended supine burials with quantities of grave goods, particularly ceramic vessels (Perttula and Nelson 1998:Table 24). Most of the apparent Titus phase elite were adult males, though at least one (Burial 19 at the Tuck Carpenter site [R. L. Turner 1992:98 and Table 17]) was an adult female.

From chronological and seriation studies, the majority of the presumed Titus phase social elite burials (in community cemeteries and the smaller family-farmstead-hamlet cemeteries) date after ca. A.D. 1550–1600. They occur across the Big Cypress basin but cluster in the Titus phase "heartland," a 60 x 20 km area along the middle reaches of Big Cypress Bayou (Perttula and Nelson 1998:Figure 150). From all indications, the large community cemeteries lasted only two or three generations, and they were used intensively only in portions of the Pineywoods, certainly ending by ca. A.D. 1680. After the community cemeteries were no longer used, most of the region was abandoned by the Caddo (Perttula 1997:172–177).

In this "heartland," community cemeteries occurred first, and the density of cemeteries and burial numbers suggest relatively high Caddo populations, higher than in other parts of the Northeast Texas region. The community cemeteries also lingered longer in use there than in any other part of the Titus phase area, while small family-farmstead-hamlet cemeteries continued to be used as long as Caddoan peoples lived in the Pineywoods (Perttula and Nelson 1998:392).

Trade

Protohistoric period Caddoan groups maintained extensive trade/exchange relationships with both agricultural and non-agricultural aboriginal groups. The Spaniards saw evidence of this in the Caddo province of Guasco on the Neches River, when they noted the Caddo peoples had cotton and turquoise items that were described as coming from the west, surely the Southwestern Pueblos.

Further testimony of a flourishing interregional trade and exchange network among the Caddo in protohistoric times comes from the wide distribution of post–A.D. 1400 Caddoan ceramics. Sherds and/or vessels of Caddo manufacture (most notably among the Ouachita and Red River Caddo and the Caddo groups living in the Neches-Angelina River basins [see Figure 4.2]) are well-documented among Lower Mississippi Valley and Arkansas River Mississippian societies (Early 1993: 233–234; House 1997; Kidder 1993), Plains Village sites in the Central and Southern Plains (Vehik and Baugh 1994); on Osage and Wichita sites (Chapman and Wiegers 1985; Perttula et al. 1995); and hunting and gathering groups in the Texas Panhandle-Plains (Boyd 1997), Central Texas (see Reese-Taylor et al. 1994), and inland regions of Southeast Texas (Aten 1983:295). Caddo ceramics comprise 20 percent or more of the ceramic assemblages on Central Texas Toyah phase sites extending to the eastern margins of the Edwards Plateau (Ricklis 1994:305 and Figure 155), and Ricklis (1994) suggests their distribution represents the southwestern extent of regular travel by Hasinai Caddo groups. Overall, the increasing evidence of Caddoan tradewares on non-Caddoan sites to the west dating after ca. A.D. 1450 appears to be related to the development of new and more intensive forms of economic interactions between the Caddo agricultural communities, Pueblo farmers of the Rio Grande, bison hunters of the southern High Plains and prairies, and horticultural communities on the Red, Washita, and Canadian rivers in Oklahoma.

Bioarchaeological Studies of Health and Disease

With respect to the study of contact between Europeans and Caddo peoples, of continuing interest has been the consideration of the effects of that contact on the nature of changes in Caddo societies. The population and disease effects on native Caddo groups is one issue that has been closely scrutinized employing both archaeological and bioarchaeological evidence (see Burnett 1993; Early 1993; Powell 1997), with the work concentrating especially on reconstructing Caddoan population histories; determining when epidemic diseases were introduced among Caddoan groups; when post-contact population declines occurred; and what were the long-term cultural impacts of disease and population declines on Caddoan societies and communities. Nevertheless, as has been argued elsewhere (see Perttula 1997), more attention should be devoted to consistently examining trends and discontinuities in those aspects of the Caddoan archaeological record (such as abandonment of regions and major sites, abrupt changes in settlement patterning, or the discontinuation of mound building) that in certain circumstances may relate to, or denote, more fundamental cultural changes in demographic or health conditions. This point is reiterated by Kealhofer and Baker (1996:210–211), who state that "changes in mortality and health patterns, and the imprint of epidemic-based demographic decline, must be correlated with the detailed settlement data and chronology."

Burnett's (1993) recent bioarchaeological study of the Ouachita River basin in southwestern Arkansas is one of the most comprehensive bioarchaeological studies of post–A.D. 1500 Caddoan skeletal remains completed in the last few years. Her work seems to suggest that between A.D. 1500–1600, Caddoan adults lived shorter lives than before, and that infection rates among sub-adults and adults were higher than at any other time in the Caddoan occupation of the basin. Might this evidence reflect population declines due to European diseases? However, Burnett detected that after A.D. 1600 infection rates declined and adult age at death increased, which she attributes to improved adaptive efficiency among these Caddoan populations; after 1700, the Caddo groups completely abandoned the Ouachita River basin.

There is no question that European epidemic diseases among the Caddo resulted in regional population declines. P. H. Wood (1989:82–84 and Table 1) has estimated that Caddoan populations declined an estimated 75 percent between 1687 and 1790 due to epidemics (see also D. Wilson and Derrick 1997). Population declines were more substantial among the Caddo groups living along the major rivers than they were among "rural" Caddoan groups (see Perttula 1997:87 and Figure 13 for locations of rural Caddoan groups in protohistoric times), and more substantial than among neighboring mobile hunter-gatherers (e.g., Ewers 1973).

The recent bioarchaeological work on protohistoric assemblages from the Red River in Northeast Texas (Lee 1997; Lippert 1997; D. Wilson 1997) provides a new view of Caddo health conditions during the Protohistoric era. These Caddo populations were generally healthy but "biologically adapted over many generations to this regimen [of a maize diet]" (Powell 1997:136). From patterns of arthritis and bone inflammations, we know their agricultural lifeway was a hard one, and patterns of infant mortality were comparable to that seen in other southeastern U.S. Mississippian societies. They suffered from endemic treponematosis, an infectious disease, and bioarchaeological studies have shown that some 11 percent of the individuals experienced severe iron deficiency anemia before the age of four (Powell 1997:137).

With one exception, there is no direct bioarchaeological evidence for the presence of epidemic diseases in any Caddoan historic bioarchaeological assemblages (Burnett 1993:194). However, acute epidemic diseases rarely leave specific direct evidence on archaeologically-recovered skeletal samples (e.g., Ortner 1992; J. W. Wood et al. 1992), limiting in this respect the interpretive significance of bioarchaeological remains to address the issue of disease impacts straightforwardly. Nevertheless, the further study of Caddoan bioarchaeological remains from post-A.D. 1500 sites, following the provisions of the Native American Graves Protection and Repatriation Act of 1990 (cf. Carter 1995b), promises to contribute important new information on the overall health and diet of Caddoan populations in the Protohistoric and early Historic eras.

Sociopolitical Relationships

Other studies have focused on how protohistoric and historic Caddo societies and sociopolitical relationships were transformed through indirect and direct contact and interaction with Europeans. One body of research in particular has concentrated on also examining how key cultural concepts and symbols of sacred and secular rituals and ceremonies were maintained by Caddo peoples amidst the European presence (see Sabo 1995a, 1995b). Sabo's ethnohistorical studies of late seventeenth- and early eighteenth-century Caddoan societies have illuminated significant structural relationships within Caddoan society—such as village organization and the hierarchical ranking of peoples—and how these relationships were extended to Europeans (Sabo 1995a:85–87). The Caddo used symbols of sacred and

62 / Timothy K. Perttula

secular rituals and greeting ceremonies (including the weeping during greeting ceremonies of the Caddo leaders noted by the de Soto chroniclers; see C. Hudson 1997:362) to draw out these relationships and "to extend to their relations with Europeans those basic principles and themes that ordered and gave shape to their own distinctive societies" (Sabo 1995a:86–87).

New historical studies of the Caddo are considering the social and political character of the Hasinai and Kadohadacho, two of the Caddo confederacies in historic times (the other being the Natchitoches), following in the tradition of historians and ethnographers such as Herbert E. Bolton, George A. Dorsey, and John R. Swanton, who pursued Caddo historical research in the early 1900s (see Dorsey 1997; F. T. Smith 1995, 1996; Tanner 1993, 1996). These studies are crucial to understanding the protohistoric and early historic (pre-1835) archaeology of the Caddo peoples.

Carter (1995a) relates present-day Caddo thoughts, rituals, and ceremonies to the past to highlight strong and pervasive continuities from the Caddo's past to modern times. Her discussion of the Turkey Dance among the modern Caddos, juxtaposed with her description of the Caddo women dancing the victory dance for Henri Joutel and companions in 1687, makes clear how the victory dance then, and the Turkey Dance now, was and is used by the Caddo to celebrate their survival, plus "recount history . . . [and] carry messages from the past" (Carter 1995a:41). Similarly, when she talks about the special place of "that kind of pole" (*Itcha kaanah*) in the context of the Ghost Dance rituals among the Caddo in the 1890s and in different ceremonies among the Nabedache Caddo in 1690, our understanding of the enduring importance of tobacco, fire, and smoke to Caddo religious rituals and ceremonies in protohistoric and historic times is broadened.

Trails and Caddoan Landscapes

Other historians and anthropologists are focusing on the routes of European explorers in Caddo country during the Protohistoric era, such as the deSoto-Moscoso *entrada* (see C. Hudson 1997; Young and Hoffman 1993) and the seventeenth- and eighteenth-century Spanish *entradas* (see Chapa 1997 and Foster 1995). These studies are helping to flesh out economic and political relationships among the Caddo, between the Caddo and other Native American groups, and between the Europeans and Caddo groups during the Protohistoric and Historic periods. Specifically, this effort is helping to locate important Caddo villages and tribal areas, as well as aboriginal trails (Corbin 1991) and sacred landscapes of Caddo mounds and connecting trails (Skiles and Perttula 1998). The trails first established by the Caddo in prehistoric times ran north-south and east-west across their lands, converging at important mound centers on the major rivers and streams. Even though Caddo populations waxed and waned, mound centers were abandoned, and groups moved about the land, the major trails were geographically stable and anchored to these ancient sacred mound centers (Skiles and Perttula 1998).

When first visited by the de Soto *entrada* in 1542, the Caddo were described as having a sometimes dense but sometimes light population that lived in scattered settlements with abundant food reserves of corn in several of the provinces (Naguatex on the Red River and Guasco near the Neches River; see C. Hudson 1997:353–379). Archaeological investigations confirm that Caddoan communities were widely dispersed throughout all of the major and minor river valleys of the region from at least A.D. 800 until the early 1700s (Figure 4.5). Their settlement and use of lands has had great permanence: a thousand years or more of living and sustaining themselves in the forested and well-watered landscape of the Trans-Mississippi South.

Caddoan communities, towns, and mound centers were never fortified, and the widely dispersed prehistoric and historic Caddoan communities do not hint of a defensive posture (C. Hudson 1997:372; Kenmotsu and Perttula 1996). Thus it is hard to credit Hickerson's (1997) assertion that the threat of Apache aggression played a major role in the formation of the Hasinai Caddo confederacy in the late seventeenth century. This is not to say that there were not conflicts between the Caddo peoples and their neighbors.

French and Spanish documents of the seventeenth and eighteenth centuries clearly show that the Caddo had many enemies; some were long-standing, like the Osage and Chickasaw to the east (see Margry n.d.), and to the west among hunter-gatherer groups. The Osage and Chickasaw ceaselessly raided the Caddo for slaves, and at the same time the Caddo became involved in the thriving traffic in Apache slaves that began about 1700 (see John and Wheat 1989).

This enmity appears to have increased after the Caddo had the horse and reliable supplies of guns (by the late seventeenth century), as the Caddo increased their bison and deer hunting in the prairies and plains well west and southwest of their territory (see Chapa 1997:136, 161, 189; Foster 1995:119, 305, fn. 20; Foster and Jackson 1993; A. V. Thoms 1997:24, 26; Weddle 1987:230) to obtain deer and bison hides for trade with the French. By the 1680s, the Caddoan societies south of the Red River were well-supplied with horses obtained in trade, such that "there were four or five about each house" (Griffith 1954:145). The acquisition and use of the horse by the Caddo facilitated the rapid movement and transportation of goods (both aboriginal and European); horses were highly sought trade items of great value, and they brought increased mobility and range to hunting forays. Thus the seemingly rapid adoption of the horse conferred a considerable selective advantage (e.g., Ramenofsky 1995:139–141) to Caddoan groups over their non-Caddoan neighbors when considered together with an increased accessibility to French guns (Perttula 1997:202–207), Spanish mission horse herds, and the expanding Southern Plains bison herds.

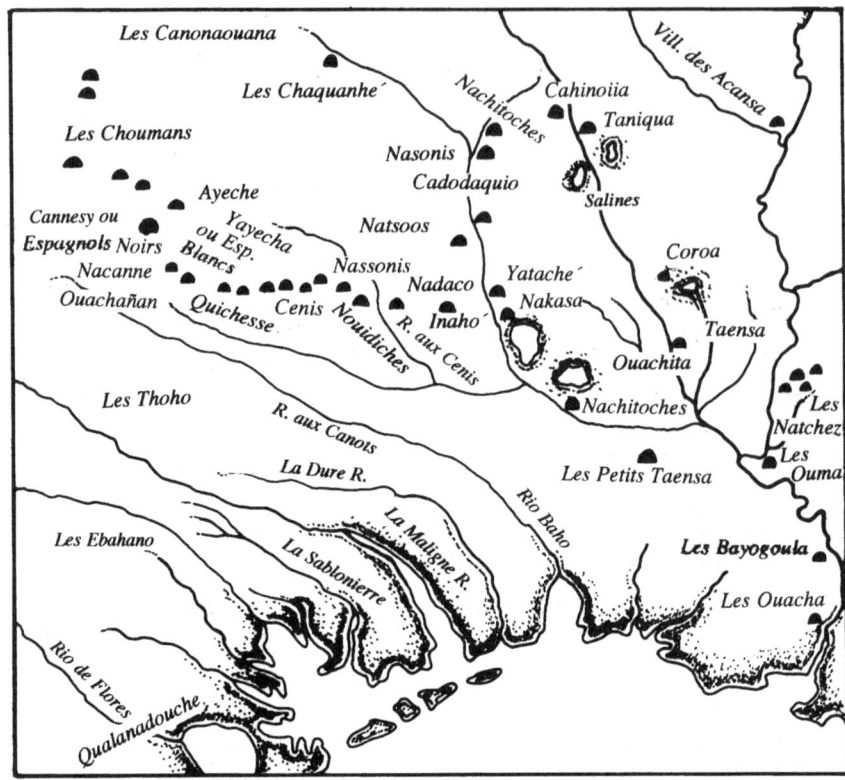

Figure 4.5 Redrawn version of Guillaume Delisle Map, 1972.

Conclusions

All these studies of the Protohistoric and Historic eras, it is fair to say, have brought a broader and more accurate appreciation of the vibrant and dynamic nature of Caddo lifeways from prehistoric times down to the present day, as well as a better understanding of the impressive social and cultural complexity and diversity that characterize Caddo native history during the Protohistoric and early Historic periods. As I mentioned earlier, the Caddos were powerful agricultural chiefdoms when visited by the Spanish *entrada* led by de Soto and Moscoso in the 1540s (see C. Hudson 1997; Young and Hoffman 1993). They were recognized as the "Great Kingdom of the Tejas," a populous nation, by the Spanish and French in the seventeenth and eighteenth centuries. And they brought these European traders and settlers into, and incorporated them within, long-standing aboriginal trading networks across the Caddoan area and beyond (see Gregory 1973).

The Spanish were unsuccessful in establishing missions among the Caddo or converting them to Catholicism. This has been attributed to the "strength of the culture of the Caddo people—their spiritual belief and long-standing customs and traditions, both for the conduct of their everyday life and the conduct of taking care of spiritual needs" (Perttula 1996a). The Caddo did not need the religion brought by the Spanish, for they had their own strong spiritual beliefs, as well as strong political and civil leaders who were also spiritual leaders in their communities (J. Miller 1996). When it suited the Caddo, they cooperated and interacted with the European intruders, mainly through trade. The Caddo traded deer hides, salt, horses, and other goods to Europeans for a variety of goods that improved the lives of the people.

The Caddo political leaders (such as the *caddis* Tinhiouen, Dehahuit, and Iesh or José Maria) were politically astute and masterful mediators and alliance-builders between European and Anglo-American explorers and colonists (Carter 1995a; F. T. Smith 1995, 1996), as well as with Native American groups such as the Comanche, Wichita, and Apache tribes. Further insights into the traditional character of Caddo life highlight important changes in their ritual beliefs and political practices that may not be apparent from either archaeological or ethnohistorical perspectives. Carter (1995a:177) notes "a startling change in governance" described by Father Gaspar José de Solís in 1768 among the Nabedache Caddo. In that community, the principal authority was a Caddo woman called Santa Adiva, not the *chenesi* and *caddi*, the hereditary male leaders. Such a change appears to be related to "epidemics decimating Hasinai villages after the coming of the missionaries or the Spanish policy of presenting the staff of leadership to an elected leader had broken the hereditary chain" (Carter 1995a:177). Even so, the hereditary chain of Caddo leadership—with strong, able, and peace- and alliance-building *caddis*—seems to have continued unbroken among the Hasinai and Kadohadacho, and this was the source of their strength. The Caddo political leaders shaped the decisive political decisions of the day to favor and strengthen the Caddo peoples, and they arranged and brought to fruition alliances between the Caddo, other powerful Native American groups, and competing European nations.

With the permanent Anglo-American settlement of the region in waves of immigration after about 1815, it was the Caddo peoples' misfortune to have been living on choice and fertile farmlands desired by the Anglo-Americans (F. T. Smith 1995:103). In a few short years, they were dispossessed of their traditional homelands. Their lands and goods were swindled from them by U.S. Federal Indian agents in the Caddo Treaty of 1835, and in 1859 they were forced to relocate from Texas to western Oklahoma (then Indian Territory).

The cultural and oral traditions of the Caddo peoples remain vibrant (Carter 1995a; Chafe 1997; Newkumet and Meredith 1988). So too do archaeological and historical studies of the Caddo. I hope that this paper on Caddo protohistory and archaeology contributes to a broader and more meaningful understanding of their past, as well as their present and future.

Notes

As with any endeavor, there are many people I would like to thank for their assistance and encouragement. First, I would like to thank Mark A. Rees and Cameron B. Wesson for the invitation to participate in the 1997 Southeastern Archaeological Conference symposium from which this paper ultimately derived. I also have to thank Mary Cecile Carter, Bo Nelson, Robert Cast, Stacy Halfmoon, Bobby Gonzalez, Bob Skiles, Diane Wilson, Mark Walters, Tom Middlebrook, Nancy A. Kenmotsu, and Dee Ann Story for their support of my research efforts. I would also like to extend my thanks to the following individuals for providing me with information and publications on Caddoan archaeology and history: J. Brett Cruse, Ann M. Early, Ross C. Fields, Jeff Girard, David H. Jurney, David B. Kelley, J. Dan Rogers, Frank F. Schambach, and F. Todd Smith.

1. Indeed, the de Soto-Moscoso *entrada* noted the agricultural capabilities of the Kadohadacho in 1542, when they pillaged the maize stores on their way west; when they returned some months later to the same villages, the maize stores had been replenished (C. Hudson 1997:361, 375).

5 / William Bartram and the Archaeology of the Appalachian Summit

Christopher B. Rodning

During the sixteenth and seventeenth centuries, tribal communities composed of several different towns and groups of towns formed out of the vestiges of the diverse Mississippian chiefdoms that rose and fell in southeastern North America from the eleventh through the sixteenth centuries (Galloway 1994, 1995; Knight 1994a; Muller 1997; J. F. Scarry 1994a, 1996a; Wesson 1999; Widmer 1994). As the seventeenth century drew to a close, the community that became known as the Cherokee formed within the cultural landscape of southwestern North Carolina and surrounding areas (Champagne 1983, 1990; Dickens 1978, 1979; Goodwin 1977; Hatley 1989, 1995; Hill 1997; Persico 1979). This paper reviews ethnohistoric evidence about native cultures and communities of southwestern North Carolina and surrounding areas in southern Appalachia and its relevance to the archaeological study of Cherokee cultural history. I concentrate especially on the travel journal of the Quaker naturalist William Bartram and his reflections on visiting the southern Appalachians during the eighteenth century.

Several crisscrossing mountain ranges in western North Carolina form the natural landscape of a cultural and geographic province known as the Appalachian Summit (Figure 5.1)(Kroeber 1939:95; Purrington 1983:83). Bartram visited the Middle Cherokee towns and surrounding countryside in these mountains on the eve of the American Revolution (Figure 5.2)(Waselkov and Braund 1995:72–88). His path of travel across southeastern North America eventually led him through several Upper Creek towns (see Braund 1993:10; Dimmick 1989:2; Lolley 1996:5). Some of his writing compares and contrasts the material culture and social structures of Iroquoian-speaking Cherokee groups and Muskogean-speaking Creek communities (Waselkov and Braund 1995:110–186).

Although his travels and journals date to the late eighteenth century, William Bartram's written descriptions of Cherokee lifeways and architecture are valuable ethnohistoric material for archaeologists interested in earlier periods (see I. W. Brown 1993:278–279; Dickens 1967:10–11; Hammett 1997:201–202; Waselkov 1997:185–187). Of course the lives of native people and communities across the Southeast had changed dramatically during the eighteenth century through their

68 / Christopher B. Rodning

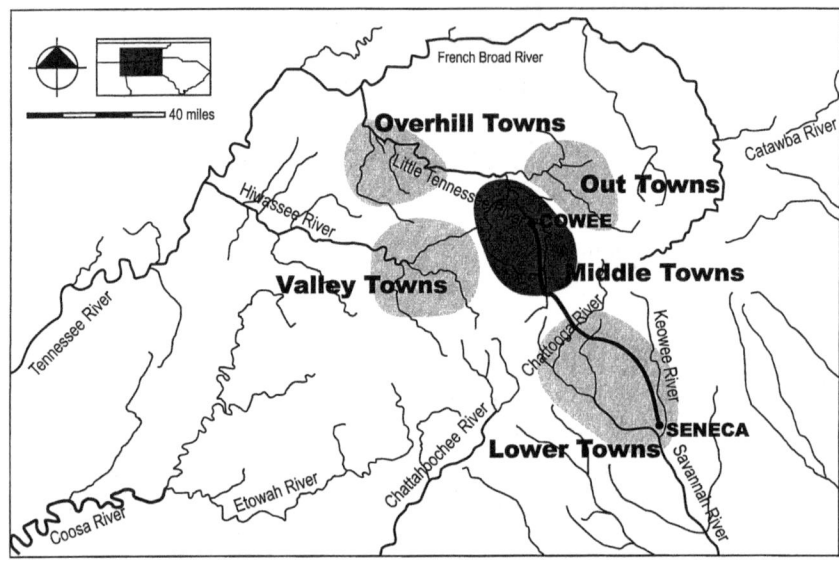

Figure 5.1 Cherokee towns and the route of William Bartram.

involvement in the deerskin trade and all the conflicts with Europeans and native allies that came with it. However, there are relatively few eyewitness accounts of native cultures and communities in the southern Appalachians between the Spanish explorations during the sixteenth century and the more permanent English presence in the mountains during the middle and late eighteenth century (see Adair 1930 [1775]; Baden 1983; Chicken 1928; Corkran 1962, 1967, 1969; Cuming 1928; Davis 1990; DePratter 1991, 1994; DeVorsey 1971, 1998; Gearing 1958, 1962; Hatley 1995; D. H. King and Evans 1977; Mereness 1916; Merrell 1989; Mooney 1887, 1891, 1900; Randolph 1973; Sattler 1995; B. A. Smith 1979; M. T. Smith 1987; Timberlake 1927). Therefore, archaeologists interested in Cherokee lifeways and the Appalachian Summit cultural landscape during the seventeenth century often rely upon ethnohistoric evidence dating to the late sixteenth or late eighteenth century, at least as starting points for archaeological research (see Beck 1997:162–163; Dickens 1967:3–5; C. Hudson 1990:94–101; M. T. Smith 1987:11–22).

This chapter concentrates on the writings of William Bartram, whose journals and essays offer a vivid portrait of what the landscapes along his path of travel looked like.[1] I relate his writing to archaeological problems and interests in the Appalachian Summit, where considerable surveys and excavations have been done and where there is great potential for further fieldwork.[2] First I trace Bartram's route of travel through the Appalachian Summit. Then I outline several anthropological

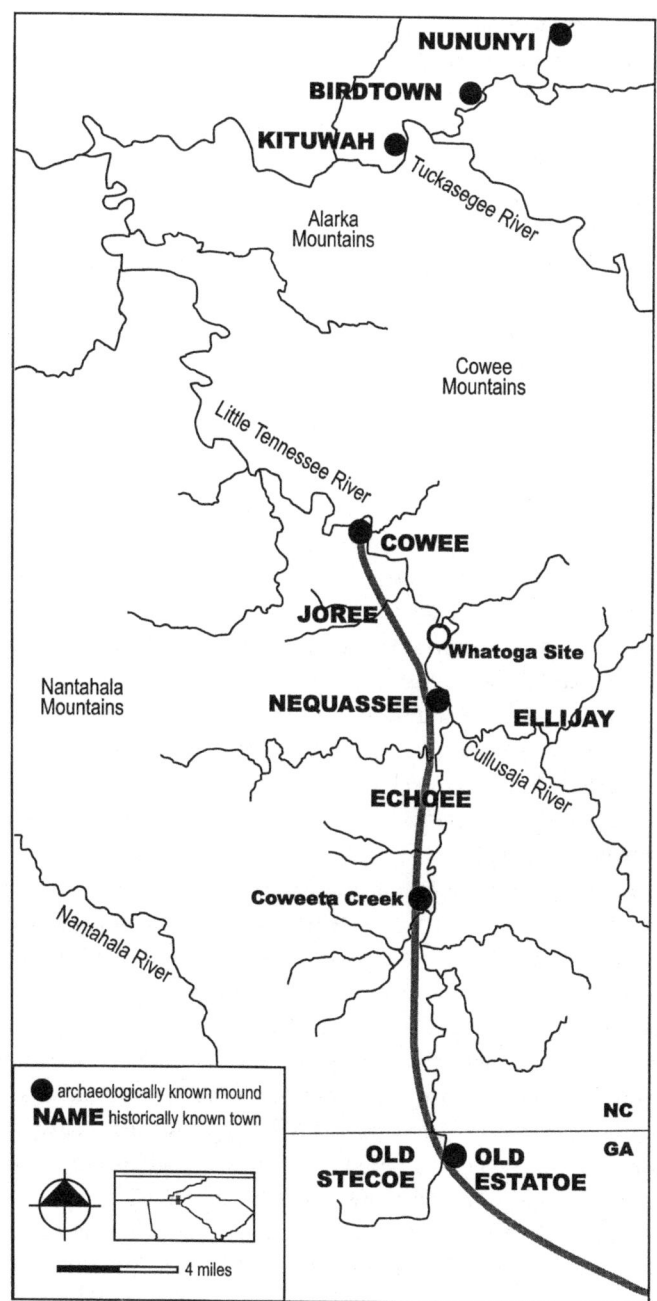

Figure 5.2 Archaeology in the upper Little Tennessee Valley, North Carolina.

topics that come up in Bartram's journal and that are worth further archaeological consideration in the Appalachian Summit. His journal offers some valuable material to compare and contrast with spatial patterns in the archaeological record of the Appalachian Summit, even though his visit to southern Appalachia came well after the Cherokee became enmeshed in the deerskin trade and other forms of interaction with European colonists. My conclusions comment on one scene from his journal that illustrates both the cultural upheaval within native communities during that century and the persistence of some traditions in the secluded cultural landscape of the Appalachian Summit, which was relatively far away from major European colonial settlements during much of the sixteenth and seventeenth centuries.

Bartram's Path

Bartram sailed from Philadelphia to Charleston in 1773. He traveled by horse to eastern Georgia and Florida and visited several ancient and abandoned mounds and villages while touring river valleys and coastal forests until March of 1774. In May of 1775 he set his course for southern Appalachia and the Cherokee towns. After visiting Cherokee country, Bartram made his way to several Creek towns along the Coosa and Tallapoosa rivers in Alabama, arriving in Mobile in July of 1775. He sailed to Pensacola and stayed there for a short while, then headed west again to explore parts of what are now southern Mississippi and southeastern Louisiana. However, he became sick and returned to Mobile by November of 1775. His journal offers excellent descriptions of native landscapes of Georgia, Alabama, and the western part of the Carolinas, but nothing about the Tennessee Valley itself and only some brief comments about the Mississippi Valley. Greg Waselkov and Kathryn Braund (1995) have written a remarkable book about his journal and its significance for archaeology in different parts of southeastern North America. Here my specific interests are Bartram's comments about native people and landscapes in and around what is now southwestern North Carolina.

Bartram traveled from a colonial outpost at the confluence of the Savannah and Broad rivers and visited Seneca as well as former Cherokee towns along the Keowee River in northwestern South Carolina (Waselkov and Braund 1995:73–75). For the most part these settlements had been abandoned, but architectural remnants of ancient villages and old townhouses were prominently visible landmarks in these areas. Traveling by horseback, Bartram then wound his way through the mountains northwest of Keowee toward the Cherokee town of Cowee (Waselkov and Braund 1995:75–76). Apparently he did not meet anybody between the Keowee and Chattooga rivers, but he saw many former settlements. He did pass through a place called Oconee somewhere west or northwest of Keowee itself, and here he noted the ruins of an ancient town.

Bartram continued to find the ruins of former towns near the headwaters of the Little Tennessee River in what is now northeastern Georgia and southwestern North Carolina (Waselkov and Braund 1995:75–76). He saw an abandoned mound that he called "Old Stecoe," which is probably at or somewhere close to the archaeologically known Dillard mound (see King and Evans 1977:289; Wynn 1990:54–55).[3] He may have been at "Old Estatoe," which perhaps was an earlier site for the historically known Lower town known by that name (see Hill 1997:68–74; King and Evans 1977:289).[4]

Bartram was intent on visiting the mound and town at Cowee along the Little Tennessee River in southwestern North Carolina (Waselkov and Braund 1995:76–79). He followed trails from near the headwaters of this river to this major town.[5] Along the way he passed through several towns and hamlets that were surrounded by fields and woods.[6]

Using Cowee as a base, Bartram traveled with a colonial trader through the Cowee Mountains east toward the Tuckasegee River, where one afternoon trek inspired some of his most lyrical prose. From overlooks above Cowee, Bartram (1955:287 [1791]) found stunning scenery—

After riding near two miles through Indian plantations of Corn, which was well cultivated, kept clean of weeds and was well advanced, being near eighteen inches in height, and the Beans planted at the Corn-hills were above ground; we leave the fields on our right, turning towards the mountains and ascending through a delightful green vale or lawn, which conducted us in amongst the pyramidal hills and crossing a brisk flowing creek, meandering through the meads which continued near two miles, dividing and branching in amongst the hills; we then mounted their steep ascents, rising gradually by ridges or steps one above another, frequently crossing narrow, fertile dales as we ascended; the air feels cool and animating, being charged with the fragrant breath of the mountain beauties, the blooming mountain cluster Rose, blushing Rhododendron and fair Lilly of the valley: having now attained the summit of this very elevated ridge, we enjoyed a fine prospect indeed; the enchanting Vale of Keowe, perhaps as celebrated for fertility, fruitfulness and beautiful prospects as the Fields of Pharsalia or the Vale of Tempe: the town, the elevated peeks [sic] of the Jore mountains, a very distant prospect of the Jore village in a beautiful lawn, lifted up many thousand feet higher than our present situation, besides a view of many other villages and settlements on the sides of the mountains, at various distances and elevations; the silver rivulets gliding by them and snow white cataracts glimmering on the sides of the lofty hills; the bold promontories of the Jore[7] mountain stepping into the Tanase[8] river, whilst his foaming waters rushed between them (Waselkov and Braund 1995:79–80).

After staying for several days at Cowee, Bartram rode toward the Overhill Cherokee towns along the lower Little Tennessee River in southeastern Tennessee, but after meeting the Overhill chief Attakullakulla in the Nantahala Mountains and learning of unrest between colonists and native groups, he returned to Cowee. While he was there, Bartram (1955:296–298 [1791]) noted many aspects of native architecture and witnessed a ritual in the townhouse—

> The town of Cowe consists of about one hundred dwellings, near the banks of the Tanase, on both sides of the river. . . . The Cherokees construct their habitations on a different plan from the Creeks, that is but one oblong four square building, of one story high; the materials consisting of logs or trunks of trees, stripped of their bark, notched at their ends, fixed one upon another, and afterwards plaistered well, both inside and out, with clay well tempered with dry grass, and the whole covered or roofed with the bark of the Chesnut tree or long broad shingles. This building is however partitioned transversely, forming three apartments, which communicate with each other by inside doors; each house or habitation has besides a little conical house, covered with dirt, which is called the winter or hot-house; this stands a few yards distance from the mansion-house, opposite the front door. . . . The council or town-house is a large rotunda, capable of accommodating several hundred people; it stands on the top of an ancient artificial mount of earth, of about twenty feet perpendicular, and the rotunda on the top of it being above thirty feet more, gives the whole fabric an elevation of about sixty feet from the common surface of the ground. But it may be proper to observe, that this mount on which the rotunda stands, is of a much ancienter date than the building, and perhaps was raised for another purpose. . . . The rotunda is constructed after the following manner, they first fix in the ground a circular range of posts or trunks of trees, about six feet high, at equal distances, which are notched at top, to receive into them, from one to another, a range of beams or wall plates; within this is another circular order of very large and strong pillars, above twelve feet high, notched in like manner at top, to receive another range of wall plates, and within this is yet another or third range of stronger and higher pillars, but fewer in number, and standing at a greater distance from each other; and lastly, in the centre stands a very strong pillar, which forms the pinnacle of the building, and to which the rafters centre at top; these rafters are strengthened and bound together by cross beams and laths, which sustain the roof or covering, which is a layer of bark neatly placed, and tight enough to exclude the rain, and sometimes they cast a thin superficies of earth over all. There is but one large door, which serves at the same time to admit light from without and the smoak to escape when a fire is kindled; but as there is but a small fire kept, sufficient to give light at

night, and that fed with dry small sound wood divested of its bark, there is but little smoak; all around the inside of the building, betwixt the second range of pillars and the wall, is a range of cabins or sophas, consisting of two or three steps, one above or behind the other, in theatrical order, where the assembly sit or lean down; these sophas are covered with matts or carpets, very curiously made of thin splints of Ash or Oak, woven or platted together; near the great pillar in the centre the fire is kindled for light, near which the musicians seat themselves, and round about this the performers exhibit their dances and other shews at public festivals, which happen almost every night throughout the year. (Waselkov and Braund 1995:84–85)

Because of the unrest between Cherokee groups and European colonists in the Overhill towns in eastern Tennessee, Bartram traveled back to Dartmouth and Fort James at the confluence of the Savannah and Broad rivers. His hosts at this European colonial outpost were preparing for meetings with Cherokee town leaders, and during his stay there he saw several stone mounds while walking through the woods close to where the town of Keowee had once stood. After a brief stay in Dartmouth, Bartram left with a group of traders bound for the Creek towns further southwest. Having visited several Lower Creek and Upper Creek towns along the Chattahoochee and Tallapoosa rivers, he described in his journal the architecture of these towns and offered clues about the history of the landscapes in which they stood.

Bartram's Journal

His journal about these travels offers a wealth of rich descriptions from which archaeologists can draw for their studies of native landscapes and lifeways in southeastern North America. It raises several topics that are worth considering in the context of archaeology in North Carolina.

A major passage in Bartram's journal to which many archaeologists have referred is his description of the Cherokee townhouse at Cowee, quoted at length above; this account has been very helpful to archaeologists interested in the evolution of Cherokee public architecture in the southern Appalachians (D. G. Moore 1990; Schroedl 1986a:220–221). Though Bartram described this public structure at Cowee as standing atop a great mound, it seems likely the townhouse stood on a modest mound that was itself built atop a much greater natural knoll beside the Little Tennessee River (Moore 1990, personal communication 1999).[9] How does archaeological evidence of southern Appalachian townhouses dating to different periods of the past compare to Bartram's description?[10] Interestingly, his representation of the Cowee council house corresponds closely to archaeological evidence of Cherokee council houses in eastern Tennessee dating to the eighteenth century. Moreover, these forms of Cherokee council houses seem to have been present in towns with some forms of household architecture showing European influences such as Bartram described.

Another interesting point about Bartram's journal is that it does not describe a mound at the place historically known as the Cherokee town of Nequassee, though he did visit a place he called Nequassee: "arrived at the town of Echoe, consisting of many good houses, well inhabited; I passed through and continued three miles farther to Nucasse" (Waselkov and Braund 1995:77). He did find a great mound and townhouse at Whatoga—

> and three more miles brought me to Whatoga: riding through this large town, the road carried me winding about through their little plantations of Corn, Beans, etc. up to the council-house, which was a very large dome or rotunda, situated on the top of an ancient artificial mount, and here my road terminated; all before me and on every side appeared little plantations of young Corn, Beans, etc. divided from each other by narrow strips or borders of grass, which marked the bounds of each one's property, their habitation standing in the midst. (Waselkov and Braund 1995:77)

Whereas Nequassee is the name of a mound along the Little Tennessee River in downtown Franklin—the current seat of Macon County (Mooney 1900:336–337)[11]—Whatoga is associated with an archaeological site in a bend of the Little Tennessee River north of Franklin, near what is now Lake Emory (Dickens 1967:7–8).[12] Did Bartram confuse or misremember these names? Did he or his publisher mistake some of the names of places along the path he traveled? My suggestion is that the place to which Bartram referred to as Whatoga is actually the mound and village known to archaeologists today as Nequassee. Perhaps when he composed his journal he mistook the order in which he visited Nequassee and Whatoga. Or perhaps place-names changed from time to time as people or whole towns moved from one place to another.[13] Cherokee place-names seem to reflect something about local environments—for example, "Keowee" refers to an abundance of mulberries (Hill 1997:9). Yet Cherokee town names often refer to "current" and "old" settings for communities—"Old Estatoe" is one example (Hill 1997:86)—and town names may apply to the "people" of a town rather than a specific "place."

It is also interesting that Bartram did not find a major town at the mouth of Coweeta Creek, where archaeologists have excavated a townhouse and village that likely date to the seventeenth century (see Dickens 1976:100; B. J. Egloff 1967:8–12; K. T. Egloff 1971:42–71; Keel 1976:234; Ward and Davis 1999:185). Glass beads and kaolin pipe stems were found with the latest stages of the Coweeta Creek council house, although non-native trade goods were not found in any burials and were very rare in all other contexts at the site (Dickens 1978:131; K. T. Egloff 1971:62–69). The native ceramics from Coweeta Creek would fit a time frame within the seventeenth or early eighteenth century, and they are comparable in many respects to Tugalo and Estatoe phase ceramics from sites farther south (Dickens 1979:22–28; B. J. Egloff 1967:27–67). Neither the Coweeta Creek archaeological locality nor archaeologically known settlements farther south in the upper Little Tennessee Valley figure prominently in the ethnohistorical literature or historical cartography of Cherokee towns,[14] supporting the conclusion that the town at Coweeta Creek predates the eighteenth century. It must have been a major town center during the seventeenth century (Ward and Davis 1999:183–187), and yet it may not have been an especially visible landmark by the middle of the eighteenth century (D. H. King and Evans 1977:297–299).

It is worth noting that Bartram offers a rich portrait of the whole landscape of the upper Little Tennessee Valley, describing trails running along the river and through the woods and fields between towns (see D. H. King and Evans 1977:283; Myer 1928:772; Waselkov and Braund 1995:77). He also depicts bustling Middle Cherokee towns and villages as well as abandoned towns and old fields, hinting that one reason Cherokee towns moved from place to place was that local supplies of firewood and other natural resources would sometimes dwindle.

Archaeological Topics

Bartram thus gives his readers striking visual images of what the cultural landscape as a whole looked like on the eve of the American Revolution, and what remnants of former towns and villages were still visible in the landscape. Of course his visit came after a century or more of trade and many forms of cultural encounter and exchange between Europeans and native people in the southern Appalachian region. He encountered both traders and some of their horses in the Middle Cherokee towns (Waselkov and Braund 1995:80), and he visited these areas after South Carolina and other colonies had waged war against native townspeople (King and Evans 1977:272). Nevertheless his descriptions of native landscapes and lifeways are a valuable window upon native southeasterners living in areas where there was a much different kind of colonial presence and perhaps greater native cultural conservatism than in many parts of the Piedmont and coastal plain provinces closer to colonial communities and outposts. Bartram offers a valuable stepping stone for comparative studies in Appalachian Summit archaeology. His descriptions of native landscapes and lifeways of the Southeast can form a contrast to archaeological patterns representing earlier eras in the Appalachian Summit or at least can suggest hypotheses that may be tested against the archaeological record.

How often did whole Cherokee communities move from one locale to another? Bartram traveled past old villages and townhouses along the Keowee River in what is now northwestern South Carolina (1955:268–271 [1791]). These were likely abandoned following encounters and conflicts with European colonists and Creek groups during the years of the slave and deerskin trades and the outbreak of epidemic diseases (see Hatley 1995:156–159; Hill 1997:74–76). He also visited deserted settlements and old fields in the Cowee Mountains of what is now southwestern North Carolina (1955:287–288 [1791]), which may have been abandoned when local supplies of natural resources dwindled. Reflecting upon visiting old fields somewhere in the mountains near Cowee, Bartram (1955:287–288 [1791]) wrote,

> After viewing this very entertaining scene we began to descend the mountain on the other side, which exhibited the same order of gradations of ridges and vales as on our ascent, and at length rested on a very expansive, fertile plain, amidst the towering hills, over which we rode a long time, through magnificent high forests, extensive green fields, meadows and lawns. Here had formerly been a very flourishing settlement, but the Indians deserted it in search of fresh planting land, which they soon found in a rich vale but a few miles distance over a ridge of hills. (Waselkov and Braund 1995:80)

How often this abandonment and movement happened is not clear. Nor is it clear how communities decided where to move or when to move. Did whole towns or just household groups within them relocate? Did different towns negotiate with each other to plan these kinds of movements? Were there changes in town spacing in different areas during different periods between the fifteenth and eighteenth centuries?[15] How might these movements have affected or been affected by politics and social interaction in the region?[16] These aspects of landscape history certainly have implications for understanding archaeological evidence of settlement patterns across southern Appalachia during the late Prehistoric and Protohistoric periods. They also relate to our understanding of how Cherokee people living in different areas interacted with each other.

What happened to Cherokee townhouses when their tenures as architectural centers of towns were over? Bartram (1955:280–281 [1791]; Waselkov and Braund 1995:76) traveled past the remnants of an old townhouse still visible atop a mound somewhere near the source of the Little Tennessee River, and of course he had seen old mounds and townhouses along the Keowee River (1955:270–271 [1791]; Waselkov and Braund 1995:75). Gardens and woods around old towns and hamlets may have been left with little thought when people moved to another place. Perhaps there were traditions for ritually ending the lives of council houses as architectural centers for towns or even groups of towns. Remembering the ancient mound and townhouse at Old Stecoe, Bartram (1955:280 [1791]) wrote, "Here was a vast Indian mount or tumulus and great terrace, on which stood the council house, with banks encompassing their circus; here were also old Peach and Plumb orchards, some of the trees appeared yet thriving and fruitful" (Waselkov and Braund 1995:76).

There is ethnohistoric evidence that old townhouses were ritually dismantled and perhaps even covered by mantles of clay (Schroedl 1986b:220; Sturtevant 1978:200). This tradition contrasts with the visible presence on the landscape of former Cherokee townhouses as described by Bartram during his tour of the southern Appalachian countryside. Perhaps this contrast represents the loss of a significant Cherokee ritual during the deerskin trade of the eighteenth century. Or maybe not all Cherokee communities performed communal rituals to end the tenure of a council house as an architectural landmark for a native township.

What impact did building and rebuilding Cherokee towns have upon the surrounding forest environment? Bartram (1955:296–298 [1791]) described the architecture of Cherokee townhouses and dwellings, and several archaeologists have referred to his accounts of architectural details (Schroedl 1986b:220–221; Waselkov and Braund 1995:84–85)—including his comments about the placement of inner support posts and rafters to hold up bark roofs. Apparently he saw (1955:296–297 [1791]) Cherokee townhouses that showed many elements of traditional architecture, although dwelling houses revealed a blend of Euroamerican and Native American influences (Schroedl 1986b:224–228; Waselkov and Braund 1995:183–186) —namely the log cabins built beside more traditional winter lodges. From his and other descriptions of Cherokee architecture and landscaping projects (see Hill 1997:68–74), it is apparent that gathering resources from the surrounding woods and gardens to build and sustain towns made a significant mark upon the forested landscape. Many historically known Cherokee names for specific places reflect characteristics of the local natural environment and its resources (see Goodwin 1977: 153–156), and it is likely that old settlements became valuable edge habitats in which to hunt deer and turkeys and gather nuts and berries.

Building and rebuilding the council house and village within the community centered at the Coweeta Creek site would have demanded considerable resources. The abandonment of Coweeta Creek and other towns may have marked the point at which dwindling local supplies of wood for architecture and firewood encouraged townspeople to move somewhere else.

What kinds of rituals were performed at Cherokee council houses and plazas? Bartram (1955:298–300 [1791]) described a ritual at the Cowee townhouse and the town common beside it; Cherokee communities likely held several of these gatherings every year (Waselkov and Braund 1995:85–86; see Adair 1930 [1775]; Corkran 1969; Wetmore 1983). Bartram (1955:284–285 [1791]) went straight to the townhouse at Whatoga after arriving there; Cherokee communities probably often received such visitors in these architectural spaces (Waselkov and Braund 1995:76–

77; see Faulkner 1978; Randolph 1973; Timberlake 1927). Members of a Cherokee community would rest in a townhouse upon their return to their hometown (see Hill 1997:73), thus renewing their places within the community (see Perdue 1998:35). It is likely that some old Cherokee men may have all but lived in townhouses (see Schroedl 1986b:224), given the involvement of many men in activities related to these architectural spaces and the historic link between women and households in this matrilineal society (see Perdue 1998:45).

The townhouse at Coweeta Creek was built and rebuilt at the same spot at least six times (K. T. Egloff 1971:51). Between it and the Coweeta Creek village was a communal plaza covered with lenses of clay and river sand (K. T. Egloff 1971:70). Artifacts and other materials found in the Coweeta Creek mound should help archaeologists reconstruct activities associated with townhouses and the events that occurred while they were being rebuilt (see VanDerwarker 1998; VanDerwarker and Detwiler 1999; G. D. Wilson et al. 1999).

What was the relationship between the Cherokee and the stone mounds or cairns found in some parts of the southern Appalachians? Bartram (1955:300 [1791]) noted the presence of stone mounds that seem to have been built many centuries earlier but that had become landmarks within the Cherokee landscape (Waselkov and Braund 1995:87). Are these related to the Swift Creek tradition of building stone mounds and cairns as has been described by archaeologists studying areas farther south (see M. Williams and Elliott 1998; M. Williams and Harris 1998)? Bartram also noted the visible presence of platform mounds in some Cherokee towns (Waselkov and Braund 1995:77). What different kinds of mounds were present in the Appalachian Summit at different points in the past (see Anderson et al. 1986; Heye et al. 1918; A. R. Kelly and de Baillou 1960; A. R. Kelly and Neitzel 1961; Lindauer and Blitz 1997; Setzler and Jennings 1941; C. Thomas 1894:333–350; Ward and Davis 1999:158–190)? The historic Cherokee certainly built townhouses on some mounds, but the mounds themselves and other landmarks that Bartram saw in southern Appalachia may have been more ancient additions to the landscape (Mooney 1887; Waselkov and Braund 1995:84).

How did members of one Cherokee township interact with other native towns in the greater southern Appalachians? Bartram (1955:298–300 [1791]) described ceremonial preparations for a ballgame against another town. Perhaps this ballgame was a form of ritual warfare that helped to keep towns at peace with each other (Waselkov and Braund 1995:85–86; see Vennum 1994:179–180, 213–235). English trader Alexander Longe (Corkran 1969:36–37) hinted that residents of several Cherokee towns cooperated to build a Cherokee council house, which seems to suggest that this kind of architectural space within a Cherokee town served as a setting for events at which people from many towns would gather. English diplomat

Henry Timberlake (1927:58–64; Randolph 1973) was welcomed at several Overhill Cherokee towns along the lower Little Tennessee River with rituals at and beside council houses, and meetings of Cherokee leaders from different towns took place in these settings. Sir Alexander Cuming (1928:125–126) met with several Cherokee town leaders at the Keowee council house upon his arrival in Cherokee country, and his later meetings at Nequassee with representatives from different Cherokee towns likely occurred in a Cherokee council house. Agent George Chicken (1928:97–102) was present at the gatherings of leaders from several different Cherokee towns at Keowee and Tanasee for trade negotiations, and my guess is that meetings like these involving representatives from different Cherokee towns would have been held in and beside council houses. Ethnohistorian Charles Hudson (1990:94–101) has described meetings between members of the Juan Pardo expedition and native town leaders from what is now southwestern North Carolina in the late sixteenth century, and these kinds of meetings very likely took place at or beside public buildings similar to historic Cherokee council houses. Bartram (1955:297–300 [1791]) saw council houses where all of these kinds of events took place—including contemporary council houses and remnants of ancient townhouses still visible on the ground (Waselkov and Braund 1995:75–76). When leaders from different Cherokee towns met, it is likely that they would gather within or beside Cherokee council houses like the ones that Bartram saw (D. G. Moore 1990; Waselkov and Braund 1995:84).

What were the shapes and dimensions of Cherokee towns? Bartram (1955:284 [1791]) described Echoee and Nequassee as villages or hamlets but noted the presence of some one hundred houses at the Cherokee town of Cowee on both sides of the river (Waselkov and Braund 1995:77, 84). He described Cowee as a "capital" and characterized Echoee as a "hamlet." From these clues it becomes apparent that larger and perhaps older Cherokee towns in southern Appalachia may have been especially prominent regional centers among the Cherokee. Did these centers shift across the landscape of southern Appalachia through time? It is also interesting to note the presence of houses on both sides of the rivers running through the communities of Cowee and Keowee. What social distinctions might have paralleled these spatial distinctions within Cherokee towns? During the eighteenth century, many Cherokee households included both a summer house and a winter lodge, and Bartram remarked on this phenomenon at Cherokee towns (Waselkov and Braund 1995:184–185). This paired architectural pattern is visible in the archaeological record of eastern Tennessee and northern Georgia (see Faulkner 1978:91; Hally and Kelly 1998:56; Polhemus 1990:130; Schroedl 1989:354; Sullivan 1987:28, 1989:110, 1995:110). Was this pattern present in southwestern North Carolina, and when?

Through time, nucleated town plans—represented by the archaeological sites of

Warren Wilson and Coweeta Creek (Dickens 1978:131)—gave way to more dispersed arrangements of households (see Wilms 1974), and this pattern is evident at the Townson and Tuckasegee sites (Dickens 1978:131). When did this dispersal happen in different river valleys and what were its social and political implications?

What kinds of paths connected Cherokee towns and farmsteads? Bartram (1955: 281 [1791]) followed trails from Echoee to Cowee and described paths leading from Cherokee towns through gardens and past hamlets to other places within the mosaic woodland landscape of southern Appalachia at the end of the eighteenth century (Waselkov and Braund 1995:76, 77). How old were these trails? Were mounds placed at crossroads or other significant points along these paths?

Native trails and routes for water travel have relatively little archaeological visibility in the Southeast (see Tanner 1989). But does the placement of towns like Nacoochee, Nequassee, Cowee, Peachtree, Coweeta Creek, and others relate at all to gaps in the mountains or the geography of historically known trails (see Myer 1928)? What patterns of interaction were there among communities in the Chattahoochee, Tugalo, Tuckasegee, Hiwassee, Little Tennessee, and other valleys? Water travel would have been relatively easy *within* groups of towns but not nearly as easy *between* one group of towns and another. The mountain landscape certainly did not prevent exchange and interaction among people from different valleys, but the terrain would have guided it in some way. Topography may have enhanced social bonds among people living in groups of neighboring towns. Furthermore, it may have heightened the effects of any conflicts that arose among close neighbors within this landscape of narrow river valleys and rugged mountain ranges.

What was the place of traders and trading houses in Cherokee communities, both socially and spatially? Some archaeological excavations have uncovered remnants of trading posts near Cherokee communities dating to the eighteenth century, and indeed the Cherokee and many of their native neighbors actively sought and encouraged trade during the early and mid-eighteenth century (Braund 1993:26–39; J. Chapman 1985; Polhemus 1979; Schroedl 1986a:5–16). Historians have noted that different traders carved their own niches within the communities of their Cherokee constituents and that many successful traders formed kinship or other social bonds within one or several Cherokee communities (Corkran 1967:11–12; Hatley 1995:43–44; J. W. Martin 1994:311; Perdue 1998:81–85). Ethnohistorian and environmental historian Tom Hatley (1995:32–51) has written a cogent review of the changing role of English traders within Cherokee communities from the earliest trade in the late seventeenth century through the end of the eighteenth century. Hatley (1989, 1995) and geographer Douglas Wilms (1991:1–3) have chronicled some of the changes in the relationship between the Cherokee and their southern Appalachian landscape introduced by opportunities and trends in the deerskin trade.

As they and geographer Gary Goodwin (1977:147–151; see also Dickens 1979: 26; Pillsbury 1983:59; Purrington 1983:150; Wilms 1974:51) have noted, settlement patterns in southern Appalachia changed dramatically due to the deerskin trade and the many forms of encounter and conflict that came with it and after it, when Cherokee communities tended to become more dispersed in their spatial layout and social fabric. Council houses still served as community centers even as households became more and more dispersed along the narrow river valleys of the Appalachians in southwestern North Carolina during the late eighteenth century. Meanwhile the social composition of native towns was changing as refugees from other native communities were moving to this relatively remote part of southeastern North America because of conflicts with European colonists. How do these changes compare to archaeologically visible changes in settlement patterns and public architecture throughout earlier centuries? How did new forms of trade change the ways that native towns and households within towns interacted with each other? How did ancient patterns of native interaction and exchange guide the ways that native people participated in the colonial trade in slaves and deerskins during the seventeenth and eighteenth centuries?

Indian agent George Chicken (1928:103; see also Cuming 1928:140; Davis 1990:31) traveled to the mountains for trade negotiations in the early eighteenth century, and it is clear that the Cherokee at times were actively interested in trade with the colonists. In time, Cherokee leaders even encouraged different colonial authorities to build forts and trading posts close to their communities. Native communities eventually became dependent upon this trade, which contributed to the breakdown of Cherokee and other native cultures and communities during the eighteenth century (Axtell 1997:69; J. N. Brown 1999:29; Corkran 1962:14; Goodwin 1977:113; Hill 1997:93; J. W. Martin 1994:316; Riggs 1989:328). The tactics and ethics of individual traders varied widely, and the policies of colonial authorities were often ineffective constraints upon the depredations of unscrupulous traders in the backcountry of southern Appalachia in the late eighteenth century (Adair 1930:242 [1775]; Axtell 1997:50; Bartram 1955:286 [1791]; Corkran 1962:34; Hatley 1995:50). How were these traders received within Cherokee towns and clans at different points during the late seventeenth and early eighteenth centuries? Did traders live within or at the edges of Cherokee communities? Did some traders have places to live in multiple Cherokee towns?

Bartram offers some clues, but not all that many (Waselkov and Braund 1995: 77–79). He observed old trading posts near the former setting of the Lower Cherokee Town of Keowee in what is now northwestern South Carolina and a trader living just south of Echoee along the upper Little Tennessee River in southwestern

North Carolina. According to Bartram, the trader at Cowee lived within that town, across the river from the council house and mound at Cowee, and he was known for his upstanding conduct and generosity to the local native community. Archaeologists have studied trading posts built close to Cherokee communities in eastern Tennessee (see J. Chapman 1985:100–110; Polhemus 1979:276–285), but they have not excavated any in western North Carolina (but see M. A. Harmon 1983, 1986), even though it is clear that traders were active in the Middle, Valley, and Out towns during the eighteenth century (Corkran 1962:192, 1967:160; Crane 1981:129–132 [1928]; Cuming 1928:132–133; Hatley 1995:17–51).

What rituals of communal renewal were performed in Cherokee towns? Many native groups of southeastern North America celebrated harvest festivals and other rituals related to their farming calendar (Bartram 1955:399 [1791]; C. Hudson 1976:374–375; Swanton 1946:769–772). Native peoples of southwestern North Carolina certainly performed rituals that created opportunities for renewing social bonds within communities (Corkran 1969:14–27; Hill 1997:83–84; Wetmore 1983:47–51). The harvest and communal renewal ceremonies known collectively at that point as the Busk which Bartram described probably bore a close relationship to rites performed in Cherokee towns in southeastern Tennessee, northeastern Georgia, and the western part of the Carolinas during the eighteenth century. These likely took place within and beside Cherokee council houses like those at Cowee, Whatoga, and other towns in the southern Appalachian region.

Bartram depicted a vibrant landscape in the upper Little Tennessee Valley, one rich in resources, yet only fifteen years before his visit South Carolina militiamen, led by James Grant, had ravaged this countryside, burning villages and fields (Adair 1930:267–268 [1775]; Hatley 1995:119–140). The social bonds within Cherokee communities in southern Appalachia survived this and the many other conflicts that erupted during the French and Indian War in the 1750s and early 1760s (Hatley 1995:155–156), though the Cherokee communities that Bartram visited would not last much longer in the form in which he saw them. Soon after his visit, during the American Revolution and its tumultuous aftermath (Dickens 1967:5–18; Hatley 1995:191–215), colonial militias again sacked native towns and landscapes in western North Carolina. The social composition of Cherokee communities changed dramatically after the depredations of colonial militias from Tennessee, Virginia, Georgia, and the Carolinas from the late 1770s through the 1780s (Hatley 1995:216–241).

Bartram's journal is certainly not the only primary ethnohistoric source about southern Appalachian cultures and communities. Journals about brief encounters between Spaniards and native groups of greater southern Appalachia in the sixteenth century are also extant (Beck 1997; DePratter 1991, 1994; C. Hudson 1990). The literature about the Cherokee as a group recognizable by that name comes mostly from English authors of the eighteenth or late seventeenth century (Baden 1983; DeVorsey 1971, 1998; Hatley 1995). During this period the French were also a significant presence throughout much of the Southeast and Midwest, and they sought to win the Cherokees as their allies and trading partners (Adair 1930:252–258 [1775]; Axtell 1997:64; Baden 1983:10–18; Hatley 1995:35). Several Christian missionaries visited native communities in the southern Appalachians and surrounding areas during the late eighteenth and early nineteenth centuries (J. N. Brown 1999:39; Schneider 1928; de Schwienitz 1928; Wilms 1991: 4–5). Yet few if any of these commentators on native cultures in the region match the rich comparative description that Bartram provided of the people and landscapes he observed.

Moreover, many ethnohistoric sources date relatively late in the time frame of Southeastern protohistory or even postdate that era. As in other parts of the Southeast there is a significant gap between the earliest European visitors to the southern Appalachians and the point at which colonists and colonial trade became a lasting presence within native communities and their ways of life.

The Comparative Perspective

Given this chronological gap in the ethnohistoric record about native cultures and landscapes in the Appalachian Summit, it is imperative that archaeologists take great care in making comparisons between ethnohistoric sources and archaeological patterns. Sites like Tuckasegee and Townson are windows upon eighteenth-century Cherokee culture (see Dickens 1967:17; Keel 1976:63–65), and thus they would make interesting comparisons with Bartram's descriptions of Cherokee households and towns. Sites like Coweeta Creek and others along the upper Little Tennessee likely represent Cherokee settlements dating to the seventeenth century, making them significant for efforts to understand native peoples of the southern Appalachians between the Spanish explorations and Bartram's visit to the Cherokee towns (see Dickens 1976:15; Hally 1994b:163). For archaeologists interested in these areas, Bartram's descriptions represent significant ethnohistoric material.

Several archaeologists and ethnohistorians have outlined problems in the application of ethnohistoric evidence toward interpreting patterns in archaeological data sets (Charlton 1981; Crumley 1974; Galloway 1989; Lightfoot 1995; Muller 1997; W. R. Wood 1990). One valuable point made by these and other scholars is that many descriptions of Native American communities and cultural practices were written after native groups had already experienced significant cultural change as a result of their encounters and interactions with Euroamerican groups, and thus these accounts are not necessarily applicable to archaeological data sets predating the sixteenth or seventeenth centuries (Galloway 1993). Another critique is that these characterizations of Native American lifeways and worldviews are biased by the Euroamerican heritage of most of the authors. Archaeologists who borrow from the ethnohistoric record certainly need to evaluate their sources as critically and carefully as they evaluate the contexts from which their archaeological evidence comes (Galloway 1991). My own approach to applying ethnohistoric evidence to archaeological problems is to frame the ethnohistoric evidence as a set of hypotheses or possibilities against which archaeological evidence can be tested. Such an approach is helpful in studying native peoples of the seventeenth century. This time frame covers the period between the earliest European explorations of the inland Southeast and the eighteenth-century trade and warfare instigated by non-native colonists.

Several archaeologists (Beck 1997; Drooker 1997; Galloway 1995; D. G. Moore 1999; M. T. Smith 1987, 1989a, 1989b; 1992, 1994a, 1994b; Waselkov 1989a, 1989b, 1993, 1997) have made major contributions to the scholarly study of native peoples in the southern Appalachians and surrounding areas—including the Creeks, Cherokees, Catawbas, and others—during the decades between Spanish explorations of the inland Southeast and the eventual spread of English trade across formerly remote areas. Ethnohistoric sources from these different forms of cultural encounter and exchange are bookends bracketing many years of cultural history for which archaeological rather than written materials offer clues about native lifeways. Sites like Coweeta Creek should help archaeologists in their quest to understand cultural continuity and change throughout the seventeenth century (see B. J. Egloff 1967:9–10). This period was certainly one of "indirect contact" between native people in southwestern North Carolina and their new colonial neighbors (see M. T. Smith 1987:6–8). During this century the Cherokee became recognizable as a tribal community by that name in southern Appalachia near the headwaters of the Savannah (Hatley 1995:16), though at this time they were not the cohesive entity they became in the early nineteenth century. At this point or soon afterward, the Creek confederacy formed as a set of alliances between towns in Alabama and Georgia (Knight 1994b:388), perhaps similarly to the ways people in different towns and groups of towns became part of the greater Cherokee community.

Although he noticed some differences, Bartram did find broad similarities in the material culture and social dynamics of Cherokee and Creek communities. The coalescence of the greater Cherokee community as such may have been a historical process comparable to the genesis of the Choctaw tribal community from several distinct but linguistically and culturally related groups just before and after the appearance of Europeans in the Mississippian world (see Galloway 1995). The historical distinction and sometime rivalry between Creek and Cherokee groups may have developed only during the tumultuous eighteenth century, and it may have been related to the rivalries between different European groups and the native towns allied to European colonial communities (see Knight 1994b).

Nevertheless, Bartram did recognize differences between the languages spoken by Cherokee and Creek people and the dialects of other native groups. The linguistic distinctions between the Creek and Cherokee are not closely correlated with differences in material culture or settlement patterns, however (see Hally 1994a: 172–173). The major differences lie in ecology and geography. During the eighteenth century, Creek towns were located along major rivers in Alabama and Georgia (Braund 1993; Dimmick 1989; Lolley 1996), whereas Cherokee communities were located in narrower river valleys of southwestern North Carolina and northwestern South Carolina and in neighboring areas of northeastern Georgia and southeastern Tennessee. Many aspects of the lifeways of different native Southeastern groups—their settlement patterns, foodways, architecture, and ritual practices—were rather similar (Swanton 1928:717). This congruence is found in the spatial layout of Mississippian and protohistoric towns, which are rather similar in many different places in the Midwest and Southeast (Hally and Kelly 1998:49–54; Lewis and Stout 1998:240–241; Schroedl 1998:73–89; Sullivan 1995:104–111). The layout of the native town at Coweeta Creek, for example (Ward and Davis 1999:185), is comparable in many respects to the layouts of Creek and Mississippian towns in other areas of southeastern North America.

Bartram's Contributions to Appalachian Summit Archaeology

The ethnohistoric material in Bartram's journal offers especially interesting clues about changes in the way that Cherokee communities were built, both literally and figuratively. He described the architecture of Cherokee dwellings and council houses, the arrangement of houses around and across the river from the Cowee mound, and the layout of former towns at Keowee and surrounding areas. There is also his description of the remnants of a townhouse near the headwaters of the Little Tennessee River itself, built atop a presumably more ancient mound.

Archaeologists know of several examples of townhouses at Cherokee towns, including the Coweeta Creek site (B. J. Egloff 1967:9–10; K. T. Egloff 1971:42–70; D. G. Moore 1990; Rodning 1996a, 1996b, 1999a, 1999b; Schroedl 1986a:534). This native architectural form may have developed during the sixteenth century or perhaps earlier, postdating the earth lodges and platform mounds as public architecture in the South Appalachian Mississippian tradition (Anderson 1994b:308–309; Crouch 1974; L. G. Ferguson 1971; Rudolph 1984:44). These communal council houses were generally larger than chiefly residences atop earlier platform mounds, and they likely reflect a relatively egalitarian social structure compared to that of earlier Mississippian chiefdoms (Anderson 1994b:302–309). Archaeological remnants of these council houses may be found at Chota, Toqua, Mialoquo, and Chattooga (J. Chapman 1985:110–114; Guthe 1977:215–217; Polhemus 1987: 242–243; Russ and Chapman 1984:51–54; Schroedl 1978, 1980, 1983, 1986b: 263–270, 1991, 1998:87; Schroedl and Riggs 1989, 1990, 1992).

Ethnohistoric sources offer some clues about how Cherokee townhouses were treated when their tenures as town centers were over, as does the archaeologically preserved townhouse at Coweeta Creek. Sturtevant (1978:200) has noted the reference by a visitor to the town of Toqua in eastern Tennessee of a ritual during which Cherokee groups would demolish an old council house and cover it with a mantle of clay. This seems to have been the case at Coweeta Creek, where former council houses were covered to create a surface for their successors, and where the sixth stage of the townhouse was dismantled and topped with a thick clay cap (Dickens 1978:123–126; B. J. Egloff 1967:9–10; K. T. Egloff 1971:58–61; D. G. Moore 1990; Rodning 1999b; Ward and Davis 1999:178–190).

Presumably this kind of ritual was not performed at the mound that Bartram found near the headwaters of the Little Tennessee River, nor in the abandoned Lower settlements in the Keowee River Valley. Throughout the eighteenth century Cherokees from the Lower towns moved north to the Middle towns or northwest to the Overhill settlements—hence the abandoned Lower Cherokee towns along the Keowee River and all the architectural remnants still visible on the landscape. Townhouses continued to serve as community centers and the architectural landmarks of towns throughout much of the eighteenth century, but perhaps some of the ritual traditions surrounding them were lost in the firestorm of cultural change within native communities of southeastern North America during that period.

Trade and warfare may not have been the only reasons Cherokee towns moved from place to place. Not everything Bartram saw in the southern Appalachians was a recent addition to the Cherokee cultural landscape. He found patches of old fields in the woods where gardens had been and abandoned towns where communities of people had lived at some point in the past (see Hammett 1992:11–23; Hill 1997:80–84; Waselkov and Braund 1995:76). He wrote that people periodically moved when resources in these patches dwindled (see Hill 1997:90–91; Waselkov 1997:188–193; Waselkov and Braund 1995:80). The southern Appalachian landscape that Bartram saw, then, reflected both recent and more ancient Cherokee lifeways. Whereas in earlier times Cherokee groups may have ritually ended the lives of old towns and council houses before moving away from them, such traditions may have faded during the eighteenth century.

Bartram did indeed visit native Southeastern people and places much changed by interaction and exchange with European groups. Yet for several reasons his journal and other reflections about his Southeastern travels are valuable resources for archaeologists studying earlier southern Appalachian groups. First, native communities in southwestern North Carolina experienced European contact differently than Piedmont and coastal groups, because they lived in rugged mountain areas distant from major colonial outposts and pathways of the seventeenth century. Second, eyewitness accounts of the cultural landscape in southwestern North Carolina before the eighteenth century are relatively rare (journals from the de Soto and

Pardo expeditions of the sixteenth century describe their explorations of parts of southern Appalachia but not the specific river valleys where historically known Cherokee towns were concentrated during the eighteenth century). Third, Bartram's journal offers vivid and even comparative descriptions of native architecture and characterizes the relationships between different towns and groups of towns spread across the southeastern landscape. Fourth, Bartram's depictions of the Southeast make some distinctions between recent and much older elements of the cultural landscape. Thus archaeologists can derive insights from his journal about what towns and their architecture looked like in the late eighteenth century, and can find clues in the southeastern landscape that Bartram described about what settlement patterns and architecture were like during the decades and perhaps even centuries before his visit. Whether as a point of comparison or contrast to archaeological patterns, the Bartram journals and other eighteenth-century ethnohistoric sources offer much for archaeologists to consider in their study of the southern Appalachian landscape of the seventeenth and earlier centuries.

Notes

This chapter is a significant revision of my conference presentation at the Southeastern Archaeological Conference in Baton Rouge focusing on William Bartram and Appalachian Summit archaeology. Thanks to Cameron Wesson and Mark Rees for the invitation to contribute to that symposium and to this book. Thanks to Jerald Milanich and Tristram Kidder for their comments as symposium discussants. Thanks to Trawick Ward, Steve Davis, David Moore, David Hally, Bennie Keel, Margie Scarry, Tony Boudreaux, Stephen Williams, Lynne Sullivan, Rob Beck, Gerald Schroedl, Brett Riggs, Vin Steponaitis, Jane Eastman, Mintcy Maxham, Greg Wilson, Amber VanDerwarker, Kathy McDonnell, and the anonymous reviewers for comments about my ideas and my writing. Thanks to Hope Spencer, Bram Tucker, and my family for their generous support and encouragement. Thanks to the NSF Graduate Research Fellowship Program for funding during my first several years of graduate school at Chapel Hill. Thanks as well for the support of the UNC Research Laboratories of Archaeology. This chapter has benefited greatly from these and other contributions. Any problems with this paper are of course my own responsibility.

1. There is currently a recreational path called the Bartram Trail that runs from Beegum Gap east of Dillard, Georgia, to Cheoah Bald just northeast of Robbinsville, North Carolina, and its seven different sections together create a trail that is some 81 miles long. The trail was established through the cooperative efforts of the U.S. Forest Service and the North Carolina Bartram Trail Society in 1977, and it generally follows the route along which Bartram traveled en route to Cowee and other Cherokee towns in southwestern North Carolina. It runs along the eastern edge of the Little Tennessee Valley across from the contemporary town of Otto and comes within two or three miles of the Coweeta Creek archaeological site, a major Cherokee town dating to some-

time in the seventeenth century (B. J. Egloff 1967; K. T. Egloff 1971; Rodning 1996a, 1996b, 1998a, 1998b, 1999a, 1999b; Ward and Davis 1999:178–190). See "One Tough Son of a Flower Picker," by T. Edward Nickens, reprinted in the September 1999 edition of *Wildlife in North Carolina,* a magazine published by the North Carolina Wildlife Resources Commission; also an article in the March 2001 issue of *National Geographic Magazine* about the travels of William Bartram across southeastern North America.

2. Much of this fieldwork was conducted as part of the Cherokee archaeological project by the UNC Research Laboratories of Anthropology (now known as the UNC Research Laboratories of Archaeology) at Chapel Hill (Coe 1961; Dickens 1976; Keel 1976; Ward and Davis 1999; Ward and Rodning 1997).

3. The Dillard mound (9RA3) in northern Georgia is close to a modern town by that name—the mound is some eight miles south of the Coweeta Creek site.

4. The map by colonial agent George Herbert (1730) shows a place called "Old Estatoe" close to the headwaters of the Little Tennessee River, along its east side (see Greene 1995, 1996). This map shows "Stecoe" just south of Old Estatoe and west of the river; another "Stecoe" is shown on maps along the Tuckasegee River.

5. Cowee is represented by archaeological site 31MA5.

6. Joree is likely represented by 31MA3 and the village of Echoee by 31MA20.

7. Brett Riggs (personal communication, 2001) associates "Old Estatoe" with the Dillard mound. The "Jore mountain" (Bartram 1955:287 [1791]) likely refers to one of the mountains west of Cowee, probably somewhere in what are now called the Nantahala Mountains.

8. The "Tanase river" (Bartram 1955:287 [1791]) flowed through Cowee, and this river is now known as the Little Tennessee River.

9. My observation of the Cowee mound from across the Little Tennessee River and photographs of it archived at the UNC Research Laboratories of Archaeology in Chapel Hill lead me to think this description is accurate—the artificial mound likely was built atop a natural platform.

10. David Hally (personal communication, 1999) has recommended comparisons between council houses at Cherokee towns in southern Appalachia and those at Creek towns farther south and west. It would also be interesting to compare the dimensions of Cherokee council houses dating to the eighteenth century with archaeologically known public buildings in southern Appalachia that predate the eighteenth century (Hally and Kelly 1998:51–52; Polhemus 1990:131–134; Schroedl 1998:69–81; Sullivan 1995:115–120; M. Williams 1994:192–193).

11. Nequassee is represented by a mound designated by site number 31MA2, which is still a prominent landmark in downtown Franklin, the current seat of Macon County (see Dickens 1967:13; Mooney 1900:337; Swanton 1952:216–217).

12. Whatoga is associated with an archaeological site designated 31MA4, an elusive site whose field notes indicate that the primary evidence of this mound are stories by local residents in areas around Franklin, who remembered a mound in the vicinity having been excavated by the Smithsonian Institution (see Dickens 1967:8; Swanton 1952:217; C. Thomas 1894:333–350).

13. Many names associated with historic Cherokee towns and other places in south-

ern Appalachia reflect influences from Iroquoian, Muskogean, and Catawban languages, and the etymology of some place names does not easily fit within current conceptions of any of these language groups (Booker et al. 1992).

14. There does not seem to be a historically known Cherokee town name that can be positively associated with the town represented by the Coweeta Creek archaeological site. However, Echoee was not far north of where Coweeta Creek meets the Little Tennessee River (see Goodwin 1977:121). Meanwhile, Tessentee old town and fields and Tessentee Creek were not far up the Little Tennessee River (see Corkran 1962:212). Other place names close to the confluence of Coweeta Creek and the Little Tennessee River are Techanto and Newuteah (B. J. Egloff 1967:19–26; B. A. Smith 1979:48–54).

15. David Hally (1993:164–165, 1994a:167–169, 1994b:246–247, 1996:97–98) has demonstrated patterns in the spacing of major mound centers across northern Georgia. Contemporary mounds less than 18 km apart are considered to represent greater and lesser centers within chiefdoms. Mounds spaced more than 32 km apart are considered to represent distinct polities.

16. Mark Williams (1994) and his colleagues have noted the movement of town communities from place to place within the Oconee Valley of northern Georgia from the eleventh through fifteenth centuries. These shifts across the landscape are related to sociopolitical dynamics within the Mississippian chiefdom in the Oconee province: the histories of individual mound centers such as Shinholser, Shoulderbone, Little River, Scull Shoals, and Dyar reflect cycling within the Oconee chiefdom and chiefdoms in neighboring regions (see Anderson 1994b; Hally 1993; Hally and Langford 1988:79–81; Hally and Rudolph 1986:63–80).

6 / "As caves below the ground"
Making Sense of Aboriginal House Form in the Protohistoric and Historic Southeast

David J. Hally

I have always found Historic period descriptions of aboriginal habitation structures in the southern Appalachian region confusing. The buildings often sound so bizarre and different from one another that I am tempted to question the observational abilities of European eyewitnesses. Houses are variously described as resembling caves, open pavilions, or European style dwellings; as being circular, octagonal, or rectangular in shape; as having subterranean floors, one or two stories, log or wattle-and-daub wall construction, and gabled or conical roofs covered with cane mats, bark, shingles, or earth—the latter bearing intentionally sewn vegetation.

The available descriptions are not, however, totally lacking in agreement. A few common characteristics can be found, including:

the distinction between summer and winter houses;
the rectangular shape of summer houses;
and the replacement through time of single-set post construction by horizontal log construction.

Despite the degree of uniformity in historical descriptions, it is difficult to know whether the architectural variability recorded there reflects change over time, differences between regions and ethnic groups, variability within single communities that are undergoing rapid acculturation, or simply observer error.

Archaeological investigations by Baden (1983), Faulkner (1978), Russ (Russ and Chapman 1984), and Schroedl (1986a, 1989), in Tennessee, and Cottier (Waselkov et al. 1990), C. T. Sheldon (1997), and Waselkov (1985) in Alabama have begun to unravel this confusion for the eighteenth- and nineteenth-century Cherokee and Upper Creek. In this paper, I would like to build on their work by looking at the late prehistoric and protohistoric antecedents of the historic period structures and by expanding the geographical area of investigation to include Georgia and the Carolinas as well as eastern Alabama and Tennessee.

Late Prehistoric and Protohistoric Domestic Architecture

The domestic architecture I am most familiar with is that of the early to mid-sixteenth century Lamar occupation of northwestern Georgia. The most easily recognizable structure type at sites where I have worked—Potts Tract (9MU103), Little Egypt (9MU102), King (9®5), and Leake (9BR2)—was typically erected in a shallow basin about 70 cm deep, had a floor plan that was square with rounded corners, and averaged about 8 m across (Figure 6.1). Exterior walls were constructed of individually set posts. These were covered on their exterior by bundles of cane or possibly split cane mats. Earth from the basin was piled against this surface, probably to a height of 1 m. Roofs were pyramidal in form and rested on exterior wall plates and beams supported by four centrally located posts. The roof had a smoke hole at its apex and was plastered with several inches of clay on its underside, from the smoke hole outward to the four support posts. Roofs were probably covered with sheets of bark or with thatch. The outer floor space was divided by partition walls into a number of alcoves that probably contained raised benches made of wood and cane. There was a hearth in the center of the floor, and human interments were placed in the outer floor space.

Given their substantial construction and depressed floors, it is highly probable that these structures were occupied primarily during the winter months. There is also a tendency for structures—or, more correctly speaking, structure locations—to be utilized for fairly long periods of time—perhaps up to 20 or 30 years. This is indicated by the habit of rebuilding structures to be rebuilt one or more times and by the number of burials interred in some structures. Structure 23 at King, for example, was rebuilt three times and contained 13 burials.

It is almost certainly this type of structure that is referred to in accounts from the de Soto, Luna, and Pardo expeditions dating between 1540 and 1566.

> Here we found a difference in the houses of the Indians; we found them as caves below the ground. (Beidma in Clayton et al. 1993:228)
>
> The winter houses are all covered with earth and they sow whatever they like over them. (Fray Domingo de la Anunciacion in Priestley 1928:239)
>
> [T]he Indians took shelter in the huts that they had inside of it [the palisade wall], which were under the ground, from which they came out to skirmish with the Spanish. (Martinez in C. Hudson 1990:320)

Biedma and Martinez are clearly referring to semi-subterranean buildings of the type described above. Biedma's reference to cave-like structures, however, also implies that houses were covered with earth—a condition more explicitly identified by Anunciacion. Archaeologists are not in agreement over the question of whether Mississippian period structures in the southern Appalachian region were earth-covered (Larson 1994; Rudolph 1984; Sears 1958; M. Williams 1993). My own opinion is that they were not. There is no indisputable archaeological evidence for earth-covered roofs, and it is questionable whether aboriginal construction techniques were sufficient to support roofs weighted down with interior and exterior layers of earth. Furthermore, erosion caused by rainfall would have been a major problem for earth-covered roofs unless they were also covered with a thick layer of vegetation. Anunciacion's reference to planting vegetation on roofs, of course, does make sense in this context.

I think it is more likely that Biedma and Anunciacion's observations reflect the practice of banking earth against exterior walls and plastering the underside of the roofs. Embankments may have given the appearance of an earth covering, and vegetation may have been planted on embankments in order to inhibit erosion. No doubt vegetation-mosses, lichens, and even grasses and bushes grew naturally on older roofs as well.

Square, semi-subterranean structures similar to those at King are very widespread in the late Prehistoric and Protohistoric periods, extending from eastern Alabama (C. T. Sheldon 1997) across Georgia (Anderson and Schuldenrein 1985; Caldwell and McCann 1941; M. T. Smith 1994a; Poplin 1990; M. Williams 1993) into Piedmont South Carolina (G. Wagner, personal communication 1997), the Blue Ridge section of North Carolina (Dickens 1976; Keel 1976, Rodning, personal communication 1997), and the Ridge and Valley section of eastern Tennessee (Polhemus 1987, Sullivan 1987)(Figures 6.1–6.6). This region encompasses the pre-contact territory of the Muskogean-speaking Upper and Lower Creek and Koasati, the Cherokee, and the Catawba (Booker et al. 1992). The structure type can be documented as early as A.D. 1400 in the Upper Savannah River drainage (Anderson and Schuldenrein 1985) and A.D. 1200 in western North Carolina (Dickens 1976). At Fusihatchee on the Lower Tallapoosa (C. T. Sheldon 1997) and Coweeta Creek in North Carolina (Rodning, personal communication), the structure type may continue into the eighteenth century.

Circular structures that may have been winter houses have been reported from three locations in the Southern Appalachian region. Substantially built circular structures are characteristic of upland sites in the Oconee River drainage of central Georgia from at least the mid-fifteenth century into the seventeenth century (Hatch 1995; Kowalewski and Williams 1989). These ranged between 8 m and 12 m in diameter, were built with either 12 or 16 exterior wall posts and 3–4 interior roof support posts, and may have had daubed exterior walls (see Figure 6.7). The existence of these structures is difficult to explain in light of the fact that square structures with depressed floors and entrance passages are represented in

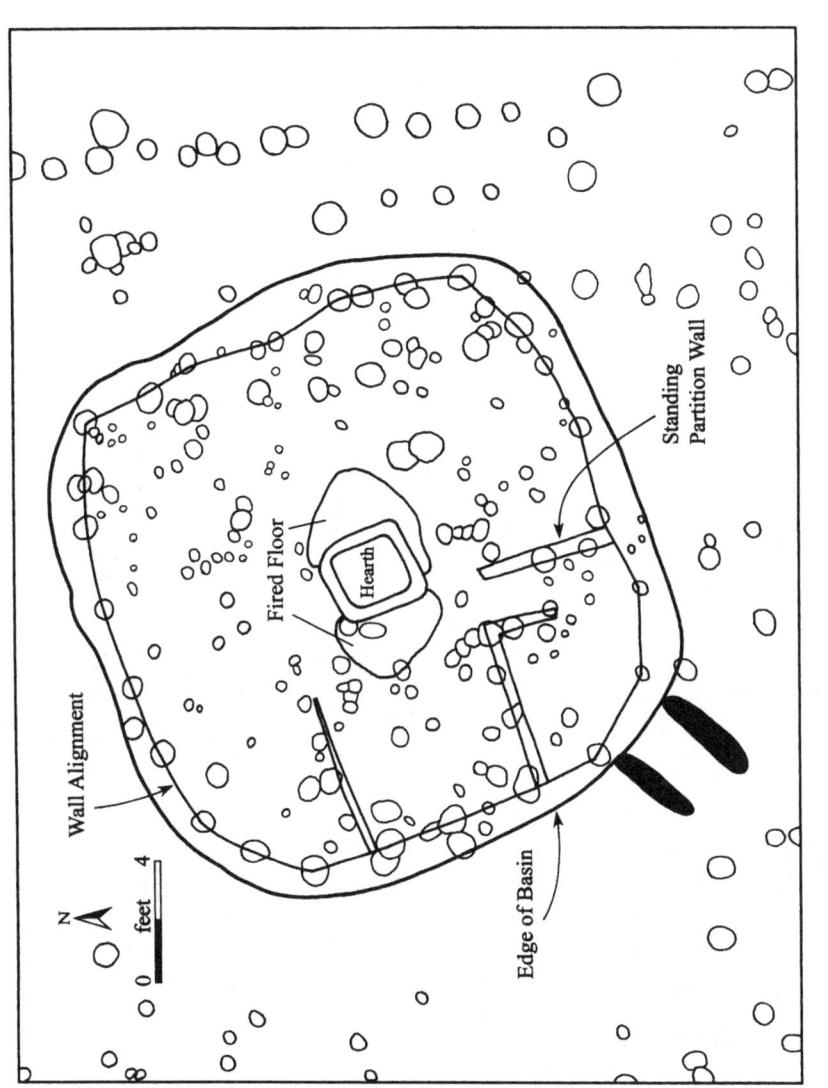

Figure 6.1 Post hole and feature map of King site winter house (structure 4).

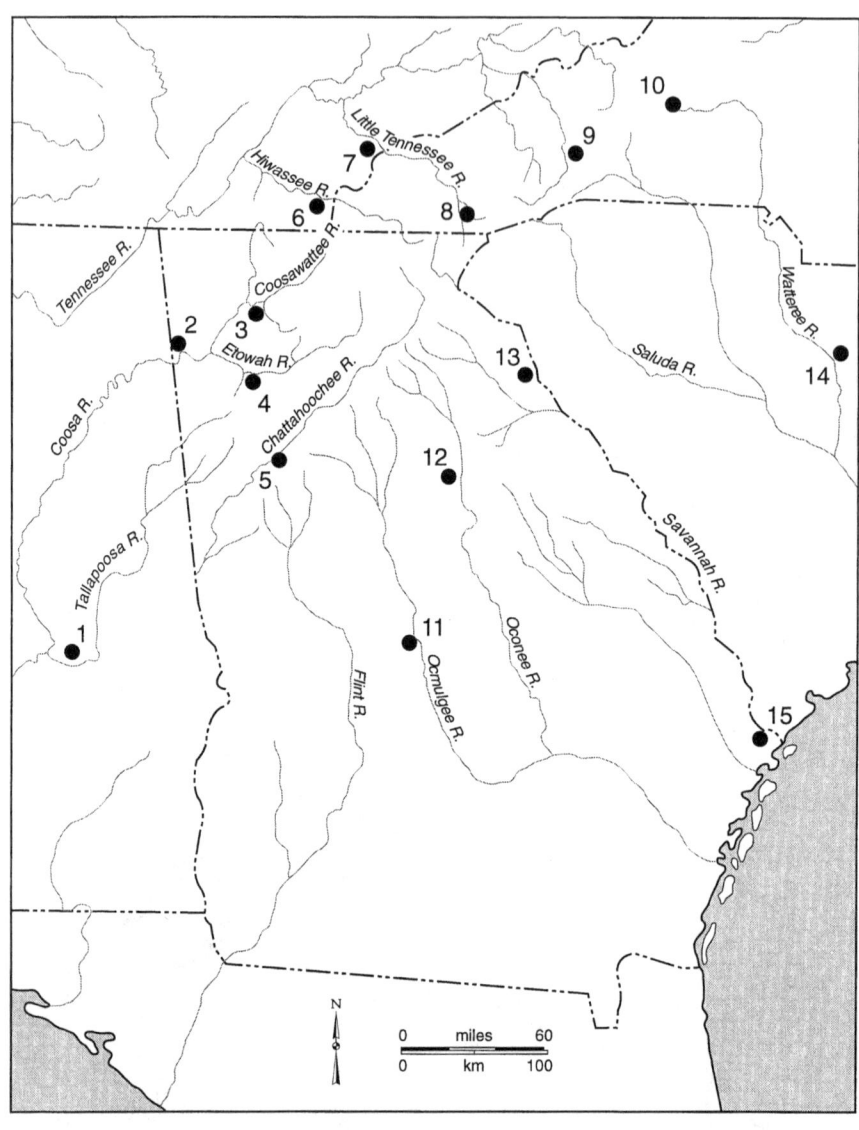

1. Fusihatchee
2. King
3. Little Egypt
4. Etowah
5. Dog River
6. Ledford Is.
7. Toqua
8. Coweeta Creek
9. Warren Wilson
10. McDowell
11. Bullard Landing
12. Dyar
13. Rucker's Bottom
14. Mulberry
15. Irene

Figure 6.2 Location of known late prehistoric and protohistoric sites with square, semi-subterranean structures.

Making Sense of Aboriginal House Form / 95

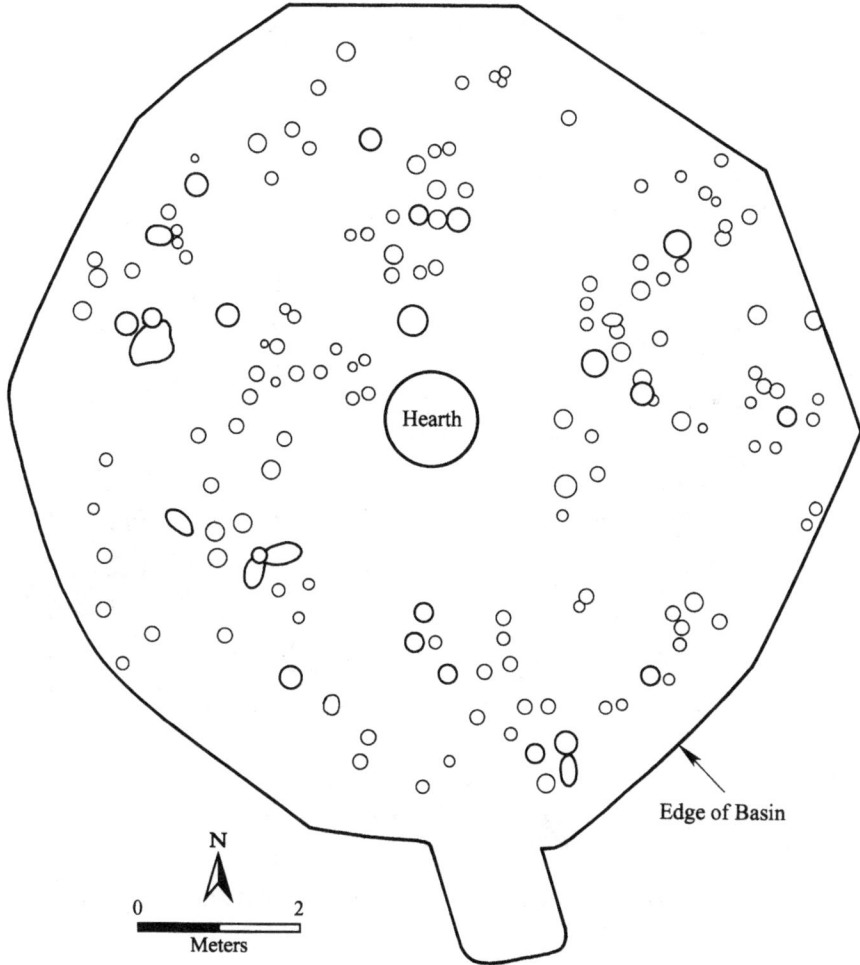

Figure 6.3 Atasi phase winter house at Fusihatchee site. Adapted from Sheldon 1997.

contemporary sites located only a mile or two distant in the floodplain of the Oconee River (M. T. Smith 1994a). It is possible that these circular structures were better suited to conditions in the uplands, where shifting cultivation may have necessitated, among other things, a more mobile residence pattern. This specific architectural form has not been reported elsewhere in the southern Appalachian region.

Anderson and Schuldenrein (1985) report circular structures from the fifteenth century Ruckers Bottom site, but they are around 4 m in diameter. The latter are similar in size to public buildings such as the council houses at King and Fusihatchee. The former are unlikely to have been winter habitations because of their

96 / David J. Hally

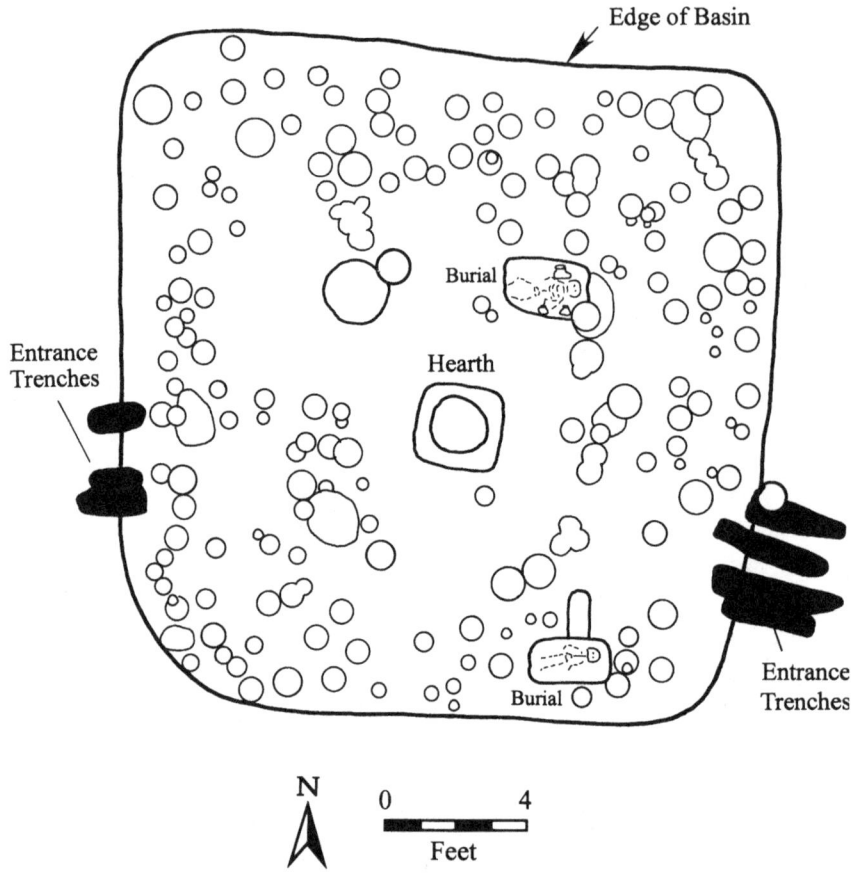

Figure 6.4 Dallas phase winter house at Toqua site. Adapted from Polhemus 1987, with permission of the author.

small size and because square, semi-subterranean structures with wall trench entrances are also represented at the site.

Finally, Knight (1985) reports a single circular structure dating to the seventeenth-century Atasi phase component at the Tukabatchee site in central Alabama. The structure measures 9.5 m in diameter and had daubed exterior walls and at least one hearth located near the center of the building. Since square structures with depressed floors and entrance passages occur at the contemporary Fusihatchee site located only 13 miles away, the significance of this structure is difficult to understand.

A second structure type represented at the King site in northwestern Georgia is rectangular[1] in floor plan and measures 4–6 m in length by 2–3 m in width (Figure 6.8). Posts forming the side walls tend to be spaced approximately 1.25 m apart,

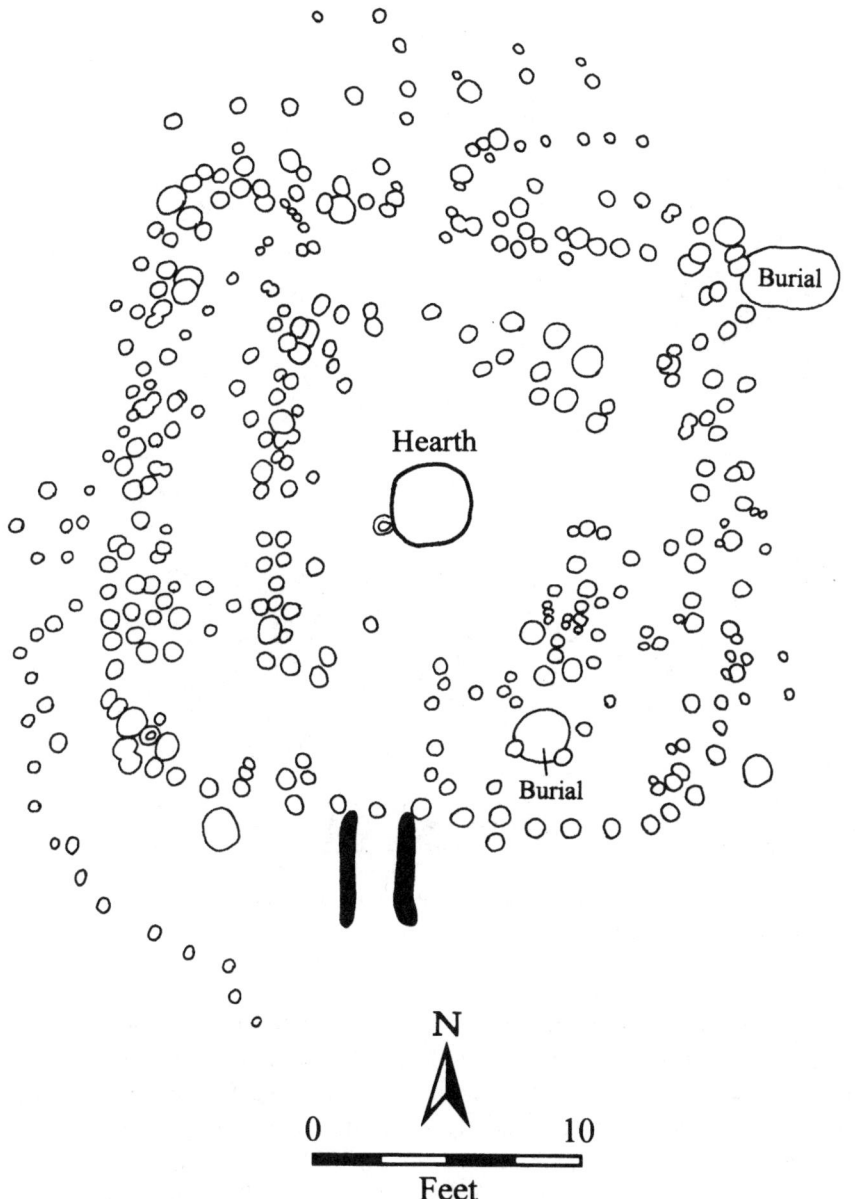

Figure 6.5 Pisgah phase winter house at Warren Wilson site. Adapted from *Cherokee Prehistory: The Pisgah Phase in the Appalachian Summit Region*, by Roy S. Dickens Jr. © University of Tennessee Press, 1976. Used by permission.

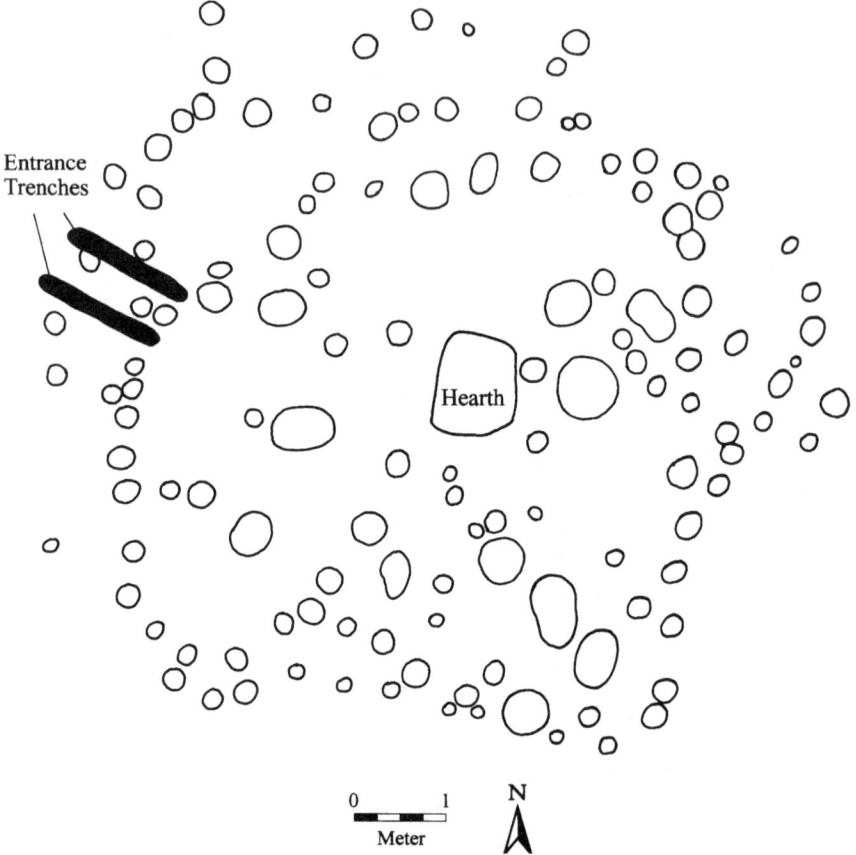

Figure 6.6 Rembert phase winter house at the Rucker's Bottom site. Adapted from Anderson and Schuldenrein 1985, with permission of the authors.

while those in the end walls are spaced approximately half that distance apart. There is no evidence of roof configuration, but it was probably gabled, with the ridge pole running parallel to the long axis of the structure. Human interments are often placed within or immediately adjacent to these structures.

This structure type was probably erected at ground level. Post spacing suggests a fairly lightly constructed building, possibly lacking solid walls on one or more sides. I interpret these structures as summer houses. Polhemus (1987) suggests that structures like these at the Toqua site in Tennessee were combination sun screens and corn cribs, the latter being raised on posts high enough above the ground to allow humans to work in the shade below. Areas of fired soil are present beneath some of the Toqua structures, suggesting that fires were built there, presumably for cooking and other domestic activities.

Making Sense of Aboriginal House Form / 99

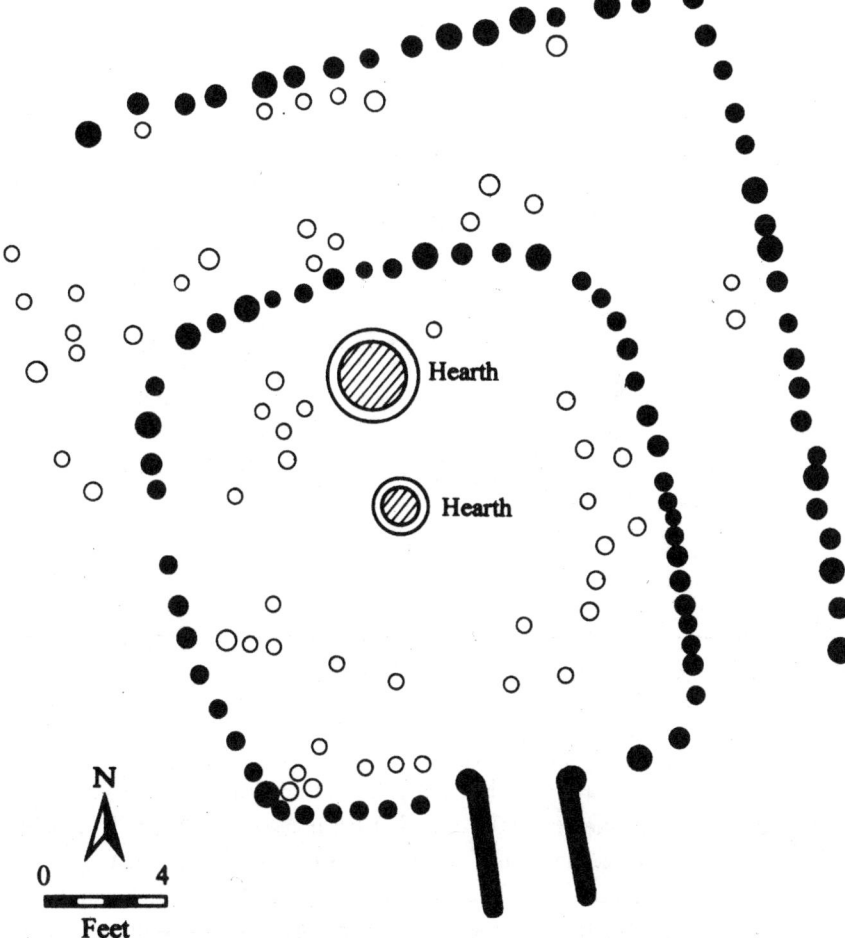

Figure 6.7 Irene phase winter house at Irene site. Adapted from Caldwell and McCann. © University of Georgia Press, 1941. Used by permission.

Similar structures are reported for the Oconee River drainage in central Georgia (Hatch 1995), the Hiwassee (Sullivan 1987) and Little Tennessee (Polhemus 1987) Rivers in eastern Tennessee, and possibly Coweeta Creek in North Carolina (Rodning, personal communication 1997) and Fusihatchee (C. T. Sheldon 1997) in eastern Alabama. Structures in the Oconee River drainage are slightly smaller than those at King; they measured on average 4.5 m long and 3 m wide, but, like King, posthole spacing appears to be greater in side walls than in end walls, and burials are present (Figure 6.9).

Wall post patterns are not clearly delineated in the Tennessee examples, making

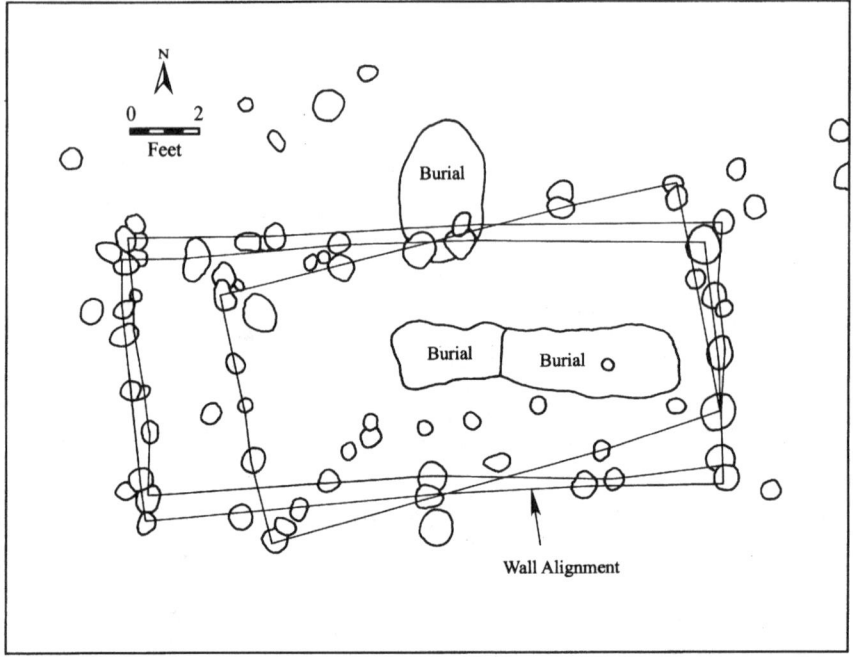

Figure 6.8 Rectangular summer house at King site.

it difficult to accurately determine their dimensions. Burials are spatially associated with structures in both the Mouse Creek and Dallas phase structures, and, as noted above, hearths are preserved in some of the Toqua site examples (Figure 6.4).

Fusihatchee site structures are the largest, with dimensions running around 7 m by 4 m (Figure 6.10). Posthole spacing appears to be quite regular, averaging 1 m in the side walls and more in end walls. C. T. Sheldon (1997) believes he can identify posts supporting a roof ridge pole. Burials as well as storage pits are identified as occurring beneath beds located at each end of the structure.

Summer houses have not been identified at other sites in the region, although two sites, Ruckers Bottom and Warren Wilson, have postholes in sufficient numbers that additional analysis would probably identify them.

In summary, winter and summer houses can be recognized in the archaeological record for the late Prehistoric and Protohistoric periods across the southern Appalachian region. Winter houses were square structures with rounded corners, depressed floors, and wall trench entrances. Structures with circular floor plans probably represent a minor variation on this basic form—one that may have been better suited to a more dispersed and shifting settlement system. Summer houses were lightly constructed, rectangular surface structures. Human interments were placed within both types of structures.

Figure 6.9 Circular house and rectangular summer house at the Sugar Creek site, central Georgia. Adapted from Hatch © University of Alabama Press, 1995.

Eighteenth- and Nineteenth-century Domestic Architecture

Following the mid-sixteenth-century Spanish explorations, there are no European accounts of aboriginal domestic architecture in the southern Appalachian region until the second half of the eighteenth century. For the Creeks, the earliest eyewitness accounts are those of Bartram (Waselkov and Braund 1995), Romans (1962

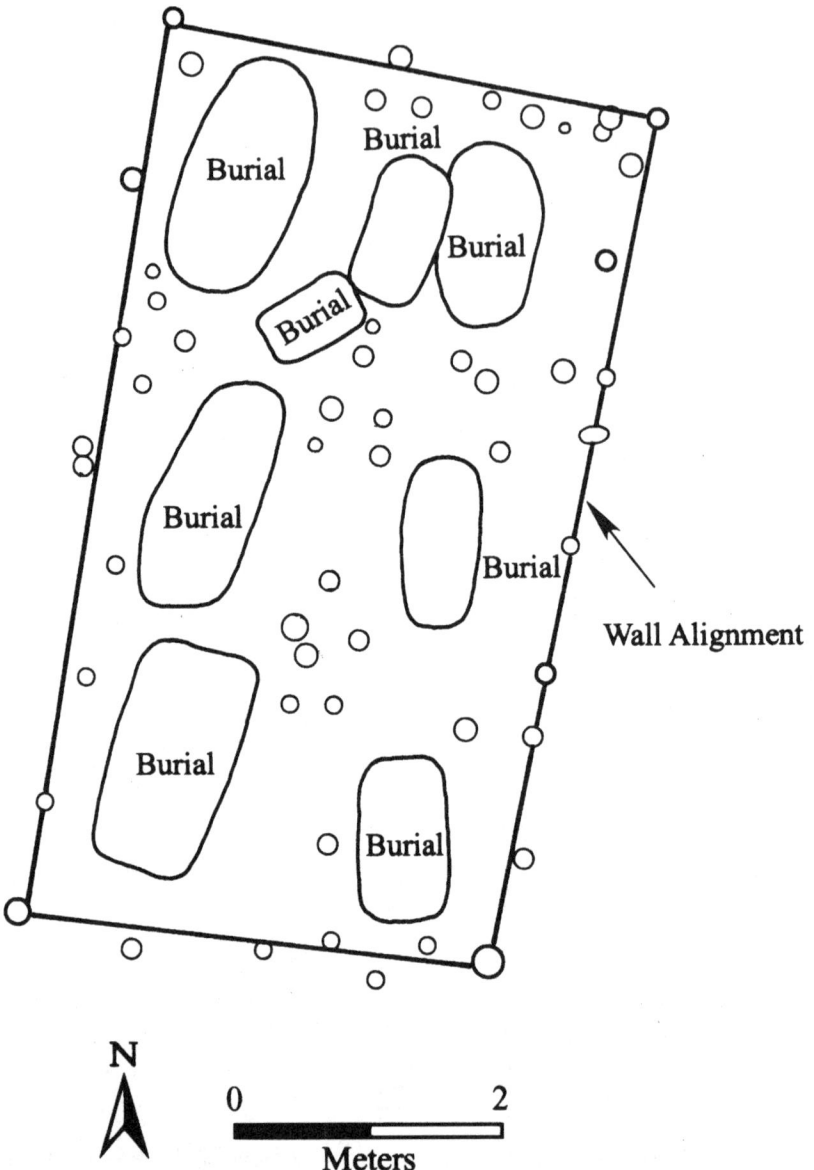

Figure 6.10 Atasi phase summer house at Fusihatchee site. Adapted from Sheldon 1997, with permission of the author.

[1775]), and Wight (Calder 1967) made in the 1770s. Summer and winter houses were still being constructed, but both were rectangular in form and there is no indication that winter houses were semi-subterranean. Exterior walls are said to be made of single set posts and wattle-and-daub, but it is not clear whether this construction technique was characteristic of both types of structures or only the winter house. Wight gives structure dimensions of 9 m by 5 m. Almost 20 years later, in 1790, Caleb Swan (Schoolcraft 1851–1857) describes similar structures, but with the addition of an exterior chimney. According to Bartram (Waselkov and Braund 1995:129), Creek domestic structures were typically arranged around the four sides of a square courtyard, and deceased household members were interred inside these structures beneath the beds.

The only archaeological research providing interpretable evidence of historic Creek domestic structures is that conducted by Sheldon, Waselkov, and Cottier at the Upper Creek towns of Fusihatchee, Hoithlewalli, and Hickory Ground located on the Lower Tallapoosa River in eastern Alabama. Waselkov (1985) found evidence of what may be circular or square structures at Hoithlewalli dating to the mid-1730s, but only rectangular structures were represented in the post-1750 component at the extensively excavated site of Fusihatchee (C. T. Sheldon 1997). At Fusihatchee, these averaged 7 m by 4 m, were constructed of single set posts, and had sub-floor burials and storage pits (Figure 6.10, Figure 6.11). There is no evidence of wattle-and-daub wall construction, but plowing may have destroyed it.

The earliest historic descriptions of Cherokee domestic structures date to the 1757–1762 period. DeBrahm (DeVorsey 1971:110) and Timberlake (L. Williams 1927:84) describe Cherokee summer houses as being rectangular and of single-set post construction with wattle-and-daub walls. These measured around 4–5 m wide and 7 m long (Timberlake says up to 20–24 m). Some had two stories.

Winter or "hot" houses were, according to DeBrahm, circular in plan, around 10 m in diameter with a conical roof 5 m high, and they had a central hearth. His statement that "two or more families join together in building a hot-house" is interesting in that it may signal a shift away from a traditional pattern in which each household had its own winter and summer structures. Also of interest is his statement that "these houses they resort to with their children in the winter nights." This suggests that the winter house no longer functioned as a regular domestic structure but rather only as a place to sleep in cold weather.

In 1775 Bartram observed rectangular Cherokee houses with exterior walls made with logs laid horizontally one above the other in log cabin style (Waselkov and Braund 1995). These walls were covered with a clay plaster. Schneider observed similar structures in 1784 but with the addition of an external chimney (L. Williams 1928).

Both individuals mention that families also had a smaller winter or hot house circular in plan and covered with earth that was located adjacent to the rectangular

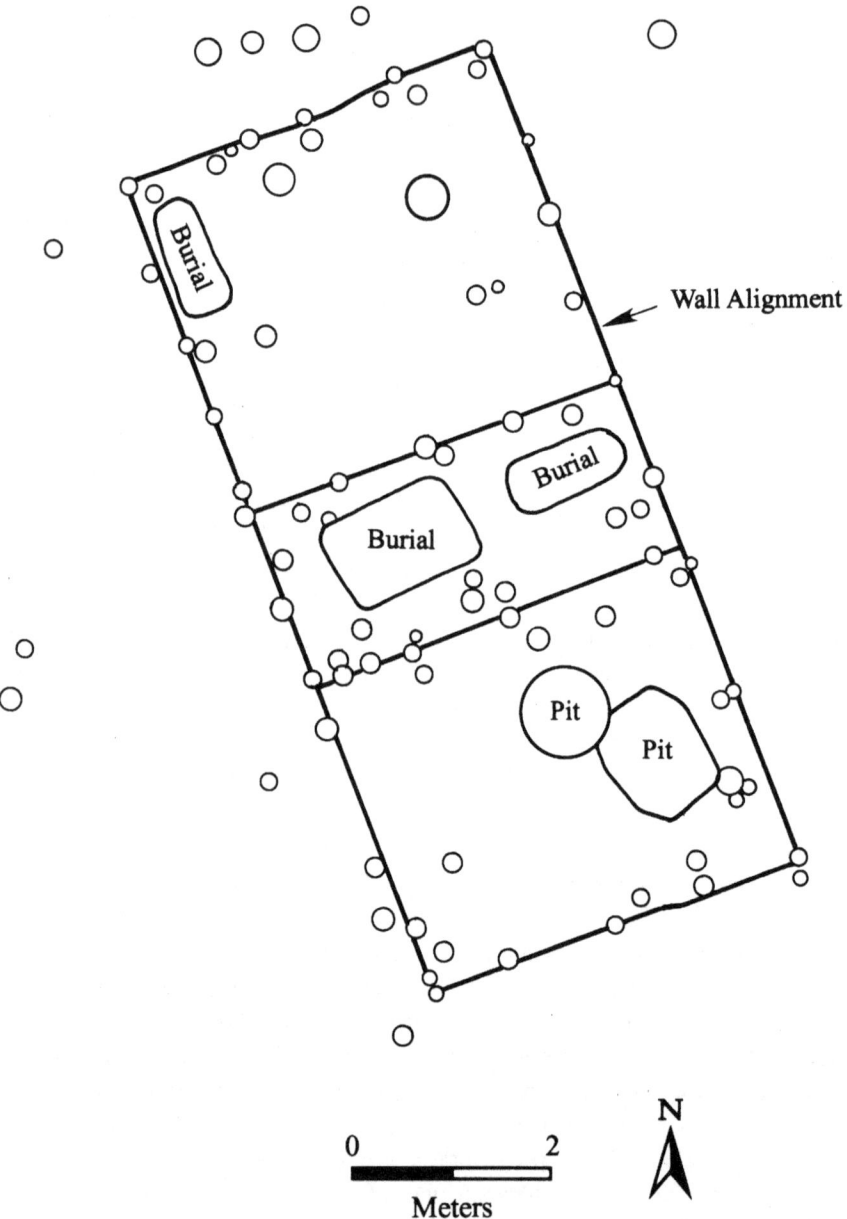

Figure 6.11 Late eighteenth-century Tallapoosa phase rectangular summer house at Fusihatchee site. Adapted from Sheldon 1997, with permission of the author.

structure. They do not say what these structures were used for, but by referring to the rectangular buildings as "dwelling houses" and "habitations" they imply that the hot house had a different or more restricted use.

Accounts by Louis-Philippe (Schroedl 1978) in 1797, Steiner and Deschweinitz (L. Williams 1928) in 1799, and L. Williams (1925–1926) in 1825 continue to describe rectangular structures of horizontal-log construction. Williams's (1925:111) statement that the houses were constructed "so they would be warm and comfortable in the winter" implies that the rectangular structure served as the primary domestic building throughout the year.

Finally, writing in 1835, Evans (1979:12–13) describes the hot house as small, low, and earth-covered, and he complains of the heat and smoke that accumulated in them during use. In addition to contrasting them to "dwellings," Evans implies that they were used primarily in the winter to escape the cold: "But during the winter months many old men spend the greater part of their time in 'hot houses' and employ themselves in roasting potatoes and parching corn. Many young people, destitute of bed clothing, find a good substitute at night in the heated air of a 'hot house.'"

I believe these accounts demonstrate that the Cherokee had, for the most part, stopped building square, semi-subterranean winter houses by the middle of the eighteenth century. With one possible exception (S. C. Williams 1930, see below), there is no mention of any kind of structure being erected in basins. I concur with Schroedl (1986b:228) that by this time or shortly thereafter the rectangular "summer" house had become a year-round residential structure. Furthermore, I believe that the small, circular, earth-covered "hot house" of the late eighteenth century is probably the architectural descendant of the square, semi-subterranean winter house, but its function shifted to that of a place of retreat during cold weather. Whether or not it also served as a sweat bath as implied by Mooney (1900) is, as Schroedl argues, debatable.

These interpretations are supported by archaeological evidence from Overhill Cherokee towns of the early to mid-eighteenth century. The architectural evidence from Chota-Tenasee matches in most respects the descriptions of winter and summer houses provided by DeBrahm and Timberlake (Schroedl 1986b, 1989). Pairs of circular[2] and rectangular structures occur in close spatial juxtaposition, the former averaging 6.8 m in diameter, the latter ranging between 8 m and 10.5 m in length and 4 m and 6 m in width (Figure 6.12). Central hearths occur in the circular structures. Differences include the smaller size of the archaeological examples (6.7 m vs. 9 m diameter, and 10.7 m vs. 21 m lengths) and the absence of evidence for wattle-and-daub wall construction. The latter discrepancy may be due to plow destruction.

Comparison of the Chota-Tenasee circular structures with the sixteenth-century square, semi-subterranean structure type reveals a number of interesting simi-

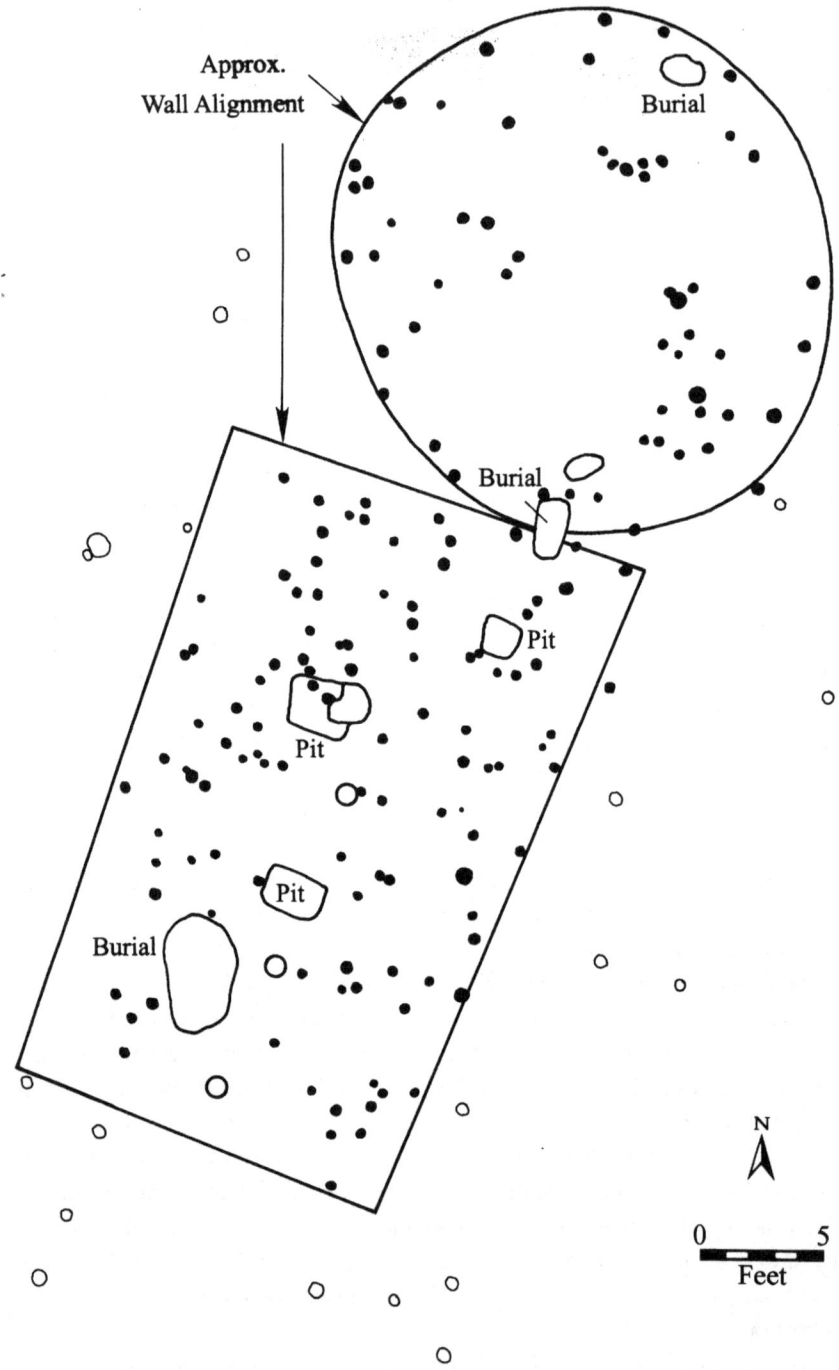

Figure 6.12 Summer and winter/hot house structures at the Chota-Tenasee site. Adapted from Schroedl 1986b, with permission of the author.

larities and differences. Overall size is approximately the same. Both have four interior roof supports and a central hearth. Burials, however, are largely absent from the later structures; evidence of burials appears in only 1 out of 11 recorded structures at Chota-Tanasee. The later structures are of course round, not square with rounded corners. Finally, with one exception (structure 5 [Schroedl 1986b:238–240]), there is no evidence that the later structures were erected in basins, though given the fact that erosion and plowing have destroyed the floor surfaces of all but one recorded structure at Chota-Tanasee, it is possible that the circular structures were in basins.

Burials were interred inside rectangular structures at Chota-Tenasee as they were in their sixteenth-century counterparts. The absence or near absence of burials from the eighteenth-century circular structures is not unexpected given the fact that mortuary patterns differed among the sixteenth-century societies as well. Mouse Creek phase winter houses, for example, contained only sub-adult burials (Sullivan 1987), while at King and Toqua (Polhemus 1987) these structures contained burials of all ages.

Adair (S. C. Williams 1930) provides the most detailed eighteenth-century description of summer and winter houses that we have. Unfortunately, it is not clear whether his account pertains to Chickasaw, Creek, or Cherokee, or to all three peoples. His description, based on observations made during the period 1735 to 1768, is nevertheless quite interesting. Summer houses are described as rectangular with gabled roofs. Winter houses are described as being circular in floor plan with four interior roof supports and an entrance passage and having clay daubed on the underside of the roof. Most interesting is the following passage: "As they usually build on rising ground, the floor is often a yard lower than the earth, which serves them as a breastwork against an enemy: and a small peeping window is level with the surface of the outside ground, to enable them to rake any lurking invaders in case of an attack" (S. C. Williams 1930: 451). I interpret this as referring to a semi-subterranean structure with earth banked against its outer walls. With the exception of the circular floor plan and curved rather than straight entrance passage, this structure is identical to the sixteenth-century semi-subterranean winter house. Adair's account indicates that at least in some areas, this structure type lasted into the middle of the eighteenth century.

A number of changes took place in domestic architecture across the south Appalachian area during the sixteenth through nineteenth centuries. These include:

1. Square, semi-subterranean winter houses ceased being constructed by the last quarter of the eighteenth century, if not earlier.
2. Among the Creek, these winter houses were replaced by (or evolved into) rectangular surface structures.
3. Among the Creek, the traditional rectangular summer house continued in use relatively unchanged.

4. Among the Cherokee, the semi-subterranean winter house apparently evolved through a circular form into the small, limited-function "hot house."
5. In the same area, the traditional rectangular summer house evolved into a year-round rectangular structure, which, by the late eighteenth century, was increasingly being constructed of horizontal logs.

Among these and other changes, the one I find most interesting is the disappearance of the square, semi-subterranean winter house. The loss of this widespread structure type has implications for change in aboriginal culture far beyond that of simple architectural form. With its depressed floor and earth-embanked walls, the square, semi-subterranean structure was better insulated against winter temperature extremes than the rectangular buildings that replaced it. Labor and material costs were probably significantly greater for the earlier structure type as well, given the necessity of excavating basins, banking earth, and spanning greater distances with pyramidal roofs. Both of these changes may be causally related to the shift toward greater residential dispersal and mobility during winter months that accompanied the growth of deer hunting and the deerskin trade (Waselkov 1988).

The square, semi-subterranean structure type appears to have been rebuilt in place more often than its late eighteenth-century counterparts. We can infer from this that later households did not endure for as long or that people no longer placed as much emphasis on household identity and continuity through time.

The sixteenth-century winter house also appears to have been used to symbolically express a number of cosmological and mythological beliefs.

1. Its square floor plan corresponded to the shape of the earth or "earth island" (Knight 1989b:287).
2. Its four walls and four roof support posts corresponded to the cardinal directions and the sacred number four (C. Hudson 1976).
3. King site structures usually have seven posts in each exterior wall regardless of structure size. Seven is a sacred number among the Cherokee that refers to, among other things, the directional divisions of the cosmos and the number of clans comprising Cherokee society. The number does not appear to have as much symbolic importance among the historic Creek, but apparently it was considered significant. Swanton (1928:488) collected an origin myth in which seven human beings were created at the time the earth was differentiated from water. The Kasi'hta migration legend, recorded in 1735, describes why Creek warriors fast for six days before departing on a raid on the seventh day (Gatschet 1884:248). The sacred plates of the Tukabatchee were seven in number and were carried in rituals by seven attendants (Gatschet 1884:505–507). Most early accounts of the busk

ceremony describe it as lasting four or eight days, but the Chiaha busk lasted seven (Gatschet 1884:551–564).
4. Physical similarities to prehistoric platform mounds—square shape, earth cover, association with human burials, rebuilding—suggest that the structure may also have represented the "earth navel" from which human ancestors emerged and to which the dead returned, as well as the notions of purification and world renewal (see Knight 1989b; Waselkov 1988).

It would have been difficult to portray some of these ideas in a rectangular building constructed in a single stage at ground level. Presumably, sometime during the eighteenth century they ceased being portrayed in domestic architecture.

Aboriginal culture in the Southeast underwent profound and far-reaching change during the Historic period. Domestic architecture was not immune to the forces driving this change. By looking at the archaeological and ethnohistoric evidence for housing at the time of earliest European contact, it has been possible to reconstruct aboriginal architectural patterns and unravel at least some of the changes in house form that occurred during the Historic period in response to European contact.

Furthermore, European accounts provide important insights into the nature of aboriginal house forms that disappeared early in the Historic period. The relationships between archaeological and ethnohistoric evidence and between prehistoric and historic cultural patterns that can be investigated in the Protohistoric make this period one of the most interesting to work in and explain why I have devoted most of my professional career to it.

Acknowledgments

I wish to thank Craig Sheldon for his assistance in the production of figures 3, 10, and 11. I would also like to thank Ian Brown, Greg Waselkov, and Gerald Schroedl for their helpful comments concerning earlier drafts of this paper.

Notes

1. Throughout this paper I will use the term "rectangular" to refer to structures that are significantly longer in one dimension than the other—i.e., oblong.
2. Schroedl (1989, personal communication) believes that the winter houses at Chota-Tenasee were actually octagonal rather than circular.

7 / Prestige Goods, Symbolic Capital, and Social Power in the Protohistoric Southeast

Cameron B. Wesson

The first Europeans to encounter Native American elites of the Southeast portrayed them as authoritative rulers exercising power over large populations and vast territories. They resided in large houses spatially segregated from the domiciles of non-elites (and frequently placed atop earthen mounds), controlled the production and exchange of high-status goods, managed the storage and provisioning of comestibles, exacted tribute from local populations and vassal provinces, commanded large military forces, supervised the construction of monumental public architecture, and presided over socioreligious ceremonies. The most powerful of these sovereigns is thought to have governed a polity extending almost 200 miles along major river systems in the present states of Alabama, Georgia, and Tennessee (De-Pratter et al. 1983; Hally et al. 1990; C. Hudson et al. 1985, 1987, 1989).

Although a number of historical documents were produced during initial contacts between Europeans and southeastern Native Americans during the sixteenth century, in many areas almost two hundred years would pass before indigenous people again were reported in detail by Europeans. Relying in part on discrepancies between sixteenth- and eighteenth-century documentary accounts, archaeologists and ethnohistorians view the Protohistoric period as a time of profound cultural change in indigenous societies. In stark contrast to earlier descriptions, later documents depict indigenous societies as politically acephalous and disintegrated, with little in the way of political, social, or economic organization (see quotes in Corkran 1967:12–13; Mereness 1916:176; Swanton 1928:279–280). This collapse is thought to have been as abrupt as it was encompassing. Within mere decades of the first contacts, the complex, hierarchical polities present during initial encounters with Europeans are believed to have vanished. For many scholars this reduction in sociopolitical complexity is representative of the complete collapse of pre-contact Native American societies (Borah 1964; Dobyns 1983, 1991; Dunnell 1991; Ramenofsky 1987, 1990; M. T. Smith 1987, 1994b).

This chapter examines archaeological data from central Alabama for evidence of the purported protohistoric collapse. Centering on the diachronic analysis of

Protohistoric and Historic period Creek households, this investigation suggests that the sociopolitics of protohistoric southeastern societies were dynamic, with individuals and small-scale social groups actively resisting the hegemonic positions of their social superiors. Rather than a precipitous protohistoric collapse, the picture that emerges is one where increasing social competition acted to continually erode the centralization of sociopolitical power throughout the Protohistoric and Historic periods.

Sociopolitics and the Protohistoric Collapse

Studies of social power in the southeast have traditionally presented a view of unquestionable elite authority, resting on a solid bedrock of communal support maintained through an elite-centered dominant ideology. The dominant ideology thesis presents us with two very different types of social and political actors—an elite responsible for developing social policy, and a non-elite responsible for carrying it out. Sociopolitical elites are depicted as shrewd and calculating, possessing almost omniscient qualities, while non-elites are passive, anemic, and apparently lacking in the ability to fully comprehend the nature of social and political relations. In this view, culture change is brought about through the actions of high-ranking members of society acting through the manipulation of social, political, and religious institutions. This elite-centered view of social agency has also spilled over into the analysis of protohistoric cultural change, only instead of an omniscient, near-omnipotent indigenous elite being responsible for social change it is the European who has seized the reigns of control.

Research addressing the nature of protohistoric culture change in the southeast has often emphasized European-introduced diseases and trade goods as the principal factors in region-wide declines in sociopolitical complexity (Axtell 1981; Blakely and Detweiler-Blakely 1989; Cotterill 1954; Crane 1981 [1928]; Dobyns 1983, 1991; Fairbanks 1952, 1958; C. Martin 1978; Mason 1963; Morris 1993; Ramenofsky 1987, 1990; Roberts 1989; M. T. Smith 1987; White 1983). Marvin Smith (1987:145), expressing a view shared by many scholars, contends that the deterioration of social complexity "corresponds almost exactly with the evidence for depopulation." He posits that with vastly reduced populations Native American societies were no longer capable of generating food surpluses, public works, large military forces, or other quintessential material characteristics of sociopolitical complexity (particularly those of complex chiefdoms). This notion of declining effectiveness is seen to stem from a disintegration of internal sociopolitical organization, which leads M. T. Smith (1987:145), for example, to conclude that not only were institutions supporting social differentiation collapsing, but Native Americans cultures as well: "the early historic period was a time of collapse; that collapse appeared by the beginning of the seventeenth century, leaving southeastern Indians in a state of 'cultural impoverishment' and leading to the rapid acculturation that took place during the eighteenth century."

Recent research has raised serious questions concerning the function of disease as the prime mover of protohistoric culture change (Baker and Kealhofer 1996; Braund 1993; Faulk 1991; Fitzhugh 1985; Galloway 1991, 1994, 1997a; C. Hudson 1990, 1994, 1997). David Henige (1998) demonstrates the considerable methodological and epistemological problems of calculating the demographic collapse brought about by the introduction of European diseases. As he incisively argues, archaeologists' standard invocations of widespread pandemics devastating local populations to the point where they lacked the numbers necessary to sustain local sociopolitical hierarchies cannot be supported a priori on empirical bases. In addition, recent research (Baker and Kealhofer 1996; Kealhofer and Baker 1996; Milner 1996b; Palkovich 1996) has demonstrated the diversity of Native American responses to European diseases and contacts.

What is clear is that much additional archaeological data on local population declines are needed to more fully evaluate claims concerning the effect of depopulation in protohistory, not simply the continued extrapolation of numbers from unreliable Spanish accounts. We can no longer accept at face value estimates of postcontact Native American population loss; instead we should continue to search for direct evidence of these declines in the archaeological record.

Along with studies of disease, examinations of Euroamerican and Native American trade have also reinforced the concept of a cultural collapse that indigenous peoples could neither alter nor control. Many studies argue that the material qualities of European goods made them irresistible to Native Americans, fostering an abandonment of indigenous production and a dependency upon European trade goods (Cotterill 1954; Crane 1981 [1928]; Fairbanks 1952, 1958; C. Martin 1978; Mason 1963; Morris 1993; R. White 1983). Such research frequently places the impetus to acquire these goods on the functional qualities of the objects themselves, with insufficient attention to the way in which these items were perceived, used, accepted, or rejected by Native Americans (see Rogers 1990 and Turnbaugh 1993 for excellent critiques of these perspectives). Often European trade goods are presented as if *they* were the animate social agents, not their Native American consumers. As Knight (1985:169–170) contends, "Standard historical treatments concerning the Indian trade in the Southeast are written, for the most part, from the European point of view.... We see portrayed here a race of primitive materialists ... vain 'children of the forest,' behaving something like a lucky youth with a five-pound note turned loose in a candy store of English vanities and trifles, thus willing to expend tremendous energies to the end of securing cheap English and French goods, items as often as not technologically useless."

This view is expressed most forthrightly by researchers such as C. Martin (1978:

8), who states that "European hardware and other trade items were immediately perceived by the Stone Age Indian as being far superior in their utility to his primitive technology and general material culture." More recently, Morris (1993) argues that Native Americans were so awed by Euroamerican trade goods that they were willing to barter for almost anything. Such approaches to the past, and the nature of the archaeological record, fail to acknowledge the nonmaterial aspects of these items, and their position in local exchanges and social relationships. Ultimately, this perspective presents us with an image of Native Americans lacking the ability to shape social phenomena, caught within and governed by forces they can neither control nor comprehend.

Such views are at odds with the nature of human society and with the inherent capacities of social actors (Bourdieu 1977, 1980; Giddens 1984; Gramsci 1971). As Giddens (1984:3) states, "To be human is to be a purposive agent, who both has reasons for his or her activities and is able, if asked, to elaborate discursively upon these reasons." All humans possess the power to not only participate in social life but, through the act of participating (or refusing to participate), to shape their social world. Even in situations where social power is highly concentrated, each member of society possesses transformative capacities which can be used to challenge the status quo and potentially alter a culture (Beaudry et al. 1991; McGuire 1992a; McGuire and Paynter 1991). As Giddens (1984:16) argues, "all forms of dependence offer some resources whereby those who are subordinate can influence the activities of their superiors."

Recent archaeological studies also have questioned traditional views of Native American and European trade (Braund 1993; Lightfoot 1995; Lightfoot et al. 1998; Rogers 1990; Rogers and Wilson 1993; Turnbaugh 1993; Waselkov 1989a, 1993). These studies demonstrate that indigenous peoples often refused to accept goods that were technologically and functionally superior to their indigenously produced counterparts (Rogers 1990; Turnbaugh 1993; Waselkov 1993). As Rogers (1990:11) states, "It may not be assumed that native peoples automatically want to acquire the technologically exotic Euroamerican trade goods, or, for that matter, accept the self-proclaimed superiority of Euroamerican customs." Many investigations traditionally focused primary attention on the items being introduced into Native American communities and households without adequately considering the use of these trade goods within indigenous contexts. It is insufficient to count the number of items being traded or report their presence in Native American archaeological contexts. Nothing short of detailed examinations of the dynamic relationships linking producers and consumers, as well as the potential social meanings of trade items for indigenous peoples, will suffice (Axtell 1979, 1981, 1992; Rogers 1990; Turnbaugh 1993).

Although disease and trade have figured prominently in most discussions of protohistoric cultural change, consideration of these factors alone constitutes an inadequate basis for developing anthropological explanations of the myriad social changes that occurred during the Protohistoric period. In truth, an overreliance on disease and trade as archaeological tropes has hindered rather than helped our understanding of protohistoric culture change. By exaggerating the European role in contact and colonial settings, such perspectives tacitly devalue the primary importance of Native American social actors in the processes of social, cultural, political, and economic change. Certainly Native Americans alone did not control and direct protohistoric culture change, but neither were they supernumeraries who merely comprised the backdrop for Europeans who strutted and fretted their hours upon the colonial stage.

In addition to problematizing the most frequently invoked explanations of protohistoric culture change, an examination of the very concept of a protohistoric cultural collapse is needed. Although the notion that southeastern societies demonstrated reduced sociopolitical complexity after the mid-sixteenth century is widely accepted, there are compelling reasons to reexamine the evidence supporting this idea. First, although some have argued that depopulation terminated social complexity in the Southeast, John Blitz (1993a:6–11) has demonstrated that the conceptualization of complexity employed in much of this research is biased toward the largest, most complex, southeastern polities. In reality, many historic southeastern societies possessed the classic characteristics of institutionalized hierarchy as defined by Service (1962, 1975) and others (Carneiro 1981; Clastres 1987; Earle 1987a, 1997; Flanagan 1989; Flannery 1972; Fried 1967, Peebles and Kus 1977). Second, as Blanton et al. (1996), Feinman (1995; 2000), and others (G. A. Johnson 1982; Renfrew 1974) demonstrate, the manifestations of social inequality vary with the particular style of leadership employed by local elites. A given society may lack the material signatures of hierarchy as traditionally defined by archaeologists (Peebles and Kus 1977), but it may, in fact, be quite sociopolitically complex (Brumfiel 1995; Clastres 1987; Crumley 1987, 1995; Gledhill 1994). Does it not seem paradoxical that during the Protohistoric period, a time argued to have witnessed a near complete collapse in indigenous sociopolitical complexity, the Southeast saw the rise of multiethnic sociopolitical confederacies that encompassed larger territories and populations than their pre-contact Mississippian predecessors (Galloway 1991, 1993; Knight 1994b)? Perhaps we have distorted not only the roles of disease and trade goods but the very nature of indigenous protohistoric sociopolitical organization as well (Muller 1997:63–116).

The sociopolitical organization of pre-contact southeastern societies has been explored most completely in the context of analyses of prestige goods economics (Anderson 1990; 1994a, 1994b; Barker 1992; Barker and Pauketat 1992a; J. A. Brown et al. 1990; Helms 1992; Muller 1997; Nassaney 1992; Pauketat 1992, 1994; Peregrine 1992; Rogers 1996; J. F. Scarry 1990a, 1996a, 1996b; B. D. Smith 1990; Welch 1991, 1996). Prestige goods economies are defined as systems in which elite political power is advanced through the control of resources that are available only through external trade (Frankenstein and Rowlands 1978:76). Prestige goods are considered valuable because they contain ideological components that make them powerful symbols of social power (*sacra*) and nonlocal contacts (Helms 1979, 1988, 1992, 1993; Knight 1986, 1990; Pauketat 1994; Peregrine 1992). Through close association with elites, prestige goods become essential components of ideologies supporting elite social aggrandizement (Knight 1985; Waselkov 1993).

As has been repeatedly demonstrated, however, much more than the simple *possession* of an object is necessary to enhance one's social power. Steponaitis (1986: 392) contends that in Native American societies, these items were "instruments of political strategy"—a form of social currency used to create prestige, impose debts, and reinforce claims to heightened social position (see Frankenstein and Rowlands 1978). Hierarchical social differentiation was bolstered further through the receipt of tribute payments of staple foods, exotic raw materials, and additional prestige goods from conquered or vassal communities (J. A. Brown et al. 1990; Dye 1995; Rees 1997 and chapter 9 this volume; Steponaitis 1978; Welch 1991; Welch and Scarry 1995).

Through the exchange of prestige goods, elites frequently inflicted debts on social rivals and created asymmetrical social relationships. Thus the real power of prestige goods economies is found in the symbolic capital that accrues from the conversion of material goods into social networks. The relationships that result are far more valuable in social terms than the material goods through which they are formed (Bourdieu 1977:179–180). The greater the investment of material resources in a social exchange, the greater the potential symbolic capital for those offering these goods. What is ultimately accumulated is not the material but "a capital of honour and prestige" (Bourdieu 1977:179). Those who successfully cultivate symbolic capital are rewarded with increased social power and with social relations who are both literally and figuratively in their debt.

Through both display and exchange, southeastern elites were thus able to use prestige goods to enhance their social status. When displayed, these items were often seen as powerful *sacra* endowed with supernatural and religious connections (Knight 1981). When exchanged, they often created debts the recipient could not repay in kind, thereby establishing and reinforcing hierarchical social relationships. Debtors were often forced to repay these gifts with loyalty, work, or services, which the recipient could then use to create new relationships of obligation (Bourdieu 1977:195). Such interactions and the symbolic capital they produced enabled southeastern elites to amass considerable power, culminating in the establishment of numerous paramount chiefdoms across the region. They also gave rise to a social ideology promoting the elite as central to cultural continuity (Wesson 1998).

When individuals and/or lineages can successfully control access to prestige goods and convert them into symbolic capital, their social power expands (Helms

1988, 1993; Kleppe 1989). In most cases, however, primary elites are not the only social segment striving to expand their symbolic capital. Other individuals and social groups are engaged in similar activities, attempting to improve their social positions as well (see Anderson 1994a, 1994b). In addition, every social exchange presents the possibility of losing material goods and existing symbolic capital. Such risk causes symbolic capital (and social position) to fluctuate between social groups and individuals, with fortunes rising or falling with each exchange (Bourdieu 1977: 56–58, 67–68). Frankenstein and Rowlands (1978:76) state that social "groups are linked to each other through the competitive exchange of wealth objects as gifts and feasting in continuous cycles of status rivalry. Descent groups reproduce themselves in opposition to each other as their leaders compete for dominance through differential access to resources and power."

Secondary elites and other social segments always present an especially potent threat to both the economic and social capital of principal elites (Ekholm 1972). Among the inherent weaknesses of prestige goods economies are that the total number of goods and their means of circulation must be tightly controlled. Increases in the number of prestige goods potentially expand the resource pools of non-elite social groups attempting to challenge elite social position (Beaudry et al. 1991; Ekholm 1972; Friedman 1982; Kleppe 1989; McGuire 1992a; McGuire and Paynter 1991; M. Williams and Shapiro 1990). As Peregrine (1992:31) states, "If a system is flooded with prestige goods, the control of them is meaningless. Alliances with individuals who have control of prestige goods are not necessary if individuals have easy access to them." In addition, by circumventing existing elite-centered mechanisms for the production, importation, display, and exchange of prestige goods, social aspirants shift the balance of social power. Such actions threaten existing social hierarchies, as "opportunistic gurus, ambitious younger sons or disgruntled minorities . . . capitalize on cultural ambiguities and discontinuities which would advance their ambitions" (Archer 1996:9). It is possible that much of the cycling in chiefly power in southeastern societies identified by Anderson (1990, 1994a, 1994b, 1996a, 1996b) and others (Blitz 1993a; Hally 1996; Williams and Shapiro 1990; J. F. Scarry 1996a) was tied to just such challenges to elite control of prestige goods systems (see Helms 1996:438).

Since individuals primarily participated in the prestige goods system through household and lineage relationships, analysis of household remains provides exceptional opportunities to evaluate the nature of prestige goods systems. Households are excellent units of analysis because they are the physical translation of a culture's sociopolitical organization, cosmology, and aesthetic principles (Bourdieu 1977; Cunningham 1973; Norberg-Schulz 1971, 1980; Rapoport 1969). The household is "a culture in microcosm . . . [where] individuals are brought to an awareness of their culture's rules, and conversely, where those rules are frequently expressed in physical form" (Deetz 1982:719). The household is also a superb arena in which to evaluate the nature of competing social ideologies and to identify acts of resistance, since it is where ideologies are most commonly formulated and put into practice (Bourdieu 1977).

Households have social, material, and behavioral correlates and "embody and underlie the organization of a society at its most basic level; they can serve as sensitive indicators of . . . [social] change" (Ashmore and Wilk 1988:1). Efforts designed to establish new social networks (or to circumvent existing ones) are manifest in household contexts and can be measured in the distribution of prestige items as mortuary goods. In addition, the size and nature of domestic structures and the increased dispersal of formerly nucleated communities reveal much concerning changing sociopolitical structure. By analyzing household data from prehistoric, protohistoric, and historic Creek sites in central Alabama, it is possible to gain a more detailed understanding of the internal forces shaping culture change during the Protohistoric period.

Analysis of Creek Households

The Creeks were sedentary agricultural groups occupying what is today the central portions of Alabama and Georgia (Figure 7.1). Although there is considerable debate concerning the origins of the Creeks (Corkran 1967:4, Fairbanks 1952; Hally 1994a; A. R. Kelly 1938; Knight 1985, 1994a, 1994b; Mason 1963; J. H. Moore 1994; H. G. Smith 1973; Swanton 1922:192, 1928:34–30), during the Protohistoric and Historic periods they were a confederacy that encompassed several distinct ethnic groups, including elements of the Alabama, Apalachee, Chickasaw, Choctaw, Hitchiti, Koasati, Natchez, Shawnee, Tunica, Yamasee, and Yuchi (Corkran 1967; J. W. Martin 1991; Swanton 1922; Wright 1986).

The Creek household (*huti*) was the smallest recognized social unit, and it was through the household that the Creeks met their basic subsistence needs. Like most southeastern groups, the Creeks traced descent matrilineally and practiced matrilocal residency. Household membership usually consisted of a matriarch, her spouse and dependent children, married daughters with their spouses and children, and, occasionally, older relatives (Swanton 1928:114). The Creek household was thus a multigenerational extended family occupying a common dwelling and cooperating in subsistence and productive activities.

Architecturally, the historic Creek household occupied a series or cluster of buildings constructed around a central courtyard (Bartram 1853:55–56). At a minimum, these structures are believed to have consisted of a summer house and a winter house; large or wealthy households added a third or fourth building for storage and other uses. Charles Hudson (1976:217–218) suggests that the number of buildings owned by a household correlates with its period of development, with established households owning more than recently established ones.

118 / Cameron B. Wesson

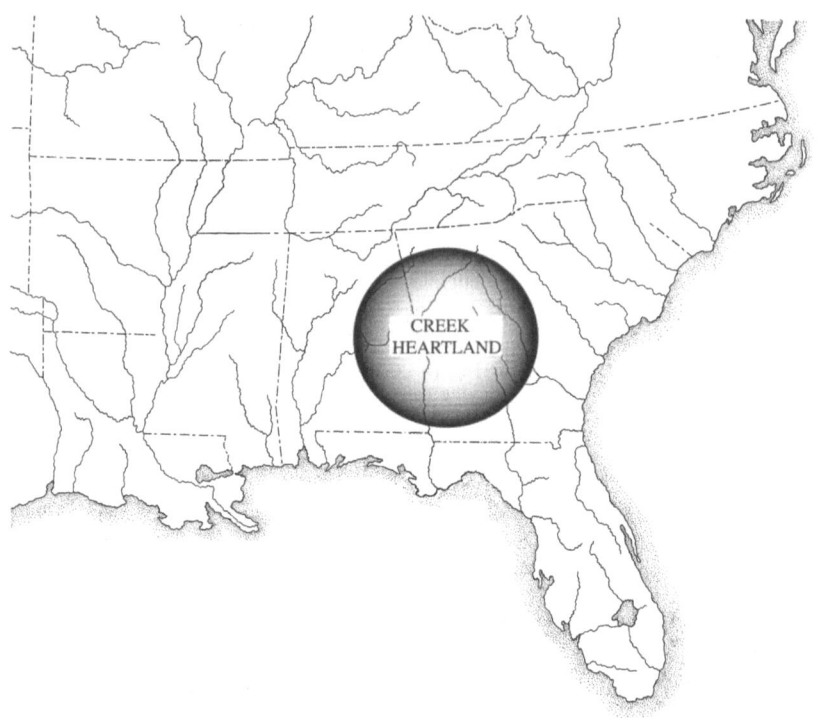

Figure 7.1 Location of the Creeks during the Historic period.

Recent archaeological research at Creek sites in central Alabama has yielded excellent household-level information on the distribution of prestige goods and the nature of sociopolitical organization during the Prehistoric, Protohistoric, and Historic periods (Cottier 1997; C. T. Sheldon 1997; Wesson 1997). In particular, data from household contexts—including burials, storage features, and village settlement patterns—allow the nature of protohistoric culture change to be evaluated diachronically (Figure 7.2). Considered in their totality, these data sources suggest a pattern of resistance to traditional elite authority and point to an increasingly household-based focus in sociopolitical and economic matters.

Analysis of burial goods as status indicators is always problematic, as has been previously demonstrated (J. A. Brown 1971; O'Shea 1984; Pearson 2000; Tainter 1975). However, if control of prestige goods is a basis of elite prerogative, then the ability of individuals to secure extra-local prestige goods for themselves would have had profound effects on chiefly authority. Like many southeastern groups, the Creeks generally buried the dead beneath the sleeping benches of their domestic structure (Swanton 1946), and Creek burial practices affirm close associations between the deceased and the sociopolitical status of the household.

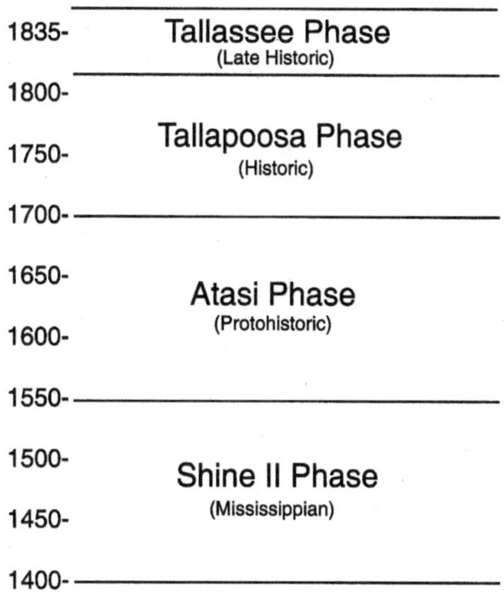

1835-	**Tallassee Phase** (Late Historic)
1800-	
1750-	**Tallapoosa Phase** (Historic)
1700-	
1650-	**Atasi Phase** (Protohistoric)
1600-	
1550-	
1500-	**Shine II Phase** (Mississippian)
1450-	
1400-	

Figure 7.2 Central Alabama cultural chronology.

Evaluation of burial furniture from Creek sites indicates an increasing number of non-prestige and prestige goods placed in burial contexts from the prehistoric Shine II, protohistoric Atasi, and historic Tallapoosa phases (Figure 7.3). In addition, analysis of burials from the protohistoric Atasi phase indicates the possible use of Euroamerican goods as status markers prior to the establishment of consistent trade relations between the Creeks and Euroamericans. By the historic Tallapoosa phase, European burial goods and prestige items were placed with almost every burial, demonstrating both the ubiquity of these items and their importance as social currency. Accompanying these trends is the apparent homogeneity of burial furniture during the Tallapoosa phase. Such similarities across the entire social spectrum lead to the conclusion that elites were no longer able to control access to Euroamerican prestige goods: individuals engaged in activities such as the deerskin trade gained greater control of these items.

Given previous stocks of symbolic capital and favorable social relationships, however, elite Creeks continued to augment their social positions through the use of prestige goods. Analysis of goods from Atasi and Tallapoosa phase burials indicates the hoarding of large numbers of prestige-related items in select burials. These burials contain significantly more prestige goods than other contemporary burials. This pattern suggests that although the control of prestige goods remained an important aspect of social status, control of these goods in large numbers was now required to intimidate one's social rivals.

Changes in household size during the Historic period provide additional evi-

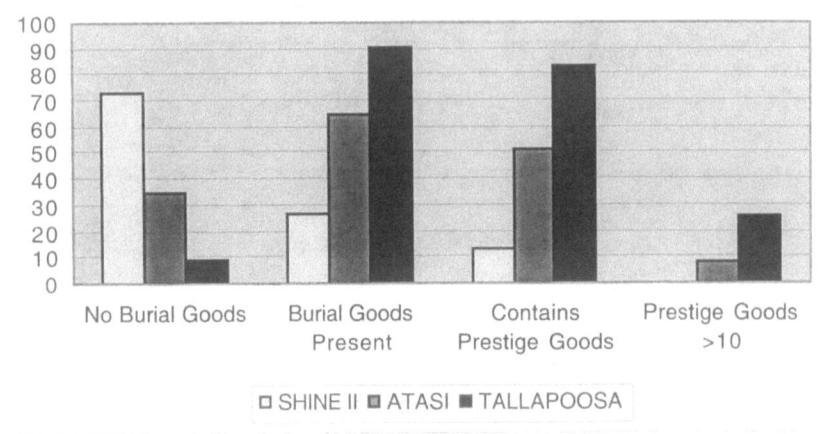

Figure 7.3 Changes in burial goods distribution from Creek sites.

dence of major changes in social organization for the Creek during the Protohistoric period. During the Prehistoric and early Protohistoric periods the Creek occupied a dual-structure household with seasonally specific structures for both the summer and winter (Cottier 1997; C. T. Sheldon 1997; Wesson 1997). During the winter months larger matrilineal groups resided together in the winter house, and during the summer months these extended families occupied their own households (C. T. Sheldon 1997; Waselkov 1993). By the end of the Atasi phase (ca. 1715), the Creek began to utilize a single domestic structure patterned after the previous summer structure. According to the evidence, construction or occupation of the winter house ceased, and a new residence pattern emerged.

The loss of the winter house and a decrease in the size of domestic structures during the Tallapoosa phase are thought to represent a reduction in economic cooperation among extended families. This pattern is also consistent with the expectation that the increased resources made available through the deerskin trade permitted new households to form. Individuals who were previously tied to the household of a matrilineally-related kin would now have been able to found their own. Moreover, by the late Tallapoosa phase (ca. 1830s) the nature of the Creek domestic structure changed to a log cabin type structure, similar to that occupied by Euroamerican colonists in the Southeast. It has been argued that these changes in household architecture had social and demographic components as well: household membership decreased, and a household social structure more like the nuclear family became the primary co-residential unit.

A comparison of the size of protohistoric and historic domestic structures reveals a general decrease in their size over time. Protohistoric Atasi phase structures were much larger and more varied than their Tallapoosa phase counterparts (Figure 7.4).

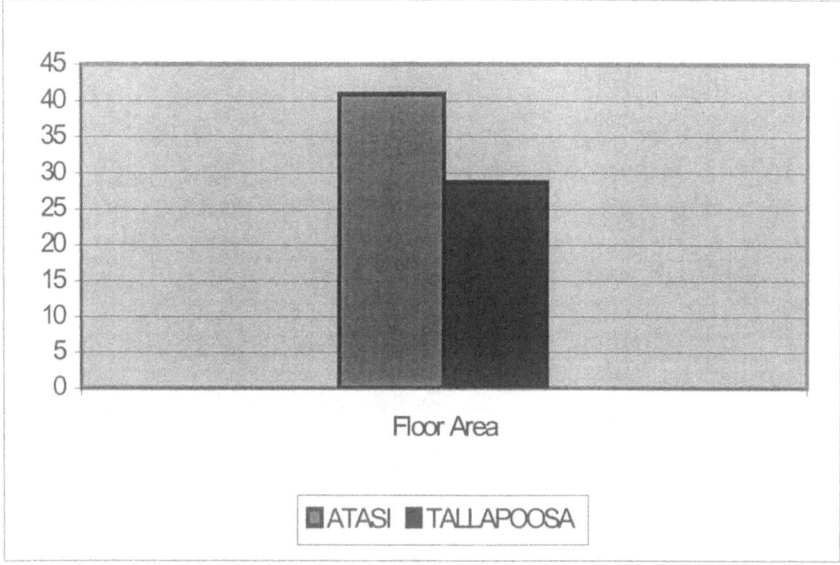

Figure 7.4 Changes in Creek domestic architecture.

These differences in size have profound implications for the understanding of social and economic practices. They suggest a dramatic decline in household occupancy from approximately six adults to three or four. Although this decrease might be ascribed to demographic collapse, these structures postdate the most lethal pandemics thought to have swept across the southeast (Knight 1994b). Although there were later waves of disease, census records indicate an increase in the number of people residing in Creek towns along the Tallapoosa River during this period (Ashley 1988; Swanton 1928). Thus, if the populations were larger and their houses were smaller, it follows that the number of domestic structures increased.

Another characteristic of household activity that bears on the nature of sociopolitical organization is food storage. One of the major roles of southeastern elites is thought to be their control and distribution of surplus foodstuffs. During the Prehistoric and early Historic periods southeastern elites supervised surplus food supplies, with each household responsible for periodic contributions to communal stores (Clayton et al. 1993; Swanton 1922, 1946:372–379). During the Protohistoric and Historic periods there was an increase in household-based storage (Wesson 1999)(Figure 7.5). Both the number and size of storage features increased dramatically over this period. The increased control of food resources by individual households is seen as an act of resistance to elite authority and a shift in the importance of household-based social, economic, and subsistence relationships. This interpretation is supported further by research by Morse (1980) and DeBoer

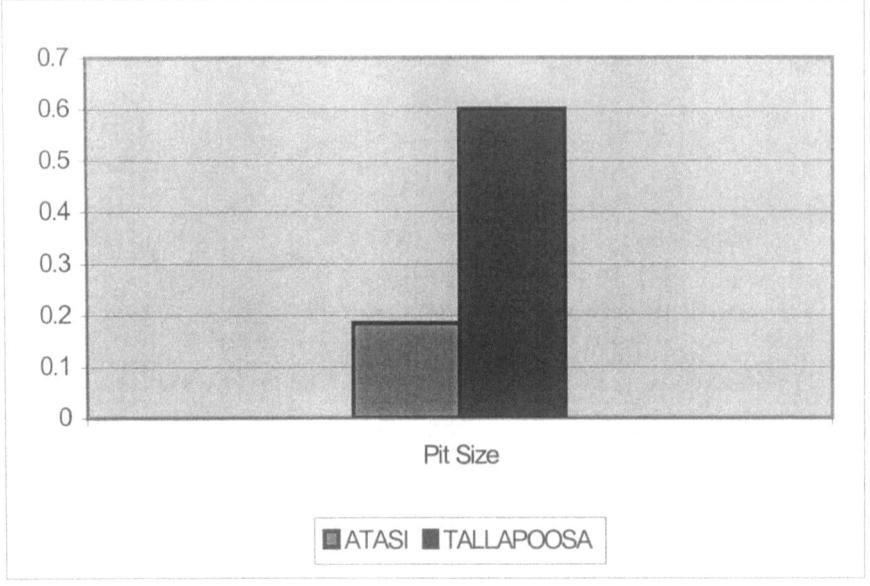

Figure 7.5 Changes in Creek domestic storage features.

(1998), who demonstrate that the advent of household-based storage hides food supplies from public knowledge and restricts their use to that of a single household.

In addition to these internal changes in Creek households, movements away from centralized communities also represented a significant source of culture change. Available evidence indicates a generalized dispersal of households within previously nucleated villages during the Protohistoric and Historic periods (Ashley 1988; Cottier 1997; Knight 1985; C. T. Sheldon 1997). Such movements are seen as efforts by households to improve their wealth and status (Ashley 1988:115)—indication of reaction against traditional communal agricultural systems and of the increasing conception of land as private property (A. Moore 1988:62–63, Swanton 1922:229; see M. Johnson 1996 for an excellent review of this concept), and of strategic movements on the part of households to place themselves in a better position to secure the resources they needed to continue their economic development (Swanton 1922:229). Removal from centralized villages also countered the effectiveness of elite-centered ideologies expressed in the spatial configuration of nucleated villages (Wesson 1998). The process of settlement dispersal heralded greater household autonomy and self-sufficiency.

As with other changes in the Creek household, alterations in settlement structures reduced the power of chiefly elites and promoted social status based on household access to Euroamerican goods. Creek elites were increasingly faced with the desertion of their population and the constant emergence of new rivals to challenge their authority. Such processes limited elite authority and eventually resulted in a dynamic sociopolitical structure that fluctuated with economic cycles and featured constant competition among rival households and families.

Taken together, these patterns of change in burial practices, domestic architecture, and spatial distribution of settlements indicate a rise in the prevalence and power of competing social ideologies and a corresponding erosion of chiefly power during the Protohistoric and Historic periods. In the end, much of the culture change experienced by the Creek and other southeastern groups during the prehistoric-historic transition was shaped by the quest for symbolic capital and by resistance to elite control of social and political institutions.

Conclusions

Although depopulation and trade fostered change in southeastern indigenous societies, local populations continued to engage in many of the same sociopolitical practices established prior to European contact. Elites continued to occupy unique social positions, holding on to control of prestige goods economies and access to supernaturally sanctioned power. Throughout the course of the Historic period, the ability of individual leaders to maintain control of these systems declined, resulting in a sharing of power with larger segments of society and the development of consensus-based governments. One mechanism thought to have precipitated declines in elite authority is the ability of individual members of society to garner directly from Euroamericans the goods they needed for social reproduction, without having to participate in the traditional elite-controlled system of exchange (Wesson 1997). A decline in elite ability to manage access to high-status prestige goods allowed individuals to increase their social prestige through participation in the deerskin trade and other exchanges with Euroamericans.

From the dominant ideology perspective, such actions were in conflict with traditional Creek culture and placed those who participated in them in opposition to existing status hierarchies. However, as previously argued, prestige goods systems are built through social competition, so resistance to dominant elites is consistent with the very rules of the game. By engaging in acts that brought them increased access to prestige goods and symbolic capital, individuals Creeks and nondominant social groups actively resisted inferior social statuses and permanently altered the nature of elite social position. As Knight (1985:182) contends,

> The nature and character of the traffic in European goods among the Creeks was not wholly imposed by Europeans. It was actively shaped by Creek individuals behaving according to an entirely indigenous moral code, a code whose origins predate the arrival of Europeans. It was a code modified at times by the history of contact with the external world, but in the end it must

be comprehended as an internal social force. It was not simply a case of the primitive passively yielding to an overwhelming exposure to superior technology and culture.

Similar patterns of change have been noted for other southeastern Native American groups. Research by Riggs (1989) and Schroedl (1986) points to numerous transitions in Cherokee culture during the Protohistoric and Historic periods that closely parallel those of the Creeks. Evidence suggests that the Cherokee abandoned long-standing patterns in domestic architecture and political economy (Davis et al. 1982; Riggs 1984; Schroedl 1986a:542–543). Schroedl (1986a:543) links these changes with transitions in other areas of Cherokee domestic organization, arguing that they were the direct outgrowth of protohistoric and historic Cherokee-Euroamerican interactions: "Beginning in the Revolutionary Period and culminating in the Federal Period, the Overhill Cherokee experienced serious disruptions to their socio-political and socio-economic patterns, reducing population size and altering its structure and distribution. The size and effectiveness of family economic and kin group networks were reduced. As this occurred, village entities collapsed, family units became more widely dispersed and the size of dwellings diminished."

These changes are almost identical to those experienced by the Creeks during this same period. As with the Creeks, these changes in Cherokee society are seen as at least partially a response to the deerskin trade, with individual hunters engaged in the competitive accumulation of prestige goods by engaging in direct trade with Europeans without the need for chiefs as intermediaries (Riggs 1989; Schroedl 1986a:542). Research also indicates increased socioeconomic competition and differentiation between households (Riggs 1989:336). These patterns are thought to have intensified as inter-household competition in trade relations with Euroamericans increased.

By examining changes in households, it is possible to view changes in indigenous protohistoric cultures as responses to internal desires to alter existing social inequalities. Individuals made decisions that fostered the accumulation of material goods and the cultivation of symbolic capital by themselves and their close kin. Such actions created an inflationary cultural spiral, where an increasing number of Euroamerican material goods were necessary for reinforcing claims to social and economic status. Even the traditional bride price was affected, with families demanding an increasing number of European goods from prospective grooms (Corkran 1967:40; Swanton 1928:369). As such, Native Americans were not dependent upon trade goods because of what Europeans professed to be their "functionally superiority" but because they had become central components in networks of social status and prestige, necessary elements for certain forms of social reproduction.

Viewed from this perspective, indigenous sociopolitical change was shaped far more profoundly by the behavior of indigenous social actors than by the traditional black boxes of European disease and trade. The selective adoption of Euroamerican material items indicates that many of the protohistoric cultural changes noted in other research were not brought about by Euroamerican design but were instead products of internal social processes. The use of Euroamerican material items in prestige goods economies indicates that such use was other than that intended by those producing or exchanging them. Instead, these items functioned within pre-existing indigenous systems for reckoning social status, simultaneously reinforcing and undermining existing mechanisms of social reproduction.

Acknowledgments

I would like to thank Mark Rees for co-organizing the original symposium on southeastern protohistory and co-editing this volume. I also wish to thank John Cottier and Craig Sheldon for all their assistance in the research efforts summarized in this chapter. In addition, much thanks is due to Maria Aviles, Shannon Freeman, and to two anonymous reviewers for their insightful comments on previous versions of this paper.

8 / Warfare in the Protohistoric Southeast
1500-1700

David H. Dye

Warfare in the Southeast evolved over the past millennia from small-scale raids and ambushes of hunter-gatherers to formal battles among competing, rival chiefdoms. Explaining the processes responsible for these changes has been a continual challenge for archaeologists, ethnohistorians, and anthropologists. In this chapter I argue that by the sixteenth and seventeenth centuries warfare had become embedded in the political activities of competing chiefly elites, who jockeyed among themselves for power. To understand the nature of the changing military system, changes in political control must be taken into account. Political control in chiefdoms is, in part, maintained and extended through the military power of competing chiefs. As Mississippian culture began to decentralize upon the impact of European contact, ruling elites throughout much of the Southeast began to lose political control over their retinue, and this in turn created new opportunities for leadership. Warfare in the Protohistoric period underwent fundamental changes within a social environment characterized by decreasing political control and centralization.

Chiefly warfare had its beginnings in the emergence of competing chiefdoms throughout much of the Southeast. The development of new styles of warfare accompanying the "Mississippian Emergence" brought about an increased need for secure alliances, strong defenses, and continual military assessment. Security, defense, and offense soon became overriding concerns to ruling elites. With European contact, however, many aspects of Mississippian warfare were altered, precipitating changes in tactics, strategies, and styles of military behavior that had evolved over the previous six centuries. Competition, generated by a new sense of political survival and exacerbated by interpolity rivalries, comprised a major focus of daily life in the sixteenth- and seventeenth-century Southeast. Considerable diversity and variation in polity structure and in warfare patterns undoubtedly existed during these two centuries, but overall a steady decline in political centralization and social control by ruling elites lead to changes in the pattern of warfare.

While political change is evident throughout the Mississippian period, particularly with regard to the cyclical rise and fall of individual polities (Anderson 1994b;

C. Hudson 1997; B. D. Smith 1986, 1996), both the scale and tempo of change accelerated considerably with the advent of sustained European contact (Dobyns 1983; C. Hudson 1997:422; Milner 1980; Purdy 1988; Ramenofsky 1987; Salisbury 1996; M. T. Smith 1987; Trigger and Swagerty 1996:364). The nature of sociopolitical change during the Protohistoric has been much discussed and debated (Anderson 1994b; Galloway 1995; C. Hudson and Tesser 1994b; Muller 1997; J. F. Scarry 1996b; M. T. Smith 1987). Despite numerous discussions of Mississippian and Colonial warfare (Anderson 1994a; DePratter 1983:44–67; Dickson 1981; Dye 1990, 1994; Gibson 1974; C. Hudson 1976:239–257; Larson 1972; Steinen 1992; Steinen and Ritson 1996; Weisman and Milanich 1976), scant attention has been paid to the transformation of indigenous patterns of warfare in the sixteenth and seventeenth centuries as a result of European colonial expansion.

The Evolution of Mississippian Warfare

Significant changes in warfare styles are evident in the Southeast prior to Western contact. Perhaps the greatest technological innovation precipitating new patterns of warfare took place as early as A.D. 600, when the bow and arrow was introduced throughout most of the Eastern Woodlands (Blitz 1988:131; Nassaney and Pyle 1999:253). Its rapid adoption appears to have resulted primarily from "competitive social relations" (Blitz 1988:137). Prior to the introduction of the bow and arrow, warfare likely resembled eighteenth-century tribal raiding parties, wherein militia kin conducted surprise raids and attacks on villages and farmsteads to increase warrior status, capture prisoners, and avenge past wrongs (C. Hudson 1976:239–257). The bow and arrow, however, apparently escalated raiding and ambushing, and ushered in new opportunities for highly formalized, standardized, and organized forms of offensive combat that necessitated changes in both defensive posturing and settlement location. The bow and arrow provided a decided advantage over the atlatl because of its greater accuracy, increased range, and higher velocity. Reduced launch time allowed more projectiles to be fired, and less body movement enabled a higher degree of concealment (Nassaney and Pyle 1999:259), thus providing greater firepower and opportunities for cover. The expansion and adoption of the bow and arrow in the seventh century A.D. resulted in "a qualitative reorganization in the scale and practice of warfare" (Nassaney and Pyle 1999:260).

By emergent Mississippian/terminal Woodland times (A.D. 900–1050) "a general climate of social circumscription, endemic warfare, and resource stress" affected a large section of the Southeast (Knight and Steponaitis 1998:10). Increased population nucleation brought about the coalescence of populations into a few relatively large, fortified villages that exhibit direct responses to bow warfare, including moats and palisades with bastions and constricted entrances (Blitz 1988; Lafferty 1973; Larson 1972).

With the development of chiefly warfare, as early as the tenth or eleventh century, increased need for security apparently resulted from widespread competition and rivalries among chiefs for control over limited resources including storable surplus (staple finance) and prestige goods (wealth finance) (Earle 1997) that fueled the Mississippian political economy and portable symbolic objects that materialized the political ideology. Fortified towns can be seen as facilities that held and protected both chiefly political funds and materialized ideology which allowed them to control and direct social labor for their own ends. Staple and wealth finance, the populations necessary for producing it, and key symbolic objects then became the primary targets of chiefly warfare. Changes in daily life are evident as early as A.D. 1100, when sites were relocated to defensible landforms, including bluff tops, islands, and river meander bends.

Another technological innovation further changed the style of Mississippian warfare. The war club, linked with warfare, personal status, and the belief system (Van Horne 1993:223), became the weapon of choice by approximately A.D. 1200. As chiefdom level warfare continued throughout the interior Southeast, warrior status became increasingly critical for legitimizing the role of specific individuals in elite hierarchical institutions. Hand-to-hand combat with war clubs provided greater killing power and may have afforded warriors the opportunity of gaining greater prestige in their quest for status in a highly charged competitive social environment than did the bow and arrow.

Chiefly warfare and the increased use of war clubs brought about differences in mortality rates and traumatic injuries directly related to site size and risk of attack. Small to medium Mississippian sites, more vulnerable to attack, exhibit the greatest levels of mortality rates and traumatic injuries. In small, undefended hamlets arrows often killed individuals, while mid-sized sites with defensive features exhibit high mortality from violence, but rarely from embedded arrow points. In mid-sized sites, high fracture rates resulted from head wounds, some of which were fatal, and the pattern of cranial trauma suggests the increased use of war clubs. Large, well-defended sites were generally secure from warfare and consequently had relatively low levels of mortality rates and traumatic injuries resulting from violence. Concomitant with these patterns is an increase in male participation in warfare, reflected in the majority of deaths being males (Bridges et al. 1999).

In the Central Mississippi Valley, fortified, civic-ceremonial centers typically surrounded by dispersed farmsteads gave way in the late thirteenth century to compact, densely occupied, fortified towns and villages with few if any adjacent farmsteads (Morse and Morse 1983). After ca. A.D. 1350–1400, large-scale warfare again increased markedly in many areas of the Southeast (Anderson 1994a:75) and may have precipitated—in conjunction with soil depletion, endemic disease, and climatic changes—the development of a "vacant quarter" (S. Williams 1990) that witnessed "a dramatic and fairly widespread episode of decline and abandonment prior to the arrival of European settlers or introduced diseases" (B. D. Smith 1996:316). The result was a pattern of population dispersal and coalescence similar to one that would be repeated in the sixteenth and seventeenth centuries. By the time of European contact warfare had developed into a well-orchestrated military program of offensive and defensive strategies and tactics. Although the details of Mississippian warfare are unknown, a pattern of surprise raids and ambushes coupled with organized, large-scale attacks is evident; to counter this, broad and extensive buffer zones were developed between polities (DePratter 1983). Milner et al.'s (1991:595) comment on the fourteenth-century Crow Creek massacre as "only one facet of intergroup hostilities featuring repeated ambushes punctuated by devastating attacks at particularly opportune moments" is noteworthy. Coordinated squadrons, often made up of allied polities, could attack their enemies with equal facility on land and water.

Early Protohistoric Warfare

Sixteenth-century Spanish (de Soto, Pardo, and Luna) and French (Laudonnière) expeditions provide convincing evidence of chiefly warfare in the mid-sixteenth century. These accounts, coupled with archaeological models, document a mosaic of political forms throughout the Southeast. Moundville, for example, had so shrunk from its former political eminence by the middle of the sixteenth century that its hereditary paramount might have lacked any real political power (Knight and Steponaitis 1998:23). The Central and Lower Mississippi Valley chiefdoms, on the other hand, appear to have been strongly centralized (Morse and Morse 1983: 305–315; B. D. Smith 1996:316–318). In the Lower Tallapoosa, Middle Coosa, and Lower Chattahoochee valleys there are "clear signs of cultural, social, and political continuity from the sixteenth through the seventeenth centuries" (Knight 1994b:385) of chiefdom-like polities. Thus, at the time of European contact a variety of political forms were evident in the Southeast, ranging from short-term chieftaincies to simple chiefdoms to various forms of complex and paramount chiefdoms whose political base was predicated on permanent regional leadership by hereditary chiefs.

In these hierarchically ranked, kin-based regional polities, chiefs actively sought political power and control through institutional governance based on inherited political offices. Chiefly political control was maintained through several power strategies, including warfare, by which political compliance was coerced from neighboring polities. Chiefs regularly extended their sphere of domination over their neighbors through warfare, which ultimately become an instrument of political expansion.

Offensive tactics of the more centralized Mississippian chiefdoms emphasized mobile attacking forces ranging from small-scale guerilla raids and ambushes to large-scale, coordinated assaults against strongly defended targets. Chiefs engaged in open field battles with opponents arranged in battle formations, including crescents (Hahn 1995:58–60) and equal arm crosses (C. Hudson 1988). Crescent formations, based on hunting strategies, enabled ambushing forces to encircle their enemies, produce an enfilade fire, and then entrap them. Equal arm crosses may have arisen to break through crescent formations with massed forces. Attacking forces were often organized into identifiable squadrons that could maneuver in formations on both land and water. Such forces were under the command of chiefs who controlled their constituent forces through the use of drums and other devices (DePratter 1983).

Defensive tactics were designed to protect fixed locations such as paramount centers and frontier villages with plastered palisades, projecting bastions, and moats (Blakely 1988; Blitz 1993a; Clay 1976; DePratter 1983; Lafferty 1973, Larson 1972; Steinen 1992; Vogel and Allan 1985). Plastered walled houses may have resulted from the Mississippian use of fire by massed warriors (DePratter 1983:47). The de Soto accounts describe large, well-organized fighting forces on both land and water (DePratter 1983:49–55; Dye 1990:220, 1994). "Static" defensive systems, incorporating palisades, bastions, and moats, may signal centralized leadership, while "active" defensive systems, based on the use of natural conditions combined with intelligence gathering and ambush tactics, may indicate less centralization of political leadership (Steinen and Ritson 1996).

Three primary political objectives of ruling elites lay at the heart of chiefly warfare. The first was the efforts of chiefs to legitimize their authority over other elites through their success in warfare and their involvement in rituals associated with warfare. Warfare and its attendant rituals provided an arena for chiefs to demonstrate and enhance their military prowess, thus bolstering their political authority and control. The second political objective was the resolution of chiefly political grudges. Chiefly grievances often arose out of interpolity political relations, sparking intense conflict, competition, and aggression among polities. Public slights, imagined or real, by chiefs, and the resulting grudges could precipitate open aggression and hostility (Reyna 1994:46). The third political objective was the facilitation of chiefly political and financial expansion. The acquisitive pursuits of chiefs prompted subjugation of neighboring polities through military means in order to amass wealth and organize labor for political currency. In turn, chiefs would be forced to defend their financial base from competing chiefs. Chiefs told French and Spanish expedition leaders that a recurring reason for initiating hostilities was rebellion by vassals who routinely provided social labor and material tribute. Although warfare does not seem to have been conducted to destroy whole populations or occupy territory (Gibson 1974:132; Steinen 1992:134), chiefly hegemonic warfare was widespread among the more centralized chiefdoms (Dye 1990:213) and often featured terror tactics and wide-scale slaughter. The goal of hegemonic warfare was the indirect control of populations for the social labor that could produce tribute in the form of staple and wealth finance and thus provide chiefs the means for further financial expansion. In other words, one source of political power in chiefdoms rested upon elite control over the production and exchange of staple and wealth finance (Earle 1997:7).

These three political objectives provided the necessary ingredients for a hostile social environment that precipitated intense and, at times, incessant warfare among neighboring chiefdoms. Where chiefly warfare took form, it generally resulted in a landscape of civic-ritual centers surrounded by moats and palisades with accompanying bastions. A major political feature of chiefly warfare was its ability to aggregate polities through subjection and incorporation (Carneiro 1994:14). Chiefs now could use violence as a "constitutive" power to "create, maintain, and transform social relations" in ways that had not been possible prior to the creation and deployment of chiefly militias (Reyna 1994:46). Through this process chiefly polities grew in size and structure. Reflecting the incorporative nature of chiefly warfare, it has been variously referred to as conquest (Earle 1997:109), aggregative (Carneiro 1994:14; Reyna 1994:47), and expansionist (Redmond 1994:53). By conquering additional territories, chiefs could expand their financial base (Barker 1992:74), but in general expansion did not entail the acquisition of land but rather improved productive facilities and social (commoner) labor that produced the surplus that, in turn, financed the political economy (Earle 1997:132).

The political dimensions of chiefly warfare seem to have given rise to several different modes or styles of warfare. At European contact there is clear documentary evidence of two basic interrelated styles of offensive chiefly warfare (Anderson 1994a:98; DePratter 1983:44–67; Dye 1990; Steinen 1992): guerilla raids/ambushes and formal battles. Guerilla or harassing raids, taking the form of hit-and-run attacks and ambushes, emphasized surprise, mobility, intelligence, and an intimate knowledge of the terrain. Although limited in their effectiveness, raids and ambushes were well suited to "reduce the effectiveness of an enemy force, demoralize a fixed population, reduce the flow of supplies, capture towns for short periods of time, or demonstrate that certain targets, such as villages and civic centers, are vulnerable" (Steinen 1992:135). Raiding parties, serving at a chief's behest, could aid in maintaining control over a tributary polity. The objective of raids was to penetrate an enemy's territory, strike quickly with the element of surprise, and then withdraw with minimal losses. To be effective raids had to be of short duration, executed swiftly, and conducted with surprise and violence (Steinen 1992:135).

Light missile weapons such as arrows were preferred by warriors on guerilla raids to impose safe distances when facing a large force. Guerilla raids provided a chief the means of harassing a more powerful enemy and avoiding hand-to-hand combat against superior numbers. Skirmish warfare—that is, preying on hunting parties and other task specific groups—could have long-term effects on tribute appropriation, chiefly authority, and population relocation (Anderson 1996b:245). An effective means of harassing and terrorizing an enemy, guerilla warfare was usually thwarted tactically by the construction of fortifications that forced some degree of population nucleation. The near impossibility of defeating guerrillas by purely military means made raiding an effective style of warfare (Keeley 1996:80). European expeditions were continuously forced to cope with guerilla warriors, and for this reason raiding is a prominent feature of most sixteenth-century documentary accounts.

When principal chiefs perceived they had an advantage over their rivals, they may have engaged them in mutually agreed upon formal battles, composed of militia-based armies of several hundred to several thousand warriors maneuvering under and coordinated by a chain of command. As a result of supply and transportation problems, organized battles were of short duration, but war foods could be prepared in advance and battles could take place near the late summer-fall harvest to partially offset these logistical problems (DePratter 1983:64–66).

Bows and arrows would have been useful in initial assaults between warring groups. Fire-tipped arrows shot over palisade walls to ignite roof thatch would have been particularly effective. Yet hand-to-hand combat with shock weapons, such as war clubs, was the preferred mode of fighting. Shock weapons possess greater striking power and accuracy over fire weapons such as arrows (Gabriel and Metz 1991:56–75; Keeley 1996:49), and their presence and longevity in southeastern iconography, beginning as early as the thirteenth century, attests to their central role in warfare. Although the bow and arrow may have been the main weapon of war, the war club was the main symbol of war (C. Hudson 1976:245).

The cornerstone of success for chiefly warfare in the early Protohistoric period was military organization. The basis of chiefly combat organization was twofold: hierarchical structure and formal institutions. The kin based, hierarchical nature of Mississippian political organization provided chiefs with a ready-made structure for their military organization. For example, hierarchical structure gave ruling elites the organizational capability to create simple but effective chains of command based on graded military statuses. The chain of command began with the chief as the commander-in-chief, while the common warrior stood at the other end of the spectrum. In between the chiefly commander and the lowest warrior lay the graded ranks of veteran warriors.

At the upper end of the ranks were the elite, experienced, principal warriors, who sat in formal war councils and served as experienced military specialists. Their status was probably ascribed, whereas lower ranking warriors' status was clearly achieved through military exploits and success. Elite warriors aided in planning campaigns and deploying warriors, and they were often military leaders of subunits, being referred to as "captains" by the French and Spanish following their own military system. These "captains," in fact, may have served roles in native military organization similar to their European counterparts, in terms of their responsibilities within the command structure for relaying orders and maintaining discipline.

Hierarchical structure also gave Mississippian paramount chiefs, as field commanders, the authority, power, and control to issue orders to subsidiary chiefs, who could relay commands to their principal warriors, who, in turn, had sufficient authority to relay orders that would be passed on to their warrior constituents. A multi-tiered command structure based on a series of graded ranks enabled principal chiefs to command hundreds if not thousands of militia warriors through an efficient and effective chain of command. The command structure also allowed chiefly commanders to maintain discipline through punishment of disobedient, recalcitrant, or careless warriors based on the combined force of the chiefly retinue. Chiefs could compel obedience to their commands through the authority and power of their office (Carneiro 1992:35), which was, in part, backed by the elite military retinue.

Hierarchical structure also allowed principal chiefs, in conjunction with their war councils, to marshal militia forces composed of the polity's able-bodied males. Militia mobilization would take place at the command of the principal chief throughout the various hamlets, villages, and towns within the polity. On numerous occasions, sixteenth-century Spanish expeditions witnessed rapid mobilization and deployment of southeastern chiefly militias by paramount chiefs in defense and offense.

Chiefly militias of complex and paramount chiefdoms with their hierarchical military command structure and formal institutions allowed chiefs to carry out sophisticated military campaigns. Southeastern militias were potent forces, as sixteenth-century French and Spanish explorers quickly learned. Chiefly militias could be rapidly summoned and then ordered to storm fortified towns during brief battles from land and water as well as oppose forces on the move, especially across barriers such as lakes and rivers.

The structure of formal battles in combination with guerilla raids gave great military strength to Mississippian principal chiefs. The institutional organization of Mississippian military power lay in the coercive force that ultimately depended upon a chief's ability to control both militia forces in formal battles and less organized groups who took part in guerilla raids. The organizational structure and control of battles and raids resided in formal Mississippian military institutions.

These formal institutions established a framework for military obligations, responsibilities, and rewards on the part of the chiefly retinue that crosscut kin relations. Two primary formal institutions underwrote the command structure of Mississippian military organization: war councils and warfare cults. War councils—formal forums composed of principal chiefs, elite warriors, and warrior priests—were instrumental in conceiving, planning, and carrying out military operations. The role of the war priests, who possessed esoteric ritual knowledge and prophetic ability, made them indispensable sources of information in war council decisions and in the spiritual or supernatural protection and guidance of warriors. They could maintain discipline and obedience by demanding adherence to strict ritual protocols. Mississippian war councils could oversee both guerilla raids and formal battles and could control the actions of warriors both on the field of battle and at home. Authority and power over warriors in ranks and upper echelon "captains" was essential in controlling the unstable coercive force available to the principal chief. A rival would quickly dispose of a chief who was unable to control both the "captains" and their militia warrior retinue. The power of military force is difficult to administer, and out of necessity chiefs generally employed a variety of means to manage their various constituent retinues.

The success of military campaigns was often based on a chief's ability to forge effective alliances through the mechanism of the war council. Alliances created forces larger than a single polity could effectively field, and allowed chiefs to concentrate and coordinate multi-polity attacks against specific towns. The initial widespread presence of fortified towns in the archaeological record may well signal the ability of principal chiefs to aggregate fighting forces through alliances with neighboring chiefs in order to attack their common rivals in overwhelming numbers. In the spring of 1543, de Soto thwarted a coalition of some twenty chiefs who were planning a massive, coordinated attack on the fortified Spanish settlement at the Central Mississippi Valley town of Aminoya (C. Hudson 1997:384).

Another formal institution, the military cult (J. A. Brown 1985:114) or warfare/cosmogony complex (Knight 1986), strengthened the principal chief's centralized authority and power by linking chiefly participation in warfare rituals and involvement and success in warfare with supernatural power. Warfare iconography, bound to military rituals, enhanced the linkage between supernatural and chiefly authority. If chiefs controlled the production and distribution of warfare related prestige goods (wealth finance) charged with iconographic representations, then the apportioning of such goods also would serve to underwrite their authority in warfare. Control over the system of wealth finance enabled chiefs to control the ideology of social ranking (Earle 1997:74) which underwrote control of the command structure and formal institutions.

Sixteenth-century Mississippian warfare, based on chiefly political objectives, distinctive warfare styles, and a highly effective, institutionalized military structure, created a formidable military machine employed by principal chiefs to further their political agendas, enhance and strengthen their political control, and protect their towns and financial systems. The early protohistoric (Mississippian) military organization was not substantially changed or altered, especially in the interior Southeast, until the late sixteenth or early seventeenth century. The demise of chiefly warfare over a large region was brought about principally through sustained Western contact in the late sixteenth/early seventeenth century, which created a "tribal zone" as a result of introduced diseases, ecological transformations, and technological changes (Ferguson and Whitehead 1992).

Late Protohistoric Warfare

The late Protohistoric period in the interior Southeast effectively begins with the second wave of Europeans, traders, priests, colonizers, explorers, and settlers in the late seventeenth century. Their accounts document changes witnessed in the late seventeenth century, but some fifty to seventy-five years of rapid social change had already been underway in many areas of the Southeast prior to their arrival. Unlike the mid-sixteenth-century expedition reports in the early Protohistoric, these later accounts are often based on longer periods of observation and a greater knowledge of native ways. Individuals such as Thomas Nairne spent extended periods of time among native polities and consequently provide greater details of social life than the earlier sixteenth-century accounts. Nairne, for example, was particularly interested in sociopolitical organization and the nature of native political power. His reporting adds significant details to the extent warfare had changed over the intervening half century.

The three precipitating factors of warfare found in the mid-sixteenth century—legitimation of chiefly authority, resolution of chiefly grudges, and facilitation of chiefly financial expansion and control—had undergone considerable alteration by the late seventeenth century. The power of the hereditary paramount, whose office was still evident, had by 1708 in many areas "dwindled away to nothing" (Nairne 1988:38). Even a century earlier on the Gulf Coast we find that the Apalachee "obey their chiefs poorly" (Hann 1988:12). With the decrease in chiefly authority and social hierarchy in many polities of the Southeast, the political objectives associated with principal chiefs changed appreciably and so, accordingly, did the objectives of warfare.

Warfare no longer served to legitimize the authority of the principal chief, whose office now had been devalued and restricted to civil matters. However, it directly enhanced the authority of the war chiefs, who "earned these Honors by the greatness of their actions" (Nairne 1988:41). War chiefs wielded considerable authority, but initially only under the conditions of warfare. Once they were back in their towns, warriors could ignore the war chief's dictates. Nairne noted in 1708 that the Chickasaw warrior "almost thinks himselfe as good as another, and only obeys so much of his superior's commands as suits with his own convenency or humor" (Nairne 1988:44). The war chief's authority evolved in the political power vacuum created after the hereditary paramount's authority and control dwindled at the end of the sixteenth century. With the gradual erosion of the ranking system, ascribed statuses, inherited offices, and social hierarchy, war chiefs garnered increasing authority based on war deeds and their generosity in distributing war booty among the warrior retinue. By the end of the seventeenth century competition for slaves, guns, and Western goods further fueled the ability of strong, opportunistic, and self-aggrandizing individuals to gain increasing authority through success in warfare. Eighteenth-century Cherokee "war parties were pecking orders, ordered by personality, in which big and aggressive men lorded it over small and less aggressive men, illegitimately and without much correspondence with the system of persons-with-role which nominally applied" (Gearing 1962:27). Cherokee war leaders coordinated behavior "through the exercise and threat of physical coercion" (Gearing 1962:47), though their power was informal and limited to warfare, and even then their authority was variable depending upon personality and charisma.

Late protohistoric combat units usually numbered between twenty and forty warriors (Adair 1930:382 [1775]); in some instances they were related, as acts of revenge were usually the responsibility of kin. When larger groups jointly pursued an enemy, they often divided into a number of smaller combat units acting independently of one another (Gearing 1962:27) and on a temporary basis. These units were not the militias of the sixteenth century called up by principal chiefs as agents of political policy; rather they were warriors who listened attentively to their wise elders in smoke-filled council chambers and then went out as war parties and did exactly as they pleased once the fighting began. In 1708 Nairne (1988:41) observed, "every private Capt. with his Followers or every single man or 2 goe a free booting at their pleasure." Rituals associated with warfare were, however, still important, and warriors were constrained to follow the protocol dictated by the war priests prior to and after engagement with the enemy.

The role of sixteenth-century chiefly grievances, as an outgrowth of political jockeying and maneuvering among competitive elites, was replaced in the seventeenth century by a pervasive sense of corporate and individual self-aggrandizement and revenge carried out informally by kin and non-kin militia whose unity was maintained and molded by ritual proscription. Guerilla raiding was often based on revenge stemming from individual or corporate grievances and aggrandizement rather than from political grudges held by chiefs as a function of public affairs. The rise of informal raids or small-scale warfare erupted as a result of the decentralization of chiefly authority. Lacking an appropriate mechanism for adjudicating grievances on an interpolity level, kin members may have been forced to handle revenge and seek economic opportunities through local kin or corporate ties. With catastrophic depopulation beginning in the late sixteenth century, greater value would have been placed on individuals whose leadership was based on personal valor and the productive role they could command in the political and ideological economy through the acquisition and distribution of European goods. In fact, competition and posturing for access to Western manufactures may have been a major factor in fostering warfare throughout the late Protohistoric period.

New elements added to the instability of the tribal zone and may have led directly to changes in warfare. Virulent European diseases in the late sixteenth century and the slave raids of the late seventeenth century brought about two waves of depopulation, which in turn resulted in changes in southeastern political organization and social structure. Population losses as early as the last quarter of the sixteenth century have been documented throughout much of the southeastern interior (Dobyns 1983; C. Hudson 1997:422; Ramenofsky 1987:67; M. T. Smith 1989a:29), and by the middle of the seventeenth-century native southeastern society again underwent fundamental population changes (M. T. Smith 1987, 1989a). In the early seventeenth century, depopulation from disease generated two critical military responses: replacement of productive members of society and displacement or destruction of one's traditional enemies who were unable to adequately defend themselves due to their own population losses. In the late seventeenth century, access to European weapons, particularly guns, became crucial for offense and defense (Hahn 1995). Guns altered the mechanics of warfare because firearms could be used at a greater distance than war clubs and arrows, but unlike either, supplies of gunpowder and lead had to be replenished from Western sources. The acquisition of slaves provided revenue for more guns and supplies and further contributed to population losses through killing and further slave raiding. Guns also brought about increased use of ambushes and reduction of open field fighting because musket balls were more difficult to dodge than arrows (Abler 1989:275; Steinen and Ritson 1996:117).

Critical members of society, women, and children—lost through depopulation—could only be replaced rapidly through warfare. While adult warriors were generally scalped and killed, women and mobile children generally were taken as captives in raids; this was in contrast to pre-contact times, when women and children were not spared in warfare (Milner 1995; Milner et al. 1991), with the possible exception of young women (Keeley 1996:68). With the advent of depopulation women and children became valued replacements for productive members of the polity who had died in epidemics or been taken as slaves. In 1700 Charles Levasseur wrote, "the greatest traffic between the English and the savages is the trade of slaves which the nations take from their neighbors whom they war with continuously, such that the men take the women and children away and sell them to the English, each person being traded for a gun" (Knight and Adams 1981:182). Thomas Nairne wrote, "no employment pleases the Chicasaws so well as slave Catching. A lucky hitt at that besides the Honor procures them a whole Estate at once, one slave brings a Gun, ammunition, horse, hatchet, and a suit of Cloathes, which would not be procured without much tedious toil a hunting. They goe a man hunting to the Chicsaws [sic; Choctaws], Down to the sea side along both sides of the great river, and 150 miles beyond it" (Nairne 1988:47–48). Captives had the added potential value of being held and later exchanged for a profitable ransom.

One attempt to increase population was to bring captives back alive rather than kill them indiscriminately for war trophies. The honors and prestige associated with war may have led to a shift from killing and dismembering individuals for the war trophies they produced to their capture and presentation at home as living war trophies and eventual incorporation as productive tribal members or being sold as slaves for weaponry and other European manufactures. What had been a relatively indiscriminate slaughter in pre-contact times and the early Protohistoric, had become by the late Protohistoric an increasingly selective procedure based on demands for social reproduction. Prestige and rank became linked to a warrior's ability to bring captives safely home, perhaps precipitating adjustments in warfare rituals and iconography.

Associated with depopulation in the mid-sixteenth century was the strong desire to avoid losing warriors in battle. War chiefs went to great measures to safeguard their warrior's lives to avoid kin retribution and loss of prestige. As a result of the increasing concern with loss of productive members, warfare rituals may have now placed even greater emphasis on spiritual aid, amulets, medicine bundles, and "holy arks" (portable shrines) to aid them in military success. While rituals and associated warfare paraphernalia promoted the principal chief's sanctity of office in the early Protohistoric, by the late Protohistoric emphasis shifted to the individual warrior's safety and protection by the war chief and a greater dependence on individual symbolic objects such as medicine bundles.

One feature of depopulation and warfare was the increased ability of a polity to destroy its enemies. The introduction of firearms in the late seventeenth century (Hahn 1995; Waselkov 1989a:120–121) transformed warfare throughout the Southeast. One's rivals, especially if they did not possess firearms, were vulnerable to decimation through killing or being carried away to the slave markets. As early as 1673, Marquette and Joliet recorded guns and other Western goods among native groups in the Central Mississippi Valley (Shea 1853:44). Woodward, at about the same time, witnessed the Westos, who were "well provided with arms, ammunition, tradeing cloath and other trade" which they had received in exchange for deerskins and young slaves (Salley 1911:133). Beginning about 1680 English slave traders on the eastern seaboard began trading guns to their native allies (P. H. Wood 1989:53). Although the trade in slaves was relatively small during the 1670s and 1680s, by 1710, "10,000 to 20,000 Indians had been shipped as slaves to New England and the Caribbean" (Haan 1982:345). The trade in guns fostered slave raiding throughout the tribal zone and served as another means of decimating one's rivals for economic ends.

Warfare contributed to demographic disruption through relocation by a polity being "pushed" by slavers and enemies who possessed guns, and being "pulled" toward the economic enticement of Western trading centers for the purchase of European technology, including guns, and for the sale of skins and slaves. Western manufactures became critical means for production and social currency, and native southeasterners traveled great distances, relocated settlements, and went to war to get them (R. B. Ferguson 1990:244). Maps portraying population movements in the seventeenth and eighteenth centuries (Brain 1988:282–283; M. T. Smith 1987:78, 1989a:24, 28, 1991:36) indicate the extent to which people relocated settlements due to disease, warfare, and the desire to obtain Western manufactures.

The style of warfare in the late Protohistoric also shows marked changes. Whereas formal battles may have taken place utilizing hundreds of warriors, guerilla warfare or small-scale, kin-based militia warfare become the preferred mode of fighting. Nairne described warfare in the early eighteenth century as "catch as catch can" (Nairne 1988:43), indicating that the formality and structure associated with large-scale battles under centralized leadership, at least in direct combat, was no longer evident.

Another aspect of late protohistoric warfare was the beginning of long-term associations of Europeans who led, organized, and instigated native military forces, sometimes in conjunction with Western forces. Slavers, such as the two English slave traders witnessed by Tonti in 1702—one of whom led a band of ten men and another of four hundred (Galloway 1982, 1995:196)—may have been typical of Europeans who led or accompanied native war parties in raids throughout the Southeast in the last quarter of the seventeenth century and well into the early eighteenth century. The objectives of these Westerners included heading and organizing slave raids, pacifying frontiers, and destroying, disrupting, and weakening their colonial rival's allies. The use of natives as mercenaries and impressed auxiliaries in the late Protohistoric period laid the ground for inciting one polity against another in the economic and political struggles of European rivals. South Carolina traders frequently fomented "perpetual warrs . . . amon[g]st the Indians for the onely reason of making slaves" (Axtell 1997:43).

Although the multi-tiered, hierarchical political structures and formal institutions associated with chiefly warfare had changed considerably by the late Protohistoric, some structure may have remained relatively intact, although it certainly varied from polity to polity and region to region. Several elements suggesting continuity are worth noting, particularly achieved military statuses and war camps. Some degree of hierarchy apparently was still evident in late protohistoric warfare, although the chain of command had weakened considerably. For example, the war organization of most southeastern polities continued to be hierarchically stratified by ranks earned through war deeds. The seventeenth-century Apalachee had a ranked series of achieved military statuses (J. F. Scarry 1992:171–172); in addition to the commander or "captain," there were four warrior ranks similar to the three Creek (C. Hudson 1976:225) and Natchez ranks (du Pratz, cited in Swanton 1911:129). The Cherokee's five warrior ranks served under a series of war officials, including "four beloved men with esoteric ritual knowledge necessary for war, war chief, war priest, speaker for war, and surgeon" (Gearing 1962:26) elected by the warriors, who in turn appointed some eight officers. In addition, there was a seven-man war council. The command structure, while hierarchical, was rudimentary. In actual practice it was a matter of militia "captains" directing their own warriors.

Another area of military continuity was almost certainly the hierarchical structure and spatial organization of the war council and war camp (Gatschet 1884:167; Knight 1998:57–58; Nairne 1988:42; Romans 1962:65 [1775]; Swan 1855:280). The structure of the typical war camp probably corresponded to Nairne's (1988:42) early eighteenth-century description of a Chickasaw war camp, in which "social distinctions were formally expressed in a spatial idiom" (Knight 1998:57). Their camp was in the form of a crescent, with the chief officers' "Lodge" in the center. In front of the officers' fires were laid red "targets" upon which were placed their individual "amulet" bags or medicine bundles. No one was allowed to light a fire until the chief officers lit theirs and delivered some of the fire to their attendants, whose fires were in front of the chief officers. The other "Capts." and their attendants likewise established a line of fires in front of the officers. All of these fires were considered sacred. After the front fires had been made, the remaining warriors lit their fires and established their camps behind the officers as they pleased.

The formal institutions of war councils and warfare cults bear brief mention. War councils were an important feature of the late protohistoric town life, but their power and authority over the various militia leaders seems problematic. The fundamental authority of the war councils was now changed from an elite policy advising body to one that had little power to enforce its jurisdiction over individuals. The warfare cult "lost its former intimate connection with the sanctity of political aristocracy" (Knight 1986:682) by the first third of the seventeenth century (M. T. Smith 1989b), but "definite warfare related cult institutions persisted in many of these same societies during the Colonial era" and they "manipulated appropriate *sacra* conforming in many respects with the earlier warfare/cosmogony complex" (Knight 1986:682). The resilience of the warfare cult institution—incorporating as *sacra* stylized, nonutilitarian war clubs and copper axes of the Chickasaw (Knight 1986:682)—suggests that some aspects of the ritual behavior continued into the seventeenth century. The war club, as one example, remained a potent symbol of military prowess and success. The Chickasaw sacred "ark," a portable shrine, likewise suggests continuity with earlier protohistoric/Mississippian warfare rituals.

Conclusion

Early protohistoric chiefdoms in the Southeast carried out chiefly warfare for clear political objectives through structured military formations, including formal battles and campaigns, and guerilla raids and ambushes. Principal chiefs of centralized polities directly benefited from warfare. It legitimized their chiefly authority and political control, gave them recourse to grievances, and provided a mechanism for incorporating neighboring sovereign polities within their own political sphere. Tribute from conquests served as a financial fund based on a surplus from which chiefs could create opportunities for control of political action. Small- and large-scale combat was successfully pursued as a result of social hierarchy, which allowed chiefs to issue orders through their retainers or principal people and maintain discipline. War councils and religious warrior cults further aided and endorsed the office of the chief in war making.

Late protohistoric polities represent a fundamental shift in warfare patterns as a result of depopulation, decentralization, and decreasing hierarchy in the late sixteenth century on the one hand and the desire for Western manufactures in the late seventeenth century on the other. Although warfare underwent substantial changes in the six hundred years of the Mississippian period, it was Western contact that was responsible as an agent of change in native warfare patterns. European diseases contributed to the precipitous drop in population, and the involvement of native polities in European capitalism based in part on the sale of slaves for European goods, particularly guns and ammunition, brought about the beginning of a wholesale transformation of southeastern native culture during the Protohistoric period.

Warfare in the late Protohistoric period continued the older Mississippian pattern of guerilla raids, but the incentive for fighting now included grudge resolution (revenge), capture of slaves for commercial export, acquisition of captives for social reproduction, and competition over access to European goods. The style of aggression resembled tribal warfare in a number of ways: it was almost solely based on temporary, small contingents of kin militia characterized by weak chains of command and informal codes of conduct. Victorious kin militias had little power to control their opponents other than to disperse them or drive them away (Carneiro 1994:14; Reyna 1994:41). By the end of the seventeenth century the chiefly warfare prevalent in the early Protohistoric had become permanently transformed into a pervasive tribal warfare generated by the rapidly expanding frontier of competing states. Native warfare would continue to change in the eighteenth century in response to the expanding political arena of mutually hostile European nations aided by indigenous auxiliaries, but it would never regain the level of military capability it had achieved at initial European contact.

9 / Elite Actors in the Protohistoric
Elite Identities and Interaction with Europeans in the Apalachee and Powhatan Chiefdoms

John F. Scarry and Mintcy D. Maxham

The Protohistoric period (the time between initial European contact and the intensive interaction of the Historic period) was an important time in eastern North America. During the Protohistoric period, native societies first experienced the dramatic transformations associated with the entry of Europeans into the region. In some cases, those transformations ultimately led to the dissolution of native societies. In other cases, they led to new social formations that characterize modern native groups. The events of the Protohistoric period also set the stage for subsequent European colonial endeavors, providing the social environments that Europeans entered in the late sixteenth and seventeenth centuries. Events of the Protohistoric period produced, in each of these cases, cultural institutions that constrained the actions of natives and Europeans alike during the early Historic period, thus shaping the historical trajectories followed by native peoples and European colonizers.

People act to achieve specific goals (individual and collective), but they act within constraints imposed by the cultural patterns established by past behavior. Their actions, in turn, produce their cultures, constrain subsequent actors and actions, and shape historical trajectories. In the Protohistoric period, native peoples also acted in response to new circumstances provided by their fellows and by Europeans. These new circumstances promoted rapid and dramatic change in native societies and cultures. Those changes in native cultures were the products of the acts of individual natives and Europeans. Native peoples were not simply passive objects who were transformed by the European invaders of their lands; they were active participants in those transformations.

We want to examine two historically important cases—the Apalachee and the Powhatan—where individuals and their actions clearly affected the course of native and European history. We choose these cases for two reasons. First, we have good information regarding these societies for the Protohistoric and early Historic periods. Second, both the Apalachee and the Powhatan had significant impacts on wider historical arenas. Not only did they affect European colonial efforts in eastern

North America, they also had significant impacts on discourses that have shaped modern American culture and American views of native peoples.

Culture and the Creation of Social Identities

Culture is constantly being created by its participants as a product of the collective practice of individuals. We cannot view it as a fixed field in which people find themselves. In fact, we need to look at cultural practices and cultural institutions as fluid media that individuals and groups of individuals manipulate and mold.

Some actions affect more people than others. In particular, political (public) acts tend to affect more people than private acts. It follows that the acts of some individuals affect more people than the acts of other individuals. Individuals who act in political ways, individuals who possess some level of authority in public spheres, and individuals who interact with people outside their own society all can act in particularly influential ways. Among the late prehistoric societies of eastern North America, individuals who acted in these ways were typically elites.

Archaeology and Past Practice

Our approach to understanding and explaining the archaeological and ethnohistorical records from Apalachee and Powhatan is based on actor-based models that focus on the production and reproduction of culture (Bourdieu 1977, 1980; Giddens 1979, 1984; Gramsci 1971; Lincoln 1989; R. Williams 1977). We have been particularly influenced by arguments stressing the importance of thinking about the production of culture rather than its reproduction (e.g., Holland and Eisenhart 1990; Willis 1981).

People, individuals and groups of individuals, create their cultures through practice. In particular, routine daily practice builds the patterns of behavior that constitute a major component of human cultures (S. B. Ortner 1984). Daily practices are, in turn, based on and reflect to some degree the ways people view and understand the structure and order of the natural and social worlds in which they live. Kent Lightfoot (Lightfoot et al. 1998:201–202) has argued that the daily practice that produces culture also produces the patterns we see in the archaeological record and that the ordering of daily practice can be seen in the organization of the archaeological record.

People also create their social identities and define the expected behaviors, meanings, and understandings attached to those identities through their day-to-day activities. Patterns in people's behavior reflect the separate social identities and the relationships among individuals possessing those identities. Because of this, patterns in the archaeological record can be used to identify distinct social identities (e.g., J. F. Scarry 1999).

Social Identities and Discourse

One very important way that people create and give meaning to social identities is through discourse—acts, patterns of acts, and use of material items that symbolize, reflect, and produce the structure of the world and of society. Discourse can take many forms. Among the more common forms are myth, ritual, and classification (Lincoln 1989), but the organization of domestic space or children's play can also be seen as discourse. Discourse shapes the ways people see and understand the world by ideological persuasion and by evoking sentiments (Lincoln 1989:8–9). It affects their views of the nature of the world, the nature of society, and the nature of individuals.

Social discourse affects the patterns of cultural change and stability in societies in several ways. Established discourses contribute to the legitimacy of cultural institutions and form part of the cultural constraints on individual action. On the other hand, there can be multiple, potentially conflicting discourses within a society. Individuals and groups of individuals may manipulate and seek to impose discourses on others, and they may acquiesce to or resist the efforts of others to impose discourses on them. Discourses that contribute to the definition of social identities are also powerful tools that individuals can use to change their own positions within society and the borders and structure of society itself (de la Cadena 1995).

Bruce Lincoln (1989:174) has suggested that during periods when dominant discourses no longer persuade, societies enter situations of fluidity and crisis where discourses are easily challenged and changed. We suggest that the Protohistoric period would have been such a period for the peoples of eastern North America. The appearance of Europeans, the disruptions to native societies caused by the depredations and settlements of the Europeans, and the impacts of diseases brought by Europeans undoubtedly produced stress and crisis in native societies. Certainly they would have weakened elites, and opened elite identities and the discourses that contributed to those identities to questioning.

Elite Actors and Relations with Europeans in Protohistoric and Early Historic Apalachee and Powhatan

In the remainder of this paper, we explore the ways that social identities constrained the actions of the Apalachee and Powhatan elites and the ways those elites manipulated social identities in attempts to maintain or alter their positions within society. We conclude with a brief examination of the circumstances that affected the success and the consequences of those efforts.

We are particularly interested in the nature of Apalachee and Powhatan views about the nature of elite individuals and political officeholders and about the nature of people and other entities outside the boundaries of Apalachee and Powhatan society (e.g., the Europeans who came to their lands). How were the elites seen? How were they expected to act? What were the relationships between the elite and other individuals in their societies? These expectations and the patterns of behavior they engendered would have affected interactions between native peoples and Europeans, and they would have contributed ultimately to the success and failure of Apalachee and Powhatan responses to European intrusion and European colonial endeavors.

The Apalachee

The Apalachee were a Muskogean-speaking people who occupied the area surrounding what is today Tallahassee, Florida (Figure 9.1) (Hann 1994; J. F. Scarry 1994a). The Apalachee of the late prehistoric Lake Jackson phase were a Mississippian polity (J. F. Scarry 1984, 1994a). Their participation in the Mississippian world was marked by similarities in material culture and subsistence economy between the Apalachee and other Mississippian societies. The spatial organization of their political centers followed a Mississippian pattern (Payne 1994b; Payne and Scarry 1998). The prestige goods found in elite burials and ceramic vessels found in probable ritual contexts in mounds provide even more explicit evidence of direct links between the Lake Jackson phase and other Mississippian polities (B. C. Jones 1982, 1994; Phillips and Brown 1978; Brain and Phillips 1996). The Apalachee of the protohistoric Velda phase and the Mission period San Luis phase were the descendants of the earlier Lake Jackson phase people. The Apalachee experienced dramatic changes during this time, although they retained much of the social and political structure of the Lake Jackson phase chiefdom (J. F. Scarry 1992).

The Protohistoric period in the Apalachee area began in the early 1500s. Spanish ships had coursed along the Gulf Coast bordering Apalachee territory early in the sixteenth century, although the first recorded interaction between Europeans and the Apalachee did not take place until 1528, when a Spanish expedition led by Panfilo de Narvaez entered the region. Narvaez and his army stayed in Apalachee territory for two months. Those two months were a period of unremitting hostility between the Apalachee and the Spanish. Following the departure of Narvaez, the Apalachee were left alone until 1539, when Hernando de Soto and his army entered Apalachee territory. The de Soto expedition stayed in Apalachee territory for five months. Again this was a period of open and constant hostility.

The Protohistoric period ended in 1633 with the establishment of the first of the Franciscan missions to the Apalachee. An Apalachee delegation traveled to San Augustín in 1608 to request that missionaries be sent to the province. In 1633, the

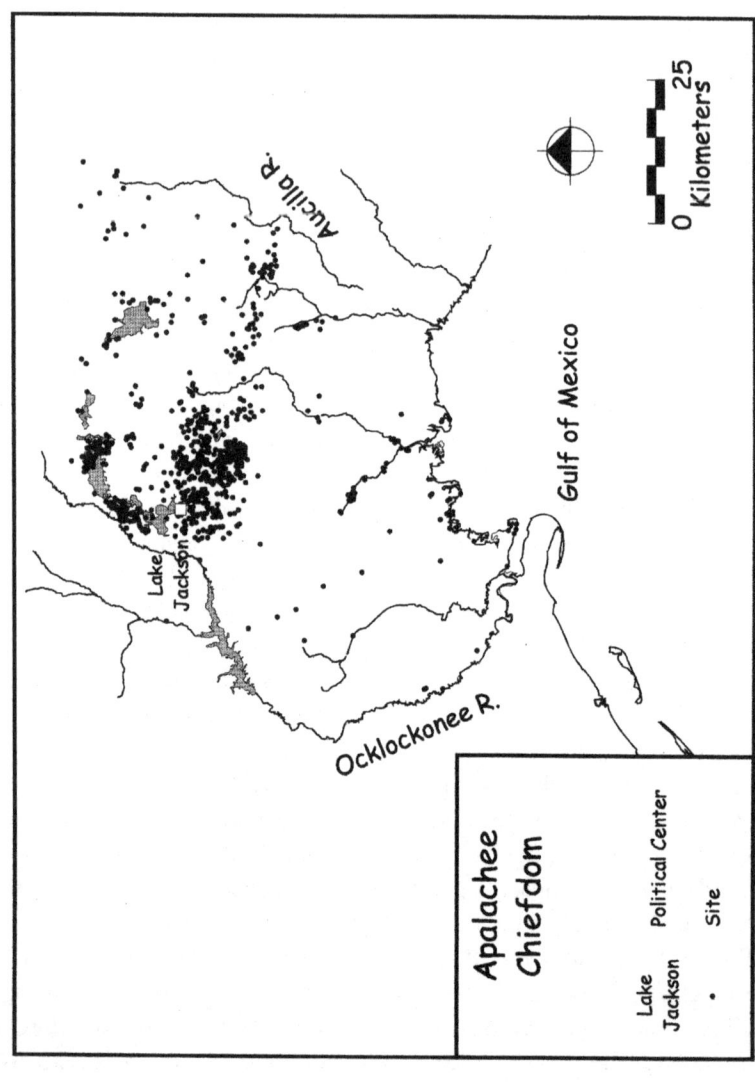

Figure 9.1 Apalachee chiefdom and settlement distribution.

first of the Apalachee missions was finally constructed (Hann 1988), marking the beginning of the San Luis phase (J. F. Scarry 1984), although there were continued contacts between 1608 and 1633. Initially, a small number of priests were stationed in the province. However, the Spanish presence increased over the course of the seventeenth century with additional priests, a lieutenant governor and his family, a small garrison, and several ranchers.

The Lake Jackson phase Apalachee chiefdom emerged around the beginning of the thirteenth century, when the initial stages of most of the mounds at the Lake Jackson site were constructed (Payne 1994a; Payne and Scarry 1998). Material culture similarities to other Mississippian polities in the region make it seem likely that the initial developments of the polity may have begun even earlier, perhaps in the twelfth century (J. F. Scarry 1990a, 1990b). The origins of the polity are not well understood (J. F. Scarry 1990a, 1990b). There do appear to be links to the local Late Woodland groups of the Tallahassee area, but there are also links to apparently earlier Mississippian societies located in the Apalachicola and Chattahoochee River valleys to the west. Just before the Protohistoric period, toward the end of the fifteenth or early in the sixteenth century, the Lake Jackson polity appears to have undergone a radical change (J. F. Scarry 1992, 1996b). The Lake Jackson center was abandoned (Payne 1994b), and Mound 3, the elite mortuary facility, was closed, perhaps with a flurry of elite burials (B. C. Jones 1982, 1994).

Apalachee Social and Political Organization

The prehistoric Lake Jackson phase Apalachee were organized as a complex chiefdom (*sensu;* Steponaitis 1978; Wright 1984). We see evidence of this organization in three important areas: settlement patterns, mortuary patterning, and material symbols. Lake Jackson phase settlements formed a multi-tiered settlement hierarchy that incorporated three or four distinct settlement types that can be placed into three hierarchically-organized community types: paramount center, regional center, and local community. The highest Lake Jackson phase elites were interred in a special, quasi-public place (Mound 3) with significant labor investments. They were accompanied by weapons, ornaments, valuables, and other material symbols (B. C. Jones 1982, 1994; J. F. Scarry 1992, 1999). The iconography of some of those symbols can be linked to Muskogean mythos (Knight 1986, 1989a) and was shared with other Mississippian societies (Brain and Phillips 1996; Phillips and Brown 1978). Many of the copper artifacts accompanying the elite were manufactured outside the Apalachee chiefdom (Leader 1988). The consistency of status markers among individuals and over time suggests that those markers were linked to one or two *institutionalized* statuses (offices) rather than to unique individuals (J. F. Scarry 1992).

The internal political structure of the historic San Luis phase Apalachee polity was *similar* to that we have described for the Lake Jackson phase, but it was *not* the same. The San Luis phase was a subject polity, a subordinate part of the Spanish colonial empire. However, if we remove the Spaniards who occupied the top of the San Luis phase political and religious hierarchies, the remaining structure does resemble that of a complex chiefdom. The political hierarchy was multi-tiered. At the top there was the principal *cacique*, who spoke for the entire province. There were subordinate *caciques* at the *doctrina* villages, and there were lesser *caciques* at villages subordinate to the *doctrina* villages. In addition to the *caciques*, there were other native officeholders, *inijas* (seconds to the *caciques*), leading men, and prominent warriors. Ethnohistorical sources indicate that the *caciques*, and probably the *inijas*, were members of a hereditary elite and that they inherited their offices. The historic sources also mention relationships among elite officeholders (often as uncle-nephew).

In the seventeenth century, the Apalachee *caciques* and *inijas* retained some authority and power, although that power was limited, particularly in the realms of external politics and religion. It is clear that they had some control over the labor or individuals not closely related to them. The *inijas* scheduled communal work groups. Members of their community worked the *caciques'* fields. The *caciques* controlled the produce of their fields and had some authority over the produce of community fields intended for widows, orphans, and other members of the community who were unable to provide for themselves.

The *caciques* also led military expeditions against other groups, although the Spaniards exercised some control over these expeditions, and individuals identified as field masters or captains by the Spaniards also occupied important positions on these expeditions. The *caciques* and the *usinulos* (sons of *caciques*) continued to play important roles in rituals surrounding the Apalachee ball game, until the ball game was banned in the late seventeenth century (Bushnell 1978; Hann 1988).

Elite Social Identities in the Apalachee Chiefdom

The Apalachee elites formed a distinct group, separate from the common Apalachee, whose social identities incorporated characteristics not associated with commoners. Five basic components contributed to that elite identity: Elites were different from commoners; they shared an ethnic identity with commoners; they mediated between commoners and the outside world (both supernatural and natural); they were powerful; and they had legitimacy and could demonstrate that legitimacy symbolically (J. F. Scarry 1999).

Several lines of evidence suggest that the Lake Jackson phase elite were differentiated from commoners in ways that reflected their elite identity. The elites (at least the highest elite) were marked by distinctions in residence, costume, and burial. The highest elite lived in distinct residences, atop earthen mounds. Much of the mortuary patterning served to reiterate and reify the distinctiveness of the elite and their separation from the common Apalachee. The elites were segregated and treated differently in death (presumably as they were in life). They were buried in a special, prominent location with considerable public investment. On the basis of dental evidence, Rebecca Storey (1991) has suggested that at least some of the elite individuals buried in Mound 3 may have been related to one another. If this were the case, the retention of position within a descent group would have also emphasized the distinction between elite and commoner.

Like their Lake Jackson phase predecessors, the San Luis phase Apalachee elites were distinct from commoners. They acted to maintain elite identity and the boundaries that separated the elite from commoners. These involved patterns of kinship and marriage that linked elites to each other. The elites intermarried, effectively maintaining themselves as a separate group.

While they were distinct from the commoners, the Lake Jackson phase elite were not outsiders. They were members of Apalachee society, public entities who belonged (in part) to the commoners (or the collective). Their space was set apart from, but partially shared with, the general public (e.g., central and public residence and burial).

The San Luis phase elites were also clearly Apalachee, like the commoners. The Apalachee ball game and the rituals surrounding it served to create boundaries and identities. They helped maintain boundaries that separated the Apalachee from other native groups and from the Spaniards, and one Apalachee community from another (the subjects of individual *caciques*). They helped maintain boundaries between the elite and commoners and reified the special status of the elite and their access to the supernatural. But the ball game also linked the commoners and the elite as members of a community separated from the outside and outsiders.

The Lake Jackson phase elites were linked to the outside world in ways that commoners were not. Many of the material symbols associated with the elite (e.g., pipes, shell gorgets, and repoussé copper plates and badges) were obtained from geographically distant sources. For instance, a copper headdress (crown) found with Burial 9K in Mound 3 was made on the same mold as the headdress found with Burial 38 at the Etowah site (Brain and Phillips 1996:181–182; Leader 1988). The absence of these artifacts in non-elite contexts suggests that the high elite monopolized the links to the sources of those artifacts (presumably the elites of other chiefdoms). The symbolism and icons associated with the elite also suggest that the elite may have claimed links to the supernatural (another external source of authority, prestige, and power).

We would argue that the Lake Jackson phase elite were mediators, neither fully Apalachee nor fully other, who could bridge the profound gap between the Apalachee and the non-Apalachee worlds (both mundane and supernatural). We would also suggest that much of their legitimacy, authority, and power derived from their identities as mediating beings. Finally, we suggest that their identity as mediating beings contributed to the importance that material symbols derived from the non-Apalachee world had as symbolic capital and in the demonstration of elite identity and legitimacy.

The San Luis phase *caciques* and other elite were not Spaniards; they were Apalachee, but they were not merely Apalachee. The use of Spanish titles (*Don* and *Cacique*) with native titles (*Holata*) and Spanish first names with Apalachee family (or clan) names (e.g., Don Patricio Hinachuba, *Cacique* and *Holata*) is a clear reflection of this intermediate identity. Amy Bushnell (1978:10) points to these multiple and mixed titles as examples of the "Hispanization of Native notables," e.g., Juan Mendoza, *holata* of San Luis, *atequi* (translator or speaker) for the church and captain in the militia, and Diego Salvador, *atequi* for the king and sergeant major in the militia.

The Lake Jackson elites were certainly powerful individuals. The near ubiquity of weapons (whether functional or not) found with the burials in Mound 3 (B. C. Jones 1982) implies some aura of coercive power. This association of the elite with force is reinforced by two repoussé plates that clearly depict armed beings, one of whom holds a severed head (B. C. Jones 1994). We would suggest that the supernatural symbolism of the repoussé plates and shell gorgets found in Mound 3 also reflects power, in this case supernatural power.

The San Luis phase Apalachee elite were also powerful individuals who claimed access to supernatural sources of power (at least before their conversion to Christianity). Juan Paiva's treatise on the Apalachee ball game (Bushnell 1978; Hann 1988) clearly links the mythical *caciques*, Ochuna Nicoguadca and Ytonanslac, with the supernatural. The legends also refer to Eslatiayupi, the grandson of Ytonanslac, as "Nicoguadca, the Lightning Bolt, son of Nicotaijuulo and Nico the Sun" (Bushnell 1978:11). They also ascribe supernatural powers to Nicoguadca.

The elites were legitimate. The Lake Jackson phase elite derived some legitimacy from the institutionalized political offices they held. They also derived legitimacy as the heirs of earlier elite. This source of legitimacy was made visible by the presence of those ancestors in Mound 3, which occupied a prominent position at the Lake Jackson site. The elite also demonstrated their legitimacy through their possession of material symbols reflecting their identity as mediators. Material symbols, whose meanings were common knowledge, were valuable commodities obtained from external sources not available to commoners.

The San Luis phase elites were also legitimate. They were elite because they were born to elite families. They inherited offices, and they received recognition from Spanish authorities.

Elite Strategies in the Apalachee Chiefdom

It is important to distinguish between the political strategies of the Apalachee elites as a group and as individuals. As a group, they were defined by sentiments of affinity and estrangement that linked them to but also separated them from the common

Apalachee. At the group level, political strategies would have been directed toward the maintenance of group status and elite identity. At the individual level, political strategies would have been directed toward maintaining or elevating individual status and obtaining political positions.

As individuals, the Apalachee elites were divided into two distinct groups, those in office and those who could aspire to office. The goals and strategies of those two kinds of individuals would have differed in significant ways. For the paramount officeholder, the primary goal would have been the maintenance of position vis-à-vis other elite. For subordinate officeholders (regional chiefs), there would have been two goals: maintenance of position vis-à-vis their subordinates and ascension to higher office. For elites with no formal political position, the goal would have been improvement of their political position and, presumably, ascension to office.

The compact geographic structure of the Apalachee polity (reflected in the short distances between centers; see Figure 9.1) would have made it relatively easy for the paramount chief to monitor subordinates' activities. It would also have made the extraction of tribute from subordinate officeholders relatively easy for the paramount. The ability to monitor and extract surplus from subordinates would have contributed to the stability of the Apalachee polity (J. F. Scarry 1991).

To the extent that subordinates (indeed all elite) relied on the demonstration of legitimacy through material symbols (within the established discourse), the ability of higher elites to control those symbols would have made subordinates reliant on their superiors. It seems unlikely that either dominant or subordinate elites would have had any interest in revolution. Subordinate elites might have had an interest in rebellion, but their opportunities would have been limited by dominant elite control of symbols required by the dominant discourse and their own need to maintain that discourse. Either they could obtain legitimating symbols independently of higher elites or they could alter the nature of acceptable symbols.

Toward the close of the late Prehistoric period we see widespread changes in regional prestige networks. These changes include the abandonment and collapse of major centers (e.g., Moundville [Knight and Steponaitis 1998] and Etowah [King 1991a, 1991b]) and regional polities. The disruption of those networks would have threatened the ability of the Apalachee elite to maintain the discourses that legitimated their identities—and hence their prestige, position, authority, and legitimacy—by removing material symbols of their links to the external world. In particular, it would have opened dominant elite to the threat of rebellion by subordinates and it might have opened all elite to resistance and perhaps revolution by commoners.

In Apalachee, the collapse of the regional prestige network coincided with a major change in the polity. The Apalachee abandoned the paramount center of Lake Jackson shortly before the beginning of the Protohistoric period (Payne 1994b). They also abandoned Mound 3 at Lake Jackson, which contained the remains of generations of Apalachee elites and all they symbolized. For the Lake Jackson phase elites, the mound and its contents must have had great symbolic importance. Its abandonment must have coincided with some change in elite identities.

Despite the dramatic transformation marked by the abandonment of Lake Jackson, the Apalachee chiefdom continued, as did an elite group within Apalachee society (even if it included different individuals).

The sixteenth century (the Protohistoric period in Apalachee) was a time of great stress for the Apalachee chiefdom and its elites. Twice the chiefdom was invaded by Spanish armies. Hernando de Soto's army occupied a portion of the chiefdom for five months in 1540. Following the departure of de Soto, we hear little about the Apalachee until the first decade of the seventeenth century, when a delegation of Apalachee elites traveled to St. Augustine. They requested that missionaries be sent to the chiefdom. It was not until 1633 that the first of the Apalachee missions were constructed, however. The delay was due, in part, to the Spaniards' assessment that many Apalachee were opposed to the missionaries and that the Apalachee chiefs could not control their followers.

It seems reasonable to interpret this action as a strategy employed by *some* Apalachee elites. One way to gain an advantage in competition with other elites would have been to gain new external sources of prestige and symbols, to successfully mediate between the Apalachee and the outside world.

During the seventeenth century, the Apalachee elites continued to occupy positions of prominence and privilege. They did so with the support of the Spanish authorities, who recognized the offices they retained. Their legitimacy was acknowledged by the representatives of the Crown. They were not subject to the same punishments as commoners (except by order of the governor) (Hann 1988:89). They continued to exert economic and political power, and they exercised some control over economic surpluses (Bushnell 1978:3).

As Bushnell (1979:3) notes, the *caciques* of Apalachee clearly played the Franciscans and Spanish secular authorities against one another. The *caciques* used chiefly stores to impose social (and economic) debts on others (Hann 1988). On occasion, members of the elite usurped offices whose legitimate heirs were elsewhere (with the connivance of the leading men of the community) (Hann 1988:103–104, 1993; J. F. Scarry 1996c:212).

The *caciques* and the *usinulos* continued to play important roles in the rituals surrounding the Apalachee ball game (until the ball game was banned in the late seventeenth century (Bushnell 1978; Hann 1988). These roles were, we believe, important elements in the discourse that framed the identities of the Apalachee elite and that helped structure Apalachee political processes.

The elites positioned themselves between the Spaniards and the common Apalachee. They spoke for their communities to Spanish authorities. Some even wrote to the king. This mediating role is evident in the person of Don Patricio Hinachuba, *holata* and *cacique* of Ivitachuco. His use of both Spanish and Apalachee names and titles clearly suggests that his identity lay in between the commoners and the Spaniards. He was, as Amy Bushnell (1979) titles him, "Defender of the Word of God, the Crown of the King, and the Little Children of Ivitachuco."

The Powhatans

The Powhatans were Algonquian speakers who lived along the lower Rappahannock and James River valleys and adjacent portions of the Virginia Coastal Plain at European contact (Figure 9.2) (Rountree 1989, 1990; Rountree and Turner 1994). The term "Powhatan" describes both the people who lived in Virginia's Coastal Plain and "the great Emperor" who took his name from the land he ruled (J. R. Smith 1986b:29 [1624]).

The Protohistoric period began in the Powhatan area in the early to mid-1500s. Spaniards had visited the region by the 1520s (Chesapeake Bay appears on Spanish maps that date to the 1520s [Potter 1993:161]), although the first recorded interaction between Europeans and the Powhatans did not take place until 1561, when a Spanish ship sailing along the Virginia coast captured an Algonquian chief's son. This young man, christened Don Luis by the Spanish, was taken to Mexico, Havana, and Spain to be "educated" and converted (Gradie 1993:166–167). In 1570 the Spanish returned with Don Luis and tried to establish a mission on the Chesapeake Bay with his help. Don Luis chose instead to reinstate himself with the Powhatans, and he joined with them to destroy the mission and drive the Spaniards away (Gradie 1993). The Protohistoric period ended in 1607 with the establishment of the English colony at Jamestown and the beginning of the Contact period.

The Powhatan chiefdom encountered by Jamestown's settlers was a relatively young polity. From conversations with Powhatan informants, English ethnographers reported that Chief Powhatan inherited six to nine "districts" in Virginia's Inner Coastal Plain in the mid- to late 1500s. A chief (*werowance*) who answered to Chief Powhatan, the paramount, ruled each of these districts. By the turn of the century, Powhatan had added up to 25 more districts through force or the threat of force, bringing the total area under his control to 16,500 km^2 (E. R. Turner 1992:115, 1993:76).

Scholars disagree about the origins of the Powhatan chiefdom. Some accept the secondhand historic accounts of the chiefdom's indigenous development. Randolph Turner (1976) and Daniel Mouer (1981), for example, believe that the ecological richness of the Powhatan core area favored population growth and that this growth stimulated the birth of the Powhatan chiefdom. On the other hand, other scholars suggest that the European presence spurred the development of the Powhatan chiefdom (e.g., Rountree 1989:141). Gallivan and Hantman (1996) contend that the conditions for the emergence of hierarchical society were in place before con-

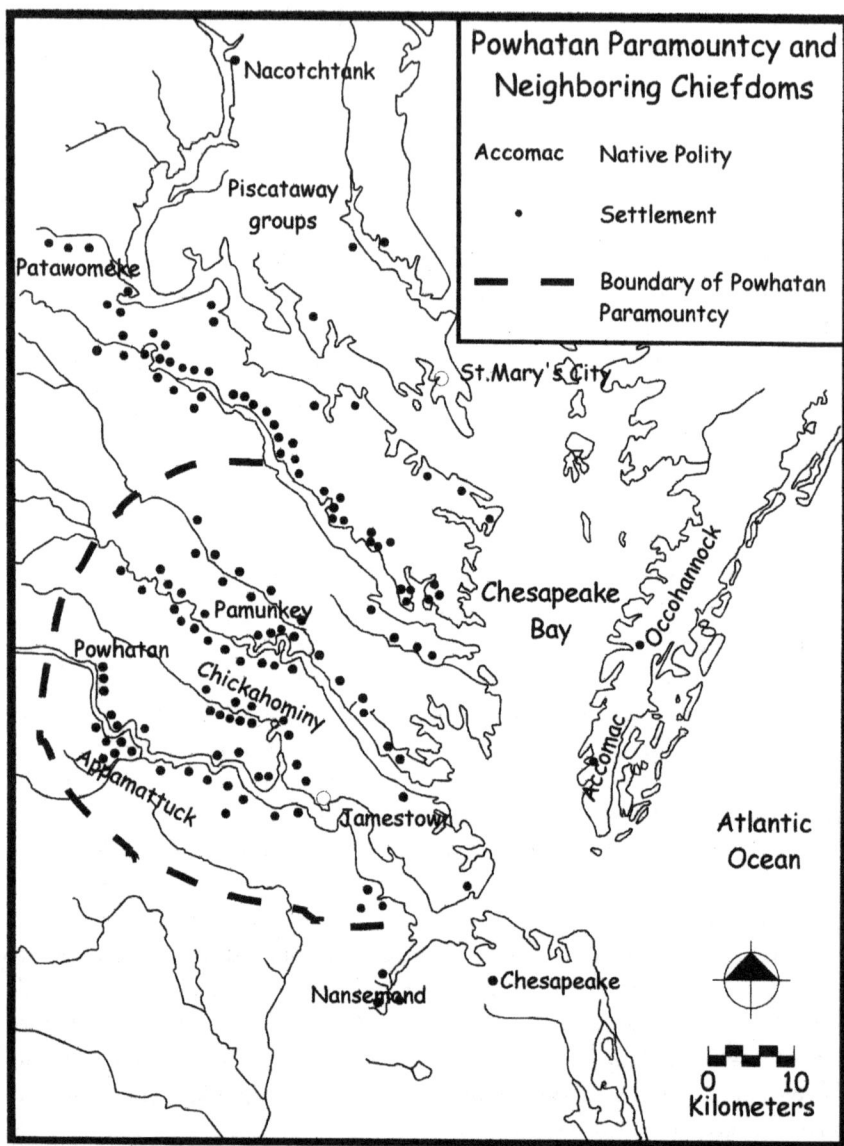

Figure 9.2 Powhatan and neighboring Virginia chiefdoms.

tact: English colonization initiated the sufficient conditions to make that transformation. Despite the debate over the timing of chiefdom development, however, almost everyone agrees that in 1607 the Powhatans were hierarchically organized.

The Powhatan chiefdom's boundaries extended from the south side of the Potomac River to the lower portion of the Eastern Shore, although many of the outlying groups in this vast territory were not fully consolidated (E. R. Turner 1993:79). Along the Eastern Shore, the south bank of the Potomac River, and the north bank of the Rappahannock River lived a series of groups Rountree (1989:14) calls Powhatan's "ethnic fringe" and Potter (Rountree 1993b:6) calls "marginal, semi-autonomous polities." At contact, these polities seem to have been part of the Powhatan chiefdom, but Powhatan's hold over them was not strong (Potter 1989: 154).

The Eastern Shore Accomacs and Occohannocks were also part of the semi-autonomous Powhatan fringe. Davidson (1993) even suggests that English reports of the tribute sent from these groups to Chief Powhatan may have been voluntary exchange. The Accomacs and Occohannocks controlled an important resource—shell—that served as a symbol of status in the Powhatan chiefdom but could not be acquired in the core area. Davidson (1993:152) argues that Accomac and Occohannock participation in the Powhatan chiefdom was probably based on mutual economic advantage.

At least one group in the Virginia Coastal Plain, the Chickahominys, successfully resisted becoming part of Chief Powhatan's paramount chiefdom (Potter 1989: 154; Rountree 1989:8; J. R. Smith 1986b:46). Even though they were located within the Powhatan core, the Chickahominys were able to maintain their independence, ruling themselves by a council of elders (Potter 1989:154; Rountree 1989:8; J. R. Smith 1986b:246). Another group, the Chesapeakes, tried to remain independent, but Powhatan exterminated them before the English arrived (Rountree 1989:120–121).

Many chiefs in the districts that were incorporated in the Powhatan paramountcy were not completely willing to surrender their autonomy. Chief Powhatan permitted some of the old chiefs to remain as district *werowances*, but where their loyalty was in serious doubt, he appointed his relatives to replace them (Rountree and Turner 1994:364). To allow more effective administrative control over his empire as a whole, Powhatan moved from his village near the falls of the James to the more centrally located village of Werowocomoco on the lower York River (Rountree and Turner 1994:365).

Of the Powhatans' immediate neighbors, the group that played one of the most significant roles in shaping foreign policy was the Monacans, Siouan speakers who lived west of the fall line. The Monacans and Powhatans were enemies on some level (J. R. Smith 1986b:73–75), but like the Eastern Shore groups, the Monacans controlled access to a commodity—copper—that Powhatan needed in order to legitimate his superordinate position (Hantman 1990; E. R. Turner 1993). Regardless of whether the source of copper was in the Virginia Blue Ridge Mountains or in the Great Lakes (the subject of some debate), copper had to pass through Monacan territory before it got to Chief Powhatan (Hantman 1990; E. R. Turner 1993). Escalating competition with the Monacans to the west and the Piscataway chiefdom to the north was probably among the primary factors that coalesced in the late sixteenth century to enable the rise of the Powhatan chiefdom (Clark and Rountree 1993; Gallivan and Hantman 1996; E. R. Turner 1992:116).

Powhatan Social and Political Organization

The writings of early colonists clearly indicate that the Powhatan political organization was hierarchical at the time the English settled at Jamestown. Captain John Smith's "Map of Virginia" shows settlement hierarchy, distinguishing "king's houses" from ordinary villages (J. R. Smith 1986a). Commoners paid chiefs tribute of skins, beads, copper, pearls, deer, turkey, and corn (J. R. Smith 1986b:174 and 169), which was stored in or near chiefs' houses (Potter 1993; J. R. Smith 1986b:169). Chiefs received different burial treatment than commoners—their bones were housed in mortuary temples with all of their wealth in a basket at their feet (J. R. Smith 1986b:169).

Almost all our knowledge about the Powhatan chiefdom comes from historic sources rather than archaeological data. The archaeological correlates of chiefdom-level organization are virtually absent in the Virginia Coastal Plain (Gallivan and Hantman 1996; see also E. R. Turner 1992:114). Archaeologists have been unable to identify settlement hierarchies or large-scale public monuments (Gallivan 1997); there is only limited evidence for prestige goods exchange (Potter 1993:198); and only two burials can be positively identified as elite (Curry 1999; Painter 1980; Potter 1989). The only clear archaeological evidence of regional polities in the Coastal Plain is the appearance of site clusters separated by buffer zones in the Late Woodland period (A.D. 900–1607) (Mouer 1981; Rountree and Turner 1998; E. R. Turner 1976, 1992, 1993).

Site clusters that correspond to the distribution of stylistically distinct ceramic assemblages may reflect the development of social or ethnic boundaries (Rountree and Turner 1994:362–363). Several scholars (e.g., MacCord 1996; Rountree and Turner 1998; E. R. Turner 1976, 1992) have suggested that the clustering of sites and increases in village size and fortifications reflect the formation of regional polities in Late Woodland Virginia. Several of the site clusters correspond to chiefdoms that were incorporated into the Powhatan polity (E. R. Turner 1992:115–116). Others correspond to what were independent chiefdoms, such as the Nansemond, Chesapeake, and Patawomeck (Rountree and Turner 1994:363).

If the archaeological data from the late Prehistoric period are obscure regarding Powhatan political organization, the available ethnohistoric data are not. They clearly indicate that the Powhatan were organized as a complex chiefdom at the time of the first English settlement in 1607.

At the top of the political hierarchy was the *Mamanatowick* (paramount chief) Powhatan. Below the paramount there were *werowances* and *werowansquas* (district chiefs). Below the district chiefs there were the lesser *werowances* (subchiefs). Each community also had other individuals with special statuses (e.g., advisors, priests, and shamans). The bulk of the chiefdom's population was composed of commoners.

Elite status was at least partially ascribed in Powhatan society. The position of chief was passed down matrilineally—Powhatan's successors were his brothers Opitchapam and Opechancanough. As Chief Powhatan expanded his political sway at the turn of the century, he placed his siblings and his sons as chiefs of subordinate districts, especially in districts where he doubted the loyalty of existing chiefs (Barker 1992). Several district chiefs also placed their siblings over satellite villages (Rountree and Turner 1994:364). But not all status in Powhatan society was ascribed. Powhatan men could achieve positions of higher status through military exploits, and success in military exploits may also have contributed to distinctions among elites and affected their access to high office (Rountree 1989:101).

The fields of the elite were planted and tended by people who lived in their communities (Rountree 1989). Chief Powhatan reportedly had rights of refusal to "eight parts in ten" of the produce of his subjects (Strachey 1953:87 [1612]). Although it seems highly unlikely that he could actually claim that much (Barker 1992; Potter 1989:153; Rountree 1989:109–110), it is clear he could extract tribute and control access to certain goods. Much of the tribute apparently took the form of display goods or labor, particularly military labor (Rountree and Turner 1998:282–284). The control that Powhatan elites exercised over access to material goods also involved prestige goods obtained from foreign sources.

Elite Identities in the Powhatan Chiefdom

Evidence, particularly ethnohistorical evidence, suggests that the elites of the Middle Atlantic Coastal Plain chiefdoms, including the Powhatan, formed a distinct social group within their societies. The evidence also suggests that the social identities of the elites incorporated characteristics not associated with commoners. Elite identities along the Middle Atlantic comprised the same crucial elements as was the case with the Apalachee (see above).

One material distinction that separated the Powhatan elite from commoners was the size of elite houses. Powhatan chiefs' houses were larger than those of commoners and chiefs' houses were partitioned (Loftfield and Jones 1995; Rountree 1989:106). Access to the innermost room was limited, and the room was associated with prestige and sacredness (Potter 1993; Rountree 1989); only guests of high status were allowed there. The outer room of chiefs' houses was the most public. Mortuary houses were similarly partitioned. The innermost room of the mortuary house served as the tomb of chiefs, priests, and other important people (Loftfield and Jones 1995:127–129).

Distinctions between commoners and elites continued beyond life. As earthly representatives of the supernatural, only elites were believed to have an afterlife (Potter 1993; Rountree and Turner 1994; J. R. Smith 1986b:172). We would expect to see evidence of these differences in commoner and elite mortuary ritual in the archaeological record, but archaeologists have struggled to reconcile archaeological evidence of Powhatan burial practices with John Smith's descriptions.

The bulk of the late Woodland mortuary data on the Virginia Coastal Plain derives from ossuaries, which are secondary burials containing the skeletal remains, usually disarticulated, of multiple individuals (Curry 1999:3). Ossuary burial is the last stage of a multi-stage burial program.

Ossuaries are often interpreted as a reflection of a corporate (kin- or community-based) political framework (e.g., Boyd and Boyd 1992; Gallivan and Hantman 1996). They emphasize the common group membership of the individuals they contain and downplay differences among the individuals within the group (Boyd and Boyd 1992; Curry 1999; Jirikowic 1990). Our interpretation of Powhatan ossuaries depends on what sectors of society received ossuary burial. Were both commoners and elites buried in ossuaries? Only commoners? Only elites? Archaeologists disagree, and historical documents are of little help—we have no accounts of commoner mortuary practices (Boyd and Boyd 1992; Gold 1999; Ubelaker 1974).

Most archaeologists, however, believe that Powhatan ossuaries comprise the remains of commoners only, because they contain people of all ages and both sexes who are rarely associated with artifacts (Jirikowic 1990; Potter 1993; cf. Loftfield and Jones 1995:127). If all individuals in ossuaries are indeed commoners, the implication is that elites received different secondary treatment, and Powhatan ossuaries therefore reflect political hierarchy (Jirikowic 1990). If, on the other hand, both commoners and elites were included in ossuaries, this practice would be consistent with descriptions of Chief Powhatan's efforts to create a regional identity. Chief Powhatan himself shunned overt displays of status, instead preferring to make his own clothes and dress like a commoner (Barker 1992:68–69).

Regardless of who was buried in ossuaries, this does not preclude pre-ossuary distinctions between elites and commoners (Potter 1989:153–154; Rountree and Turner 1998:267–270). Ethnohistorical accounts of mortuary rituals and treatments of elites that differed from the treatments of commoners (e.g., interment in mortuary temples) certainly suggest this may be the case (Potter 1989:153–154; Rountree and Turner 1998:267–270).

Two graves near Indian Point in the Patawomeck chiefdom, a chiefdom semi-independent of the Powhatan paramountcy (Rountree 1993b:4), are often cited as evidence of elite burial in the Coastal Plain. Both are primary interments that post-date 1607 (Potter 1989:162; Potter 1993:213). The first contained a diverse assemblage of material goods, including a crescent-shaped copper breastplate, copper beads, and bone pins, and possibly glass beads (Potter 1989:162). The second grave contained twelve individuals interred with items interpreted as prestige goods: aboriginally manufactured shell beads accompanied eleven of the individuals; the twelfth was interred with *Busycon* maskettes, shell gorgets, copper gorgets, flush-loop copper bells, a metal crucifix, and copper, bone, ceramic, shell, and glass beads (Potter 1989:162–165). While clearly the individuals in both these burials received special treatment (they were not in ossuaries and were accompanied by grave goods), these two primary interments cannot be brought to bear on precontact mortuary treatment in the Powhatan core area because they are not representative numerically, temporally, or geographically. In fact, "prestige goods" in contact period burials may be a product of greater native access to European items and the declining influence of *werowances*, not status.

The second source of information concerning Late Woodland elite identities in Virginia consists of prestige or display goods found at some Late Woodland sites. Across the region we see evidence of the exchange of a limited set of raw materials and finished goods that appear in a few special burials and that are mentioned in historic documents as being concentrated in the hands of the elite (Rountree 1993b; Rountree and Turner 1998:282–284). Marine shells (e.g., *Busycon* whelks) have been recovered from interior sites. Freshwater pearls have been found at coastal sites. Native copper (from sources to the west) has been recovered from both piedmont and coastal plain sites. Historic accounts note the importance of copper for the elite (Hantman 1990; Rountree and Turner 1998:283), and it appears in the rich Patawomeke burials as well (Potter 1989:161–164). Among the artifacts recovered from the presumed elite burials from Patawomeke was a South Atlantic style shell gorget (Brain and Phillips 1996:39–40). Most of the gorgets of this style come from the Irene site, a Mississippian site near the mouth of the Savannah River in Georgia. The concentration of these gorgets at Irene may indicate that Irene was the source of the gorgets found elsewhere, including Virginia.

Prestige or display goods were particularly important to the elites of the Virginia chiefdoms (e.g., Hantman 1990; Rountree and Turner 1994, 1998). Copper and shell were important media for elite display and mortuary ritual (Rountree and Turner 1998:283–284), but they were not the only materials used in early historic times by Powhatan and other Coastal Plain elites. Pigments (e.g., powdered antimony from the Patawomeke near the Potomac River and the red pigment *puccoon* [*Lithospermum caroliniense*] from the Nottoway south of the James River) figure prominently in historic accounts (Rountree and Turner 1998:284).

Chiefly and commoner identities were clearly distinguished in Powhatan society. Rountree and Turner (1994:365) suggest that chiefs were considered to be semi-divine. The distinction between chiefs and commoners was marked by dress, differential access to display goods (e.g., beads, copper, pearls, and *puccoon*) and exclusive access to copper, the paying of obeisance, and servants who attended the chiefs. Chiefs' houses were also larger than commoners' houses (Loftfield and Jones 1995). The distinctions continued beyond life. Chiefs were interred in special temples, with material symbols of their status. Access to these chiefly mortuary facilities was limited to the elite (chiefs and priests).

It seems clear that the Powhatan and other Late Woodland elites of the Coastal Plain were individuals set apart from the other members of their societies. They made significant efforts to mark that distinction during their lives, and the distinctions continued to be marked after their deaths. The distinctions were marked through daily practice involving the use of space and material symbols.

While the Powhatan elites were different from commoners, the elites and commoners were linked. The linkage between elites and commoners took the form of a common ethnic identity. Chief Powhatan was different from commoners, but he and they were Powhatan: he was not a "foreigner." There appears to have been a deliberate, conscious effort to forge this common identity. Powhatan elites were not always easily distinguished from commoners (Barker 1992; Gallivan and Hantman 1996; J. R. Smith 1986b:170). Barker (1992) has argued that Chief Powhatan deliberately dressed like a commoner to mask the differences between himself and commoners and create that common identity. Rountree and Turner (1998:285–286) note that "setting his subjects against 'outsiders'" was one of Powhatan's most effective methods for forging what they call a "supradistrict ethnic identity" that was crucial in the establishment of the Powhatan paramountcy. We note that the creation of such an identity links elite and commoners, forming what we see as an important part of Powhatan elite identities.

The Powhatan elites occupied mediating positions between the Powhatan commoners and the outside world. Powhatan chiefs and the religious practitioners (priests) associated with them controlled access to sacred knowledge and symbols, including the mortuary temples containing the remains of the chiefs' ancestors. Chiefs were seen as semidivine individuals who, unlike commoners, had an afterlife beyond death (Rountree and Turner 1998:271). Chief Powhatan also attempted to monopolize interaction (or at least exchange) with the English (Strachey 1953:107, 114 [1612]; cited in Rountree and Turner 1998:283).

The Powhatan elites were powerful. Chiefs were military figures and leaders, and this aspect of elite identity can be clearly seen in the actions of Chief Powhatan and his successor, Opechancanough. Chief Powhatan directed military actions to bring other groups into the Powhatan paramountcy, and both he and his brother directed attacks against the English. Rountree suggests that warfare was an important part of the social reproduction of masculine gender among the Powhatan. He (1989:85) also stresses the importance of military prowess in establishing and maintaining chiefly status. Adam King and Jennifer Freer (1995:275) suggest that elites manipulated this aspect of Powhatan discourse to their advantage by encouraging their followers to strive for such status (and in the process increase the prestige and status of the elites).

The Powhatan elites were legitimate, deriving their legitimacy by their membership in elite families or matrilineal descent groups. Chiefs inherited their positions or were appointed by higher officeholders. But legitimacy also depended in part on the demonstration of power and elite character (conformity to established patterns of elite identity) in discourses or overt actions. These components of legitimacy could be demonstrated by actions in war, by command of resources or people, and by possession and use of material symbols (e.g., prestige goods). Many of the material symbols associated with elite identity in Powhatan society were derived from the outside world and demonstrated the mediating role of the elite.

Elite Strategies in Powhatan

The Powhatan chiefdom was a post-1571 union of previously independent polities orchestrated by one charismatic individual, Chief Powhatan. Not all the polities Chief Powhatan sought to control became part of the chiefdom. Some were able to successfully resist being absorbed into the paramountcy (Potter 1989:154; Rountree 1989:8; J. R. Smith 1986b:246). In those politics that were incorporated, Chief Powhatan permitted some of the old chiefs to remain as district *werowances*, but in districts where loyalty was in doubt, he appointed his relatives as petty chiefs (Rountree and Turner 1994:364).

The Siouan-speaking Monacans in Virginia's Piedmont were important players in the Powhatan political arena because they controlled access to the copper that Powhatan chiefs needed to legitimize their superordinate positions (Hantman 1990, 1993; E. R. Turner 1993). The Eastern Shore Accomacs and Occohannocks likewise controlled an important wealth item—shell. The Monacans and Powhatans were enemies (see J. R. Smith 1986a:73–75), but the Algonquian-speaking Accomacs and Occohannocks were part of what Rountree (1989:14) calls Powhatan's "ethnic fringe." Members of these outlying districts identified themselves as Powhatans to the English, but their allegiance to the paramount chief was tenuous. Powhatan continued to hold on to these fringe districts not only because they feared military retaliation, but also because Powhatan controlled the distribution of prestige goods they needed to cement social transactions and to pay social debts.

Copper and shell were essential to the creation and maintenance of social identity in the Powhatan world—for both elites and commoners (see Frankenstein and Rowlands 1978:76). Powhatan doled out copper to purchase assistance from his districts in warfare and to reward lesser elites and warriors for jobs well done; elites also gave copper to commoners to complete funerary rites (Potter 1993; Rountree 1989:111). Powhatan elites and commoners alike used copper and shell to mark life transitions and cement relationships within and between descent groups. By controlling access to prestige goods necessary for social reproduction, Chief Powhatan kept his populace in his debt.

Because both copper and shell came from distant sources, Powhatan could easily monopolize their distribution (Davidson 1993; see also Brumfiel and Earle 1987). Powhatan thus served as the intermediary between Powhatan commoners and the outside world. Shell and copper symbolized Powhatan's foreign connections—in this world, the Monacans, Accomacs, and Occohannocks, but more generally, the supernatural (see Helms 1979; J. F. Scarry 1999). These prestige goods were thus tied to elite identity and status—elites possessed more copper and shell goods than commoners. In life, elites signified their foreign connections and status by wearing copper plates on their heads or around their necks (Potter 1989:153). At death, goods that embodied elite status were placed in mortuary temples with chiefs and priests.

Given the importance of shell and copper in this life and beyond, it is reasonable to expect that both commoners and elites saw the opportunity to acquire copper from the English as a means of enhancing their prestige. Lesser elites probably also looked at copper as a means of recreating their previous identities as leaders independent of Chief Powhatan. Chief Powhatan tried to monopolize European copper in an effort to circumvent both the Monacans and lesser Powhatan elites vying for autonomy.

When the English established Jamestown, Chief Powhatan's initial reaction was to destroy the English, just as the Powhatans had destroyed the earlier Spanish mission (Potter 1989:151), but he soon realized the opportunities an English alliance promised. If he could maintain friendly relations with the English colonists, he would have a more reliable source of copper and could end his dependence on the hostile Monacans to the west (Gallivan and Hantman 1996; Hantman 1990). To preserve his position as paramount and continue to control copper exchange, Powhatan attempted to position himself between the English and lesser Powhatan elites and commoners.

The English initially traded copper for Powhatan's maize, allowing Powhatan to maintain his monopoly on prestige goods. Soon, however, lesser Powhatan elites started trading directly with the English (Rountree 1993a:179). This arrangement benefited both *werowances* seeking autonomy and the English. The English saw that the fringe groups were more "friendly" to their settlements and that trading with lesser elites more distant from the Powhatan core weakened the chiefdom (Potter 1989:154, 158; Rountree 1993a:180). Once *werowances* were able to acquire copper without the intervention of the paramount chief, Powhatan could no longer keep lesser elites in his debt.

For a time, native elites (both lesser and paramount elites) were able to maintain and even enhance their superordinate statuses by controlling the distribution of copper within the Powhatan world (Potter 1989:156). *Werowances* in more geographically distant districts claimed independence from the Powhatan core. Eventually, however, the English started trading directly with commoners (Potter 1993), and within two years the English saturated the copper market, causing copper to lose its prestige value (Potter 1989:157).

By 1610 the English had grown in size and strength. Because they no longer needed the core Powhatan groups for subsistence (Potter 1989:159), they had little to lose by expanding their colony into Powhatan's core territory. The English raided the Powhatan core village of Paspahegh, and core districts responded by integrating more tightly (Rountree 1993a: 183). By 1611 the Monacans had allied with the Powhatan core against the English (Potter 1993:183; Rountree 1989, 1990; Strachey 1953:105–106 [1612]), and in 1616 the Chickahominys joined the Powhatan paramountcy. But because the English had not yet encroached on the lands of the fringe groups, these districts remained relatively uninvolved in English-Powhatan conflicts and continued to trade with the English.

In 1622 and again in 1644, the Powhatans launched massive attacks on the English colonists. By 1644 the fringe groups felt the pressure of the growing colony and decided to join the Powhatan core to fight the English. The English prevailed. The subsequent treaty restricted Powhatan territory to the land north of the York River and established the Powhatans as subjects of the English (Rountree 1990:87). The Powhatans all but vanished soon after.

The English were lucky to arrive in the Chesapeake during a period of political disequilibrium in the Powhatan world. Chief Powhatan was in the midst of a struggle to complete the consolidation of his chiefdom, and elites in outlying districts were looking for a way out. Both groups of native elites viewed the arrival of the English as an opportunity to use the colonists as pawns in their ascent to power. For Chief Powhatan, the English were a new source of copper that would end his reliance on the increasingly hostile Monacans to the west. For the lesser elites on the Powhatan periphery the English were a source of copper that would allow them to circumvent Powhatan.

Mere interaction with the English—the Other—increased the prestige of these lesser elites in the short term, elevating them to direct mediators between earthly and supernal realms. The real struggle, then, was not for copper but for what copper represented—status and supernatural connections; in other words, identity. The English quickly understood the importance of copper and were able to use competition for it to bring about the demise of the already fragile Powhatan paramountcy.

Comparing the Apalachee and Powhatan Cases

The Apalachee and the Powhatans were farming peoples who grew corn and a variety of other crops. Their societies were organized as complex chiefdoms, at least in the late sixteenth and early seventeenth centuries. However, there were important differences between the two. The Apalachee were a Mississippian people, with historical, cultural, and linguistic links to other Mississippian peoples of the Southeast. The Powhatans were a Late Woodland people, whose cultural patterns resembled those of Woodland peoples along the Middle Atlantic Coastal Plain and regions to the north rather than the Mississippian peoples to the south. This distinction reflects deep historical divides that must be considered in any comparison of the Apalachee and the Powhatans.

The Apalachee and Powhatan cases are similar in several respects. These similarities reflect similar patterns of behavior on the part of individuals striving to achieve a degree of social ascendancy over others in the absence of any real concentration of coercive force. However, the cases also differ in several important respects. The differences reflect the very real differences in the histories of the Apalachee and the Powhatans and the very real differences between Spanish and English colonists.

Common Patterns

In both Apalachee and Powhatan societies, certain individuals had social identities that set them apart from the majority of their fellows. In both societies, these elite individuals had greater access to institutionalized social positions that were linked to rights that included some degree of legitimate authority over the labor of commoners and the products of that labor. They also had greater access to exotic valuables that had some (often significant) symbolic content. Those materials (and the identities they signified and perhaps validated) can be seen as symbolic capital (Bourdieu 1980). Greater access to that capital was crucial to the legitimacy of chiefs and aspiring elites. (They can also be seen as wealth in a system of wealth finance [Brumfiel and Earle 1987:7–8; Rountree and Turner 1998:269].)

In both Apalachee and Powhatan societies, the Protohistoric and early Historic periods of the sixteenth and seventeenth centuries were times of great social and political change and upheaval. In both cases, elite individuals sought to maintain their position and status during the flux of the Protohistoric and Historic periods. They did so in part by manipulating their social identities. However, those social identities were created and recreated within existing systems of meaning, limiting the actions elites could take.

During the Protohistoric and early Historic periods, the elites of both Apalachee and Powhatan sought to position themselves as mediators between Europeans and other members of their societies (a role clearly in keeping with past practice). They interacted and negotiated with the European invaders of their lands and treated them as powerful but rational (in their world) outsiders. In turn, they expected the Europeans to treat them in accordance with their status. They gave to the Europeans but they expected things in return. In particular, they expected acknowledgment and recognition of their status. They also sought European goods as material symbols of their position and status (again keeping with past practice).

However, while there were similarities in social structure and elite identities between Apalachee and Powhatan and in the strategies used by their elites during interactions with Europeans, there were some important differences. The consequences of the strategies followed by the Apalachee and Powhatan elites were also quite different. Those distinctions resulted from differences in the contexts in which the elites acted.

Differing Contexts and Consequences

The complex Powhatan chiefdom that the English colonists encountered in 1607 appears to have been a relatively late development. It seems to have emerged after 1571 as the result of the incorporation of several previously independent simple chiefdoms into a single political unit under the leadership of Chief Powhatan (Rountree 1990). Thus, unlike the Apalachee, the Powhatan chiefdom had a limited time depth (at least as a complex chiefdom). By contrast, the Apalachee had been a complex chiefdom for hundreds of years, during which both ethnic and elite identities were created and strengthened. Lacking that depth of history, the identity of the Powhatan paramountcy was not well established. Powhatan (the paramount) was linked by marriage to previously autonomous chiefdoms under his sway but not by shared identities (although he attempted to create such an identity). Hence his legitimacy (particularly in the eyes of rivals) was less well established than that of the Apalachee *caciques*. His rivals and subordinates were, not surprisingly, willing to act to weaken him and create or reclaim long-standing positions for themselves. Finally, Powhatan's paramountcy (at least the incorporation of recently independent polities) was largely founded on coercive power. The English actively sought to limit that power, at least in later times—and particularly after the Powhatan attack of 1622. But even before that, the English had raided the core Powhatan village Paspahegh in 1610 (Rountree 1993a:183).

The second major difference between the Apalachee and the Powhatan cases lies in the reactions of the Spanish and English to the actions of the native elite. The Spanish secular authorities acted as outsiders should act, through the mediators of the Apalachee elite. They acknowledged the legitimacy of the elite and accorded them privileges not granted to commoners. They conferred titles and positions. The story is different for the Franciscan missionaries, although they too acknowledged the legitimacy of the elite as political beings. The friars eventually confronted those aspects of elite identity linked to the supernatural (e.g., the roles of *caciques* and *usinulos* in the ball game [Bushnell 1978; Hann 1988]).

In Virginia, the English were not so accommodating. They countered Chief Powhatan's attempts to monopolize and control the movement of copper by bypassing the paramount and dealing directly with lesser elite and commoners. They encouraged rivals and the elites of recently subordinated polities to resist Chief Powhatan and his successors, consciously allying themselves with groups on Powhatan's fringe that were less closely tied to the chiefdom. Not only did the acts of the English weaken the high Powhatan elite politically, economically, and militarily, the English also subverted the identity of the elite (Potter 1989:158; Rountree 1993b:18). That part of the legitimacy of the elite that rested on their positions as mediators between commoners and the outside was clearly confounded by the actions of the English.

Thomas Håkansson (1998:265) has pointed to a pattern between control of valuables needed for social payments and the degree of political centralization. Where valuables are profuse and cannot be controlled, political organization is competitive and poorly centralized; where valuables are limited and exchange can be controlled, political organization is centralized and hierarchical. The material symbols of chiefly status and identity in both Apalachee and Powhatan were limited and controlled by the high elite during prehistoric times. However, while material and other symbols of chiefly status in Apalachee continued to be restricted in the seventeenth century (and chiefly authority was maintained to a degree), such was not the case in Powhatan. The English made symbolic goods, such as copper, available to rivals to the established elite (for a price, usually maize early in the colony's history).

Given the different historical and social contexts in which they operated, we should not be surprised to see differing consequences resulting from similar strategies. Thus it is not surprising that the Apalachee high elites managed to maintain their identity and a portion of their authority. It is also not surprising that the Powhatan high elites failed to maintain either their positions or their identity.

Conclusion

Our examination of the Apalachee and Powhatan chiefdoms in the Protohistoric points to similarities and differences that reflect similarities in processes and differences in historical contingencies. Our study also has implications for our reading of the archaeological record.

Implications for the Study of Agency

Clearly, we think it is possible to examine questions of agency using archaeological data. The archaeological record reflects past practice and that record can be interpreted. We can also approach questions related to the construction of social identities and the meanings attached to those identities. However, there are also things we cannot do—or at least that we cannot be confident about.

Unlike the Apalachee, the Powhatans left few archaeological sites on the landscape that reflect their obvious importance at contact. Further, the archaeological record is silent on their political organization during the Protohistoric period (Gallivan and Hantman 1996; see also E. R. Turner 1992). The historic record of the Virginia Coastal Plain fits with the model of a complex chiefdom: three-tiered political hierarchy of paramount, lesser chiefs, and commoners; settlement hierarchy;

tribute sent to elites by commoners; prestige goods under elite control; and different burial treatment for elite individuals. Without historic data, we would classify the Powhatan as independent, tribally-organized communities. There is no archaeological evidence of settlement hierarchies, elite mortuary temples, chiefly storage facilities, or a prestige goods economy.

For at least one moment in time, we know that the peoples of the Virginia Tidewater were organized hierarchically. The short lifespan of the Powhatan chiefdom is likely the primary reason for its archaeological invisibility. The communities of the Coastal Plain may have been hierarchical at other moments in time even before the Protohistoric period. Gallivan and Hantman's (1996) model of a fluid organization, cycling between hierarchy and egalitarianism, fits with both the historic and archaeological data. A group of communities does not have to be *either* hierarchical *or* egalitarian—it can be both (see also Crumley 1987, 1995). In the Powhatan case, we might not have been able to detect its hierarchical state without English documentation.

The benefit of having historic records is that we can consider the role individuals played in the early contact period. Chief Powhatan was a charismatic and influential person who aspired to create a regional polity and to convince the people of the Virginia Coastal Plain that they should share a common identity. Captain John Smith's actions were designed to increase his own prestige in England. Add to Powhatan and Smith dozens of *werowances* and colonial leaders with their own personalities and agendas. How might the Virginia colonial endeavor have been different if the Powhatan chief were not so driven, if district *werowances* didn't feel so oppressed, or if the colonial leaders were more concerned with understanding and tolerating native ways of life?

The Powhatan case raises significant issues for archaeologists interested in studying agency. Given that the Powhatan chiefdom never reached the level of archaeological visibility, we must ask ourselves how often we might miss short-lived or failed attempts to institutionalize social and political inequalities. How many polities rise and fall without leaving an archaeological signature? While the archaeological record certainly reflects daily practice, the sum of individual actions, how many significant actions and decisions never make it into the archaeological record?

Agency and Identity in Protohistoric Apalachee and Powhatan

The Protohistoric period was a time of flux and fluidity for both the Apalachee and Powhatan, as it was for all native societies. The Powhatans appear to have been subject to a greater degree of flux during this period. It is unclear whether the flux the Powhatan experienced during this time was unusual or a normal state of affairs (Gallivan and Hantman 1996). The Apalachee and Powhatan elites reacted to the uncertainty that characterized the Protohistoric in ways that were intended to maintain or enhance their own social positions. One aspect of their efforts involved the (continued) recreation of elite identities. This was nothing new, but the ways they did it were different because of the appearance of new actors and circumstances.

In both societies the elites turned to Europeans and attempted to use their links to these new actors to their advantage. They positioned themselves as mediators between the Europeans and their fellows. They sought material symbols associated with elite identities from the European colonists. They used traditional and new material symbols to signify their identities as individuals who were not common Apalachee or Powhatan, but who were not Europeans either. They positioned themselves as intermediates, linked to both. Moreover, the efforts of the Apalachee and Powhatan elites were constrained by prior practice and established patterns of discourse.

The successes and failures of the elites of Powhatan and Apalachee were partially the results of the actions of the different others with whom they interacted and partially the result of the actions of their subordinates and rivals. For the Apalachee, the Spaniards acted in ways that conformed to the patterns established in native discourses concerning the relationship between elites and the outside world. As a result, the Apalachee elites were relatively successful in maintaining both their own positions and the organizational integrity of their societies. For the Powhatan, the English acted in ways that did not conform to the established or expected patterns. As a result, the Powhatan elite encountered internal rebellion and resistance that threatened their positions and the fragile structure of the paramountcy. Too, the actions of the Spanish tended to maintain the control the Apalachee elite held over important forms of symbolic capital, while the actions of the English disrupted the control the Powhatan elite held over their symbolic capital.

The Protohistoric period was important, both for the profound changes in native societies that took place during the period and because the events of that time set the stage for later European colonial endeavors. The events of the Protohistoric were particularly critical at the first Spanish and English settlements. Apalachee contributed to the relative success of the colony of La Florida as an economic and military enterprise. The Powhatans directly affected the course of British colonial efforts, particularly interactions with other native groups.

The impact of the Apalachee and Powhatan cases extends up until today. In both cases, the actions of the native elites and the Europeans they dealt with affected the discourses that have shaped modern American culture and American views of native peoples (Apalachee through their absence from those discourses and the Powhatan through their presence).

Initial encounters with Europeans, or with information about European explorers, affected the Apalachee and the Powhatan in many important ways. Those encounters challenged existing native pictures of the nature of the world and its inhabitants. The encounters also affected the native leaders and elites of Apalachee and Powhatan—on the one hand threatening their positions and sources of legitimacy, and on the other hand providing them with opportunities to tap new sources of power and legitimacy.

In both Apalachee and Powhatan, the Protohistoric period was a time of instability, fluidity, and flux. For this reason, there were opportunities for individuals and various collectivities to actively work to change the discourses that shaped their societies.

The actions of individuals were crucial to the transformations of the native societies in the Protohistoric: in Apalachee, in Powhatan, and in other societies as well. But those actions are not, and presumably were not, random. In the Protohistoric, individuals acted according to their individual personalities within constraints imposed by past patterns of practice in their societies. They acted in response to new circumstances provided by their fellows and by the Europeans by attempting to achieve specific goals (individual and collective).

Particularly important actors were the native elites, whose social and political positions enabled them to exert greater influence over cultural institutions and general social discourses. Their actions were more or less successful in achieving their conscious goals. But our actions typically have consequences that we do not anticipate (and that we may not desire). Such was the case for the native elites. Their actions changed (recreated) their cultures, constrained subsequent practice, and shaped historical trajectories.

Regardless of the ultimate outcome of their actions, the inescapable conclusion is that the native peoples were not simply passive objects to be transformed by the European invaders of their lands. They were *active* participants in the changes that mark the Protohistoric and that continued through the early Historic period. Indeed, they were active participants in creating the history of the Colonial period.

The Powhatan and Apalachee cases provide an interesting comparison, illustrating similarities and differences in the ways in which both native and European peoples responded to contact. Some of the differences in Apalachee and Powhatan responses are likely related to the greater time depth of the Apalachee chiefdom. (The Powhatan chiefdom was a more recent and therefore less stable political entity.) Others may reflect differences among individual actors—their goals and capabilities. Differences between the Spanish and English responses can be explained in part by their unique colonial histories and the goals of their respective crowns.

Acknowledgments

We would like to thank Mark Rees and Cameron Wesson for organizing the symposium and inviting us to participate. We also want to thank Marisol de la Cadena and Dorothy Holland of the University of North Carolina at Chapel Hill, who suggested readings that helped shape our thinking about political identities and political actors.

10 / Subsistence Economy and Political Culture in the Protohistoric Central Mississippi Valley

Mark A. Rees

Surveying the prehistory and protohistory of the Lower Mississippi Valley a half-century ago, Philip Phillips wrote of the importance of identifying "late archaeological complexes with living peoples," setting the standard for archaeological and ethnohistorical research in the southeastern United States (Phillips et al. 1951:347; e.g., Galloway 1995; C. Hudson 1997; Krause 1985; Morse and Morse 1983; articles in Dye and Cox 1990, C. Hudson and Tesser 1994b, McNutt 1996a, Young and Hoffman 1993). Anthropological archaeologists working in the Americas have subsequently defined a discipline based on the contrasts between prehistory and history, egalitarian and complex societies, chiefdom and state. At the same time, there has been an abiding interest in the explanation of long-term historical development, under the guise of either culture historical phases and periods or neo-evolutionary sociopolitical types and stages. In the first instance culture change has been attributed to migrations, diffusion, or innovation, while in the latter cultural adaptation, productive intensification, and general evolutionary trends have taken center stage (Lyman et al. 1997; cf. Willey 1985).

The culture historical approach advanced by Phillips, Ford, and Griffin (1951) and others (e.g., Ford 1936, 1938, 1952; Griffin 1952a, 1952c; Phillips 1970; Willey and Phillips 1958) had a profound and lasting influence on the archaeology of the Central Mississippi Valley as well as the entire Southeast, to the extent that Dunnell (1990:19) remarked that southeastern archaeologists have made little contribution to a neo-evolutionary, processual archaeology. Archaeologists working in the Southeast did, however, expand on neo-evolutionary concepts such as sociopolitical types, cultural adaptation, subsistence strategies, and cultural ecology, particularly with reference to Mississippi period hierarchically-ranked societies or "chiefdoms" (e.g., Lewis 1974; Peebles 1971, 1974; Peebles and Kus 1977; B. D. Smith 1975, 1978b; articles in B. D. Smith 1978a). While archaeological research in the Central Mississippi Valley has retained a strong culture historical orientation and methodology following Phillips, Ford, and Griffin's (1951) groundbreaking study, it is uncertain whether the future advancement of archaeological research heralds the long deferred "fall" of culture history (i.e., Lyman et al. 1997). As a discipline founded on the study of extensive time spans, archaeology must inevitably address the development and decline of local level and regional polities, what has been referred to as long-term historical trajectories or the rise and fall of civilizations (Daniel 1964; Johnson and Earle 1987; Peebles 1987; Steponaitis 1991; Trigger 1989a:397–398). In its broadest sense, identifying the archaeological record with living peoples requires taking into account regional, historical variations in political economy and ideology, as well as exogenous sources of social interaction (Earle 1991b; Trigger 1991).

As a point of departure, I reexamine documentary evidence for mid-sixteenth-century Native American interaction with Spanish conquistadors in the Central Mississippi Valley, from the perspective of current ethnohistorical reconstruction and ethnological theory. Focusing on a specific event described in the narratives of the de Soto expedition, I examine the potential implications of gift-giving in Mississippian societies, in terms of both subsistence economy and political process. In contrast with the results of other studies in the Central Mississippi Valley and Southeast, faunal remains from the Upper Nodena site in northeastern Arkansas provide evidence for a local subsistence economy that was ultimately interrelated with regional political culture. The Upper Nodena site has been associated by many researchers with the historically documented province of Pacaha (C. Hudson 1985, 1994; C. Hudson et al. 1990; D. F. Morse 1990; D. F. Morse and P. A. Morse 1983, 1990b; cf. Brain et al. 1974; Swanton 1985 [1939]). Evidence that the site of Parkin may have been the central town of Casqui offers additional support for this position (Mitchem 1996; P. A. Morse 1981, 1990, 1993). Rather than associating particular archaeological complexes or phases with historically documented provinces, emphasis is placed on the relevance of subsistence economy in understanding regional and macro-regional variations in political culture. In order to advance an understanding of regional political development and decline, it is crucial that explanations of protohistoric political economy take into account indigenous sources of stability and change, as well as potential responses to European exploration, epidemic disease, and subsequent demographic upheaval (e.g., Blakely and Detweiler-Blakely 1989; Kidder 1993; M. T. Smith 1987, 1994b). In examining the relationship between subsistence economy and political culture in the Central Mississippi Valley, attention is drawn to social relations of authority rather than cultural homogeneity or sociopolitical types, to regional political processes rather than evolution or selection.

Political Economy, Culture, and Process

While strains of evolutionism can be identified in archaeology as early as the nineteenth century, it was the positivistic, neo-evolutionary anthropology of the mid-twentieth century that gave rise to the evolutionary perspectives of a systemic, processual archaeology (e.g., Binford 1962, 1965, 1968; Watson et al. 1971; cf. Lyman et al. 1997). On the basis of the social Darwinism of Herbert Spencer (1862, 1967

[1898]) and different interpretations of cultural evolution by Leslie White (1959) and Julian Steward (1955), long-term developmental differences throughout prehistory were characterized by Carneiro (1973:90) as "change from a relatively indefinite, incoherent homogeneity to a relatively definite, coherent heterogeneity, through successive differentiations and integrations." Throughout the 1960s and 1970s the specific political and economic implications of these "successive differentiations and integrations" were explored in detail (e.g., Cohen and Service 1978; Flannery 1972; Fried 1967; Friedman and Rowlands 1978; Sanders and Price 1968; Service 1962, 1975). Sahlins (1960) addressed perceived discrepancies between regional, culture historical contexts and broad evolutionary trends by distinguishing specific from general evolution; other scholars have called attention to the distinction between multilinear and unilinear evolution (Steward 1955:15–19; cf. Blanton et al. 1996; Sanders and Webster 1978).

While debate continues, the study of prehistoric political economy is usually subsumed under a neo-evolutionary concept of progressive cultural development (Hirth 1996; Stein 1998). Historical variations in regional and macro-regional political economy are generally explained in terms of sociopolitical evolution and the adaptiveness of culture, overlooking or misinterpreting evidence for regional political decentralization and decline. From this view, the development of regional political economy represents a systemic response to environmental or demographic factors, facilitated by economic management or technological advances and ultimately debilitated by maladaptation, systemic disequilibrium, or "hypercoherence" (Flannery 1972; Rappaport 1978; Renfrew 1978). Such managerial, adaptationist perspectives have been criticized as inadequate for advancing further understanding of long-term historical trajectories, including explanation of political process and social change (Brumfiel and Earle 1987; Feinman 1995; Feinman and Neitzel 1984; McGuire 1983, 1992a; Saitta 1989; C. S. Spencer 1987).

One outcome of the neo-evolutionary critique has been increased interest in selectionist or Darwinian approaches to complexity and culture change. The concepts of "cultural adaptation" and "cultural systems" have come under scrutiny, and the importance of variation, selection, transmission, and decision-making have been emphasized (e.g., Barton and Clark 1997b; Dunnell 1989; Maschner 1996; O'Brien 1996; O'Brien and Holland 1990, 1992; Rindos 1985, 1989a, 1989b; Teltser 1995). While there has been a concerted effort to purge functionalist, systemic lines of reasoning from evolutionary archaeology, the potential relevance of such an approach to long-term political development and decline has only begun to be explored (e.g., Braun 1990; Maschner and Patton 1996; Neiman 1997). Dunnell (1989:49) proffered Darwinian evolution as a rallying point for anthropology, in order to once and for all "ground archaeology in science," yet there remains a fundamental divergence between natural selection and human agency, political process and evolution (e.g., Barton 1997; Barton and Clark 1997a; O'Brien 1996:18;

O'Brien et al. 1998; cf. C. S. Spencer 1997). Observations by Trigger (1989b) and others that archaeology and history have common interests and goals point toward a more productive synthesis, an approach that has already been explored in cultural anthropology, political economy, and cultural history (e.g., Burke 1990; Cobb 1991; Comaroff and Comaroff 1991; Duke 1992; Feinman 1997; Kertzer 1996; Lightfoot 1995; Peebles 1991; Roseberry 1989; Wolf 1982).

Following Wolf (1982:80), studies of noncapitalist political economy in prehistory have focused on social relations of production and exchange as a political process (e.g., Cobb 1993; Earle 1991b, 1997; Feinman 1991; Gilman 1991; Saitta 1997). Regional political economies are based in part on the intensification of local subsistence economies and the control of labor, production, or exchange—what essentially represents a political process; Johnson and Earle (1987:13) describe regional political economy as "growth oriented in a highly competitive political domain, and thus inherently unstable." Subsistence economy has in turn been characterized as striving for sufficiency on the household level, what Sahlins (1972) refers to as the "domestic mode of production" (cf. Earle 1997:203). Earle (1987a) contrasts an adaptationist approach with political control established through wealth or staple finance, more recently characterized as "prestige-good chiefdoms" and "staple-finance chiefdoms" (Earle 1997:209–210; cf. Brumfiel and Earle 1987). While Earle (1997:207) points out that "sources of power are intertwined and interdependent," considerable archaeological research has been aimed at distinguishing the influences of discrete political, military, economic, and ideological factors (e.g., Blanton et al. 1996; Brumfiel and Earle 1987; DeMarrais et al. 1996; Earle 1987b, 1990; 1991a, 1997; Earle and D'Altroy 1989; Joyce and Winter 1996; Peregrine 1995).

Subsistence economy is transformed through the expropriation of social relations of production and expansion of legitimate authority in social reproduction (Johnson and Earle 1987:11–15; cf. Sahlins 1972:92–95). The emergence of a regional political economy is *politically* instituted, through subversion of the principles of reciprocity and creation of indebtedness (Sahlins 1972:123–148). Resource accumulation and distribution are thus simultaneously political-symbolic factors in social relations of authority (Cohen 1974; Kertzer 1988; Wolf 1982:80). In light of the apparently unstable and contested nature of authority in regional polities, the political-economic development of chiefdoms has been described as episodic or cyclical (Anderson 1994a, 1994b, 1996a, 1996b; Johnson and Earle 1987:13; Wright 1984). Although this presents a fundamentally different interpretation of multilinear evolution, cycling between "simple" and "complex" chiefdoms does not appear to be a recurrent phenomena in all long-term historical trajectories of regional political development and decline (e.g., Hally 1996:125; Knight 1997; Milner 1990, 1996a; Peebles 1986, 1987).

Taking a cue from anthropological political economy, archaeological studies of prehistoric political economy should emphasize the developmental relationships between political action, authority, and structure (Roseberry 1988:170–172; cf. S. B. Ortner 1984:141–144). Interest in local level cultural histories as an integral component of regional political development and decline should not be mistaken for the particularistic stance of an earlier culture historical approach. Nor should these political economies be conflated with the economizing, macro-regional histories of capitalist global expansion. Noncapitalist social formations are "cultural economies," and it is counterproductive to analytically detach economic behavior from social relations of authority (Halperin 1994:74–75, 191–204). What such an approach elicits is clearly less "world-system" than a neo-Marxist critique of noncapitalist social relations, symbolic legitimation, political domination, and resistance—what amounts to the historical development of "nonstate political hegemonies" (Pauketat 1994:11). In considering a range of multi-scalar interactions that are transformed through political actions, it may be more productive to treat prehistoric political economy as a form of cultural reproduction—what has been referred to as political culture (Cohen 1974:129; Marquardt 1992:101–113; Pauketat 1997b:7; Sahlins 1985:144; R. W. Wilson 1992:11–24).

Recent research in the American Bottom of the Mississippi River suggests that regional political development and decline can be explained through such a historical-processual approach rather than neo-evolutionary, systemic-processual, or selectionist models of human behavior (e.g., Emerson 1997a, 1997b; Pauketat 1992, 1994, 1997a, 1998; Pauketat and Emerson 1991, 1997b; M. T. Smith 1992). Earlier definitions of Mississippian culture as a particular "adaptive niche" emphasized the homogeneity of subsistence economy, settlement patterns, and sociopolitical systems, with less concern for regional variations or social heterogeneity (B. D. Smith 1975, 1978a, 1978c:486). As a result, the "Mississippian pattern of subsistence" has become an archetype for cultural adaptation in the late prehistoric Southeast, with undue emphasis frequently placed on the economic significance of intensive maize agriculture (B. D. Smith 1985:67; cf. Fritz 1992; Lopinot 1997). Recognizing that political, economic, and symbolic factors are interrelated in social relations of authority, it is suggested that this historical process is central to our understanding of regional political development and decline (Pauketat 2001b; Pauketat and Emerson 1997b:21). In examining Central Mississippi Valley protohistory, an area long associated with a culture historical approach, it is fitting to consider regional political culture from a historical-processual perspective.

Ethnohistorical and Ethnological Perspectives

Originally proposed as the anthropological integration of historical, ethnological, and archaeological research, ethnohistory has in some respects fallen short of this interdisciplinary goal (Brain et al. 1974; Jennings 1982; Sturtevant 1966; Trigger

1982, 1986). A broader definition of ethnohistory involves combining various lines of evidence in advancing anthropological theories of history—what has come to be known as anthropological history or historical anthropology (Krech 1991, 1996; Lightfoot 1995; Simmons 1988). The ways in which regional and macro-regional interactions were interconnected with local level histories have become a major focus of historical anthropology (e.g., S. B. Ortner 1984; Sahlins 1994). The protohistoric Southeast (ca. A.D. 1521–1704) is particularly suitable for this sort of approach: it was an era of significant political and economic change, yet available historical documentation is sparse and at best sporadic.

Although there are interpretive problems in their ethnohistorical application, the narratives of the sixteenth-century de Soto expedition provide a critical source of information on protohistoric political culture in the southeastern United States (Galloway 1993, 1997b). The precise route of various segments of the de Soto *entrada* has been disputed, leaving doubt as to the locations of different named towns and provinces, as well as the potential identification of archaeological sites (e.g., Brain 1985a; C. Hudson et al. 1990; Weinstein 1985). The association of certain provinces visited by the Spaniards with major topographical features is more certain, however, such as Coosa in the Southern Appalachians and Casqui in the Central Mississippi Valley (C. Hudson 1994). Future research will undoubtedly continue to expand upon and revise interpretations of sixteenth-century Native American–Spaniard interactions.

The de Soto narratives are of primary interest here in their potential relevance to understanding Mississippian subsistence economy and political culture, thereby advancing explanations of regional political development. Avoiding largely extraneous arguments regarding sociopolitical taxonomy and cultural classification, it can be assumed that provinces such as Coosa and Pacaha described in the de Soto narratives represented regional Mississippian polities (i.e., Johnson and Earle 1987: 21–22). The existence of regional polities is further supported by comparative ethnographic evidence for social interactions that transcend local-level politics and domestic economy, involving the monumental architecture and coercive authority of centralized political economies (Feinman and Neitzel 1984; Johnson and Earle 1987:207–245; Sahlins 1972:101–148; Wright 1984). The de Soto narratives are used here as a backdrop for a reexamination of gift-giving as it relates to the historical development of subsistence economy and political culture in the Central Mississippi Valley.

"A Gift of Many Fish"

Having forced its way through the present-day southeastern United States over a period of two years, the de Soto expedition entered the Central Mississippi Valley in May of 1541 (Biedma 1993:238; Elvas 1993:111–112 [1557]; Rangel 1993:299–

300; Swanton 1985:326 [1939]). Upon reaching the province of Casqui the Spaniards formed an alliance against the province of Pacaha, which had apparently been in conflict with Casqui for some time. Bolstered by the considerable military presence of the conquistadors, the Casquins defeated Pacaha and the main town was seized by de Soto. Many of the residents escaped, fleeing to an island in the river. After a combined Spaniard-Casquin raid on the island, the Casquins broke with the Spaniards, ostensibly apprehensive that they would be forced to surrender their newly gained plunder. Angered by this desertion, de Soto quickly sent a messenger to engage Pacaha in an alliance against his former Casquin allies (Elvas 1993:113–119 [1557]; see Dye 1994:46–48).

The chief (*cacique*) of Pacaha first attempted to mislead the Spaniards by sending an impersonator in his place. The hesitancy of Pacaha to take de Soto at his word is understandable, given the recent turn of events (Elvas 1993:118–119 [1557]). The narrative of a "Gentleman of Elvas" relates how the defeated Pacaha finally went out to greet de Soto:

> Next day came the cacique accompanied by many Indians bringing *a gift of many fish, skins, and blankets.* He made a talk which all were glad to hear and concluded by saying that even though his lordship [de Soto] had wrought damage to his land and vassals without him having deserved it, nevertheless he would not cease to be his, and would always be at his service. The governor ordered his brother and some others of the principal Indians whom he had captured to be released. (Elvas 1993:119 [1557], emphasis added)

In light of the problems in extending narrative histories to archaeological contexts and anthropological explanation (Elbl and Elbl 1997; Galloway 1997a, 1997b), how are we to interpret the purported actions of Pacaha? The narratives of the de Soto expedition describe an exceptional series of events at the onset of European exploration and present a "window" into the Mississippian Southeast prior to the long-term effects of European introduced pathogens (Johnson 1997; cf. Phillips et al. 1951:347). What possible conclusions can be drawn from this brief encounter between de Soto and Pacaha? The de Soto narratives indicate that Native Americans provided various gifts of food and other items to the Spaniards throughout the Southeast, whether voluntary or coerced. Once the de Soto expedition entered the Central Mississippi Valley, fish appear to have been a common offering (Rees 1997). Considering the gift of Pacaha from a political perspective has the potential to shed light on the historical dynamics of regional political culture, or the ways in which events were "integrated into the history of the long term" (Galloway 1997a:291).

That Pacaha is described as bearing "a gift of many fish, skins, and blankets" may at first glance seem inconsequential or trivial. As the leader of a powerful and obviously foreign military force, de Soto may have been dealt with by some southeastern polities as an invading paramount, being accorded the appropriate offerings of conquest or alliance (M. T. Smith and Hally 1992). In the pursuit of peace rather than continued hostilities, gifts of food and material goods may have been an attempt at appeasement or allegiance, an ostensibly spontaneous gesture of tribute (Dye 1995). This fits with earlier interpretations of Mississippian chiefdoms as prestige-good oriented economies and expectations that the mobilization of tribute and provisioning of an elite with foodstuffs are central organizational components in regional political economy (J. A. Brown et al. 1990; Johnson and Earle 1987:21, 207–312; Steponaitis 1978; Welch 1991; Welch and Scarry 1995; Wolf 1982:79–88).

Interpreting the actions of Pacaha as the singular prestation of tribute would seem to imply a specific category of sociopolitical complexity, a topic of recent debate (Mainfort and Carroll 1996; O'Brien 1995). Although sociopolitical complexity in the Central Mississippi Valley has only begun to be systematically addressed, studies of monumental architecture, settlement patterns, and historical sources suggest a scale of regional political economy comparable to other Mississippian societies in the late prehistoric Southeast (D. F. Morse 1989, 1990; P. A. Morse 1981, 1990; D. F. Morse and P. A. Morse 1990b). Spanish interactions with native polities throughout the Southeast were based in part on their ability to militarily dominate the people they encountered, exerting an often violent, coercive force to procure food, critical resources, guides, porters, and vital information. Gifts of food and portable items at crucial junctures in political mediation are likely to have symbolized allegiances and new alliances, but simply categorizing such gifts as tribute provides little further understanding of political process.

In searching for a systemic link between sociopolitical types and economic institutions, there is a potential for glossing over significant regional and macroregional variations among Mississippian polities. Accounting for political process in terms of social relations of authority requires evaluating the conceptual schema upon which social relations of production and regional political authority were based (e.g., Feinman and Neitzel 1984; Marquardt 1987, 1988; McGuire and Saitta 1996). In short, the political contexts and political-symbolic acts of gift-giving are of interest here, not whether tribute was characteristic of Mississippian political economy, or whether tribute, provisioning, or prestige goods correspond with a certain level of complexity or sociopolitical type. In light of the above quotation from the Gentleman of Elvas, it is worthwhile to reexamine in a comparative, cross-cultural sense the political-symbolic implications of the gift.

The Symbolic Capital of the Gift

The "gift of Pacaha" falls within a range of economic and political actions documented among societies throughout the world, in which reciprocity is embedded in social relations of authority (Mauss 1967; Sahlins 1972:149–275). It is in attempting to explain the nature of such social relations that we might arrive at a more incisive understanding of the long-term historical trajectories of political development and decline. Gift-giving holds a central place in social relations of authority and political process, encompassing a broad spectrum of so-called "economic behavior," from generalized reciprocity to trade (Malinowski 1961:166–194; Sahlins 1972:185–230). To caricature gift-giving solely as economic behavior in noncapitalist societies is shortsighted, however, taking human agency out of its political-symbolic and moral contexts. The very notion of the gift entails obligations that ultimately define social relations between individuals and groups (Malinowski 1996:15). The "productive capacity" of the gift, according to Mauss (1967:43, 73, 80), compels obligations, creates prestige, and reinforces solidarity: "Likewise the payments to chiefs are tribute; the distributions of food (*sagali*) are payments for labour or ritual accomplished, such as work done on the eve of a funeral. Thus basically as these gifts are not spontaneous so also they are not really disinterested. They are for the most part counter-prestations made not solely in order to pay for goods or services, but also to maintain a profitable alliance which it would be unwise to reject" (Mauss 1967:71).

Insofar as gifts are "not really disinterested," they comprise a political medium of exchange in which social relations of authority are actively negotiated. The observation that there are no "pure" or "free" gifts is nowhere more apparent than during the precipitous moments of initial encounters, in which the expectations and interests of each group are inevitably at risk (Douglas 1989; Malinowski 1996). Evidence of gift-giving in the transcultural realm of first encounters has considerable potential to further our understanding of regional variations in political culture. In such instances, self-interest is merely one dimension of a political-symbolic process that transcends the econocentric behavior of methodological individualism (Giddens 1979:94–95; Halperin 1994:13–26; Mauss 1967:75). Political action (practice) is embedded in multi-scalar interactions not reducible to individual interest (Bourdieu 1977:171–183; 1980:112–121).

The concept of reciprocity becomes ambiguous through kinship obligations and subsistence economy, imposing political expectations and social inequalities upon seeming generosity (Sahlins 1972:130–134). Social relations of authority may be expanded through such generosity, using kinship obligations to create indebtedness and prestige. This involves the cultural production of value through social transactions, blurring distinctions between a prestige goods economy, redistribution, and tributary mode of production (Pauketat 1997b:8–11). Foodstuffs, prestige goods, and other forms of "wealth" represent a form of "political currency" in regional and macro-regional interactions, made even more decisive in contexts involving warfare, organized violence, or coercive force (Dye 1995:292; cf. Kipp and Schortman 1989). A political-administrative hierarchy may eventually be established through such gift-giving, based on the existing social heterogeneity of competing coalitions and factions rather than on the mere "production of surplus" (Sahlins 1972:140). Since "to give is to show one's superiority," the attached value is not simply economic profit or commodification but political and symbolic capital (Bourdieu 1977: 171–183, 1980:112–121; Lévi-Strauss 1996:19; Mauss 1967:72).

Gift-giving is a central component in actions that reproduce a social order by initiating, maintaining, or disrupting social relations of authority, providing a launching pad for regional political culture (Komter 1996:9–10). While social relations of authority are sustained through political ideologies, authority can also be expanded or altered through coercive force. Political strategies aimed at reducing disparities in the acquisition and distribution of resources may in some instances have magnified existing social relations of authority (Sahlins 1972:139–145). Warfare, alliances, and gift-giving are interrelated, alternative means of interaction that are simultaneously political, economic, and symbolic (Dalton 1977). In the context of competitive feasting, gifts of food represent one means of "fighting with property" and are often closely associated with warfare (Blitz 1993a; Codere 1950; Dye 1990, 1995). Herein lies the interrelatedness of gift-giving and political process in noncapitalist societies. As Sahlins (1972:182) eloquently surmised, the gift carries with it a "political burden of reconciliation."

Although the "productive capacity" of gift-giving may transcend the solidarity of household and kinship organizations through control of craft goods production or long-distance exchange, it is generally associated with subsistence economy (Helms 1993; Peregrine 1991; cf. Johnson and Earle 1987). Food was a common gift in noncapitalist societies, holding strategic importance in ritual feasts, ceremonial exchanges between groups, and prestations to a centralized authority (Ames 1995; Blitz 1993a, 1993b; Sahlins 1972:187–191, 263–275; Welch and Scarry 1995). In the Trobriand Islands of Melanesia, periodic gifts of large quantities of fish regularly established and reproduced social relations of authority.

> Such large quantities of fish are always acquired only in connection with big distributions of food (*sagali*). It is remarkable that in the inland villages these distributions must be carried out in fish, whereas in the Lagoon villages, fish never can be used for ceremonial purposes, vegetables being the only article considered proper. Thus the motive for exchange here [is] not to get food in order to satisfy the primary want of eating, but in order to satisfy the social need of displaying large quantities of conventionally sanctioned eatables. Often when such a big fishing takes place, great quantities of fish perish by becoming rotten before they reach the man for whom they are finally destined. But being rotten in no way detracts from the value of fish in a *sagali*. (Malinowski 1961:187)

Comparable occasions of gift-giving were recorded among polities along the northwest coast of North America and may have had parallels in ceremonial feasts of the protohistoric Natchez in the Lower Mississippi Valley (Drucker and Heizer 1967; C. Hudson 1976:365–366; Kan 1986, 1989; Swanton 1911:110–123, 129–130).

The political and symbolic value of food is not confined to a surplus, however, as "value" is defined through social relations of giving and receiving. Among the Tikopia in Polynesia, certain *kinds* of foods and their preparation held crucial importance in social relations of authority. "Cooked food has a direct bearing on kinship in that so many obligations are fulfilled in terms of food, and to some extent the nature and quality of the dish are indices of the timbre, as it may be called, of the relationship" (Firth 1957:103).

The value of foods in gift-giving and feasting is thus fundamentally political-symbolic and should not be considered solely in terms of economic determination (Dalton 1977:208–209). This contrasts starkly with models of redistribution as a form of economic integration (e.g., Polanyi 1957; Sahlins 1958:248). Giving away food in ritual feasts or through prestation may have been as formidable a political process in prehistory as acquiring or distributing "wealth" in the form of craft goods or nonlocal resources, although the greater archaeological visibility of the latter has in many instances detracted attention from the former. The issue to be addressed is how subsistence economy and symbolic presentations of food were transformed through political actions involving "conventionally sanctioned eatables" (Malinowski 1961:187).

During the early eighteenth century in the Lower Mississippi Valley, the Natchez are reported to have held a "war feast" in which particular dishes of prepared foods were meticulously arranged (Swanton 1911:129–130). While cooked maize, deer, and dog had positive significations intended to be "consumed" by the warriors, other foods such as buffalo and fish had negative connotations and were apparently avoided. The ritual avoidance of fish in the Natchez war feast, also noted among the Cherokee, seems unusual considering the historical references to fish in the Central Mississippi Valley two centuries earlier (Elvas 1993:112, 117–118 [1557]; C. Hudson 1976:128, 158, 281). The use of fish in mortuary ceremonialism and representations in ceramic effigy vessels in the Central Mississippi Valley implies that ethnographic analogies with the Natchez may be only generally relevant, in that certain kinds of foods were imbued with meanings that were to be symbolically consumed (Rees 1997). As gift-giving was a central component in social relations of authority, the likelihood that fish were integral to political culture in the protohistoric Central Mississippi Valley suggests a historical trajectory somewhat unique in the Mississippian Southeast. In the context of ceremonial feasts or negotiations, gifts of fish may have represented a political currency available to chiefs in establishing or maintaining alliances, making restitution, or negotiating the termination of warfare (Dye 1995:306).

Previous models of Mississippian political economy have stressed prestige goods distribution and the mobilization of foodstuffs (J. A. Brown et al. 1990; Peregrine 1992; Steponaitis 1978; Welch 1991; Welch and Scarry 1995). The significance of maize has long been appreciated and associated with subsistence intensification, the emergence of social complexity, and ascribed social status (Griffin 1952b:361, 1985:59; D. F. Morse and Morse 1996a:11–12; B. D. Smith 1985:71–75, 1986:53–57; Steponaitis 1986:387–393). Recent studies of faunal remains have suggested that deer and other game animals were also important in ritual feasting and the provisioning of an elite (Bogan and Polhemus 1987; Jackson and Scott 1995a, 1995b; L. S. Kelly 1997; Michals 1990; Welch 1991). There is additional evidence to suggest that status-related differences in animal use and consumption may have included certain rare species of animals that legitimized and sanctified authority (Jackson and Scott 1995b). Rather than approaching subsistence economy from an adaptationist or systemic perspective, it is useful to examine the evidence for qualitative differences in local foodways as reflecting social heterogeneity in Mississippian political culture (Blau 1977; Crumley 1987, 1995; McGuire 1983; Stein 1998). An understanding of gift-giving as a political-symbolic transaction suggests a middle ground between a tributary mode of production and redistribution, in which certain kinds of foods served as politically legitimating "symbols of authority" (Pauketat 1997b:9). I turn now to a consideration of subsistence economy through an examination of the archaeological evidence from late prehistoric and protohistoric sites in the Southeast.

The Central Mississippi Valley

What is usually referred to as the Central Mississippi Valley was described by Phillips as comprising the northern and central divisions of the Lower Mississippi Alluvial Valley, ranging from the confluence of the Ohio River on the north to the Arkansas River on the south (Phillips et al. 1951:5–20). This includes the White and St. Francis river drainages and their tributaries in the western and eastern lowlands, a hydrographically complex region of braided stream surfaces, alluvial deposits, meander belts, minor drainages, and backwater sloughs separated by Crowley's Ridge and loosely bounded on the west and east by the Ozark Escarpment and loess bluffs of the Mississippi River (D. F. Morse and Morse 1983:1–13; Saucier 1994). While this topographic description suggests a formal or "homogeneous" region, it should be distinguished from a spatially or temporally defined range of social interactions based on archaeological evidence and historical documentation (Burton et al. 1996; Crumley 1979:143; Hassig 1996).

Available information on settlement patterns, site distributions, and material culture in the late prehistoric-protohistoric Central Mississippi Valley points toward the "interrelatedness of diverse elements," suggesting a functional or "heterogeneous" region—an interpretation also supported by available historical documentation (Crumley 1979:143; McNutt 1996b; D. F. Morse and Morse 1983, 1990a, 1996b). As Crumley (1979:143) suggests, this concept of region involves "an arbitrary areal classification whose limits are defined . . . for the purpose of studying phenomena within its boundaries." The Central Mississippi Valley is consequently defined here by a range of political-economic interactions that appear to be broadly reflected in archaeological complexes in the eastern and western lowlands and adjacent uplands (Griffin 1952c; Mainfort 1996, 1999; Mainfort and Moore 1998; D. F. Morse 1990; D. F. Morse and Morse 1983:271–301; P. A. Morse 1990). That individual phases do not precisely conform to a region is ultimately a problem of methodology and terminology on the part of archaeologists, as local groups integrated by political and economic interactions are by definition "regional" polities (Crumley 1979:143–145; Phillips 1970:923–940).

Subsistence Economy

The Upper Nodena site (3MS4) is located near a relict channel of the Mississippi River in Mississippi County, Arkansas (Figure 10.1). The site has undergone extensive excavations by avocational and professional archaeologists during the past century (D. F. Morse 1989, 1990). The Alabama Museum of Natural History and the University of Arkansas Museum conducted excavations at the site in 1932, focusing on the excavation of burials and recovery of artifacts (D. F. Morse 1989). Of the approximately 1,755 burials excavated during this time, only a small fraction of the skeletal remains were preserved for further study (D. Morse 1990:75; Powell 1989:65, 1990:99). Much of what is known about the Upper Nodena site is based on fragmentary evidence and secondary sources, including a map drawn from a photograph of a scale model (Figure 10.2; D. F. Morse 1989, 1990:70). Systematic analyses of Upper Nodena artifact assemblages have only recently begun to appear (Carroll 1997; Mainfort and Carroll 1996).

On the basis of available information, Upper Nodena was a multiple mound complex, with at least five mounds that appear to have been organized around a central plaza and enclosed by a palisade wall (D. F. Morse 1989:72–73; D. F. Morse and Morse 1983:287). A fortified, tightly nucleated village plan fits with historically documented descriptions for the provinces of Pacaha and Casqui during the mid-sixteenth century (Biedma 1993:238–240; Elvas 1993:113–120 [1557]; Rangel 1993:300–304). The Upper Nodena site occupation appears to date from approximately A.D. 1400 until the time of the de Soto expedition (D. F. Morse 1990:76–77). This is supported by late Mississippian ceramic assemblages, decorative ceramic styles, the recovery of Spanish trade goods in succeeding contexts at other sites, the absence of such items at Upper Nodena, and the scarcity of end scrapers (Brain 1985a; Dye 1998; Mainfort 1996; D. F. Morse and Morse 1983:287, 1996b:133; P. A. Morse 1981; Phillips 1970:933–936; Price and Price 1990). Occupation of

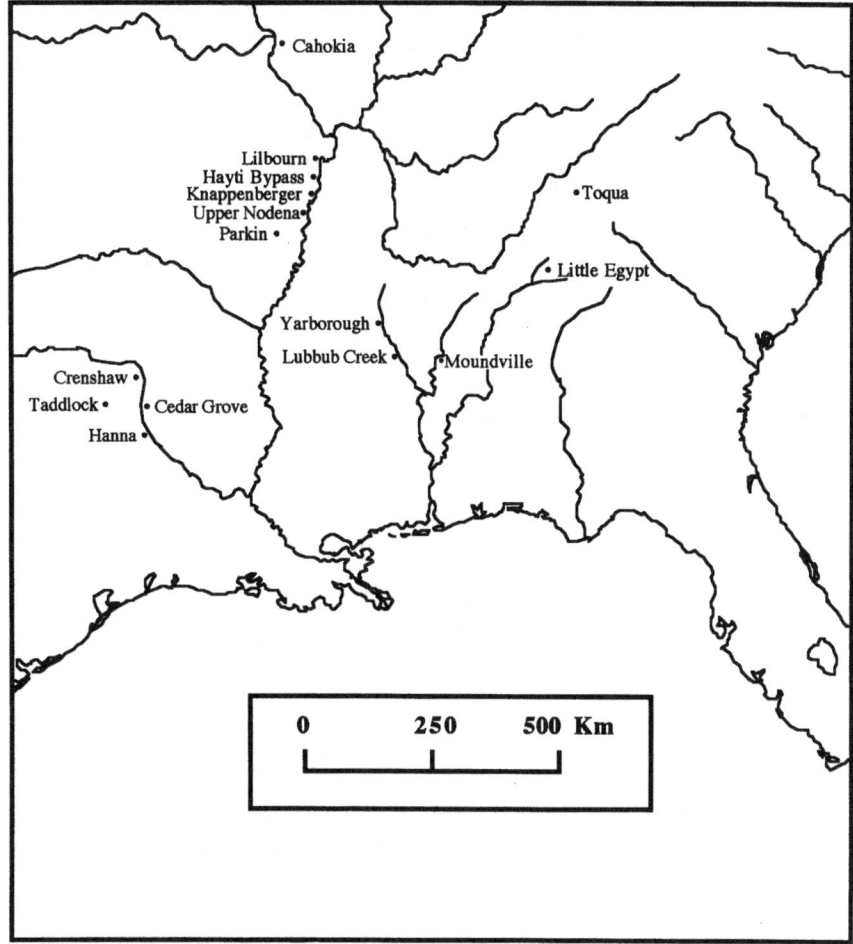

Figure 10.1 Locations of sites mentioned in the text.

the nearby Middle Nodena site (3MS3) appears to have occurred slightly later (D. F. Morse 1990:77, personal communication 1998).

In 1973 a combined Arkansas State University and University of Arkansas field school returned to the Upper Nodena site with the goal of obtaining information on settlement patterns, economic organization, and site structure (D. F. Morse 1973, 1989). Given the severity of site destruction and continued looting of sites in the region, assemblages from the 1973 excavations represent a crucial source of information on Nodena phase households and subsistence. The field school excavations at Upper Nodena focused on Blocks A, B, and C, located on the northeastern side of the site (see Figure 10.2). Late prehistoric and protohistoric deposits from

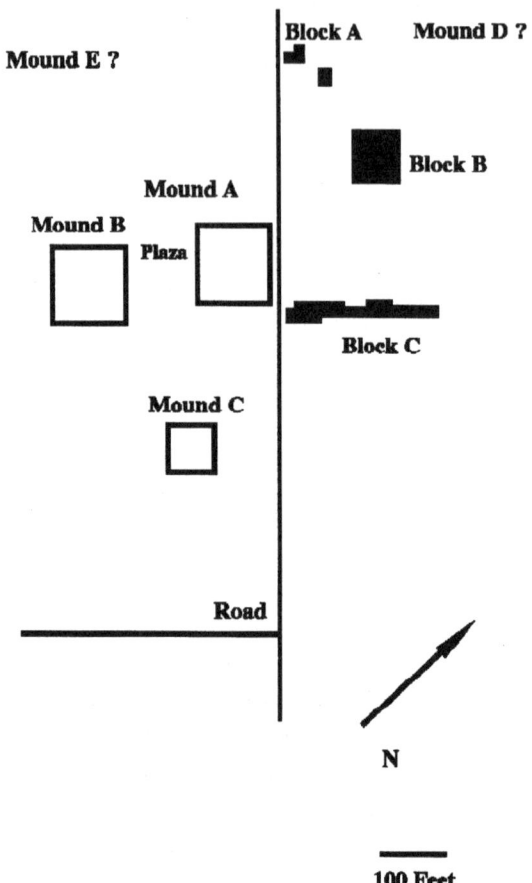

Figure 10.2 Map of the Upper Nodena site.

Block A appear to have been disturbed by historic buildings, indicated by the recovery of historic artifacts (D. F. Morse 1990:73). Trench excavations in Block C produced the greatest quantity of faunal remains during the 1973 field season. However, their context is uncertain. Here I focus on Block B, in which two superimposed episodes of wall-trench building were documented (Figure 10.3). The faunal remains from Block B appear to represent sequential domestic contexts within the first century and a half of the Nodena phase (ca. A.D. 1400–1650).

Based on the site reconstruction, Block B was located approximately 45 m north of Mound A. The first wall-trench structure measured approximately 5.3 by 5.2 m, while the second was slightly larger, 5.8 by 5.7 m. The Block B excavations covered an area of approximately 88.5 m. Midden in this area did not exceed a depth of 0.4 m (D. F. Morse 1989, 1990; D. F. Morse and P. A. Morse 1983:287). Large

Subsistence Economy and Political Culture / 185

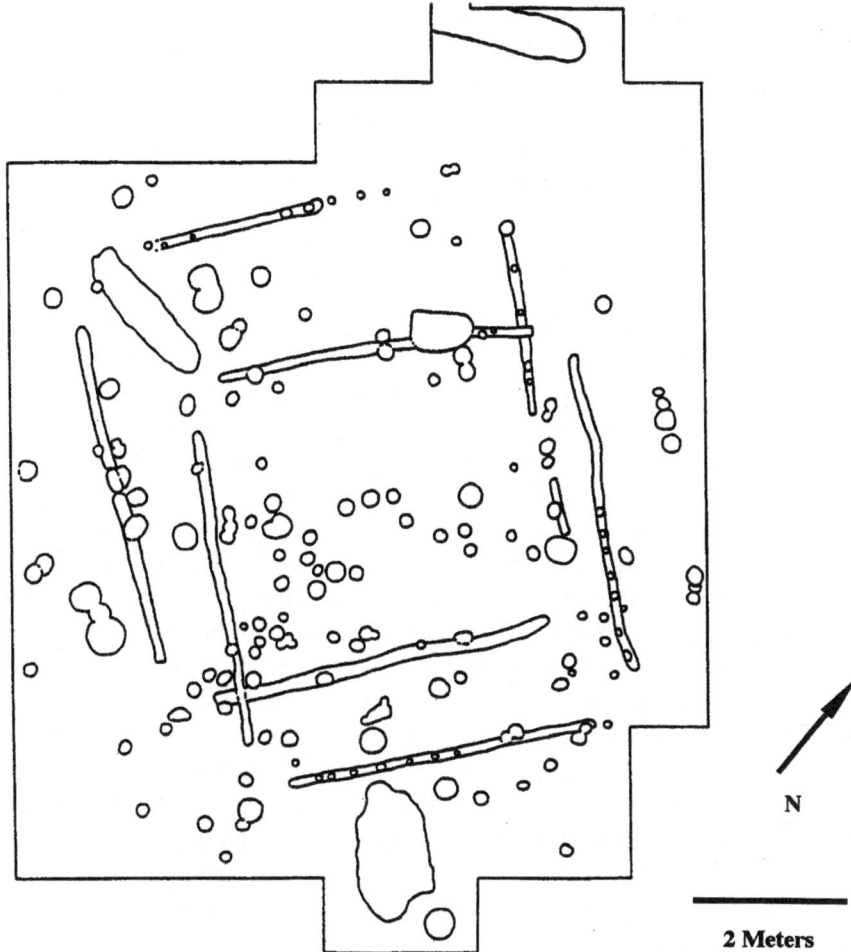

Figure 10.3 Plan view of the Block B excavations at the Upper Nodena site.

amounts of daub were recovered from Block B and interior roof supports of wall-trench buildings were represented by post molds (D. F. Morse 1990:74–75). Numerous features were documented within the wall trenches, including a burial and pit-shaped feature (Feature 1) that intruded into a northern wall.

Ethnobotanical remains from the Upper Nodena site include a large amount of burned maize, some of which was apparently from an above-ground granary or corn crib (D. F. Morse 1990:75). Beans (*Phaseolus vulgaris*), hickory nut shells (*Carya* sp.), persimmon seeds (*Diospyros virginiana*) and black walnut shells (*Juglans nigra*) were also recovered, along with small quantities of other wild plant foods. Maize from the corn crib exhibited relatively larger cobs and cupules, as well as a higher occurrence of 12-rowed cobs (Blake and Cutler 1979). Blake and Cutler (1979:53) interpreted intrasite variation in maize cupule and cob size as reflecting either differential selection for storage or the result of a "particularly competent family or group." While it is also conceivable that such variation was produced by feasting activities or the preferential provisioning of an elite, the social contexts of corn crib and village area have not been independently established (see Crabtree 1990:177; Welch and Scarry 1995).

Maize agriculture is well-documented in the de Soto narratives and skeletal analyses suggest that maize was a dietary staple at Upper Nodena (Powell 1989, 1990:113–115). While it might have provided food surpluses for regional centralization and demographic nucleation, it is no longer thought to be the prime mover in political consolidation and social complexity (Fritz 1992; Fritz and Kidder 1993; Kidder and Fritz 1993; Lopinot 1997; C. M. Scarry 1993a). Furthermore, ethnobotanical and bone chemistry analyses suggest variation in crop production and maize consumption throughout the Southeast (Greenlee 1998; C. M. Scarry 1993b). Recent analysis of skeletal data by Greenlee (1998:320) suggests greater variation between communities in the Central Mississippi Valley, as well as lower levels of maize consumption than elsewhere in the Mississippian Southeast (cf. Lynott et al. 1986). Given the documented occurrence of maize agriculture in the region, there are obvious political and economic variables that might account for such variation, including the role of different foods in feasting and gift-giving (cf. Greenlee 1998:323). Increased warfare among polities in the Central Mississippi Valley might have constrained the use of maize in ritual feasts or as a form of expedient political currency, just as alliances associated with the cessation of warfare might have led to increased availability of certain prestige goods or nonlocal items (cf. Dye 1995:293). Maize also might have been particularly vulnerable to raiding parties, as the Casquins are described as having destroying the crops of Pacaha, either in retaliation or as a strategic military maneuver (de la Vega 1993:400).

As recent studies of Mississippian subsistence have shown, animals also played a central role in status-related food consumption and political symbolism. Deer and preferential cuts of deer appear to have been particularly significant as a political medium of exchange, either in gift-giving, feasting, or in the provisioning of an elite (Blitz 1993a; Bogan 1983; Bogan and Polhemus 1987; Jackson and Scott 1995a, 1995b; L. S. Kelly 1997; Michals 1990; S. L. Scott 1982, 1983; Welch 1991:77–103). Ritual feasting, food storage, and food presentation in Mississippian societies appear to have taken place at specified locations, associated with platform mound ceremonialism and political-symbolic central places (Blitz 1993b; Knight 1989b; M. T. Smith and Williams 1994; Welch and Scarry 1995). Although subsistence data should ideally be associated with well-defined social contexts, inconsistent and unsystematic recovery techniques presently make this unfeasible. A more detailed, comparative analysis of faunal assemblages is hindered by poor preservation and the often fragmentary condition of the remains, as well as by inconsistent units of measurement used in archaeological site reports. Nonetheless, the overall importance of different kinds of foods in gift-giving, feasting, and the political mobilization of subsistence should be evident in the diversity of fauna at different sites, both in terms of the number of identified specimens (NISP) and relative percentages of major faunal classes recovered (e.g., L. S. Kelly 1997:73). While there are other more informative units of measurement, percent NISP of major faunal classes is a broadly applicable index that can be derived from the available data for comparative purposes (Brewer 1992; Grayson 1979, 1984).

The overall importance of deer is reflected in the faunal assemblages from three sites east of the Central Mississippi Valley, in which deer and unidentified large mammal elements comprise an overwhelming majority of the percent NISP for major faunal classes recovered (Figure 10.4). Faunal remains from the Little Egypt site in northwest Georgia, Lubbub Creek in west-central Alabama, and the Yarborough site in eastern Mississippi indicate the prominent role of deer in local subsistence economies (Roth 1980; S. L. Scott 1982, 1983). The Little Egypt and Lubbub Creek sites are both described as regional political-administrative mound centers, the latter located on the Tombigbee River and dating to the Summerville I–IV phases of ca. A.D. 1000–1600 (Blitz 1993a:56; Hally 1980; Jackson and Scott 1995b:112; Peebles 1983). The Little Egypt site is located on the Coosawattee River and has been associated with the protohistoric province of Coosa documented in the de Soto narratives (Hally 1980, 1994b; Hally et al. 1990; C. Hudson 1994; C. Hudson et al. 1985). The Yarborough site is a late Mississippian farmstead on a tributary of the Tombigbee River, dating to the second half of the fifteenth century (Jackson and Scott 1995a:184; Solis and Walling 1982:170). The faunal remains from these sites suggest the use of large and small mammals, reptiles, amphibians, and birds, as well as the relative de-emphasis of fish. There is additional evidence from Lubbub Creek and the Yarborough site suggesting the seasonal provisioning of an elite with deer meat (Jackson and Scott 1995b). As indicated by percent NISP for major faunal classes, local subsistence economies appear to be similar in terms of the kinds of animals being consumed at mound centers and farmsteads.

A relatively minor percent NISP of deer remains were recovered in the Upper Nodena site faunal assemblage, a trend noted during the 1973 excavations (D. F. Morse 1990:77). In Block B at Upper Nodena, identifiable elements of deer comprise approximately 1 percent NISP. Even when combined with unidentified large mammal specimens, many of which are most likely small fragments of deer elements, this increases to only 6.6 percent NISP (Figure 10.5). Other species of small mammal, including rabbit, squirrel, raccoon, coyote, and various unidentified mammal comprise approximately 11.7 percent NISP. In contrast, fish are the principal

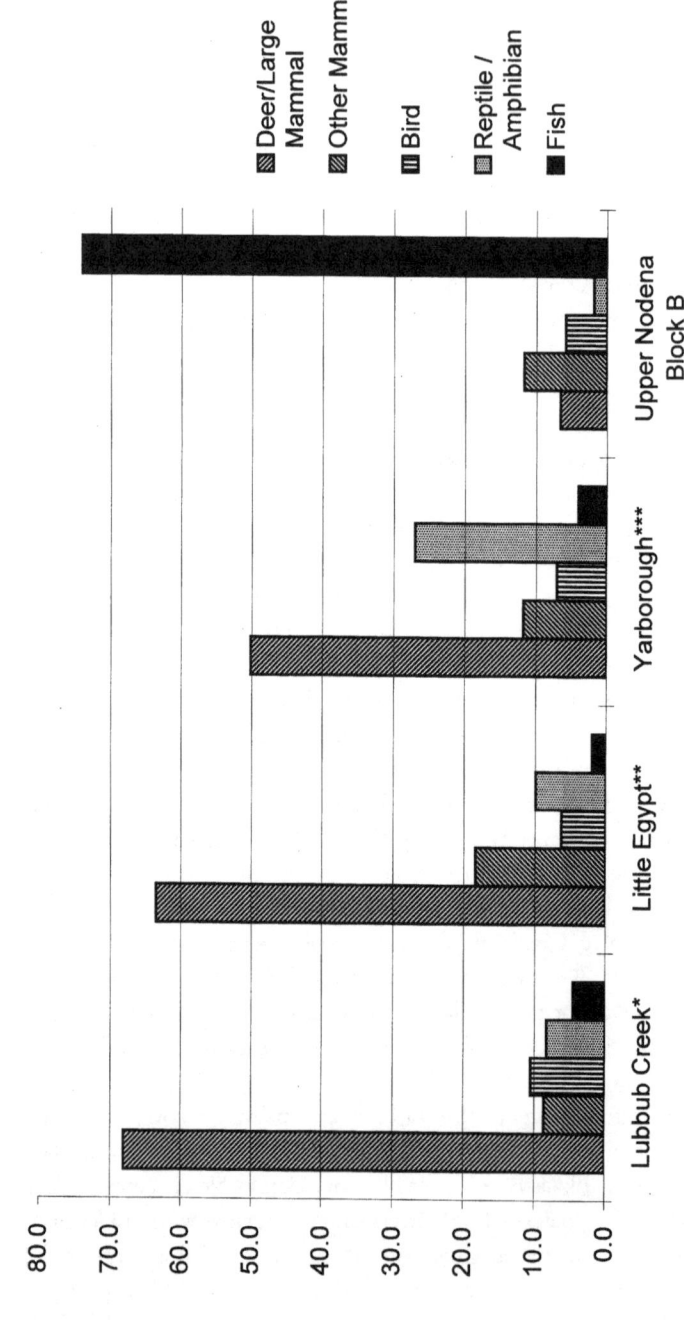

Figure 10.4 Percent NISP for faunal classes from various Mississippian sites (*Scott 1983; **Roth 1980; ***Scott 1982).

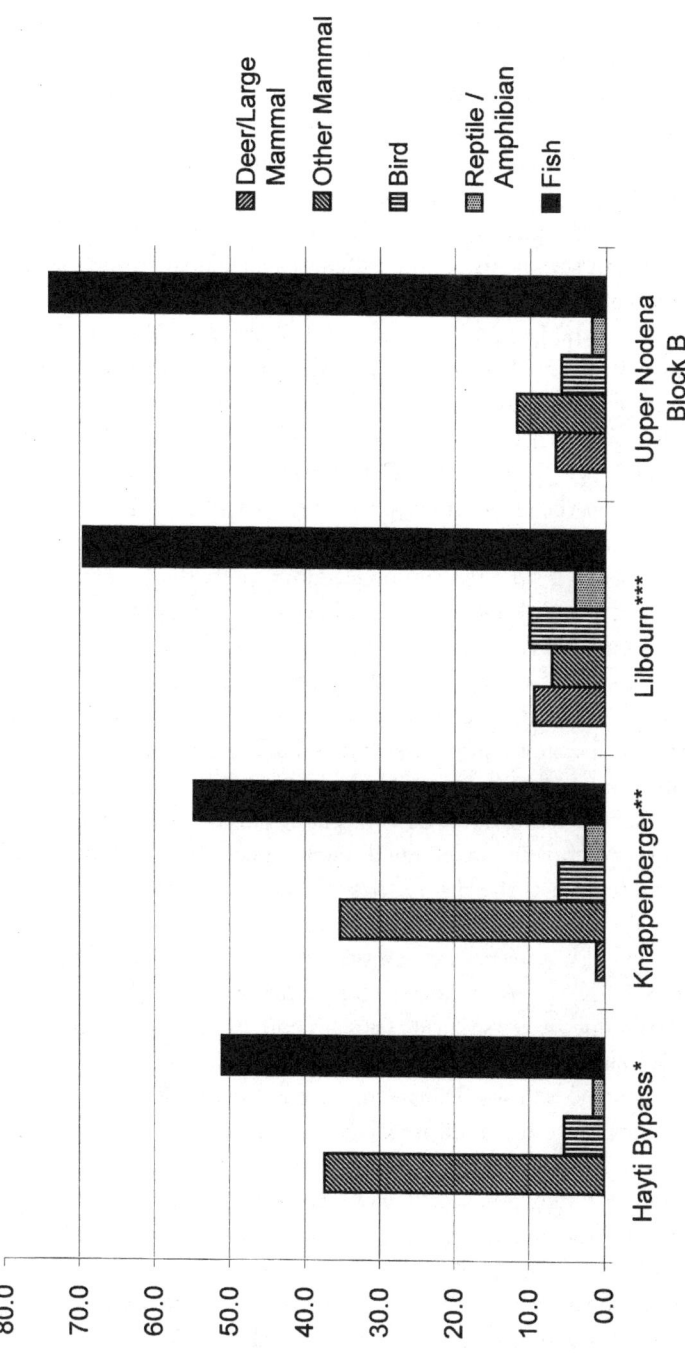

Figure 10.5 Percent NISP for major faunal classes from sites in the Central Mississippi Valley (*Deer/large mammal included as other mammal, in Yelton 1995:278; **Bogan 1974:74–75; ***Smith 1975:181–195).

taxa represented in Block B at Upper Nodena, at approximately 74 percent NISP. Various species of bird (5.9 percent NISP) and reptile and amphibian (1.8 percent NISP) comprise the remainder of identifiable taxa. While the relative quantity of fish is probably inflated by the fragmentary nature of these elements, their greater prevalence is particularly notable given their generally poorer preservation and the fact that recovery techniques are generally biased against the collection of smaller bone fragments (Casteel 1976; Colley 1990).

When comparing the percent NISP of major faunal classes from various contexts at Mississippian sites in the Central Mississippi Valley with the sites to the east, an unambiguous pattern begins to emerge (Figure 10.6). Faunal procurement and consumption in the late prehistoric Central Mississippi Valley is reflected in assemblages from the Hayti Bypass, Lilbourn, and Knappenberger sites, the latter of which is a single mound site located on a relict channel of the Mississippi River in northeast Arkansas. Knappenberger appears to have been partially contemporaneous with the Upper Nodena site (Bogan 1974; Klinger 1974; B. D. Smith 1975:175–195; Yelton 1995). Hayti Bypass has been described as a small Mississippian community, and the Lilbourn site is a large multi-mound center that has been the focus of investigations since the mid-nineteenth century (Conner et al. 1995:1; B. D. Smith 1975:175–181). Both are located on the Mississippi River flood plain in southeast Missouri. Occupations at Hayti Bypass span the Woodland and early Mississippian periods, ca. A.D. 0–1000, while those at Lilbourn are slightly later, between ca. A.D. 1000 and 1350 (Conner et al. 1995:1; D. F. Morse and P. A. Morse 1983:249; B. D. Smith 1975:175–177; cf. Lafferty and Price 1996:13).

Fish remains comprise between 51 and 69 percent NISP from these sites, while deer and large mammal elements are notably sparse. This trend is even more apparent where recovery techniques were geared toward systematic sampling of features for smaller faunal remains at the Hayti Bypass and Upper Nodena sites (e.g., Yelton 1995:278–281). In Feature 1 at the Upper Nodena site, from which a soil sample was water-screened, fish elements were particularly abundant, comprising approximately 86.6 percent NISP. The position of this feature in the northern wall trench of the second structure suggests that it postdates both building episodes. The cranium of a mink (*Mustela vison*) was also recovered from Feature 1, in a context with otherwise few mammal remains. Differential preservation of fish elements in this feature does not appear to be a mitigating factor in the percent NISP of major faunal classes represented, particularly since elements of other taxa were recovered (cf. Yelton 1995:275). Flotation sampling of a basin-shaped pit (Feature 63) associated with the Mississippian occupation at Hayti Bypass similarly yielded 73.8 percent NISP of fish (Yelton 1995:288).

Given the dissimilar hydrographic environments of the site assemblages represented in Figures 10.5 and 10.6, it is tempting to conclude that regional differences in percent NISP of major faunal classes merely reflect ecological variation in local

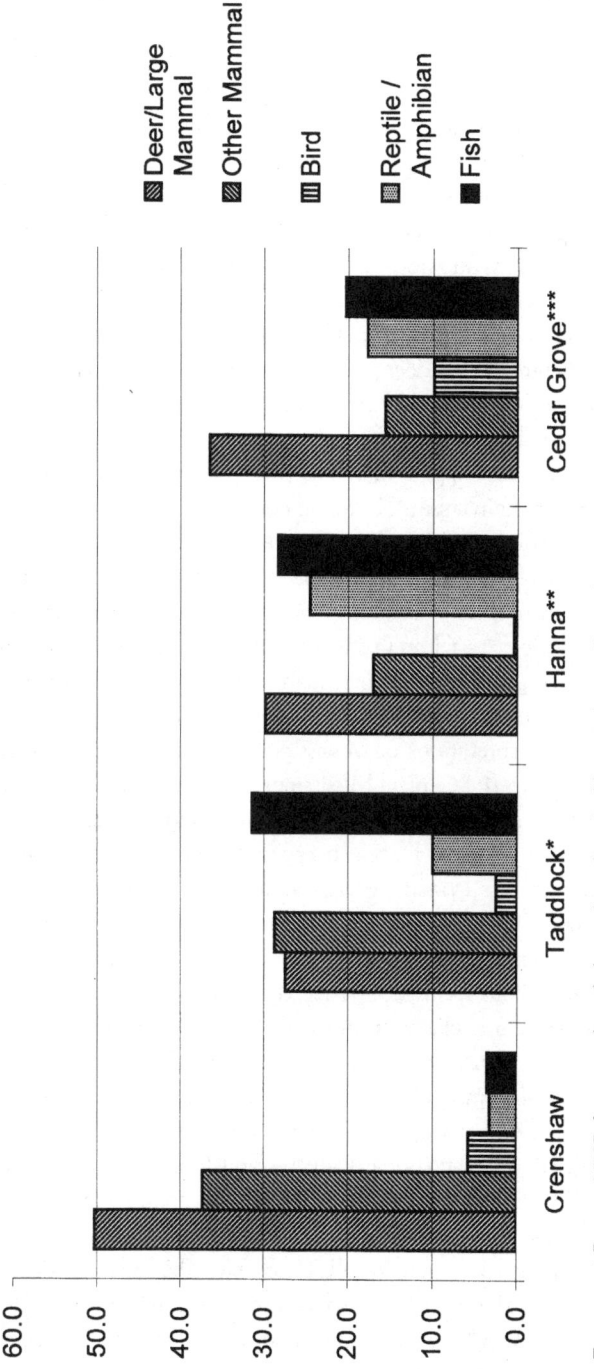

Figure 10.6 Percent NISP for major faunal classes from four Caddo sites (*Perttula et al. 1982; **Byrd 1980; ***Styles and Purdue 1984; in Jackson and Scott 1995b:112).

subsistence economies. Cursory examination of faunal assemblages dating from earlier time periods at sites in the Red and Mississippi river valleys lends little support for this argument. Fish remains are notably scarce in an early Caddo (ca. A.D. 900–1100) faunal assemblage from the multi-mound Crenshaw site on the Red River, whereas they occur more frequently in the assemblages from three Caddo residential sites (Figure 10.6; K. M. Byrd 1980; Perttula et al. 1982; Styles and Purdue 1984; in Jackson and Scott 1995b:109–112). Given the location of the Crenshaw site on an abandoned channel of the Red River, Jackson and Scott (1995b:111) attribute the paucity of fish remains and non-mammalian taxa at the Crenshaw site to "ritual proscriptions which largely precluded their consumption." It is notable that deer appear to have had a ceremonial or political-symbolic significance, as reflected in the provisioning of preferential deer parts, the percent NISP of major faunal classes, and recovery of deer antlers at the Crenshaw site (Jackson and Scott 1995b:109–112; Schambach 1982).

In contrast to the Mississippian faunal assemblages from Hayti Bypass and Upper Nodena, the faunal remains from Woodland contexts at Hayti Bypass are conspicuous for the relative paucity of fish elements (Figure 10.7; Yelton 1995:281). Flotation sampling at the Hayti Bypass site emphasizes even more clearly a proportionate increase in fish consumption between Woodland and Mississippian occupations (Yelton 1995:279–289). As Yelton (1995:287, 289) states, this may indicate a trend toward the harvesting of fish in larger quantities, even as "the representation of bird, reptile, and amphibian remains does not drastically change." This tends to support prevalent interpretations of Mississippian subsistence and settlement patterns, based on work in the Central Mississippi Valley by Bruce Smith (1975:121–146) that suggests a riverine-floodplain adaptation and annual cycle of seasonal animal exploitation (see also B. D. Smith 1978b, 1978c; 1985). Similarities in subsistence economy are less evident when the faunal assemblages from sites in the Central Mississippi Valley are contrasted with those from the Tombigbee, Coosawattee, and Red River drainages.

Temporal variations in local subsistence economy are also reflected in the percent NISP for major faunal classes from the Cahokia site in the American Bottom (Figure 10.4). Located south of the confluence of the Mississippi and Missouri rivers, Cahokia was a multi-mound center of such enormity and influence that it has redefined and exceeded characterizations of the Mississippian Southeast (Anderson 1997; Knight 1997; Pauketat 1997a; Pauketat and Emerson 1997b). In emergent Mississippian Edelhardt phase (ca. A.D. 1000–1050) contexts from Cahokia, fish remains are extremely well represented at approximately 77 percent NISP, but they decrease proportionally to 10 percent NISP following the rapid political consolidation of the Lohmann phase (ca. A.D. 1050–1100) (Figure 10.7; L. S. Kelly 1997; see Pauketat 1994, 1997a). At the same time, the NISP for deer increases from approximately 6 percent to 63 percent. Lucretia Kelly (1997:79–82) suggests that

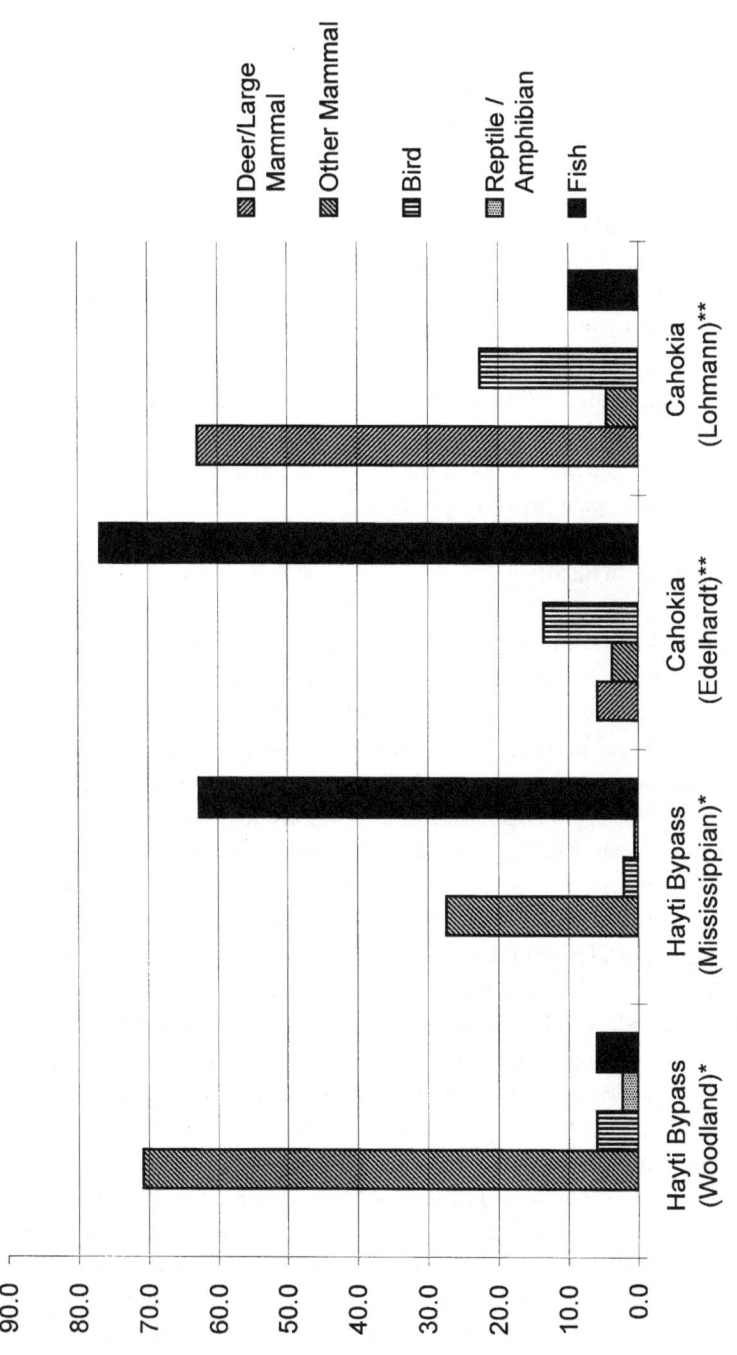

Figure 10.7 Percent NISP for major faunal classes from Hayti bypass and Cahokia sites (*Deer/large mammal included as other mammal, flotation sample in Yelton 1995:281; **Kelly 1997:79, reptile/amphibian not included).

this reflects a proportionate increase in consumption of deer meat and that additional evidence indicates the provisioning of a Cahokian elite with preferential cuts of deer. This contrasts sharply with the increased use of fish and aquatic resources following the Woodland-Mississippian transition in the Central Mississippi Valley, as well as documentary and archaeological evidence for the importance of fish at Upper Nodena (Rees 1997; Yelton 1995:286). In light of the preceding comparisons, systemic definitions of Mississippianism as an "adaptive niche" with a "similar subsistence subsystem" no longer seem sufficient to explain variations in subsistence economy (B. D. Smith 1978c:486). While it may still be tempting to posit an ecological "prime mover" in each of these instances, the complexity of temporal and spatial variations in the Central Mississippi Valley and throughout the Southeast suggests that local subsistence economies were purposefully mediated through regional political culture. While the long-term consequences may have been unintended, people clearly brought to bear the preexisting intentions, expectations, and inclinations of different regional traditions. In doing so, they reproduced and transformed Mississippian political culture.

Summary and Conclusion

Just as the significance of maize and maize agriculture in southeastern societies has recently come under reexamination (e.g., Fritz 1992; Lopinot 1997; Rose et al. 1991:21; C. M. Scarry 1993b:90), it is worthwhile to unpack the wide range of regional political and economic dynamics associated with Mississippian culture, subsistence, and settlement patterns in order to assess long-term historical development in terms of social heterogeneity and political action. Systemic-processual and eco-functionalist approaches are generally inadequate in accounting for the historical trajectories of regional polities. Studies of prehistoric political economy have thus moved away from adaptationist perspectives toward a consideration of the variable sources of political power (Brumfiel and Earle 1987; e.g., articles in Earle 1991a and 1997). While various economic models have been proposed, research should be guided by an understanding of the interrelatedness of political-symbolic and economic factors. A historical-processual perspective is based on the methodological advances of culture historical and systemic processual archaeology, recognizing that regional variations in political economy are not reducible to ecological systems, cultural adaptation and homogeneity, or economic institutions.

The regional development and decline of Mississippian polities involved historical variations in political economy and ideology that defy simplistic taxonomic categories and functionalist concepts of cultural adaptation (Pauketat 1992). Rather than investigate whether certain archaeological complexes represent certain stages or types of sociopolitical complexity and were thus similar, it will be more productive to explore the political-symbolic processes that affected long-term historical trajectories. The historical development of cultural traditions is ultimately a political process in which local level, regional, and macro-regional interactions should be understood in terms of political culture and human agency. This historically situated political process, referred to by Sahlins (1985:152) as the "structure of the conjuncture," presents archaeologists with a multi-scalar, anthropological approach to the study of noncapitalist political economy (cf. Giddens 1979:49–95). Concern for political culture should not be mistaken for cultural relativism or methodological individualism (Giddens 1979:95). The concept of regional political culture unites economy and ideology or "materialist and idealist traditions" through an examination of power relations and political actions (Barker and Pauketat 1992a:3; Pauketat 1992:34).

From this perspective, the emergence and decline of Mississippian polities in the late prehistoric and protohistoric Southeast can be understood as the long-term, historical development of regional political culture. Political culture in the Central Mississippi Valley involved the purposeful manipulation of local subsistence economies and social relations—what has been referred to as staple finance and redistribution. The analysis of faunal remains from the Upper Nodena site suggests that fish played a central role in local subsistence economy. Relying on a comparison of percent NISP for major faunal classes at various sites throughout the Southeast, it is suggested that the importance of fish in local subsistence economy was directly related to regional political culture in the Central Mississippi Valley. In light of ethnological perspectives of gift-giving, an event described in the narratives of the de Soto expedition holds particular significance. Gifts of fish represented a political-symbolic medium of exchange in which social relations of authority were actively negotiated and reproduced.

While Mississippian elite were provisioned with maize and deer in some regions of the Southeast, gifts of fish appear to have held symbolic capital in the late prehistoric and protohistoric Central Mississippi Valley, either in the provisioning of an elite or competitive feasting. In the context of regional warfare and alliances, this political currency was the basis for a range of social interactions that had the potential to transform social relations of authority. Subsistence economy and political culture were thus interrelated through human agency as a historical dialectic, in which regional centralization confronted the decentralizing tendencies of political factionalism and conflict (Anderson 1994a; Brumfiel 1989, 1994, 1995; Helms 1994; Marquardt 1992; Pauketat 1992:40–43; Saitta 1994; C. S. Spencer 1994). From this perspective, the development and decline of Mississippian polities can be understood as "a chain of historically linked events" in which multi-scalar political-symbolic interactions or "linkages" defined the nature of those relationships (Knight 1997:234). While geographically expansive polities such as Cahokia and Moundville appear to have forged somewhat parallel historical trajectories culminating in regional stability (Knight 1997), other Mississippian polities were fraught with political conflict, warfare, and instability (Anderson 1990, 1994b; cf. J. F. Scarry 1990a). Through examining the archaeological correlates of subsistence economy it is possible to begin to understand the range of regional variations in Mississippian political culture, variations in ideology and identity that ultimately constituted divergent historical trajectories of development and decline (Friedman 1992).

The idea that historical and processual explanations provide complementary lines of inquiry in archaeology is not new (e.g., Trigger 1978:28–36; Willey 1985). Productive application of this approach to the study of regional political culture requires that archaeologists critically reassess programmatic caricatures of culture history as overly particularistic. In order to address political process from prehistory to protohistory, more fine-grained regional chronologies are needed and comparable data on subsistence economy must be associated with discrete archaeological contexts. By bringing together knowledge of long-term historical trajectories and concern for political culture and process, archaeologists can yet make unique contributions to contemporary anthropological theory.

This paper began with an observation by Phillips on the importance of identifying "living peoples" with the late prehistory of the Southeast; his remark is all the more prescient in light of recent debates regarding the cultural patrimony of the past (Phillips et al. 1951:347; e.g., McGuire 1992b; Zimmerman 1989). The identification of archaeological sites and material culture with historic tribes is an immense task that has barely begun (e.g., M. P. Hoffman 1990, 1993; cf. D. F. Morse 1991; D. F. Morse and P. A. Morse 1996b:133–134). Nevertheless, it is important to recognize the relevance of human agency in historical processualism (Pauketat 2001b). While determination of cultural affiliation is often problematic, it may be even more advantageous to archaeology as a historical, anthropological science to begin addressing the Native American past as an integral part of American cultural history (e.g., Pauketat 2001a; Pauketat and Emerson 1997a:278; Trigger 1980:672–673, 1984:287–295; Wolf 1974). Although protohistoric Mississippian societies were "nine-tenths submerged in the prehistoric past" (Phillips 1970:19), a focus on regional political culture counterbalances subsequent histories of European encroachment, demographic disintegration, and colonialism. Because protohistoric archaeology crosses the threshold between prehistory and history, it is ideally situated to pursue the goals of historical processualism.

Acknowledgments

An earlier version of this paper was presented in a symposium on protohistory and archaeology at the 54th annual meeting of the Southeastern Archaeological Conference in Baton Rouge, Louisiana, November 5–8, 1997. I would like to thank Cameron Wesson for co-chairing the symposium and working to make this publication a reality. I am indebted to Dan Morse for his suggestion that I look at the Upper Nodena site collections and I appreciate his and Phyllis's generosity and hospitality and encouragment. Dan Morse also provided comments on the manuscript. Timothy Pauketat offered critical insight, making my thoughts and writing more intelligible. The Oklahoma Archeological Survey generously provided access to its comparative faunal collections. I would like to acknowledge the assistance of Jeremy Watson in the analysis of faunal remains from the Upper Nodena site. This research was supported by grants from the University of Oklahoma Graduate College and Graduate Student Senate. As always, my research benefited from the encouragement and inspiration of Johanna, Sarah, and Jennifer Rees.

References

Abler, T. B.
1989   European Technology and the Art of War in Iroquoia. In *Cultures in Conflict: Current Archaeological Perspectives*, edited by D. C. Tkaczuk and B. C. Vivian, pp. 273–282. Archaeological Association of the University of Calgary, Calgary.

Adair, J.
1930   [1775] *History of the American Indians*. Edited by S. Williams. Originally published by Charles Dilley, London. Reprinted by Watauga Press, Johnson City, Tennessee.

Adams, P. G.
1967   [1929] Introduction to the Dover edition of William Byrd's *Histories of the Dividing Line Betwixt Virginia and North Carolina*. Reprinted. Dover, New York.
1980   *Travelers and Travel Liars 1660–1800*. Dover, New York.

Adkins, L., and R. A. Adkins
1982   *A Thesaurus of British Archaeology*. David and Charles, London.

Aharon, P.
1982   Stable Oxygen and Carbon Isotope Technique in Archaeology and Museum Studies: A Review. In *Archaeometry: An Australian Perspective*, edited by W. Ambrose and P. Duerden, pp. 156–172. Australian National University Press, Canberra.

Ames, K. M.
1995   Chiefly Power and Household Production on the Northwest Coast. In *Foundations of Social Inequality*, edited by G. M. Feinman, pp. 155–187. Plenum Press, New York.

Anderson, D. G.
1990   Stability and Change in Chiefdom-Level Societies: An Examination of Mississippian Political Evolution on the South Atlantic Slope. In M. Williams and Shapiro, eds., *Lamar Archaeology*, pp. 187–213.
1994a   Factional Competition and the Political Evolution of Mississippian Chiefdoms in the Southeastern United States. In Brumfiel and Fox, eds., *Factional Competition*, pp. 61–76.
1994b   *The Savannah River Chiefdoms: Political Change in the Late Prehistoric Southeast*. University of Alabama Press, Tuscaloosa.
1996a   Chiefly Cycling and Large Scale Abandonments as Viewed from the Savannah River Basin. In J. F. Scarry, ed., *Political Structure and Change*, pp. 150–191.
1996b   Fluctuations between Simple and Complex Chiefdoms: Cycling in the Late

Prehistoric Southeast. In J. F. Scarry, ed., *Political Structure and Change*, pp. 231–252.
1997 The Role of Cahokia in the Evolution of Southeastern Mississippian Society. In Pauketat and Emerson, eds., *Cahokia*, pp. 248–268.

Anderson, D. G., D. J. Hally, and J. L. Rudolph
1986 The Mississippian Occupation of the Savannah River Valley. *Southeastern Archaeology* 5:32–51.

Anderson, D. G., and J. Schuldenrein (editors)
1985 *Prehistoric Human Ecology along the Upper Savannah River: Excavations at the Rucker's Bottom, Abbeville, and Bullard Site Groups*. Russell Papers 1985, Archaeological Services-Atlanta. National Park Service, Atlanta.

Anderson, D. G., D. W. Stahle, and M. K. Cleaveland
1995 Paleoclimate and the Potential Food Reserves of Mississippian Societies: A Case Study from the Savannah River Valley. *American Antiquity* 60:258–286.

Anghiera, P. M. d'
1964 *Decades del Nuevo Mundo*. Edited by E. O'Gorman. Porrua, Mexico City.

Archer, M. S.
1996 *Culture and Agency: The Place of Culture in Social Theory*. Cambridge University Press, Cambridge.

Ashley, K. H.
1988 Effects of European and American Colonization of the Southeast on Upper Creek Settlement Patterns: 1700–1800. Unpublished Master's thesis, Department of Anthropology, Florida State University, Tallahassee.

Ashmore, W., and R. Wilk
1988 Household and Community in the Mesoamerican Past. In *Household and Community in the Mesoamerican Past*, edited by W. Ashmore and R. Wilk, pp. 1–27. University of New Mexico Press, Albuquerque.

Aten, L. E.
1983 *Indians of the Upper Texas Coast*. Academic Press, New York.

Avalle-Arce, J. B.
1997 Gonzalo Fernández de Oviedo y Valdés: Chronicler of the Indies. In Galloway, ed., *Hernando de Soto Expedition*, pp. 369–379.

Avery, G.
1996 Eighteenth-Century Spanish, French, and Caddoan Interactions as Seen from Los Adaes. *Journal of Northeast Texas Archaeology* 7:27–68.

Axtell, J.
1979 Ethnohistory: An Historian's Viewpoint. *Ethnohistory* 26:1–13.
1981 *The European and the Indian: Essays in the Ethnohistory of Colonial North America*. Oxford University Press, New York.
1992 *Beyond 1492: Encounters in Colonial North America*. Oxford University Press, New York.
1997 *The Indians' New South: Cultural Change in the Colonial Southeast*. Louisiana State University Press, Baton Rouge.

Baden, W. W.
1983 *Tomotley: An Eighteenth-Century Cherokee Village*. University of Tennessee, Department of Anthropology Report of Investigations 36, Knoxville.

Badger, R. R., and L. A. Clayton (editors)
1985 *Alabama and the Borderlands: From Prehistory to Statehood*. University of Alabama Press, Tuscaloosa.

Baker, B. J., and L. Kealhofer
1996a   Assessing the Impact of European Contact on Aboriginal Populations. In Baker and Kealhofer, eds., *Bioarchaeology*, pp. 1–14.
Baker, B. J., and L. Kealhofer (editors)
1996b   *Bioarchaeology of Native American Adaptation in the Spanish Borderlands.* University Press of Florida, Gainesville.
Barker, A. W.
1992   Powhatan's Pursestrings: On the Meaning of Surplus in a Seventeenth-Century Algonkian Chiefdom. In Barker and Pauketat, eds., *Lords of the Southeast*, pp. 61–80.
Barker, A. W., and T. R. Pauketat
1992a   Introduction: Social Inequality and the Native Elites of Southeastern North America. In Barker and Pauketat, eds., *Lords of the Southeast*, pp. 1–10.
Barker, A. W., and T. R. Pauketat (editors)
1992b   *Lords of the Southeast: Social Inequality and the Native Elites of Southeastern North America.* Archaeological Papers of the American Anthropological Association Number 3. American Anthropological Association, Washington, D.C.
Barton, C. M.
1997   Preface. In Barton and Clark, eds., *Rediscovering Darwin*, pp. iii–v.
Barton, C. M., and G. A. Clark
1997a   Evolutionary Theory in Archaeological Explanation. In Barton and Clark, eds., *Rediscovering Darwin*, pp. 3–18.
Barton, C. M., and G. A. Clark (editors)
1997b   *Rediscovering Darwin: Evolutionary Theory and Archaeological Explanation.* Archaeological Papers of the American Anthropological Association No. 7. American Anthropological Association, Arlington, Virginia.
Bartram, W.
1853   *Observations on the Creek and Cherokee Indians.* Transactions of the American Ethnological Society 3.
1955   [1791] *Travels of William Bartram.* Edited by M. Van Doren. Reprint of 1928 Macy-Masius edition. Originally published by James & Johnson, Philadelphia. Reprinted by Dover, New York.
Beaudry, M. C. (editor)
1988   *Documentary Archaeology in the New World.* Cambridge University Press, Cambridge.
Beaudry, M. C., L. J. Cooke, and S. A. Mrozowski
1991   Artifacts and Active Voices: Material Culture as Social Discourse. In *The Archaeology of Inequality*, edited by R. H. McGuire and R. Paynter, pp. 150–191. Basil Blackwell, Cambridge.
Beck, R. A., Jr.
1997   From Joara to Chiaha: Spanish Exploration of the Appalachian Summit Area, 1540–1568. *Southeastern Archaeology* 16:162–169.
Bender, B.
1989   The Roots of Inequality. In D. Miller et al., eds., *Domination and Resistance*, pp. 83–95.
Benson, A. B. (editor)
1987   *Peter Kalm's Travels in North America: The English Version of 1770.* Dover, New York.

Beverley, R.
1947 [1705] *The History and Present State of Virginia.* Edited by L. B. Wright. University of North Carolina Press, Chapel Hill.

Biedma, L. H. de
1993 Relation of the Island of Florida. Translated and edited by J. E. Worth. In Clayton et al., eds., *De Soto Chronicles,* Vol. 1, pp. 221–246.

Binford, L. R.
1962 Archaeology as Anthropology. *American Antiquity* 28:217–225.
1965 Archaeological Systematics and the Study of Cultural Process. *American Antiquity* 31:203–210.
1968 Some Comments on Historical versus Processual Archaeology. *Southwestern Journal of Anthropology* 24:267–275.

Bintliff, J.
1991 The Contribution of Annaliste/Structural History Approach to Archaeology. In *Annales School and Archaeology,* edited by J. Bintliff, pp. 1–33. Leicester University Press, New York.

Blake, L. W.
1981 Early Acceptance of Watermelon by Indians of the United States. *Journal of Ethnobiology* 1:193–199.
1986 Corn and Other Plants from Prehistory into History in the Eastern United States. In *The Protohistoric Period in the Mid-South: 1500–1700.* Proceedings of the 1983 Mid-South Archaeological Conference, edited by D. H. Dye and R. C. Brister, pp. 3–13. Archaeological Report No. 18. Mississippi Department of Archives and History, Jackson.

Blake, L. W., and H. C. Cutler
1979 Plant Remains from the Upper Nodena Site (3MS4). *Arkansas Archaeologist* 20:53–58.

Blakely, R. L. (editor)
1988 *The King Site.* University of Georgia Press, Athens.

Blakely, R. L., and B. Detweiler-Blakely
1989 The Impact of European Diseases in the Sixteenth-Century Southeast: A Case Study. *Midcontinental Journal of Archaeology* 14:62–89.

Bland, E.
1966 [1651] *The Discovery of New Brittaine.* Readex Microprint Edition.

Blanton, R. E., G. M. Feinman, S. A. Kowalewski, and P. N. Peregrine
1996 A Dual-Processual Theory for the Evolution of Mesoamerican Civilization. *Current Anthropology* 37:1–14.

Blau, P. M.
1977 *Inequality and Heterogeneity: A Primitive Theory of Social Structure.* Free Press, New York.

Blitz, J. H.
1988 Adoption of the Bow in Prehistoric North America. *North American Archaeologist* 9:123–145.
1993a *Ancient Chiefdoms of the Tombigbee.* University of Alabama Press, Tuscaloosa.
1993b Big Pots for Big Shots: Feasting and Storage in a Mississippian Community. *American Antiquity* 58:80–96.
1999 Mississippian Chiefdoms and the Fission-Fusion Process. *American Antiquity* 64:577–592.

Bogan, A. E.
1974   Appendix II: A Preliminary Faunal Sample from the Knappenberger Site (3MS53). *Arkansas Archeologist* 15:73–75.
1983   Evidence for Faunal Resource Partitioning in an Eastern North American Chiefdom. In *Animals and Archaeology 1: Hunters and Their Prey*, edited by J. Clutton-Brock and C. Grigson, pp. 305–324. BAR International Series, No. 163. Oxford.

Bogan, A. E., and R. R. Polhemus
1987   Faunal Analysis. In *The Toqua Site: A Late Mississippian Dallas Phase Town*, edited by R. R. Polhemus, pp. 971–1111. University of Tennessee, Department of Anthropology, Report of Investigations No. 41, Tennessee Valley Authority Publications in Anthropology No. 44, Knoxville.

Booker, K. M., C. M. Hudson, and R. L. Rankin
1992   Place Name Identification and Multilingualism in the Sixteenth-Century Southeast. *Ethnohistory* 39:399–451.

Borah, W.
1964   America as Model: The Demographic Impact of European Expansion upon the Non-European World. *Actas y Memorias del XXXV Congresso Internacional de Americanistas*, Mexico, 1962, 3:79–87.

Bourdieu, P.
1977   *Outline of a Theory of Practice*. Translated by R. Nice. Cambridge University Press, Cambridge.
1980   *The Logic of Practice*. Translated by R. Nice. Stanford University Press, Stanford.

Boyd, D. C., and C. C. Boyd
1992   Late Woodland Mortuary Variability in Virginia. In *Middle and Late Woodland Research in Virginia: A Synthesis*, edited by T. Reinhart and M. E. Hodges, pp. 249–276. Special Publication 29. Archaeological Society of Virginia, Richmond.

Boyd, D. K.
1997   *Caprock Canyonlands Archeology: A Synthesis of the Late Prehistory and History of Lake Alan Henry and the Texas Panhandle-Plains*. Report of Investigations No. 110. 2 vols. Prewitt and Associates, Austin.

de Brahm, J. W. G.
1928   John William Gerard DeBrahm's Account. In S. C. Williams, ed., *Early Travels*, pp. 187–194.

Brain, J. P.
1985a The Archaeology of the Hernando de Soto Expedition. In Badger and Clayton, eds., *Alabama and the Borderlands*, pp. 96–107.
1985b Introduction: Update of De Soto Studies since the United States De Soto Expedition Commission Report. In *Final Report of the United States De Soto Expedition Commission*, by John R. Swanton, pp. xi–lxxii. Smithsonian Classics of Anthropology reprint, originally issued 1939. Smithsonian Institution Press, Washington, D.C.
1988   *Tunica Archaeology*. Harvard University, Papers of the Peabody Museum of American Archaeology and Ethnology 77, Cambridge.

Brain, J. P., and P. Phillips
1996   *Shell Gorgets: Styles of the Late Prehistoric and Protohistoric Southeast*. Peabody Museum Press, Cambridge, Massachusetts.

Brain, J. P., A. Toth, and A. Rodriguez-Buckingham
1974 Ethnohistoric Archaeology and the de Soto Entrada into the Lower Mississippi Valley. *Conference on Historic Site Archaeology Papers* 7:232–289.

Braley, C. O., L. D. O'Steen, and I. R. Quitmyer
1986 Archaeological Investigations at 9MC141, Harris Neck National Wildlife Refuge, McIntosh County, Georgia. Southeastern Archaeological Services, Athens, Georgia.

Brasser, T. J.
1978 Early Indian-European Contacts. In *Handbook of North American Indians*, vol. 15, *Northeast*, edited by B. G. Trigger, pp. 78–88. Smithsonian Institution Press, Washington, D.C.

Braudel, F.
1980 *On History*. Translated by S. Matthews. University of Chicago Press, Chicago.

Braun, D. P.
1990 Selection and Evolution in Nonhierarchical Organization. In *The Evolution of Political Systems: Sociopolitics in Small-Scale Sedentary Societies*, edited by S. Upham, pp. 62–86. Cambridge University Press, Cambridge.

Braund, K. E. H.
1993 *Deerskins and Duffels: The Creek Indian Trade with Anglo-America, 1685–1815*. University of Nebraska Press, Lincoln.

Brettell, C. B.
1986 Introduction: Travel Literature, Ethnography, and Ethnohistory. *Ethnohistory* 33:127–138.

Brewer, D. J.
1992 Zooarchaeology: Method, Theory, and Goals. *Archaeological Method and Theory* 4:195–244.

Bridges, P. S., K. P. Jacobi, and M. L. Powell
1999 Warfare-Related Trauma in the Late Prehistory of Alabama. In *Bioarchaeological Studies of Life in the Age of Agriculture*, edited by P. Lambert. University of Alabama Press, Tuscaloosa.

Brown, I. W.
1985 *Natchez Indian Archaeology: Culture Change and Stability in the Lower Mississippi Valley*. Archaeological Report 15. Mississippi Department of Archives and History, Jackson.
1993 William Bartram and the Direct Historical Approach. In *Archaeology of Eastern North America: Essays in Honor of Stephen Williams*, edited by J. B. Stoltman, pp. 277–282. Archaeological Report 25. Mississippi Department of Archives and History, Jackson.
1994 Recent Trends in the Archaeology of the Southeastern United States. *Journal of Archaeological Research* 2:45–111.

Brown, J. A.
1975 Spiro Art and Its Mortuary Contexts. In *Death and Afterlife in Pre-Columbian America*, edited by E. P. Benson, pp. 1–32. Dumbarton Oaks, Washington, D.C.
1985 The Mississippian Period. In *Ancient Art of the American Woodland Indians*, pp. 92–145. Harry N. Adams, New York.
1996 *The Spiro Ceremonial Center: The Archaeology of Arkansas Valley Caddoan Culture in Eastern Oklahoma*. 2 vols. Memoirs of the Museum of Anthropology 29. University of Michigan, Ann Arbor.

Brown, J. A. (editor)
1971   Approaches to the Social Dimensions of Mortuary Practices. Society for American Archaeology, Washington, D.C.

Brown, J. A., R. A. Kerber, and H. D. Winters
1990   Trade and the Evolution of Exchange Relations at the Beginning of the Mississippian Period. In *The Mississippian Emergence*, edited by B. D. Smith, pp. 251–280. Smithsonian Institution Press, Washington, D.C.

Brown, J. N.
1999   Steadfast and Changing: The Apparent Paradox of Cherokee Kinship. *Journal of Cherokee Studies* 20:3–26.

Brown, J. S. H.
1991   Ethnohistorians: Strange Bedfellows, Kindred Spirits. *Ethnohistory* 38:113–123.

Brumfiel, E. M.
1989   Factional Competition in Complex Society. In D. Miller et al., eds., *Domination and Resistance*, pp. 127–139.
1992   Breaking and Entering the Ecosystem: Gender, Class, and Faction Steal the Show. *American Anthropologist* 94:551–567.
1994   Factional Competition and Political Development in the New World: An Introduction. In Brumfiel and Fox, eds., *Factional Competition*, pp. 3–13.
1995   Heterarchy and the Analysis of Complex Societies: Comments. In *Heterarchy and the Analysis of Complex Societies*, edited by R. M. Ehrenreich, C. L. Crumley, and J. E. Levy, pp. 125–31. Archaeological Papers of the American Anthropological Association, No. 6. American Anthropological Association, Arlington, Virginia.

Brumfiel, E. M., and T. K. Earle
1987   Specialization, Exchange, and Complex Societies: An Introduction. In *Specialization, Exchange, and Complex Societies*, edited by E. M. Brumfiel and T. K. Earle, pp. 1–9. Cambridge University Press, Cambridge.

Brumfiel, E. M., and J. W. Fox (editors)
1994   *Factional Competition and Political Development in the New World*. Cambridge University Press, Cambridge.

Burke, P.
1990   Historians, Anthropologists and Symbols. In *Culture through Time: Anthropological Approaches*, edited by Emiko Ohnuki-Tierney, pp. 268–283. Stanford University Press, Palo Alto.

Burnett, B. A.
1993   Adaptive Efficiency of Arkansas Populations. In *Caddoan Saltmakers in the Ouachita Valley: The Hardman Site*, edited by A. M. Early, pp. 187–223. Research Series No. 43. Arkansas Archeological Survey, Fayetteville.

Burton, M. L., J. W. M. Whiting, and A. K. Romney
1996   Regions Based on Social Structure. *Current Anthropology* 37:87–123.

Bushnell, A. T.
1978   "That Demonic Game": The Campaign to Stop Indian Pelota Playing in Spanish Florida, 1675–1684. *Americas* 35:1–19.
1979   Patricio de Hinachuba: Defender of the Word of God, the Crown of the King, and the Little Children of Ivitachuco. *American Indian Culture and Research Journal* 3:1–21.

Byrd, K. M.
1980   Zooarchaeological Analysis of the Hanna Site: An Alto Focus Occupation in Louisiana. *Louisiana Archaeology* 5:235–265.

Byrd, W.
1967 [1929] *Histories of the Dividing Line Betwixt Virginia and North Carolina.* Edited by W. K. Boyd. Originally published by the North Carolina Historical Commission. Reprinted by Dover, New York.

de la Cadena, M.
1995 *Race, Ethnicity, and the Struggle for Self-representation: Deindianization in Cuzco, Peru.* Ph.D. dissertation, University of Wisconsin, Madison. University Microfilms, Ann Arbor.

Calder, I. M. (editor)
1967 Journals of Sargeant Wight, 1771: Journal of the Passage of Serj't Wight to the Upper Creek Nation 1771. In *Colonial Captivities, Marches and Journeys,* pp. 236–243. Kennikat Press, Port Washington, New York.

Caldwell, J. R., and C. McCann
1941 *Irene Mound Site, Chatham County, Georgia.* University of Georgia Press, Athens.

Carneiro, R. L.
1973 The Four Faces of Evolution: Unilinear, Universal, Multilinear, and Differential. In *Handbook of Social and Cultural Anthropology,* edited by J. L. Honigmann, pp. 89–110. Rand McNally, Chicago.
1981 The Chiefdom: Precursor to the State. In *Transitions to Statehood in the New World,* edited by G. J. and R. Kantz, pp. 37–79. Cambridge University Press, Cambridge.
1992 The Calusa and the Powhatan, Native Chiefdoms of North America. *Reviews in Anthropology* 21:27–38.
1994 War and Peace: Alternating Realities in Human History. In *Studying War: Anthropological Perspectives,* edited by S. P. Reyna and R. E. Downs, pp. 3–27. Gordon and Breach, New York.

Carroll, R. F.
1997 Sociopolitical Organization at Upper Nodena (3MS4) from a Mortuary Perspective. Unpublished Master's thesis, Department of Anthropology, University of Arkansas, Fayetteville.

Carter, C. E.
1995a *Caddo Indians: Where We Come From.* University of Oklahoma Press, Norman.
1995b Archaeology, the Caddo Indian Tribe, and the Native American Graves Protection and Repatriation Act. *Journal of Northeast Texas Archaeology* 5:4–8.

Casteel, R. W.
1976 *Fish Remains in Archaeology.* Academic Press, New York.

Catesby, M.
1771 *The Natural History of Carolina, Florida, and the Bahama Islands.* Benjamin White, London.

Chafe, W. L.
1997 Introduction to the paperback edition. In *Traditions of the Caddo,* by G. A. Dorsey, pp. vii–xxiv. University of Nebraska Press, Lincoln.

Champagne, D.
1983 Symbolic Structure and Political Change in Cherokee Society. *Journal of Cherokee Studies* 8:87–96.
1990 Institutional and Cultural Order in Early Cherokee Society: A Sociological Interpretation. *Journal of Cherokee Studies* 15:3–26.

Chapa, J. B.
1997   *Texas and Northeastern Mexico, 1630–1690*. Edited with an introduction by W. C. Foster. University of Texas Press, Austin.

Chapman, C. H., and R. P. Wiegers
1985   Archaeological Investigations on Historic Missouri, Little Osage, and Big Osage Village Sites. In *Osage and Missouri Indian Life Cultural Change: 1675–1825*, assembled by C. H. Chapman, pp. 273–379. Final Performance Report on National Endowment for the Humanities Research Grant RS-20296.

Chapman, J.
1985   *Tellico Archaeology: Twelve Thousand Years of Native American History*. Department of Anthropology, University of Tennessee, Report of Investigations 43, Knoxville.

Chapman, J., P. A. Delcourt, P. A. Cridlebaugh, A. B. Shea, and H. R. Delcourt
1982   Man-Land Interaction: 10,000 Years of American Indian Impact on Native Ecosystems in the Lower Little Tennessee River Valley. *Southeastern Archaeology* 2:115–121.

Chapman, J., and A. B. Shea
1981   The Archaeobotanical Record: Early Archaic Period to Contact in the Lower Little Tennessee River Valley. *Tennessee Anthropologist* 6:61–84.

Charlton, T. H.
1981   Archaeology, Ethnohistory, and Ethnology: Interpretive Interfaces. *Advances in Archaeological Method and Theory* 4:129–176.

Chicken, G.
1928   Journal of Colonel George Chicken. In S. C. Williams, ed., *Early Travels*, pp. 93–104.

Clark, W. E., and H. C. Rountree
1993   The Powhatans and the Maryland Mainland. In Rountree, ed., *Powhatan Foreign Relations*, pp. 112–135.

Clastres, P.
1987   *Society against the State*. Zone Books, New York.

Clay, R. B.
1976   Tactics, Strategy, and Operations: The Mississippian System Responds to its Environment. *Midcontinental Journal of Archaeology* 1:137–162.

Clayton, L. A., V. J. Knight, and E. C. Moore (editors)
1993   *The De Soto Chronicles: The Expedition of Hernando de Soto to North America in 1539–1543*. 2 vols. University of Alabama Press, Tuscaloosa.

Cleland, C. E.
2001a Historical Archaeology Adrift? *Historical Archaeology* 35:1–8.
2001b Reply to Douglas V. Armstrong, Lu Ann De Cunzo, Gregory A. Waselkov, Donald L. Hardesty, and Robert S. Greenwood. *Historical Archaeology* 35:28–30.

Cobb, C. R.
1991   Social Reproduction and the *Longue Durée* in the Prehistory of the Midcontinental United States. In *Processual and Postprocessual Archaeologies: Multiple Ways of Knowing the Past*, edited by R. W. Preucel, pp. 168–182. Center for Archaeological Investigations, Southern Illinois University at Carbondale.
1993   Archaeological Approaches to the Political Economy of Nonstratified Societies. *Archaeological Method and Theory* 5:43–100.

Codere, H.
1950 Fighting with Property: A Study of Kwakiutl Potlatching and Warfare, 1792–1930. University of Washington Press, Seattle.

Coe, J. L.
1961 Cherokee Archaeology. In *The Symposium on Cherokee and Iroquois Culture*, edited by W. N. Fenton and J. Gulick, pp. 51–60. Bureau of American Ethnology Bulletin 180. Smithsonian Institution, Washington, D.C.

Cohen, A.
1974 Two-Dimensional Man: An Essay on the Anthropology of Power and Symbolism in Complex Society. University of California Press, Berkeley.

Cohen, R., and E. R. Service (editors)
1978 *Origins of the State: The Anthropology of Political Evolution*. Institute for the Study of Human Issues, Philadelphia.

Colley, S. M.
1990 The Analysis and Interpretation of Archaeological Fish Remains. *Archaeological Method and Theory* 2:207–253.

Comaroff, J., and J. Comaroff
1991 *Of Revelation and Revolution: Christianity, Colonialism, and Consciousness in South Africa*, Vol. 1. University of Chicago Press, Chicago.
1992 *Ethnography and the Historical Imagination*. Westview Press, Boulder, Colorado.

Conner, M. D., N. H. Lopinot, and J. H. Ray
1995 Introduction. In *Woodland and Mississippian Occupations at the Hayti Bypass Site, Pemiscot County, Missouri*, edited by M. D. Conner, pp. 1–30. Special Publication No. 1, Center for Archaeological Research. Southwest Missouri State University, Springfield.

Cook, F. C.
1980 Aboriginal Mortality on the Georgia Coast During the Early Historic Period. *South Carolina Antiquities* 12:36–42.
1988 Archaeological Evidence for the Distribution of Sixteenth-Century Irene/Guale People on the Georgia Coast and Relationships to Socio-political Organizations. *Early Georgia* 16:1–27.

Cook, F. C., and Charles E. Pearson
1989 The Southeastern Ceremonial Complex on the Georgia Coast. In *The Southeastern Ceremonial Complex: Artifacts and Analysis*, edited by P. Galloway, pp. 147–165. University of Nebraska Press, Lincoln.

Cook, F. C., and F. Snow
1983 Southeastern Ceremonial Complex Symbolism on the Georgia Coast during the Late Irene Phase of Two Sixteenth-Century Spanish Contact Sites. *Chesopiean* 21:2–14.

Corbin, J. E.
1991 Retracing the Camino de los Tejas from the Trinity River to Los Adaes: New Insights into East Texas History. In *A Texas Legacy: The Old San Antonio Road and the Caminos Reales, A Tricentennial History, 1691–1991*, edited by A. J. McGraw, J. W. Clark, Jr., and E. A. Robbins, pp. 191–219. Texas Department of Highways and Public Transportation, Austin.

Corkran, D. H.
1957 *The Cherokee Frontier, 1740–1762*. University of Oklahoma Press, Norman.
1962 *The Cherokee Frontier: Conflict and Survival, 1740–1762*. University of Oklahoma Press, Norman.

1967   *The Creek Frontier, 1540–1783*. University of Oklahoma Press, Norman.

Corkran, D. H. (editor)

1969   A Small Postscript on the Ways and Manners of the Indians Called Cherokees, by A. Longe. *Southern Indian Studies* 21:3–49.

Cotterill, R. S.

1954   *The Southern Indians: The Story of the Five Civilized Tribes before Removal*. University of Oklahoma Press, Norman.

Cottier, J. W.

1997   Fringes of a Creek Community: Margin Configurations along the Edges of an Archaeological Site. Paper presented at the 62nd Annual Meeting of the Society for American Archaeology, Nashville.

Crabtree, P. J.

1990   Zooarchaeology and Complex Societies: Some Uses of Faunal Analysis for the Study of Trade, Social Status, and Ethnicity. *Archaeological Method and Theory* 2:155–205.

Crane, V. W.

1981   [1928] *The Southern Frontier, 1670–1732*. Norton Publishers, New York.

Creel, D. G.

1996   Hatchel-Mitchell Site. In *The New Handbook of Texas*, Vol. 3, edited by R. Tyler, pp. 504–505. Texas State Historical Association, Austin.

Crook, R. R.

1978   Mississippian Period Community Organization on the Georgia Coast. Unpublished Ph.D. dissertation, Department of Anthropology, University of Florida, Gainesville.

1986   *Mississippi Period Archaeology of the Georgia Coastal Zone*. Laboratory of Archaeology Series Report No. 23. Georgia Archaeological Research Design Papers, No. 1. University of Georgia, Athens.

Crosby, A.

1986   *Ecological Imperialism: The Biological Expansion of Europe, 900–1900*. Cambridge University Press, Cambridge.

Crouch, D.

1974   South Appalachian Earth Lodges. Unpublished Master's thesis, Department of Anthropology, University of North Carolina, Chapel Hill.

Crumley, C. L.

1974   *Celtic Social Structure: The Generation of Archaeologically Testable Hypotheses from Literary Evidence*. University of Michigan Museum of Anthropology, Archaeological Papers 54, Ann Arbor.

1979   Three Locational Models: An Epistemological Assessment for Anthropology and Archaeology. *Advances in Archaeological Method and Theory* 2:141–173.

1987   A Dialectical Critique of Hierarchy. In *Power Relations and State Formation*, edited by T. C. Patterson and C. W. Gailey, pp. 155–169. American Anthropological Association, Washington, D.C.

1995   Heterarchy and the Analysis of Complex Societies. In *Heterarchy and the Analysis of Complex Societies*, edited by R. M. Ehrenreich, C. L. Crumley, and J. E. Levy, pp. 1–6. Archaeological Papers of the American Anthropological Association, Number 6. American Anthropological Association, Arlington, Virginia.

Cuming, A.

1928   Journal of Sir Alexander Cuming. In S. C. Williams, ed., *Early Travels*, pp. 115–143.

Cunningham, C.
1973 Order in the Atoni House. In *Right and Left: Essays on Dual Symbolic Classification*, edited by R. Needham, pp. 204–238. University of Chicago Press, Chicago.

Curry, D. C.
1999 *Feast of the Dead: Aboriginal Ossuaries in Maryland*. Archaeological Society of Maryland, Crownsville, Maryland.

Cusick, J. G. (editor)
1998 *Studies in Culture Contact: Interaction, Culture Change, and Archaeology*. Center for Archaeological Investigations, Southern Illinois University, Carbondale.

Dalton, G.
1977 Aboriginal Economies in Stateless Societies. In *Exchange Systems in Prehistory*, edited by T. K. Earle and J. E. Ericson, pp. 191–212. Academic Press, New York.

Daniel, G. E.
1964 *The Idea of Prehistory*. Penguin Books, Harmondsworth.

Davidson, T. E.
1993 Relations between the Powhatans and the Eastern Shore. In Rountree, ed., *Powhatan Foreign Relations*, pp. 136–153.

Davis, R. P. S., Jr. (editor)
1990 The Travels of James Needham and Gabriel Arthur through Virginia, North Carolina, and Beyond, by A. Wood. *Southern Indian Studies* 39:31–55.

Davis, R. P. S., Jr., L. R. Kimball, and W. Baden
1982 *An Archaeological Survey and Assessment of Aboriginal Settlement within the Lower Little Tennessee River Valley*. Submitted to Report on File with the Tennessee Valley Authority.

Day, G. M.
1953 The Indian as an Ecological Factor in the Northeastern Forest. *Ecology* 34:329–346.

Deagan, K. A.
1982 Avenues of Inquiry in Historical Archaeology. In *Advances in Archaeological Method and Theory*, 5:151–177. Academic Press, New York.
1985 Spanish-Indian Interaction in Sixteenth-Century Florida and Hispaniola. In Fitzhugh, ed., *Cultures in Contact*, pp. 281–318.
1988 The Archaeology of the Spanish Contact Period in the Caribbean. *Journal of World Prehistory* 2:187–233.
1990 Sixteenth-Century Spanish-American Colonization in the Southeastern United States and the Caribbean. In D. H. Thomas, ed., *Columbian Consequences*, Vol. 2, pp. 225–250.
1996 Environmental Archaeology and Historic Archaeology. In *Case Studies in Environmental Archaeology*, edited by E. J. Reitz, L. A. Newsom, and S. J. Scudder, pp. 359–376. Plenum Press, New York.
1997 Cross-Disciplinary Themes in the Recovery of the Colonial Middle Period. *Historical Archaeology* 31:1–8.
1998. Rethinking Modern History. *Archaeology* 51:54–60, 82.

DeBoer, W. R.
1998 Subterranean Storage and the Organization of Surplus: The View from Eastern North America. *Southeastern Archaeology* 7:1–20.

Deetz, J. F.
1960   An Archaeological Approach to Kinship Change in Eighteenth Century Arikara Culture. Unpublished Ph.D. dissertation, Department of Anthropology, Harvard University, Cambridge, Massachusetts.
1982   Households. *American Behavioral Scientist* 25:717–724.
1988   History and Archaeological Theory: Walter Taylor Revisited. *American Antiquity* 53:13–22.

Delcourt, P. A., H. R. Delcourt, P. A. Cridlebaugh, and J. Chapman
1986   Holocene Ethnobotanical and Paleoecological Record of Human Impact on Vegetation in the Little Tennessee River Valley, Tennessee. *Quaternary Research* 25:330–349.

Deloria, V.
1995   *Red Earth, White Lies: Native Americans and the Myth of Scientific Fact*. Scribner's, New York.

Delorit, R., and C. R. Gunn
1986   *Seeds of Continental United States Legumes (Fabaceae)*. Agronomy Publications, River Falls, Wisconsin.

DeMarrais, E., L. J. Castillo, and T. Earle
1996   Ideology, Materialization, and Power Strategies. *Current Anthropology* 37:15–31.

DePratter, C. B.
1983   *Late Prehistoric and Early Historic Chiefdoms in the Southeastern United States*. Ph.D. dissertation, University of Georgia. University Microfilms, Ann Arbor.
1991   *Late Prehistoric and Early Historic Chiefdoms in the Southeastern United States*. Garland, New York.
1994   The Chiefdom of Cofitachequi. In C. Hudson and Tesser, eds., *Forgotten Centuries*, pp. 197–226.

DePratter, C., C. M. Hudson, and M. T. Smith
1983   The Route of Juan Pardo's Explorations in the Interior Southeast, 1566–1568. *Florida Historical Quarterly* 62:125–158.

Derrick, S. M., and D. Wilson
1997   Cranial Modeling as an Ethnic Marker among the Prehistoric Caddo. *Bulletin of the Texas Archeological Society* 68:139–146.

DeVorsey, L., Jr.
1966   The Colonial Southeast on "an accurate general map." *Southeastern Geographer* 6:20–32.
1971   *DeBrahm's Report of the General Survey in the Southern District of North America*. University of South Carolina Press, Columbia.
1977   Early Maps as a Source in the Reconstruction of Southern Indian Landscapes. In *Red, White, and Black: Symposium on Indians in the Old South*, edited by C. M. Hudson, pp. 12–30. Southern Anthropological Society and University of Georgia Press, Athens.
1998   American Indians and Early Mapping. In *The Southeast in Early Maps*, third edition, edited by W. P. Cumming, pp. 65–98. University of North Carolina Press, Chapel Hill.

Dickens, R. S., Jr.
1967   The Route of Rutherford's Expedition against the North Carolina Cherokees. *Southern Indian Studies* 19:3–24.
1976   *Cherokee Prehistory: The Pisgah Phase in the Appalachian Summit Region*. University of Tennessee Press, Knoxville.

1978   Mississippian Settlement Patterns in the Appalachian Summit Area: The Pisgah and Qualla Phases. In B. D. Smith, ed., *Mississippian Settlement Patterns*, pp. 115–139.
1979   The Origins and Development of Cherokee Culture. In B. D. Smith, ed., *Cherokee Indian Nation*, pp. 3–32.

Dickson, D. B.
1981   The Yanomamö of the Mississippi Valley? Some Reflections on Larson (1972), Gibson (1974), and Mississippian Period Warfare in the Southeastern United States. *American Antiquity* 46:909–916.

Dimmick, F. R.
1989   A Survey of Upper Creek Sites in Alabama. *Journal of Alabama Archaeology* 35.

Dirks, N. B.
1992   Introduction: Colonialism and Culture. In *Colonialism and Culture*, edited by N. B. Dirks, pp. 1–25. University of Michigan Press, Ann Arbor.

Dobyns, H. F.
1983   *Their Number Become Thinned: Native American Population Dynamics in Eastern North America*. University of Tennessee Press, Knoxville.
1991   New Native World: Links between Demographic and Cultural Changes. In D. H. Thomas, ed., *Columbian Consequences*, Vol. 3, pp. 541–559.

Dorsey, G. A.
1997   *Traditions of the Caddo*. University of Nebraska Press, Lincoln.

Douglas, M.
1989   Foreword: No Free Gifts. In *The Gift: The Form and Reason for Exchange in Archaic Societies*, by M. Mauss, translated by W. D. Halls, pp. vii–xviii. Routledge, New York.

Dowd, D. L.
1964   French Florida Four Centuries Later. In *Jean Ribaut: The Whole & True Discourerye of Terra Florida*, pp. xiii–lxvi. Florida State Historical Society, Deland.

Drooker, P. B.
1997   *The View from Madisonville: Protohistoric Western Fort Ancient Interaction Patterns*. University of Michigan, Memoirs of the Museum of Anthropology 31, Ann Arbor.

Drucker, P., and R. F. Heizer
1967   *To Make My Name Good: A Reexamination of the Southern Kwakiutl Potlatch*. University of California Press, Berkeley.

Duke, P.
1992   Braudel and North American Archaeology: An Example from the Northern Plains. In Knapp, ed., *Archaeology, Annales, and Ethnohistory*, pp. 99–111.

Dunnell, R. C.
1989   Aspects of the Application of Evolutionary Theory in Archaeology. In Lamberg-Karlovsky, ed., *Archaeological Thought*, pp. 35–49.
1990   The Role of the Southeast in American Archaeology. *Southeastern Archaeology* 9:11–22.
1991   Methodological Impacts of Catastrophic Depopulation on American Archaeology and Ethnology. In D. H. Thomas, ed., *Columbian Consequences*, Vol. 3, pp. 561–580.

Dye, D. H.
1989   Death March of Hernando de Soto. *Archaeology* 42:26–31.

1990   Warfare in the Sixteenth-Century Southeast: The de Soto Expedition in the Interior. In D. H. Thomas, ed., *Columbian Consequences*, Vol. 2, pp. 211–222.
1994   The Art of War in the Sixteenth-Century Central Mississippi Valley. In *Perspectives on the Southeast: Linguistics, Archaeology, and Ethnohistory*, edited by P. B. Kwachka, pp. 44–60. Southern Anthropological Society Proceedings, No. 27. University of Georgia Press, Athens.
1995   Feasting with the Enemy: Mississippian Warfare and Prestige-Goods Circulation. In Nassaney and Sassaman, eds., *Native American Interactions*, pp. 289–316.
1998   An Overview of Walls Engraved Pottery in the Central Mississippi Valley. In O'Brien and Dunnell, eds., *Changing Perspectives*, pp. 80–98.

Dye, D. H., and R. C. Brister (editors)
1986   *The Protohistoric Period in the Mid-South: 1500–1700: Proceedings of the 1983 Mid-South Archaeological Conference*. Archaeological Report No. 18, Mississippi Department of Archives and History, Jackson.

Dye, D. H., and C. A. Cox (editors)
1990   *Towns and Temples along the Mississippi*. University of Alabama Press, Tuscaloosa.

Earle, T. K.
1987a Chiefdoms in Archaeological and Ethnohistorical Perspective. *Annual Review of Anthropology* 16:279–308.
1987b Specialization and the Production of Wealth: Hawaiian Chiefdoms and the Inka Empire. In *Specialization, Exchange, and Complex Societies*, edited by E. M. Brumfiel and T. K. Earle, pp. 64–75. Cambridge University Press, Cambridge.
1990   Style and Iconography as Legitimation in Complex Chiefdoms. In *The Uses of Style in Archaeology*, edited by M. Conkey and C. Hastorf, pp. 73–81. Cambridge University Press, Cambridge.
1991a Property Rights and the Evolution of Chiefdoms. In Earle, ed., *Chiefdoms*, pp. 71–99.
1991b The Evolution of Chiefdoms. In *Chiefdoms*, pp. 1–15.
1997   *How Chiefs Come to Power: The Political Economy in Prehistory*. Stanford University Press, Palo Alto.

Earle, T. K. (editor)
1991   *Chiefdoms: Power, Economy, and Ideology*. Cambridge University Press, Cambridge.

Earle, T. K., and T. N. D'Altroy
1989   The Political Economy of the Inka Empire: The Archaeology of Power and Finance. In Lamberg-Karlovsky, ed., *Archaeological Thought*, pp. 183–204.

Early, A. M.
1988   *Standridge: Caddoan Settlement in a Mountain Environment*. Research Series No. 29. Arkansas Archeological Survey, Fayetteville.

Early, A. M. (editor)
1993   *Caddoan Saltmakers in the Ouachita Valley: The Hardman Site*. Research Series No. 43. Arkansas Archeological Survey, Fayetteville.

Egloff, B. J.
1967   An Analysis of Ceramics from Historic Cherokee Towns. Unpublished Master's thesis, Department of Anthropology, University of North Carolina, Chapel Hill.

214 / References

Egloff, K. T.
1971 Methods and Problems of Mound Excavation in the Southern Appalachian Area. Unpublished Master's thesis, Department of Anthropology, University of North Carolina, Chapel Hill.

Ekholm, K.
1972 *Power and Prestige: The Rise and Fall of the Kongan Kingdom.* Uppsala University Press, Uppsala.

Elbl, M. M., and I. Elbl
1997 The Gentleman of Elvas and His Publisher. In Galloway, ed., *Hernando de Soto Expedition*, pp. 45–97.

Elliott, J. H.
1970 *The Old World and the New, 1492–1650.* Cambridge University Press, Cambridge.

Elvas, Gentleman of
1993 [1557] The Account of the Gentleman from Elvas. Translated and edited by J. A. Robertson. In Clayton et al., eds., *De Soto Chronicles*, Vol. 1, pp. 19–220.

Emerson, T. E.
1997a *Cahokia and the Archaeology of Power.* University of Alabama Press, Tuscaloosa.
1997b Cahokian Elite Ideology and the Mississippian Cosmos. In Pauketat and Emerson, eds., *Cahokia*, pp. 190–228.

Erickson, E. C., and J. E. Corbin
1996 *Archaeological Survey and Cultural Resource Assessment of Mission Tejas State Historical Park, Houston County, Texas.* Public Lands Division, Cultural Resource Program, Texas Parks and Wildlife Department, Austin.

Euler, R. C.
1972 Ethnohistory in the United States. *Ethnohistory* 19:201–207.

Evans, J. P.
1979 Sketches of Cherokee Characteristics. *Journal of Cherokee Studies* 4:10–20.

Ewen, C. R.
1996 Continuity and Change: De Soto and the Apalachee. *Historical Archaeology* 30:41–53.
1997 The Search for Coronado's Contemporary: The Discovery, Excavation, and Interpretation of Hernando de Soto's First Winter Encampment. In *The Coronado Expedition to Tierra Nueva: The 1540–1542 Route across the Southwest*, edited by R. Flint and S. C. Flint, pp. 116–134. University Press of Colorado, Niwot.

Ewers, J. C.
1973 The Influence of Epidemics on the Indian Populations and Cultures of Texas. *Plains Anthropologist* 18:104–115.

Fairbanks, C. H.
1952 Creek and Pre-Creek. In *Archaeology of Eastern United States*, edited by J. B. Griffin, pp. 285–300. University of Chicago Press, Chicago.
1958 Some Problems of the Origins of Creek Pottery. *Florida Archaeologist* 11:53–64.

Faulk, L. (editor)
1991 *Historical Archaeology in Global Perspective.* Smithsonian Institution Press, Washington, D.C.

Faulkner, C. H.
1978 Origin and Evolution of the Cherokee Winter House. *Journal of Cherokee Studies* 3:87–94.

Feinman, G. M.
1991   Demography, Surplus, and Inequality: Early Political Formations in Highland Mesoamerica. In Earle, ed., *Chiefdoms*, pp. 229–262.
1995   The Emergence of Inequality: A Focus on Strategies and Processes. In *Foundations of Social Inequality*, edited by T. D. Price and G. M. Feinman, pp. 255–279. Plenum Press, New York.
1997   Thoughts on New Approaches to Combining the Archaeological and Historical Records. *Journal of Archaeological Method and Theory* 4:367–377.
2000   Dual-Processual Theory and Social Formations in the Southwest. In *Alternative Leadership Strategies in the Prehispanic Southwest*, edited by B. J. Mills, pp. 207–224. University of Arizona Press, Tucson.

Feinman, G. M., and J. Neitzel
1984   Too Many Types: An Overview of Sedentary Prestate Societies in the Americas. *Advances in Archaeological Method and Theory*, Vol. 7, edited by M. Shiffer, pp. 39–102. Academic Press, New York.

Ferguson, L. G.
1971   South Appalachian Mississippian. Unpublished Ph.D. dissertation, Department of Anthropology, University of North Carolina, Chapel Hill.

Ferguson, R. B.
1990   Blood of the Leviathan: Western Contact and Warfare in Amazonia. *American Ethnologist* 17:237–257.

Ferguson, R. B., and N. L. Whitehead
1992   The Violent Edge of Empire. In *War in the Tribal Zone: Expanding States and Indigenous Warfare*, edited by R. B. Ferguson and N. L. Whitehead, pp. 1–30. School of American Research, Santa Fe.

Firth, R.
1957   *We, The Tikopia: A Sociological Study of Kinship in Primitive Polynesia*. Second edition. Beacon Press, Boston.

Fitzhugh, W. W.
1985   Introduction. In Fitzhugh, ed., *Cultures in Contact*, pp. 1–15.

Fitzhugh, W. W. (editor)
1985   *Cultures in Contact: The European Impact on Native Cultural Institutions in Eastern North America, A.D. 1000–1800*. Smithsonian Institution Press, Washington, D.C.

Flanagan, J.
1989   Hierarchy in Simple "Egalitarian" Societies. *Annual Review of Anthropology* 18:245–266.

Flannery, K. V.
1972   The Cultural Evolution of Civilizations. *Annual Review of Ecology and Systematics* 3:399–426.

Ford, J. A.
1936   *Analysis of Indian Village Site Collections from Louisiana and Mississippi*. Anthropological Study No. 2. Department of Conservation, Louisiana State Geological Survey, Baton Rouge.
1938   A Chronological Method Applicable to the Southeast. *American Antiquity* 3:260–264.
1952   Measurements of Some Prehistoric Design Developments in the Southeastern States. *Anthropological Papers of the American Museum of Natural History*, 44:313–384.

Foster, W. C.
1995 Spanish Expeditions into Texas, 1689–1768. University of Texas Press, Austin.
Foster, W. C., and J. Jackson (editors) and N. F. Brierley (translator)
1993 The 1693 Expedition of Governor Salinas Varona to Sustain the Missionaries among the Tejas Indians. *Southwestern Historical Quarterly* 97:264–311.
Frankenstein, S. M., and M. J. Rowlands
1978 The Internal Structure and Regional Context of Early Iron Age Society in Southwestern Germany. *Bulletin of the Institute of Archaeology* 15:73–112.
Fried, M. H.
1967 *The Evolution of Political Society*. Random House, New York.
Friedman, J. A.
1982 Catastrophe and Continuity in Social Evolution. In *Theory and Explanation in Archaeology: The Southampton Conference*, edited by M. J. R. Colin Renfew, and B. A. Seagraves, pp. 175–196. Academic Press, New York.
1989 Culture, Identity, and World Process. In D. Miller et al., eds., *Domination and Resistance*, pp. 246–260.
1992 The Past in the Future: History and the Politics of Identity. *American Anthropologist* 94:837–859.
Friedman, J. A., and M. J. Rowlands
1978 Notes towards an Epigenetic Model of the Evolution of "Civilisation." In *The Evolution of Social Systems*, edited by J. Friedman and M. J. Rowlands, pp. 201–276. Duckworth, London.
Fritz, G. J.
1992 "Newer," "Better" Maize and the Mississippian Emergence: A Critique of Prime Mover Explanations. In *Late Prehistoric Agriculture: Observations from the Midwest*, edited by W. I. Woods, pp. 19–43. Studies in Illinois Archaeology Number 8. Illinois Historic Preservation Agency, Springfield.
Fritz, G. J., and T. R. Kidder
1993 Recent Investigations into Prehistoric Agriculture in the Lower Mississippi Valley. *Southeastern Archaeology* 12:1–14.
Gabriel, R., and A. Metz
1991 *From Sumer to Rome: The Military Capabilities of Ancient Armies*. Greenwood Press, New York.
Gallivan, M. D.
1997 Reinterpreting Late Prehistoric Political Dynamics in the Chesapeake from the Household. Unpublished ms.
Gallivan, M. D., and J. L. Hantman
1996 Rethinking Chieftaincy: Powhatan and Monacan Ethnohistory and Archaeology. Paper presented at the 61st annual meeting of the Society for American Archaeology, New Orleans.
Galloway, P.
1982 Henri de Tonti du Village des Charles: The Beginning of the French Alliance. In *La Salle and His Legacy: Frenchmen and Indians in the Lower Mississippi Valley*, edited by P. Galloway, pp. 146–175. University Press of Mississippi, Jackson.
1986 The Direct Historical Approach and Early Historical Documents: The Ethnohistorian's View. In *The Protohistoric Period in the Mid-South: 1500–1700. Proceedings of the 1983 Mid-South Archaeological Conference*, edited by D. H. Dye

and R. C. Brister, pp. 14–23. Archaeological Report No. 18, Mississippi Department of Archives and History, Jackson.
1989 "The Chief Who Is Your Father": Choctaw and French Views of the Diplomatic Relation. In P. H. Wood et al., eds., *Powhatan's Mantle*, pp. 254–278.
1991 The Archaeology of Ethnohistorical Narrative. In D. H. Thomas, ed., *Columbian Consequences*, Vol. 3, pp. 453–469.
1993 Ethnohistory. In *The Development of Southeastern Archaeology*, edited by J. K. Johnson, pp. 78–108. University of Alabama Press, Tuscaloosa.
1994 Confederacy as a Solution to Chiefdom Dissolution: Historical Evidence in the Choctaw Case. In C. Hudson and Tesser, eds., *Forgotten Centuries*, pp. 393–420.
1995 *The Choctaw Genesis: 1500–1700*. University of Nebraska Press, Lincoln.
1997a Conjoncture and Longue Durée: History, Anthropology, and the Hernando de Soto Expedition. In Galloway, ed., *Hernando de Soto Expedition*, pp. 283–294.
1997b The Incestuous Soto Narratives. In Galloway, ed., *Hernando de Soto Expedition*, pp. 11–44.

Galloway, P. (editor)
1997 *The Hernando de Soto Expedition: History, Historiography, and "Discovery" in the Southeast*. University of Nebraska Press, Lincoln.

Gatschet, A. S.
1884 *A Migration Legend of the Creek Indians, With a Linguistic, Historic and Ethnographic Introduction*. D. G. Brinton, Philadelphia.

Gearing, F. O.
1958 The Structural Poses of the Eighteenth-Century Cherokee Villages. *American Anthropologist* 60:1148–1157.
1962 *Priests and Warriors: Social Structures for Cherokee Politics in the Eighteenth Century*. Memoir 93:1–124. American Anthropological Association, Washington, D.C.

Gellner, E.
1995 *Anthropology and Politics: Revolutions in the Sacred Grove*. Blackwell, Cambridge.

Gibson, J. L.
1974 Aboriginal Warfare in the Protohistoric Southeast: An Alternative Perspective. *American Antiquity* 39:130–133.

Giddens, A.
1979 *Central Problems in Social Theory: Action, Structure and Contradiction in Social Analysis*. University of California Press, Berkeley.
1984 *The Constitution of Society: Outline of a Theory of Structuration*. Polity Press, Cambridge.

Gilman, A.
1991 Trajectories towards Social Complexity in the Later Prehistory of the Mediterranean. In Earle, ed., *Chiefdoms*, pp. 146–168.

Girard, J. S.
1997 Historic Caddoan Occupation in the Natchitoches Area: Recent Attempts to Locate Residential Sites. *Caddoan Archeology* 8:19–31.

Gledhill, J.
1994 *Power and Its Disguises: Anthropological Perspectives on Politics*. Pluto Press, Boulder.

218 / References

Gold, D. L.
1999   Subsistence, Health and Emergent Inequality in Late Prehistoric Interior Virginia. Unpublished Ph.D. dissertation, Department of Anthropology, University of Michigan.

Goodwin, G. C.
1977   *Cherokees in Transition: A Study of Changing Culture and Environment Prior to 1775.* Research Paper 181, Department of Geography, University of Chicago, Chicago.

Gradie, C. M.
1993   The Powhatans in the Context of the Spanish Empire. In Rountree, ed., *Powhatan Foreign Relations*, pp. 154–172.

Gramsci, A.
1971   *Selections from the Prison Notebooks of Antonio Gramsci.* Translated by Q. Hoare and G. N. Smith. International Publishers, New York.

Grayson, D. K.
1979   On the Quantification of Vertebrate Archaeofaunas. *Advances in Archaeological Method and Theory* 2:199–237.
1984   *Quantitative Zooarchaeology: Topics in the Analysis of Archaeological Faunas.* Academic Press, Orlando.

Greenblatt, S.
1993   Introduction: New World Encounters. In *New World Encounters*, edited by S. Greenblatt, pp. vii–xviii. University of California Press, Berkeley.

Greene, L. K.
1995   Culture Change in the Historic Cherokee Out Towns. Paper presented at the 52nd Annual Meeting of the Southeastern Archaeological Conference, Knoxville.
1996   The Archaeology and History of the Cherokee Out Towns. Unpublished Master's thesis, Department of Anthropology, University of Tennessee, Knoxville.

Greenlee, D. M.
1998   Prehistoric Diet in the Central Mississippi Valley. In O'Brien and Dunnell, *Changing Perspectives*, pp. 299–324.

Gregory, H. F.
1973   Eighteenth-Century Caddoan Archaeology: A Study in Models and Interpretation. Unpublished Ph.D. dissertation, Department of Anthropology, Southern Methodist University, Dallas.

Gremillion, K. J.
1989   *Late Prehistoric and Historic Period Paleoethnobotany of the North Carolina Piedmont.* Ph.D. dissertation, University of North Carolina, Chapel Hill.
1993a Adoption of Old World Crops and Processes of Cultural Change in the Historic Southeast. *Southeastern Archaeology* 12:15–20.
1993b Paleoethnobotanical Evidence of Change and Continuity in Piedmont Subsistence. In *Indian Communities on the North Carolina Piedmont, A.D. 1000 to 1700*, edited by H. T. Ward and R. P. S. Davis, Jr., pp. 455–466. Monograph No. 2, Research Laboratories of Anthropology, University of North Carolina, Chapel Hill.
1995   Comparative Paleoethnobotany of Three Native Southeastern Communities of the Historic Period. *Southeastern Archaeology* 14:1–16.
1996a Diffusion and Adoption of Crops in Evolutionary Perspective. *Journal of Anthropological Archaeology* 15:183–204.

1996b   Archaeobotany at Old Mobile. Paper presented at the 53rd Annual Meeting of the Southeastern Archaeological Conference, Birmingham.

Gremillion, K. J. (editor)
1997   *People, Plants, and Landscapes: Studies in Paleoethnobotany.* University of Alabama Press, Tuscaloosa.

Gremillion, K. J., and E. J. Reitz
1997   Toward an Understanding of Creek Subsistence. Paper presented at the 62nd Annual Meeting of the Society for American Archaeology, Nashville.

Griffin, J. B.
1952b   Culture Periods in Eastern United States Archeology. In Griffin, ed., *Archeology of Eastern United States,* pp. 352–364.
1952c   Prehistoric Cultures of the Central Mississippi Valley. In Griffin, ed., *Archeology of Eastern United States,* pp. 226–238.
1985   Changing Concepts of the Prehistoric Mississippian Cultures of the Eastern United States. In Badger and Clayton, eds., *Alabama and the Borderlands,* pp. 40–63.

Griffin, J. B. (editor)
1952a   *Archeology of Eastern United States.* University of Chicago Press, Chicago.

Griffith, W. J.
1954   *The Hasinai Indians of East Texas as Seen by Europeans, 1687–1772.* Philological and Documentary Studies, Vol. 2, No. 3. Middle American Research Institute, Tulane University, New Orleans.

Guthe, A. K.
1977   The Eighteenth-Century Overhill Cherokee. In *For the Director: Research Essays in Honor of James Griffin,* edited by C. E. Cleland, pp. 112–129. University of Michigan, Museum of Anthropology, Anthropological Papers 61, Ann Arbor.

Haan, R. L.
1982   The "Trade Doe's Not Flourish as Formerly": The Ecological Origins of the Yamassee War of 1715. *Ethnohistory* 28:341–358.

Hadley, D., T. H. Naylor, and M. K. Schuetz-Miller (editors)
1997   *The Presidio and Militia on the Northern Frontier of New Spain: A Documentary History,* Vol. 2, Part 2: *The Central Corridor and the Texas Corridor, 1700–1765.* University of Arizona Press, Tucson.

Hahn, Steven C.
1995   A Miniature Arms Race: The Role of the Flintlock in Initiating Indian Dependency in the Colonial Southeastern United States, 1656–1730. Unpublished Master's thesis, University of Georgia, Athens.

Håkansson, N. T.
1998   Rulers and Rainmakers in Precolonial South Pare, Tanzania: Exchange and Ritual Experts in Political Centralization. *Ethnology* 37:263–283.

Hally, D. J.
1980   Archaeological Investigation of the Little Egypt Site (9MU102), Murray County, Georgia 1970–72 Seasons. Report submitted to the Heritage Conservation and Recreation Service, United States Department of the Interior.
1993   The Territorial Size of Mississippian Chiefdoms. In *Archaeology of Eastern North America: Papers in Honor of Stephen Williams,* edited by J. B. Stoltman, pp. 143–168. Mississippi Department of Archives and History, Report 15, Jackson.

1994a   An Overview of Lamar Culture. In Hally, ed., *Ocmulgee Archaeology*, pp. 144–174.
1994b   The Chiefdom of Coosa. In C. Hudson and Tesser, eds., *Forgotten Centuries*, pp. 227–253.
1996   Platform Mound Construction and the Instability of Mississippian Chiefdoms. In J. F. Scarry, ed., *Political Structure and Change*, pp. 92–127.

Hally, D. J. (editor)
1994c   *Ocmulgee Archaeology, 1936–1986*. University of Georgia Press, Athens.

Hally, D. J., and H. Kelly
1998   The Nature of Mississippian Towns in Northern Georgia: The King Site Example. In Lewis and Stout, eds., *Mississippian Towns*, pp. 49–63.

Hally, D. J., and J. B. Langford, Jr.
1988   *Mississippi Period Archaeology of the Georgia Valley and Ridge Province*. University of Georgia, Laboratory of Archaeology Series, Report 25, Athens.

Hally, D. J., and J. L. Rudolph
1986   *Mississippi Period Archaeology of the Georgia Piedmont*. University of Georgia, Laboratory of Archaeology Series, Report Number 24, Athens.

Hally, D. J., M. T. Smith, and J. B. Langford, Jr.
1990   The Archaeological Reality of de Soto's Coosa. In D. H. Thomas, ed., *Columbian Consequences*, Vol. 2, pp. 121–138.

Halperin, R. H.
1994   *Cultural Economies Past and Present*. University of Texas Press, Austin.

Hammett, J. E.
1992   Ethnohistory of Aboriginal Landscapes in the Southeastern United States. *Southern Indian Studies* 41.
1997   Interregional Patterns of Land Use and Plant Management in Native North America. In Gremillion, ed., *People, Plants, and Landscapes*, pp. 195–216.

Hann, J.
1988   *Apalachee: The Land between the Rivers*. University Presses of Florida, Gainesville.
1993   The Visitation Records of 1677–1678. In *Visitations and Revolts in Florida, 1656–1695*, by J. Hann, pp. 77–146. Florida Bureau of Archaeological Research, Tallahassee.
1994   The Apalachee of the Historic Era. In C. Hudson and Tesser, eds., *Forgotten Centuries*, pp. 327–354.

Hantman, J. L.
1990   Between Powhatan and Quirank: Reconstructing Monacan Culture and History in the Context of Jamestown. *American Anthropologist* 92:676–690.
1993   Powhatan's Relations with the Piedmont Monacan. In *Powhatan's Foreign Relations, 1500–1722*, edited by H. Rountree, pp. 94–111. University Press of Virginia, Charlottesville.

Harmon, A. M., and J. C. Rose
1989   Bioarchaeology of the Louisiana and Arkansas Study Area. In *Archeology and Bioarcheology of the Lower Mississippi Valley and Trans-Mississippi South in Arkansas and Louisiana*, by M. D. Jeter, J. C. Rose, G. I. Williams, Jr., and A. M. Harmon, pp. 323–468. Arkansas Archeological Survey Research Series No. 37, Fayetteville.

Harmon, M. A.
1983   Cherokee Acculturation in Northwestern South Carolina. Paper presented at

the 40th Annual Meeting of the Southeastern Archaeological Conference, Columbia.
1986 *Eighteenth-Century Lower Cherokee Adaptation and Use of Material Cultures.* South Carolina Institute of Archaeology and Anthropology, Volumes in Historical Archaeology 2, Columbia.

Harriot, T.
1972 [1590] *A Briefe and True Report of the New Found Land of Virginia.* The complete 1590 Theodor de Bry edition, with an introduction by P. Hulton. Dover, New York.

Hassig, R.
1996 Regional Analysis. In *Encyclopedia of Cultural Anthropology*, Vol. 3, edited by D. Levinson and M. Ember, pp. 1081–1086. Henry Holt and Company, New York.

Hastorf, C. A., and V. S. Popper (editors)
1988 *Current Paleoethnobotany: Analytical Methods and Cultural Interpretations of Archaeological Plant Remains.* University of Chicago Press, Chicago.

Hatch, J. W.
1995 Lamar Period Upland Farmsteads of the Oconee River Valley, Georgia. In Rogers and Smith, eds., *Mississippian Communities and Households*, pp. 135–155.

Hatcher, M. A.
1932 The Expedition of Don Domingo Teran de los Rios into Texas. *Preliminary Studies of the Texas Catholic Historical Society* 2:3–62.

Hatley, M. T.
1989 The Three Lives of Keowee. In P. H. Wood et al., eds., *Powhatan's Mantle*, pp. 223–248.
1995 *The Dividing Paths: Cherokees and South Carolinians through the Revolutionary Era.* Oxford University Press, Oxford.

Hawke, D. F. (editor)
1970 *Captain John Smith's History of Virginia.* Bobbs-Merrill, Indianapolis.

Heizer, R. F.
1941 The Direct-Historical Approach in California Archaeology. *American Antiquity* 7:98–122.

Helms, M. W.
1979 *Ancient Panama: Chiefs in Search of Power.* University of Texas Press, Austin.
1988 *Ulysses' Sail.* Cambridge University Press, Cambridge.
1992 Long-Distance Contacts, Elite Aspirations, and the Age of Discovery in Cosmological Context. In *Resources, Power, and Interregional Interaction*, edited by E. M. Schortman and P. A. Urban, pp. 157–174. Plenum Press, New York.
1993 *Craft and the Kingly Ideal: Art, Trade, and Power.* University of Texas Press, Austin.
1994 Chiefdom Rivalries, Control, and External Contacts in Lower Central America. In Brumfiel and Fox, eds., *Factional Competition*, pp. 55–60.
1996 Review: *The Savannah River Chiefdoms: Political Change in the Late Prehistoric Southeast*, by D. G. Anderson. *American Antiquity* 61:437–438.

Hendry, G.
1934 The Source Literature of Early Plant Introduction into Spanish America. *Agricultural History* 8:64–71.

Henige, D.
1986 Primary Source by Primary Source? On the Role of Epidemics in New World Depopulation. *Ethnohistory* 33:293–312.

1998 *Numbers from Nowhere: The American Indian Contact Population Debate.* University of Oklahoma Press, Norman.

Herbert, J. M., and L. C. Steponaitis
1998 Estimating the Season of Harvest of Eastern Oysters (*Crassostrea virginica*) with Shells from Chesapeake Bay. *Southeastern Archaeology* 17:53:71.

Heye, G. G., F. W. Hodge, and G. H. Pepper
1918 *The Nacoochee Mound in Georgia.* Contributions of the Museum of the American Indian 4, New York.

Hickerson, D. A.
1997 Historical Processes, Epidemic Disease, and the Formation of the Hasinai Confederacy. *Ethnohistory* 44:31–52.

Hickerson, H.
1970 *The Chippewa and Their Neighbors: A Study in Ethnohistory.* Holt, Rinehart and Winston, New York.

Hill, S. H.
1997 *Weaving New Worlds: Southeastern Cherokee Women and Their Basketry.* University of North Carolina Press, Chapel Hill.

Hirth, K. G.
1996 Political Economy and Archaeology: Perspectives on Exchange and Production. *Journal of Archaeological Research* 4:203–239.

Hodder, I.
1987 The Contribution of the Long-Term. In *Archaeology as Long-Term History*, edited by I. Hodder, pp. 1–8. Cambridge University Press, Cambridge.

Hoffman, M. P.
1983 Changing Mortuary Patterns in the Little River Region, Arkansas. In *Southeastern Natives and Their Pasts*, edited by D. G. Wycoff and J. L. Hoffman, pp. 163–182. Studies in Oklahoma's Past No. 11. Oklahoma Archaeology Survey, Norman.
1990 The Terminal Mississippian Period in the Arkansas River Valley and Quapaw Ethnogenesis. In Dye and Cox, eds., *Towns and Temples*, pp. 208–226.
1993 Identification of Ethnic Groups Contacted by the de Soto Expedition in Arkansas. In *The Expedition of Hernando de Soto West of the Mississippi, 1541–1543*, edited by G. A. Young and M. P. Hoffman, pp. 132–142. University of Arkansas Press, Fayetteville.

Hoffman, P. E.
1984 The Chicora Legend and Franco-Spanish Rivalry in La Florida. *Florida Historical Quarterly* 62:419–438.
1990 *A New Andalucia and a Way to the Orient: The American Southeast during the Sixteenth Century.* Louisiana State University Press, Baton Rouge.
1993 Introduction: The de Soto Expedition, A Cultural Crossroads. In Clayton et al., eds., *De Soto Chronicles*, Vol. 1, pp. 1–18.
1994 Lucas Vázquez de Ayllón's Discovery and Colony. In C. Hudson and Tesser, eds., *Forgotten Centuries*, pp. 36–49.
1997 Did Coosa Decline between 1541 and 1560? *Florida Anthropologist* 50:25–30.

Holland, D. C., and M. A. Eisenhart
1990 *Educated in Romance: Women, Achievement, and College Culture.* University of Chicago Press, Chicago.

Holland, T. D., and M. J. O'Brien
1997 Parasites, Porotic Hyperostosis, and the Implications of Changing Perspectives. *American Antiquity* 62:183–193.

House, J. H.
1997   Noble Lake: A Protohistoric Archeological Site on the Lower Arkansas River. *Arkansas Archeologist* 36:47–97.

Hudson, C.
1973   The Historical Approach in Anthropology. In *Handbook of Social and Cultural Anthropology*, edited by J. L. Honigmann, pp. 111–141. Rand McNally, Chicago.
1976   *The Southeastern Indians*. University of Tennessee Press, Knoxville.
1977   James Adair as Anthropologist. *Ethnohistory* 24:311–328.
1985   De Soto in Arkansas: A Brief Synopsis. *Field Notes* 205:3–12. Arkansas Archeological Society.
1988   A Spanish-Coosa Alliance in Sixteenth-century North Georgia. *Georgia Historical Quarterly* 62:599–626.
1990   *The Juan Pardo Expeditions: Exploration of the Carolinas and Tennessee, 1566–1568*. Smithsonian Institution Press, Washington, D.C.
1994   The Hernando de Soto Expedition, 1539–1543. In C. Hudson and Tesser, eds., *Forgotten Centuries*, pp. 74–103.
1997   *Knights of Spain, Warriors of the Sun: Hernando de Soto and the South's Ancient Chiefdoms*. University of Alabama Press, Tuscaloosa.

Hudson, C., C. DePratter, and M. T. Smith
1984   The Hernando de Soto Expedition: From Apalachee to Chiaha. *Southeastern Archaeology* 3:66–77.

Hudson, C., M. T. Smith, and C. B. DePratter
1990   The Hernando de Soto Expedition: From Mabila to the Mississippi River. In Dye and Cox, eds., *Towns and Temples*, pp. 181–207.

Hudson, C., M. T. Smith, C. B. DePratter, and E. Kelley
1989   The Tristán de Luna Expedition, 1559–1561. *Southeastern Archaeology* 8:31–45.

Hudson, C., M. T. Smith, D. Hally, R. Polhemus, and C. DePratter
1985   Coosa: A Chiefdom in the Sixteenth-Century Southeastern United States. *American Antiquity* 50:723–737.
1987   In Search of Coosa: Reply to Schroedl and Boyd. *American Antiquity* 52:840–857.

Hudson, C., and C. C. Tesser
1994a   Introduction. In C. Hudson and Tesser, eds., *Forgotten Centuries*, pp. 1–14.

Hudson, C., and C. C. Tesser (editors)
1994b   *The Forgotten Centuries: Indians and Europeans in the American South, 1521–1704*. University of Georgia Press, Athens.

Hudson, J. (editor)
1993   *From Bones to Behavior: Ethnoarchaeological and Experimental Contributions to the Interpretation of Faunal Remains*. Occasional Paper No. 21. Center for Archaeological Investigations, Southern Illinois University, Carbondale.

Hulton, P.
1972   Introduction to the Dover edition of *A Briefe and True Report of the New Found Land of Virginia*, by T. Harriot. Dover, New York.

Hutchinson, D. L., C. S. Larsen, L. Norr, and M. J. Schoeninger
2000   Agricultural Melodies and Alternative Harmonies in Florida and Georgia. In *Bioarchaeological Studies of Life in the Age of Agriculture: A View from the Southeast*, edited by P. M. Lambert, pp. 96–115. University of Alabama Press, Tuscaloosa.

Hutchinson, D. L., C. S. Larsen, M. J. Schoeninger, and L. Norr
  1998   Regional Variation in the Pattern of Maize Adoption and Use in Florida and Georgia. *American Antiquity* 63:397–416.
d'Iberville, P. L. M.
  1981   *Iberville's Gulf Journals*. Edited and translated by R. G. McWilliams. University of Alabama Press, Tuscaloosa.
Iggers, G. G.
  1997   *Historiography in the Twentieth Century: From Scientific Objectivity to Postmodern Challenge*. Wesleyan University Press, Hanover, New Hampshire.
International Association for Plant Taxonomy
  1998   www.bgbm.fu-berlin.de/iapt/ncu/geneva/. *Names in Current Use, Electronic Version 1.0 (NCU 3–e)*. Edited by W. Greuter, B. Zimmer, and W. Berendsohn. Accessed 2/13/98.
Iscan, M. Y., and M. H. Kessel
  1997   Giant Amerindians: Facts or Fantasy? *Southeastern Archaeology* 16:73–78.
Jackson, H. E., and S. L. Scott
  1995a Mississippian Homestead and Village Subsistence Organization: Contrasts in Large Mammal Remains from Two Sites in the Tombigbee Valley. In Rogers and Smith, eds., *Mississippian Communities and Households*, pp. 181–200.
  1995b The Faunal Record of the Southeastern Elite: The Implications of Economy, Social Relations, and Ideology. *Southeastern Archaeology* 14:103–119.
Jennings, F.
  1982   A Growing Partnership: Historians, Anthropologists and American Indian History. *Ethnohistory* 29:21–34.
Jirikowic, C.
  1990   The Political Implications of a Cultural Practice: A New Perspective on Ossuary Burial in the Potomac Valley. *North American Archaeologist* 11:353–374.
John, E. A. H. (editor), and J. Wheat (translator)
  1989   *Views from the Apache Frontier: Report on the Northern Provinces of New Spain by José Cortes, Lieutenant in the Royal Corps of Engineers, 1799*. University of Oklahoma Press, Norman.
Johns, T.
  1994   Ambivalence to the Palatability Factors in Wild Food Plants. In *Eating on the Wild Side: The Pharmacologic, Ecologic, and Social Implications of Using Noncultigens*, edited by N. L. Etkin, pp. 46–61. University of Arizona Press, Tucson.
Johnson, A. W., and T. Earle
  1987   *The Evolution of Human Societies: From Foraging Group to Agrarian State*. Stanford University Press, Stanford.
Johnson, G. A.
  1982   Organizational Structure and Scalar Stress. In *Theory and Explanation in Archaeology: The Southampton Conference*, edited by C. Renfrew, M. Rowlands, and B. Segraves, pp. 389–421. Academic Press, New York.
Johnson, J. K.
  1997   From Chiefdom to Tribe in Northeast Mississippi: The de Soto Expedition as a Window on a Culture in Transition. In Galloway, ed., *Hernando de Soto Expedition*, pp. 295–312.
Johnson, M.
  1996   *An Archaeology of Capitalism*. Blackwell, Oxford.

Jones, B. C.
1982   Southern Cult Manifestations at the Lake Jackson Site, Leon County, Florida: Salvage Excavation of Mound 3. *Midcontinental Journal of Archaeology* 7:1–50.
1994   The Lake Jackson Mound Complex (8LE1): Stability and Change in Fort Walton Culture. *Florida Anthropologist* 45:120–146.

Jones, G. D.
1978   The Ethnohistory of the Guale Coast through 1684. In *The Anthropology of St. Catherines Island 1: Natural and Cultural History*, by D. H. Thomas, G. D. Jones and R. S. Durham, pp. 178–209. Anthropological Papers of the American Museum of Natural History, Vol. 55: Part 2, New York.

Josselyn, J.
1972   [1672] *New-Englands Rarities Discovered*. Reprinted by the Massachusetts Historical Society, Boston.

Joyce, A. A., and M. Winter
1996   Ideology, Power, and Urban Society in Pre-Hispanic Oaxaca. *Current Anthropology* 37:33–47.

Kan, S.
1986   The Nineteenth-Century Tlingit Potlatch: A New Perspective. *American Ethnologist* 13:191–212.
1989   *Symbolic Immortality*. Smithsonian Institution Press, Washington, D.C.

Kealhofer, L., and B. J. Baker
1996   Counterpoint to Collapse: Depopulation and Adaptation. In Baker and Kealhofer, eds., *Bioarchaeology*, pp. 209–222.

Keel, B. C.
1976   *Cherokee Archaeology: A Study of the Appalachian Summit*. University of Tennessee Press, Knoxville.

Keeley, L. H.
1996   *War before Civilization: The Myth of the Peaceful Savage*. Oxford University Press, New York.

Kelley, D. B. (editor)
1994   *The McLelland and Joe Clark Sites: Protohistoric-Historic Caddoan Farmsteads in Southern Bossier Parish, Louisiana*. Coastal Environments, Baton Rouge.
1997   *Two Caddoan Farmsteads in the Red River Valley: The Archeology of the McLelland and Joe Clark Sites*. Research Series No. 51. Arkansas Archeological Survey, Fayetteville.

Kelley, D. B., D. G. Hunter, P. S. Gardner, D. C. Weinand, A. Tine, and L. L. Tieszen
1996   The McLelland and Joe Clark Sites: Protohistoric-Historic Caddo Farmsteads in the Red River Valley of Northwest Louisiana. *Southeastern Archaeology* 15:81–102.

Kelly, A. R.
1938   *A Preliminary Report on Archaeological Excavations at Macon, Georgia*. Bureau of American Ethnology Bulletin 119. Smithsonian Institution, Washington, D.C.

Kelly, A. R., and C. de Baillou
1960   Excavation of the Presumptive Site of Estatoe. *Southern Indian Studies* 12:3–30.

Kelly, A. R., and R. S. Neitzel
1961   *The Chauga Site, Oconee County, South Carolina*. Laboratory of Anthropology Report 3, Department of Anthropology, University of Georgia, Athens.

Kelly, L. S.
1997   Patterns of Faunal Exploitation at Cahokia. In Pauketat and Emerson, eds., *Cahokia*, pp. 69–88.

Kenmotsu, N. A., and T. K. Perttula
1996   "Historical Processes and the Political Organization of the Hasinai Caddo Indians": A Reply. *Caddoan Archeology* 7:9–24.

Kertzer, D. I.
1988   *Ritual, Politics, and Power*. Yale University Press, New Haven.
1996   *Politics and Symbols: The Italian Communist Party and the Fall of Communism*. Yale University Press, New Haven.

Kidder, T. R.
1992   Coles Creek Period Social Organization and Evolution in Northeast Louisiana. In Barker and Pauketat, eds., *Lords of the Southeast*, pp. 145–162.
1993   The Glendora Phase: Protohistoric-Early Historic Culture Dynamics on the Lower Ouachita River. In *Archaeology of Eastern North America: Papers in Honor of Stephen Williams*, edited by J. B. Stoltman, pp. 231–260. Archaeological Report No. 25. Mississippi Department of Archives and History, Jackson.

Kidder, T. R., and G. J. Fritz
1993   Investigating Subsistence and Social Change in the Lower Mississippi Valley: The 1989 and 1990 Excavations at the Reno Brake and Osceola Sites, Tensas Parish, Louisiana. *Journal of Field Archaeology* 20:281–297.

King, A.
1991a Excavations at Mound B, Etowah: 1954–1958. Unpublished Master's thesis, Department of Anthropology and Linguistics, University of Georgia, Athens.
1991b What's New (or Old) from Etowah. *LAMAR Briefs* 18:9–12.

King, A., and J. A. Freer
1995   The Mississippian Southeast: A World-Systems Perspective. In Nassaney and Sassaman, *Native American Interactions*, pp. 266–288.

King, D. H., and E. R. Evans (editors)
1977   Memoirs of the Grant Expedition against the Cherokees, 1761. *Journal of Cherokee Studies* 2:272–337.

Kipp, R. S., and E. M. Schortman
1989   The Political Impact of Trade in Chiefdoms. *American Anthropologist* 91:370–385.

Kleppe, E. J.
1989   Divine Kingship in Northern Africa: Material Manifestations of Social Institutions. In *The Meaning of Things: Material Culture and Symbolic Expression*, edited by I. Hodder. Unwin-Hyman, Winchester, Massachusetts.

Klinger, T. C.
1974   Report on the 1974 Test Excavations at the Knappenberger Site, Mississippi County, Arkansas. *Arkansas Archeologist* 15:45–75.

Knapp, A. B.
1992   Archaeology and *Annales*: Time, Space, and Change. In Knapp, ed., *Archaeology, Annales, and Ethnohistory*, pp. 1–21.

Knapp, A. B. (editor)
1992   *Archaeology, Annales, and Ethnohistory*. Cambridge University Press, Cambridge.

Knight, V. J., Jr.
1981   *Mississippian Ritual*. Ph.D. dissertation, University of Florida, Gainesville. University Microfilms, Ann Arbor.

1985   Tukabatchee: Archaeological Investigations at an Historic Creek Town, Elmore County, Alabama. Report of Investigations No. 45. Office of Archaeological Research, Alabama State Museum of Natural History, University of Alabama, University.
1986   The Institutional Organization of Mississippian Religion. *American Antiquity* 51:675–687.
1989a   Some Speculations on Mississippian Monsters. In *The Southeastern Ceremonial Complex: Artifacts and Analysis*, edited by P. Galloway, pp. 205–210. University of Nebraska Press, Lincoln.
1989b   Symbolism of Mississippian Mounds. In P. H. Wood et al., eds., *Powhatan's Mantle*, pp. 279–291.
1990   Social Organization and the Evolution of Hierarchy in Southeastern Chiefdoms. *Journal of Anthropological Research* 46:1–23.
1994a   Ocmulgee Fields Culture and the Historical Development of Creek Ceramics. In Hally, ed., *Ocmulgee Archaeology*, pp. 181–189.
1994b   The Formation of the Creeks. In C. Hudson and Tesser, eds., *Forgotten Centuries*, pp. 373–392.
1997   Some Developmental Parallels between Cahokia and Moundville. In Pauketat and Emerson, eds., *Cahokia*, pp. 229–247.
1998   Moundville as a Diagrammatic Ceremonial Center. In *Archaeology of the Moundville Chiefdom*, edited by V. J. Knight, Jr., and V. P. Steponaitis, pp. 44–62. Smithsonian Institution Press, Washington, D.C.

Knight, V. J., Jr., and S. L. Adams
1981   A Voyage to the Mobile and Tomeh in 1700, with Notes on the Interior of Alabama. *Ethnohistory* 28:179–194.

Knight, V. J., Jr., and V. P. Steponaitis
1998   A New History of Moundville. In *Archaeology of the Moundville Chiefdom*, edited by V. J. Knight and V. Steponaitis, pp. 1–25. Smithsonian Series in Archaeological Inquiry. Smithsonian Institution Press, Washington, D.C.

Komter, A. E.
1996a   Introduction. In Komter, ed., *Gift*, pp. 3–12.

Komter, A. E. (editor)
1996b   *The Gift: An Interdisciplinary Perspective*. Amsterdam University Press, Amsterdam.

Kosso, P.
1991   Method in Archaeology: Middle Range Theory as Hermeneutics. *American Antiquity* 56:621–627.

Kowalewski, S., and M. Williams
1989   The Carroll Site: Analysis of 1936 Excavations at a Mississippian Farmstead in Georgia. *Southeastern Archaeology* 8:46–67.

Krause, R. A.
1985   Trends and Trajectories in American Archaeology: Some Questions about the Mississippian Period in Southeastern Prehistory. In Badger and Clayton, eds., *Alabama and the Borderlands*, pp. 17–39.

Krech, S.
1991   The State of Ethnohistory. *Annual Review of Anthropology* 20:345–375.
1996   Ethnohistory. In *Encyclopedia of Cultural Anthropology*, Vol. 2, edited by D. Levinson and M. Ember, pp. 422–429. Henry Holt, New York.

Kroeber, A. L.
1939   *Cultural and Natural Areas of Native North America*. University of California, Publications in American Archaeology and Ethnology 38, Berkeley.

Lafferty, R. H., III
1973   An Analysis of Prehistoric Southeastern Fortifications. Unpublished Master's thesis, Southern Illinois University, Carbondale.

Lafferty, R. H., and J. E. Price
1996   Southeast Missouri. In McNutt, ed., *Prehistory of the Central Mississippi Valley*, pp. 1–45.

Lamberg-Karlovsky, C. C. (editor)
1989   *Archaeological Thought in America*. Cambridge University Press, Cambridge.

Larsen, C. W., and L. E. Sering
2001   Inferring Iron-Deficiency Anemia from Human Skeletal Remains: The Case of the Georgia Bight. In *Bioarchaeological Studies of Life in the Age of Agriculture: A View from the Southeast*, edited by P. M. Lambert, pp. 16–133. University of Alabama Press, Tuscaloosa.

Larson, L. H.
1972   Functional Considerations of Warfare in the Southeast during the Mississippian Period. *American Antiquity* 37:383–392.
1978   Historic Guale Indians of the Georgia Coast and the Impact of the Spanish Mission Effort. In *Tacachale: Essays on the Indians of Florida and Southeastern Georgia during the Historic Period*, edited by J. Milanich and S. Proctor, pp. 120–140. University Press of Florida, Gainesville.
1980   *Aboriginal Subsistence Technology on the Southeastern Coastal Plain during the Late Prehistoric Period*. University Presses of Florida, Gainesville.
1994   The Case for Earth Lodges in the Southeast. In *Ocmulgee Archaeology: 1936–1986*, edited by David J. Hally, pp. 105–115. University of Georgia Press, Athens.

Laudonnière, R.
1975   [1586] *Three Voyages*. Translated by C. Bennett. University Presses of Florida, Gainesville.

Lawson, J.
1967   [1709] *A New Voyage to Carolina*. Edited by H. T. Lefler. University of North Carolina Press, Chapel Hill.

Leader, J.
1988   The Lake Jackson Site (8LE1): A Discussion of Trade and Metalworking at a North Florida Mississippian Period Site. Paper presented at the 45th Annual Southeastern Archaeological Conference, New Orleans.

Lederer, J.
1966   [1672] *The Discoveries of John Lederer*. Readex Microprint Edition. Originally published by Sir William Talbot, London.

Lee, C.
1997   Paleopathology of the Hatchel-Mitchell-Moores Sites, Bowie County, Texas. *Bulletin of the Texas Archeological Society* 68:161–177.

Leonard, R. D.
1993   The Persistence of the Explanatory Dilemma in Contact Period Studies. In *Ethnohistory and Archaeology: Approaches to Postcontact Change in the Americas*, edited by J. D. Rogers and S. M. Wilson, pp. 31–48. Plenum Press, New York.

Le Page du Pratz, A. S.
1975   [1774] *The History of Louisiana*, edited by J. J. G. Tregle. Originally published in French in 1758. Louisiana State University Press, Baton Rouge.

Lévi-Strauss, C.
1996   The Principle of Reciprocity. In Komter, ed., *Gift*, pp. 18–25.
Lewis, R. B.
1974   Mississippian Exploitative Strategies: A Southeast Missouri Example. Missouri Archaeological Society *Research Series* No. 11.
Lewis, R. B., and C. B. Stout
1998a   Town as Metaphor. In Lewis and Stout, eds., *Mississippian Towns*, pp. 227–241.
Lewis, R. B., and C. B. Stout (editors)
1998b   *Mississippian Towns and Sacred Spaces: Searching for an Architectural Grammar*. University of Alabama Press, Tuscaloosa.
Lightfoot, K. G.
1995   Culture Contact Studies: Redefining the Relationship Between Prehistoric and Historical Archaeology. *American Antiquity* 60:199–217.
Lightfoot, K. G., A. Martinez, and A. M. Schiff
1998   Daily Practice and Material Culture in Pluralistic Social Settings: An Archaeological Study of Culture Change and Persistence from Fort Ross, California. *American Antiquity* 63:199–222.
Lincoln, B.
1989   *Discourse and the Construction of Society: Comparative Studies of Myth, Ritual, and Classification*. Oxford University Press, New York.
Lindauer, O., and J. H. Blitz
1997   Higher Ground: The Archaeology of North American Platform Mounds. *Journal of Archaeological Research* 5:169–207.
Lindgren, W. H. III
1972   Agricultural Propaganda in Lawson's *A New Voyage to Carolina*. *North Carolina Historical Review* XLIX:333–344.
Linton, R. (editor)
1940   *Acculturation in Seven American Indian Tribes*. Appleton-Century-Crofts, New York.
Lippert, D. T.
1997   A Combination of Perspectives on Caddo Indian Health. Unpublished Ph.D. dissertation, University of Texas at Austin.
Little, B. J.
1992   Text-Aided Archaeology. In *Text-Aided Archaeology*, edited by B. J. Little, pp. 1–8. CRC Press, Boca Raton, Florida.
1996   People with History: An Update on Historical Archaeology in the United States. In *Images of the Recent Past: Readings in Historical Archaeology*, edited by C. E. Orser, Jr., pp. 42–78. Altamira Press, Walnut Creek, California.
Loftfield, T. C., and D. C. Jones
1995   Late Woodland Architecture on the Coast of North Carolina: Structural Meaning and Environmental Adaptation. *Southeastern Archaeology* 14:120–135.
Lolley, T. L.
1996   Ethnohistory and Archaeology: A Map Method for Locating Historic Upper Creek Indian Towns and Villages. *Journal of Alabama Archaeology* 42:1–93.
Lopinot, N. H.
1997   Cahokian Food Production Reconsidered. In Pauketat and Emerson, eds., *Cahokia*, pp. 52–68.
Lyman, R. L.
1982   Archaeofaunas and Subsistence Studies. *Advances in Archaeological Method and Theory* 5:331–393.

Lyman, R. L., M. J. O'Brien, and R. C. Dunnell
1997   *The Rise and Fall of Culture History*. Plenum Press, New York.

Lynott, M. J., T. W. Buotton, J. E. Price, and D. E. Nelson
1986   Stable Carbon Isotopic Evidence for Maize Agriculture in Southeast Missouri and Northeast Arkansas. *American Antiquity* 51:51–65.

MacCord, H. A., Sr.
1996   Prehistoric Territoriality in Virginia. *Southern Indian Studies* 45:57–77.

MacEachern, S., D. J. W. Archer, and R. Gavin (editors)
1989   *Households and Communities*. University of Calgary, Archaeological Association of Calgary Proceedings 21, Calgary.

Magoon, D., L. Norr, D. L. Hutchinson, and C. R. Ewen
2001   An Analysis of Human Skeletal Materials from the Snow Beach Site (8WA52). *Southeastern Archaeology* 20:18–30.

Mainfort, R. C., Jr.
1996   Late Period Chronology in the Central Mississippi Valley: A Western Tennessee Perspective. *Southeastern Archaeology* 15:172–180.
1999   Late Period Phases in the Central Mississippi Valley: A Multivariate Approach. In *Arkansas Archaeology: Essays in Honor of Dan and Phyllis Morse*, edited by R. C. Mainfort and M. D. Jeter, pp. 143–167. University of Arkansas Press, Fayetteville.

Mainfort, R. C., Jr., and R. Carroll
1996   The Nodena Phase: Research Potential of Museum Collections. Paper presented at the 61st Annual Meeting of the Society for American Archaeology, New Orleans.

Mainfort, R. C., Jr., and M. C. Moore
1998   Graves Lake: A Late Mississippian-Period Village in Lauderdale County, Tennessee. In O'Brien and Dunnell, eds., *Changing Perspectives*, pp. 99–123.

Malinowski, B.
1961   *Argonauts of the Western Pacific: An Account of Native Enterprise and Adventure in the Archipelagoes of Melanesian New Guinea*. E. P. Dutton, New York.
1996   The Principle of Give and Take. In Komter, ed., *Gift*, pp. 15–17.

Margry, P.
n.d.   *Découvertes et établissements des Français dans l'ouest et dans le sud de l'Amérique Septentrionale (1614–1754)*. 6 vols. on three microfilm rolls. English translation in Burton Historical Collections, Detroit Public Library, Detroit, Michigan.

Marquardt, W. H.
1987   The Calusa Social Formation in Protohistoric South Florida. In *Power Relations and State Formation*, edited by T. C. Patterson and C. W. Gailey, pp. 98–116. American Anthropological Association, Washington, D.C.
1988   Politics and Production among the Calusa of South Florida. In *Hunters and Gatherers I: History, Evolution, and Social Change*, edited by T. Ingold, D. Riches, and J. Woodburn, pp. 161–188. St. Martin's Press, New York.
1992   Dialectical Archaeology. *Archaeological Method and Theory* 4:101–140.

Martin, C.
1978   *Keepers of the Game: Indian-Animal Relationships and the Fur Trade*. University of California Press, Berkeley.

Martin, J. W.
1991   *Sacred Revolt: The Muskogee's Struggle for a New World*. Beacon Press, Boston.

1994   Southeastern Indians and the English Trade in Skins and Slaves. In C. Hudson and Tesser, eds., *The Forgotten Centuries*, pp. 304–324.

Martyr, P. (see Anghiera, P. M. d').

Maschner, H. D. G. (editor)
1996   *Darwinian Archaeologies*. Plenum Press, New York.

Maschner, H. D. G., and J. Q. Patton
1996   Kin Selection and the Origins of Hereditary Social Inequality: A Case Study from the Northern Northwest Coast. In Maschner, ed., *Darwinian Archaeologies*, pp. 89–107.

Mason, C. I.
1963   Eighteenth-Century Culture Change among the Lower Creeks. *Florida Anthropologist* 16:65–80.

Mauss, M.
1967   *The Gift: Forms and Functions of Exchange in Archaic Societies*. Translated by I. Cunnison. W. W. Norton, New York.

McGuire, R. H.
1983   Breaking Down Cultural Complexity: Inequality and Heterogeneity. *Advances in Archaeological Method and Theory* 6:91–142.
1992a   *A Marxist Archaeology*. Academic Press, New York.
1992b   Archaeology and the First Americans. *American Anthropologist* 94:816–836.

McGuire, R. H., and R. Paynter (editors)
1991   *The Archaeology of Inequality*. Basil Blackwell, Cambridge.

McGuire, R. H., and D. J. Saitta
1996   Although They Have Captains, They Obey Them Badly: The Dialectics of Prehispanic Western Pueblo Social Organization. *American Antiquity* 61:197–216.

McNutt, C. H.
1996b   The Central Mississippi Valley: A Summary. In McNutt, ed., *Prehistory of the Central Mississippi Valley*, pp. 187–257.

McNutt, C. H. (editor)
1996a   *Prehistory of the Central Mississippi Valley*. University of Alabama Press, Tuscaloosa.

McWilliams, R. G.
1981   Introduction. In *Iberville's Gulf Journals*, edited by R. G. McWilliams, translated by R. G. McWilliams, pp. 1–16. University of Alabama Press, Tuscaloosa.

Mereness, N. D.
1916   *Travels in the American Colonies*. Macmillan, New York.

Merrell, James H.
1989   "Our Bond of Peace": Patterns of Intercultural Exchange in the Carolina Piedmont, 1650–1750. In P. H. Wood et al., eds., *Powhatan's Mantle*, pp. 196–222.

Michals, L.
1990   Faunal Exploitation and Chiefdom Organization at Moundville, Alabama. Paper presented at the 55th Annual Meeting of the Society for American Archaeology, Las Vegas.

Milanich, J. T.
1994a   Franciscan Missions and Native Peoples in Spanish Florida. In C. Hudson and Tesser, eds., *Forgotten Centuries*, pp. 276–303.
1994b   *Archaeology of Precolumbian Florida*. University Press of Florida, Gainesville.

Milbrath, S.
1989   Old World Meets New: Views Across the Atlantic. In *First Encounters: Spanish*

Explorations in the Caribbean and the United States, 1492–1570, edited by J. T. Milanich and S. Milbrath, pp. 183–210. University of Florida Press, Gainesville.

Miller, D., M. Rowlands, and C. Tilley
1989a Introduction. In D. Miller et al., eds., *Domination and Resistance*, pp. 1–26.

Miller, D., M. Rowlands, and C. Tilley (editors)
1989b *Domination and Resistance*. Unwin Hyman, Boston.

Miller, J.
1996 Changing Moons: A History of Caddo Religion. *Plains Anthropologist* 41:243–259.

Milner, G. R.
1980 Epidemic Disease in the Postcontact Southeast: a Reappraisal. *Midcontinental Journal of Archaeology* 5:39–56.
1990 The Late Prehistoric Cahokia Cultural System of the Mississippi River Valley: Foundations, Florescence, and Fragmentation. *Journal of World Prehistory* 4:1–43.
1995 An Osteological Perspective on Prehistoric Warfare. In *Regional Approaches to Mortuary Analysis*, edited by L. A. Beck, pp. 221–244. Plenum Press, New York.
1996a Development and Dissolution of a Mississippian Society in the American Bottom, Illinois. In J. F. Scarry, ed., *Political Structure and Change*, pp. 27–52.
1996b Prospects and Problems in Contact-Era Research. In Baker and Kealhofer, eds., *Bioarchaeology*, pp. 198–208.

Milner, G. R., E. Anderson, and V. G. Smith
1991 Warfare in Late Prehistoric West-Central Illinois. *American Antiquity* 56:581–603.

Mitchem, J. M.
1996 Investigations of the Possible Remains of de Soto's Cross at Parkin. *Arkansas Archeologist* 35:87–95.

Mooney, J.
1887 Cherokee Mound Building. *American Anthropologist* 2:161–171.
1891 *Sacred Formulas of the Cherokees*. Bureau of American Ethnology Annual Report 7:301–409. Smithsonian Institution, Washington, D.C.
1900 *History, Myths, and Sacred Formulas of the Cherokees*. Bureau of American Ethnology Annual Report 19:3–548. Smithsonian Institution, Washington, D.C.

Moore, A.
1988 *Nairne's Muskhogean Journal: The 1708 Expedition to the Mississippi River*. University Press of Mississippi, Jackson.

Moore, D. G.
1990 An Overview of Historic Aboriginal Public Architecture in Western North Carolina. Paper presented at the 47th Annual Meeting of the Southeastern Archaeological Conference, Mobile.
1999 Late Prehistoric and Early Historic Period Settlement in the Catawba Valley, North Carolina. Unpublished Ph.D. dissertation, Department of Anthropology, University of North Carolina, Chapel Hill.

Moore, J. H.
1994 Ethnoarchaeology of the Lamar Peoples. In *Perspectives on the Southeast: Linguistics, Archaeology, and Ethnohistory*, edited by P. B. Kwachka, pp. 126–141. University of Georgia Press, Athens.

Morris, M. J.
1993 The Bringing of Wonder: Creek and Euroamerican Trade in the Seventeenth Century. Ph.D. dissertation, Auburn University. University Microfilms, Ann Arbor.

Morse, D. F.
1973 The 1973 Field School Excavations at Upper Nodena. *Field Notes* 106:3–8.
1980 The Big Lake Household and the Community. In *Zebree Archaeological Project*, edited by D. F. Morse and P. A. Morse. Arkansas Archaeological Survey, Fayetteville.
1989 The Nodena Phase. In *Nodena: An Account of 90 Years of Archaeological Investigation in Southeast Mississippi County, Arkansas,* edited by D. F. Morse, pp. 97–114. Arkansas Archaeological Survey Research Series No. 30, Fayetteville.
1990 The Nodena Phase. In Dye and Cox, eds., *Towns and Temples*, pp. 69–97.
1991 On the Possible Origin of the Quapaws in Northeast Arkansas. In *Arkansas before the Americans,* edited by H. A. Davis, pp. 40–54. Arkansas Archeological Survey Research Series No. 40, Fayetteville.

Morse, D. F., and P. A. Morse
1983 *Archaeology of the Central Mississippi Valley.* Academic Press, New York.
1990a Emergent Mississippian in the Central Mississippi Valley. In *The Mississippian Emergence,* edited by B. D. Smith, pp. 153–174. Smithsonian Institution Press, Washington, D.C.
1990b The Spanish Exploration of Arkansas. In D. H. Thomas, ed., *Columbian Consequences,* Vol. 2, pp. 197–210.
1996a Changes in Interpretation in the Archaeology of the Central Mississippi Valley Since 1983. *North American Archaeologist* 17:1–35.
1996b Northeast Arkansas. In McNutt, ed., *Prehistory of the Central Mississippi Valley,* pp. 119–136.

Morse, P. A.
1981 Parkin: The 1978–1979 Archeological Investigations of a Cross County, Arkansas Site. Arkansas Archaeological Survey *Research Series* No. 13.
1990 The Parkin Site and the Parkin Phase. In Dye and Cox, eds., *Towns and Temples,* pp. 118–34.
1993 The Parkin Archaeological Site and Its Role in Determining the Route of the de Soto Expedition. In Young and Hoffman, eds., *Expedition of Hernando de Soto,* pp. 58–67.

Mouer, L. D.
1981 Powhatan and Monacan Regional Settlement Hierarchies: A Model of the Relationship between Social and Environmental Structures. *Quarterly Bulletin of the Archaeological Society of Virginia* 36:1–21.

Mrozowski, S. A.
1993 The Dialectics of Historical Archaeology in a Post-Processual World. *Historical Archaeology* 27:106–111.

Muller, J.
1997 *Mississippian Political Economy.* Plenum Press, New York.

Muller, J., and J. E. Stephens
1991 Mississippian Sociocultural Adaptations. In *Cahokia and the Hinterlands,* edited by T. E. Emerson and R. B. Lewis, pp. 297–310. University of Illinois Press, Urbana.

Myer, W. E.
1928 Indian Trails of the Southeast. Smithsonian Institution, *Bureau of American Ethnology Report* 41:727–857, Washington, D.C.

Nairne, Thomas
1988 *Nairne's Muskhogean Journals: The 1708 Expedition to the Mississippi River*. University Press of Mississippi, Jackson.

Nassaney, M. S.
1992 Communal Societies and the Emergence of Elites in the Prehistoric American Southeast. In Barker and Pauketat, eds., *Lords of the Southeast*, pp. 111–143.

Nasseney, M. S., and K. Pyle
1999 The Adoption of the Bow and Arrow in Eastern North America: A View from Central Arkansas. *American Antiquity* 64:243–263.

Nasseney, M. S., and K. E. Sassaman (editors)
1995 *Native American Interactions: Multiscalar Analyses and Interpretations in the Eastern Woodlands*. University of Tennessee Press, Knoxville.

Neiman, F.
1997 Conspicuous Consumption as Wasteful Advertising: A Darwinian Perspective on Spatial Patterns in Classic Maya Terminal Monument Dates. In Barton and Clark, eds., *Rediscovering Darwin*, pp. 267–290.

Newkumet, V. B., and H. L. Meredith
1988 *Hasinai: A Traditional History of the Caddo Confederacy*. Texas A&M University Press, College Station.

Norberg-Schulz, C.
1971 *Existence, Space and Architecture*. Praeger, New York.
1980 *Genius Loci: Towards a Phenomenology of Architecture*. Rizzoli, New York.

Norr, L., and D. L. Hutchinson
1998 Constructing Prehistoric Subsistence in South Florida (Abstract). *Florida Anthropologist* 51:163.

Nye, W. S.
1968 *Plains Indian Raiders: The Final Phases of Warfare from the Arkansas to the Red River, with Original Photographs by William S. Soule*. University of Oklahoma Press, Norman.

O'Brien, M. J.
1995 Archaeological Research in the Central Mississippi Valley: Culture History Gone Awry. *Review of Archaeology* 16:23–36.
1996 The Historical Development of an Evolutionary Archaeology: A Selectionist Approach. In Maschner, ed., *Darwinian Archaeologies*, pp. 17–32. Plenum Press, New York.

O'Brien, M. J., and R. C. Dunnell (editors)
1998 *Changing Perspectives on the Archaeology of the Central Mississippian Valley*. University of Alabama Press, Tuscaloosa.

O'Brien, M. J., and T. D. Holland
1990 Variation, Selection, and the Archaeological Record. *Archaeological Method and Theory* 2:31–79.
1992 The Role of Adaptation in Archaeological Explanation. *American Antiquity* 57:36–59.

O'Brien, M. J., R. L. Lyman, and R. D. Leonard
1998 Basic Incompatibilities between Evolutionary and Behavioral Archaeology. *American Antiquity* 63:485–498.

Ortner, D. J.
1992 Skeletal Paleopathology: Probabilities, Possibilities, and Impossibilities. In *Disease and Demography in the Americas,* edited by J. W. Verano and D. H. Ubelaker, pp. 5–13. Smithsonian Institution Press, Washington, D.C.

Ortner, S. B.
1984 Theory in Anthropology since the Sixties. *Comparative Studies in Society and History* 26:126–166.

O'Shea, J. M.
1984 *Mortuary Variability: An Archaeological Investigation.* Academic Press, New York.

Oviedo y Valdés, G. F. de
1959 *Historia General y Natural de las Indias.* 5 vols. Biblioteca de Autores Españoles, vols. 117–121. Graficas Orbe, Madrid.

Painter, F.
1980 The Great King of Great Neck: A Status Burial from Coastal Virginia. *Chesopiean* 18:74–75.

Palkovich, A. M.
1996 Historic Population in the American Southwest: Issues of Interpretation and Context-Embedded Analysis. In Baker and Kealhofer, eds., *Bioarchaeology,* pp. 179–197.

Parsons, E. C.
1941 *Notes on the Caddo.* Memoir No. 57. American Anthropological Association, Washington, D.C.

Pauketat, T. R.
1992 The Reign and Ruin of the Lords of Cahokia: A Dialectic of Dominance. In Barker and Pauketat, eds., *Lords of the Southeast,* pp. 31–51.
1994 *The Ascent of Chiefs: Cahokia and Mississippian Politics in Native North America.* University of Alabama Press, Tuscaloosa.
1997a Cahokian Political Economy. In Pauketat and Emerson, eds., *Cahokia,* pp. 30–51.
1997b Specialization, Political Symbols, and the Crafty Elite of Cahokia. *Southeastern Archaeology* 16:1–15.
1998 Refiguring the Archaeology of Greater Cahokia. *Journal of Archaeological Research* 6:45–89.
2001a A New Tradition in Archaeology. In *Archaeology of Traditions: Agency and History before and after Columbus,* edited by T. R. Pauketat, pp.1–16. University Press of Florida, Gainesville.
2001b Practice and History in Archaeology: An Emerging Paradigm. *Anthropological Theory* 1:73–98.

Pauketat, T. R., and T. E. Emerson
1991 The Ideology of Authority and the Power of the Pot. *American Anthropologist* 93:919–941.
1997a Conclusion: Cahokia and the Four Winds. In Pauketat and Emerson, eds., *Cahokia,* pp. 269–278.
1997b Introduction: Domination and Ideology in the Mississippian World. In Pauketat and Emerson, eds., *Cahokia,* pp. 1–29.

Pauketat, T. R., and T. E. Emerson (editors)
1997 *Cahokia: Domination and Ideology in the Missisippian World.* University of Nebraska Press, Lincoln.

Payne, C.
1994a Fifty Years of Archaeological Research at the Lake Jackson Site. *Florida Anthropologist* 47:107–119.
1994b *Mississippian Capitals: An Archaeological Investigation of Precolumbian Political Structure*. Ph.D. dissertation, University of Florida. University Microfilms, Ann Arbor.

Payne, C., and J. F. Scarry
1998 Town Structure at the Edge of the Mississippian World. In Lewis and Stout, eds., *Mississippian Towns*, pp. 22–48.

Paynter, R.
1989 The Archaeology of Equality and Inequality. *Annual Review of Anthropology* 18:369–99.

Pearsall, D. M.
1989 *Paleoethnobotany: A Handbook of Procedures*. Academic Press, San Diego.

Pearson, M. P.
2000 *Archaeology of Death of Burial*. Texas A&M Press, College Station.

Peebles, C. S.
1971 Moundville and Surrounding Sites: Some Structural Considerations of Mortuary Practices. In *Approaches to the Social Dimension of Mortuary Practices*, edited by J. A. Brown, pp. 68–91. Society for American Archaeology, Memoir 15. Washington, D.C.
1974 *Moundville: The Organization of a Prehistoric Community and Culture*. Ph.D. dissertation, University of California, Santa Barbara. University Microfilms, Ann Arbor.
1983 *Prehistoric Agricultural Communities in West Central Alabama*. U.S. Army Corps of Engineers, Mobile District. National Technical Information Services, Springfield, Virginia.
1986 Paradise Lost, Strayed and Stolen: Prehistoric Social Devolution in the Southeast. In *The Burden of Being Civilized: An Anthropological Perspective on the Discontents of Civilization*, edited by M. Richardson and M. C. Webb, pp. 24–40. Southern Anthropological Society Proceedings, no. 18. University of Georgia Press, Athens.
1987 The Rise and Fall of the Mississippian in Western Alabama: The Moundville and Summerville Phases, A.D. 1000 to 1600. *Mississippi Archaeology* 22:1–31.
1991 *Annalistes*, Hermeneutics and Positivists: Squaring Circles or Dissolving Problems. In *The Annales School and Archaeology*, edited by J. Bintliff, pp. 108–124. New York University Press, New York.

Peebles, C. S., and S. M. Kus
1977 Some Archaeological Correlates of Ranked Societies. *American Antiquity* 42:421–448.

Perdue, T.
1998 *Cherokee Women: Gender and Culture Change, 1700–1835*. University of Nebraska Press, Lincoln.

Peregrine, P.
1991 Some Political Aspects of Craft Specialization. *World Archaeology* 23:1–11.
1992 *Mississippian Evolution: A World-System Perspective*. Prehistory Press, Madison.
1995 Networks of Power: The Mississippian World System. In Nassaney and Sassaman, *Native American Interactions*, pp. 247–265.

Persico, J. R., Jr.
1979 Early Nineteenth-Century Cherokee Political Organization. In B. D. Smith, ed., *Cherokee Indian Nation*, pp. 92–110.

Perttula, T. K.
1982 A Consideration of Caddoan Subsistence. *Southeastern Archaeology* 1:89–102.
1994 French and Spanish Colonial Trade Policies and the Fur Trade among the Caddoan Indians of the Trans-Mississippi South. In *The Fur Trade Revisited: Selected Papers of the Sixth North American Fur Trade Conference, Mackinac Island, Michigan, 1991*, edited by J. S. H. Brown, W. J. Eccles, and D. P. Heldman, pp. 71–91. Michigan State University Press, East Lansing.
1996a (moderator) Two Worlds Meet: The Caddoan People and Missions. *Journal of Northeast Texas Archaeology* 7:69–91.
1996b Caddoan Area Archaeology since 1990. *Journal of Archaeological Research* 4:295–348.
1997 "The Caddo Nation": Archaeological and Ethnohistoric Perspectives. Paperback edition. University of Texas Press, Austin.

Perttula, T. K., L. E. Albert, A. M. Early, and J. S. Girard
1998 *Bibliography of Caddoan Archaeology and Bioarchaeology, Ethnography and Ethnohistory, and History*. Special Publication. Friends of Northeast Texas Archaeology, Fayetteville, Arkansas.
1999 *Caddoan Bibliography: Archaeology and Bioarchaeology, Ethnography and Ethnohistory, and History*. Technical Paper 10, Arkansas Archaeological Survey, Fayetteville.

Perttula, T. K., and J. E. Bruseth (editors)
1998 *The Native History of the Caddo: Their Place in Southeastern Archaeology and Ethnohistory*. Studies in Archaeology. Texas Archeological Research Laboratory, University of Texas at Austin.

Perttula, T., C. Crane, and J. E. Bruseth
1982 A Consideration of Caddoan Subsistence. *Southeastern Archaeology* 1:89–102.

Perttula, T. K., M. R. Miller, R. A. Ricklis, D. J. Prikryl, and C. Lintz
1995 Prehistoric and Historic Aboriginal Ceramics in Texas. *Bulletin of the Texas Archeological Society* 66:175–235.

Perttula, T. K., and B. Nelson
1998 Titus Phase Mortuary Practices in the Northeast Texas Pineywoods and Post Oak Savanna. In *Analysis of the Titus Phase Mortuary Assemblage at the Mockingbird or "Kahbakayammaahin" Site (41TT550)*, by T. K. Perttula, M. Tate, H. Neff, J. W. Cogswell, M. D. Glasscock, E. Skokan, S. Mulholland, R. Rogers, and B. Nelson, pp. 328–401. Document No. 970849. Espey, Huston and Associates, Austin.

Phillipe, L.
1928 Tour of the Duke of Orleans, Later Louis Phillipe, King of the French. In S. C. Williams, eds., *Early Travels*, pp. 433–441.

Phillips, P.
1970 Archaeological Survey in the Lower Yazoo Basin, Mississippi, 1949–1955. *Papers of the Peabody Museum of American Archaeology and Ethnology*, Vol. 60, Parts 1 and 2. Peabody Museum Press, Cambridge, Massachusetts.

Phillips, P., and J. A. Brown
1978 *Pre-Columbian Shell Engravings from the Craig Mound at Spiro, Oklahoma, Part 1*. Peabody Museum Press, Cambridge, Massachusetts.

Phillips, P., J. A. Ford, and J. B. Griffin
1951   Archaeological Survey in the Lower Mississippi Alluvial Valley, 1940–47. *Papers of the Peabody Museum of American Archaeology and Ethnology*, Vol. 25. Harvard University Press, Cambridge, Massachusetts.

Pillsbury, R.
1983   The Europeanization of the Cherokee Settlement Landscape Prior to Removal: A Georgia Case Study. In *Historical Archaeology of the Eastern United States*, edited by R. W. Neuman, pp. 59–69. Louisiana State University, Geoscience and Man Vol. 23, Baton Rouge.

Polanyi, K.
1957   The Economy as Instituted Process. In *Trade and Market in the Early Empires*, edited by K. Polanyi, C. Arensberg, and W. H. Pearson, pp. 243–270. Free Press, New York.

Polhemus, R. P.
1979   Archaeological Investigations of the Tellico Blockhouse Site: A Federal Military and Trade Complex. University of Tennessee, Department of Anthropology Report of Investigations 26, Knoxville.
1987   *The Toqua Site: A Late Mississippian Dallas Phase Town*. University of Tennessee, Department of Anthropology, Report of Investigations No. 41, Knoxville.
1990   Dallas Phase Architecture and Sociopolitical Structure. In M. Williams and Shapiro, eds., *Lamar Archaeology*, pp. 125–138.
1998   Activity Organization in Mississippian Households: A Case Study from the Loy Site in East Tennessee. Unpublished Ph.D. dissertation, Department of Anthropology, Univesity of Tennessee, Knoxville.

Poplin, E. C.
1990   Prehistoric Settlement in the Dog River Valley: Archaeological Recovery at 9D034, and 9D045, Douglas County, Georgia. Report prepared by Brockington and Associates for the Douglasville-Douglas County Water and Sewage Authority. Manuscript on file, Laboratory of Archaeology, University of Georgia, Athens.

Potter, S. R.
1989   Early English Effects on Virginia Algonquian Exchange and Tribute in the Tidewater Potomac. In P. H. Wood et al., *Powhatan's Mantle*, pp. 151–172.
1993   *Commoners, Tribute, and Chiefs: The Development of Algonquian Culture in the Potomac Valley*. University Press of Virginia, Charlottesville.

Powell, M. L.
1989   The Nodena People. In *Nodena: An Account of 90 Years of Archaeological Investigation in Southeast Mississippi County, Arkansas*, edited by D. F. Morse, pp. 65–95. Arkansas Archaeological Survey Research Series No. 30, Fayetteville.
1990   Health and Disease at Nodena: A Late Mississippian Community in Northeastern Arkansas. In Dye and Cox, eds., *Towns and Temples*, pp. 98–117.
1997   Foreword for Special Papers on Caddoan Bioarcheological Research. *Bulletin of the Texas Archeological Society* 68:135–138.

Preucel, R. W. (editor)
1991   *Processual and Postprocessual Archaeologies: Multiple Ways of Knowing the Past*. Center for Archaeological Investigations, Southern Illinois University, Carbondale.

Price, J. E., and C. R. Price
1990   Protohistoric/Early Historic Manifestations in Southeastern Missouri. In Dye and Cox, eds., *Towns and Temples*, pp. 59–68.

Priestley, H. I.
1928   *The Luna Papers: Documents Relating to the Expedition of Don Tristan de Luna y Arellano for the Conquest of La Florida in 1559–1561*. Florida Historical Society, Deland.

Purdy, B.
1988   American Indians after A.D. 1492: A Case Study. *American Anthropologist* 90:640–655.

Purrington, B. L.
1983   Ancient Mountaineers: An Overview of the Prehistoric Archaeology of North Carolina's Western Mountain Region. In *The Prehistory of North Carolina: An Archaeological Symposium*, edited by M. A. Mathis and J. L. Crow, pp. 83–180. North Carolina Division of Archives and History, Raleigh.

Quitmyer, I. R., H. S. Hale, and D. S. Jones
1985   Paleoseaonality Determination Based on Incremental Shell Growth in the Hard Clam, *Mercenaria mercenaria*, and Its Implications for the Analysis of Three Southeast Georgia Coastal Shell Middens. *Southeastern Archaeology* 4:27–40.

Quitmyer, I. R., and D. S. Jones
1997   The Schlerochronology of Hard Clams, *Mercenaria* spp., from the South-Eastern U.S.A.: A Method of Elucidating the Zooarchaeological Records of Seasonal Resource Procurement and Seasonality in Prehistoric Shell Middens. *Journal of Archaeological Sciences* 24:825–840.

Radford, A. E., H. Ahles, and C. R. Bell
1968   *Manual of the Vascular Flora of the Carolinas*. University of North Carolina Press, Chapel Hill.

Ramenofsky, A. F.
1987   *Vectors of Death: The Archaeology of European Contact*. University of New Mexico Press, Albuquerque.
1990   Loss of Innocence: Explanations of Differential Persistence in the Sixteenth-Century Southeast. In D. H. Thomas, ed., *Columbian Consequences*, vol. 2, pp. 31–48.
1991a Beyond Disciplinary Bias: Future Directions in Contact Period Studies. In D. H. Thomas, ed., *Columbian Consequences*, Vol. 3, pp. 431–436.
1991b Historical Science and Contact Period Studies. In D. H. Thomas, ed., *Columbian Consequences*, Vol. 3, pp. 437–452.
1995   Evolutionary Theory and Native American Artifact Change in the Postcontact Period. In Teltser, ed., *Evolutionary Archaeology: Methodological Issues*, pp. 129–147.

Ramenofsky, A. F., and P. Galloway
1997   Disease and the de Soto Entrada. In Galloway, ed., *Hernando de Soto Expedition*, pp. 259–282.

Randolph, J. R.
1973a Henry Timberlake and the Cherokees. In Randolph, ed., *British Travelers*, pp. 142–154.

Randolph, J. R. (editor)
1973b *British Travelers among the Southern Indians, 1660–1763*. University of Oklahoma Press, Norman.

Rangel, R.
1993   Account of the Northern Conquest and Discovery of Hernando de Soto. Translated and edited by J. E. Worth. In Clayton et al., eds., *De Soto Chronicles*, Vol. 1, pp. 245–306.

Rapoport, A.
1969   *House Form and Culture*. Prentice-Hall, Englewood Cliffs, New Jersey.

Rappaport, R. A.
1978   Maladaption in Social Systems. In *The Evolution of Social Systems*, edited by J. Friedman and M. J. Rowlands, pp. 49–72. Duckworth, London.

Redfield, R., R. Linton, and M. J. Herskovits
1936   Memorandum for the Study of Acculturation. *American Anthropologist* 38: 149–152.

Redmond, E. M.
1994   *Tribal and Chiefly Warfare in South America*. University of Michigan, Museum of Anthropology, Memoir 28. Ann Arbor.

Rees, M. A.
1997   Coercion, Tribute, and Chiefly Authority: The Regional Development of Mississippian Political Culture. *Southeastern Archaeology* 16:113–133.

Reese-Taylor, K., J. Hageman, and R. A. Ricklis
1994   Preliminary Paste Analyses of Ceramic Samples from the Mustang Branch Site (41HY209) and Barton Site (41HY202). In *Archaic and Late Prehistoric Human Ecology in the Middle Onion Creek Valley, Hays County, Texas*, by R. A. Ricklis and M. B. Collins, pp. 549–568. Studies in Archeology 19. 2 vols. Texas Archeological Research Laboratory, University of Texas at Austin.

Reitz, E. J.
1982   Availability and Use of Fish along Coastal Georgia and Florida. *Southeastern Archaeology* 1:65–88.
1987   Coastal Adaptations in Georgia and the Carolinas. Paper presented at the 44th Annual Meeting of the Southeastern Archaeological Conference, Charleston.

Reitz, E. J., and C. M. Scarry
1985   *Reconstructing Historic Subsistence with an Example from Sixteenth-Century Spanish Florida*. Special Publication Series Number 3, Society for Historical Archaeology, Ann Arbor.

Renfrew, C.
1974   Beyond a Subsistence Economy: The Evolution of Social Organization in Prehistoric Europe. In *Reconstructing Complex Societies: an Archaeological Colloquium*, edited by C. B. Moore, pp. 69–85. Supplement to the Bulletin of the American Schools of Oriental Research, No. 20. Ann Arbor.
1978   Trajectory Discontinuity and Morphogenesis: The Implications of Catastrophe Theory for Archaeology. *American Antiquity* 43:203–222.

Reyna, S. P.
1994   A Mode of Domination Approach to Organized Violence. In *Studying War: Anthropological Perspectives*, edited by S. P. Reyna and R. E. Downs, pp. 29–65. Gordon and Breach, New York.

Ribault, J.
1964   [1563] *The Whole and True Discouerye of Terra Florida: A Facsimile Reprint of the London Edition of 1563*. University of Florida Press, Gainesville.

Ricklis, R. A.
1994   Toyah Components: Evidence for Occupation in the Project Area during the

Latter Part of the Late Prehistoric Period. In *Archaic and Late Prehistoric Human Ecology in the Middle Onion Creek Valley, Hays County, Texas*, by R. A. Ricklis and M. B. Collins, pp. 207–316. Studies in Archeology 19. Texas Archeological Research Laboratory, University of Texas at Austin.

Riggs, B. H.
1984 The Bell Rattle Cabin Site (40MR6): A Case Study in Cherokee Acculturation. Paper presented at the Second Symposium on Uplands Archaeology in the East. James Madison University, Harrisonburg, Virginia.
1989 Ethnohistorical and Archaeological Dimensions of Early Nineteenth-Century Cherokee Intrahousehold Variation. In MacEachern et al., eds., *Households and Communities*, pp. 328–338.

Rindos, D.
1985 Darwinian Selection, Symbolic Variation, and the Evolution of Culture. *Current Anthropology* 26:65–88.
1989a Diversity, Variation, and Selection. In *Quantifying Diversity in Archaeology*, edited by R. D. Leonard and G. T. Jones, pp. 13–23. Cambridge University Press, Cambridge.
1989b Undirected Variation and the Darwinian Explanation of Culture Change. *Archaeological Method and Theory* 1:1–45.

Rindos, D., and S. Johannessen
1991 Human-Plant Interactions and Cultural Change in the American Bottom. In *Cahokia and the Hinterlands*, edited by T. E. Emerson and R. B. Lewis, pp. 35–45. University of Illinois Press, Urbana.

Roberts, L.
1989 Disease and Death in the New World. *Science* 246:1245–1247.

Robertson, J. A. (translator and editor)
1993 "True Relation of the Hardships Suffered by Governor Hernando De Soto & Certain Portuguese Gentlemen During the Discovery of the Province of Florida, Now Newly Set Forth by a Gentleman of Elvas." In Clayton et al., eds., *De Soto Chronicles*, Vol. 1, pp. 19–219.

Rodning, C. B.
1996a *Towns and Clans: Social Institutions and Organization of Native Communities on the Appalachian Summit*. Unpublished fourth semester paper for the Department of Anthropology, University of North Carolina, Chapel Hill.
1996b Gender and Social Institutions of Native Communities of the Appalachian Summit. Paper presented at the 53rd Annual Meeting of the Southeastern Archaeological Conference, Birmingham.
1996c Trends in Intrasite Settlement Patterning in the Appalachian Summit Region during Late Precontact and Early Postcontact Times. Paper presented at the Conference on Integrating Appalachian Highlands Archaeology, Albany.
1998a Spatial Patterning in the Archaeology of the Upper Little Tennessee Valley. Poster presented at the 63rd Annual Meeting of the Society for American Archaeology, Seattle.
1998b Mortuary Patterns at Coweta Creek in the Upper Little Tennessee Valley. Poster presented at the 55th Annual Meeting of the Southeastern Archaeological Conference, Greenville, South Carolina.
1999a Archaeological Perspectives on Gender and Women in Traditional Cherokee Society. *Journal of Cherokee Studies* 20:3–27.
1999b Landscaping Communal Space at the Coweeta Creek Site. Paper presented at

the 56th Annual Meeting of the Southeastern Archaeological Conference, Pensacola.

Rogers, D. J.
1990 *Objects of Change: The Archaeology and History of Arikara Contact with Europeans.* Smithsonian Institution Press, Washington, D.C.
1995 Dispersed Communities and Integrated Households: A Perspective from Spiro and the Arkansas Basin. In Rogers and Smith, *Mississippian Communities and Households,* pp. 81–98.
1996 Markers of Social Integration: The Development of Centralized Authority in the Spiro Region. In J. F. Scarry, ed., *Political Structure and Change,* pp. 53–68.

Rogers, D. J., and B. D. Smith (editors)
1995 *Mississippian Communities and Households.* University of Alabama Press, Tuscaloosa.

Rogers, D. J., and S. M. Wilson (editors)
1993 *Ethnohistory and Archaeology: Approaches to Postcontact Change in the Americas.* Plenum Press, New York.

Rollings, W. H.
1995 Living in a Graveyard: Native Americans in Colonial Arkansas. In *Cultural Encounters in the Early South: Indians and Europeans in Arkansas,* compiled by J. Whayne, pp. 38–60. University of Arkansas Press, Fayetteville.

Romans, B.
1962 [1775] *A Concise Natural History of East and West Florida.* Facsimile reproduction of the 1775 edition. University of Florida Press, Gainesville.

Rose, J. C., M. K. Marks, and L. L. Tieszen
1991 Bioarchaeology and Subsistence in the Central and Lower Portions of the Mississippi Valley. In *What Mean These Bones: Studies in Southeastern Bioarchaeology,* edited by M. L. Powell, P. S. Bridges, and A. M. W. Mires, pp. 7–21. University of Alabama Press, Tuscaloosa.

Roseberry, W.
1988 Political Economy. *Annual Review of Anthropology* 17:161–185.
1989 *Anthropologies and Histories: Essays in Culture, History, and Political Economy.* Rutgers University Press, New Brunswick, New Jersey.

Roth, J. A.
1980 Analysis of Faunal Remains. In *Archaeological Investigation of the Little Egypt Site (9MU102), Murray County, Georgia 1970–72 seasons,* pp. 570–591. Report submitted to the Heritage Conservation and Recreation Service, United States Department of the Interior.

Rountree, H. C.
1989 *The Powhatan Indians of Virginia: The Traditional Culture.* University of Oklahoma Press, Norman.
1990 *Pocahontas's People: The Powhatan Indians of Virginia through Four Centuries.* University of Oklahoma Press, Norman.
1993a The Powhatans and the English: A Case of Multiple Conflicting Agendas. In Rountree, ed., *Powhatan Foreign Relations,* pp. 173–205.
1993b Who Were the Powhatans and Did They Have a Unified "Foreign Policy"? In Rountree, ed., *Powhatan Foreign Relations,* pp. 1–19.

Rountree, H. C. (editor)
1993c *Powhattan Foreign Relations 1500–1722.* University Press of Virginia, Charlottesville.

Rountree, H. C., and E. R. Turner III
1994   On the Fringe of the Southeast: The Powhatan Paramount Chiefdom in Virginia. In C. Hudson and Tesser, eds., *Forgotten Centuries*, pp. 355–372.
1998   The Evolution of the Powhatan Paramount Chiefdom in Virginia. In *Chiefdoms and Chieftaincy in the Americas,* edited by E. M. Redmond, pp. 265–296. University Press of Florida, Gainesville.

Rozin, P.
1987   Psychobiological Perspectives on Food Preferences and Avoidances. In *Food and Evolution: Toward a Theory of Human Food Habits,* edited by M. Harris and E. B. Ross, pp. 181–206. Temple University Press, Philadelphia.

Rudolph, J. L.
1984   Earthlodges and Platform Mounds: Changing Public Architecture in the Southeastern United States. *Southeastern Archaeology* 3:33–45.

Ruhl, D. L.
1993   Old Customs and Traditions in New Terrain: Sixteenth- and Seventeenth-Century Archaeobotanical Data from La Florida. In C. M. Scarry, ed., *Foraging and Farming,* pp. 255–284.

Russ, K. C., and J. Chapman
1984   *Archaeological Investigations at the Eighteenth-Century Overhill Cherokee Town of Mialoqua.* University of Tennessee, Department of Anthropology, Report of Investigations 37. Knoxville.

Russo, M. A.
1991   A Method for the Measurement of Season and Duration of Oyster Collection: Two Case Studies from the Prehistoric Southeast U.S. Coast. *Journal of Archaeological Science* 18:205–221.
1992a   Chronologies and Cultures of the St. Marys Region of Northeast Florida and Southeast Georgia. *Florida Anthropologist* 45:107–126.
1992b   *The Timucuan Ecological and Historic Preserve Phase III Final Report.* Florida Museum of Natural History, Gainesville.

Russo, M. A., and R. Saunders
1999   *Identifying the Early Use of Coastal Fisheries and the Rise of Social Complexity in Shell Rings and Arcuate Middens on Florida's Northeast Coast.* Final Report Submitted to the National Geographic Society, Grant #6018–97.

Sabo, G., III
1995a   Rituals of Encounter: Interpreting Native American Views of European Explorers. In *Cultural Encounters in the Early South: Indians and Europeans in Arkansas,* compiled by J. Whayne, pp. 76–87. University of Arkansas Press, Fayetteville.
1995b   Encounters and Images: European Contact and Caddo Indians. *Historical Reflections/Reflexions Historiques* 21:217–242.

Sahlins, M.
1958   *Social Stratification in Polynesia.* University of Washington Press, Seattle.
1960   Evolution: Specific and General. In *Evolution and Culture,* edited by M. D. Sahlins and E. R. Service, pp. 12–44. University of Michigan Press, Ann Arbor.
1972   *Stone Age Economics.* Aldine Atherton, Chicago.
1985   *Islands of History.* University of Chicago Press, Chicago.
1993   Goodbye to Tristes Tropes: Ethnography in the Context of Modern World History. *Journal of Modern History* 65:1–25.

1994 Goodbye to Tristes Tropes: Ethnography in the Context of Modern World History. In *Assessing Cultural Anthropology*, edited by R. Borofsky, pp. 377–393. McGraw Hill, New York.

Saitta, D. J.
1989 Dialectics, Critical Inquiry, and Archaeology. In *Critical Traditions in Contemporary Archaeology*, edited by V. Pinsky and A. Wylie, pp. 38–43. Cambridge University Press, Cambridge.
1994 Agency, Class, and Archaeological Interpretation. *Journal of Anthropological Archaeology* 13:1–27.
1997 Power, Labor, and the Dynamics of Change in Chacoan Political Economy. *American Antiquity* 62:7–26.

Salisbury, N.
1996 Native People and European Settlers in Eastern North America, 1600–1783. In Trigger and Washburn, eds., *Cambridge History of the Native Peoples*, pp. 399–460.

Salley, A. S., Jr. (editor)
1911 *Narratives of Early Carolina, 1650–1708*. Charles Scribner's Sons, New York.

Sanders, W. T., and B. Price
1968 *Mesoamerica: the Evolution of a Civilization*. Random House, New York.

Sanders, W. T., and D. Webster
1978 Unilinealism, Multilinealism, and the Evolution of Complex Societies. In *Social Archaeology: Beyond Subsistence and Dating*, edited by R. L. Redman, M. J. Berman, E. V. Curtin, W. T. Langhorne, Jr., N. M. Versaggi, and J. C. Wanser, pp. 249–302. Academic Press, New York.

Sattler, R. A.
1995 Women's Status among the Muskogee and Cherokee. In *Women and Power in Native North America*, edited by L. F. Klein and L. A. Ackerman, pp. 214–229. University of Oklahoma Press, Norman.

Saucier, R. T.
1994 *Geomorphology and Quaternary Geologic History of the Lower Mississippi Valley*. U.S. Army Corps of Engineers Waterways Experiment Station, Vol. 1, Vicksburg, Mississippi.

Saunders, R.
1992a Continuity and Change in Guale Indian Pottery, A.D. 1350–1702. Unpublished Ph.D. dissertation, Department of Anthropology, University of Florida, Gainesville.
1992b Guale Indian Pottery: A Georgia Legacy in Northeast Florida. *Florida Anthropologist* 45:139–147.
1992c The Lost Colony of San Miguel de Gualdape, Past and Present. Paper submitted for *The Search for San Miguel*, edited by D. H. Thomas. Anthropological Papers of the American Museum of Natural History, New York.
1998 The Lost Colony of San Miguel de Gualdape, Past and Present. In *The Search for San Miguel*, edited by D. H. Thomas. Anthropological Papers of the American Museum of Natural History, New York.
2000a *Continuity and Change in Guale Indian Pottery, A.D. 1300–1702*. University of Alabama Press, Tuscaloosa.
2000b The Guale Indians of the Lower Atlantic Coast: Change and Continuity. In *Indians of the Greater Southeast during the Historic Period*. University Press of Florida, Gainesville.

Saunders, R., and M. A. Russo
1988 Meeting House Fields: Irene Phase Material Culture and Seasonality of St. Catherines Island. Report submitted to the American Museum of Natural History, New York.

Scarry, C. M.
1986 Change in Plant Procurement and Production during the Emergence of the Moundville Chiefdom. Unpublished Ph.D. dissertation, Department of Anthropology, University of Michigan, Ann Arbor.
1993a Agricultural Risk and the Development of the Moundville Chiefdom. In C. M. Scarry, ed, *Foraging and Farming*, pp. 157–181.
1993b Variability in Mississippian Crop Production Strategies. In C. M. Scarry, ed., *Foraging and Farming*, pp. 78–90.

Scarry, C. M. (editor)
1993c *Foraging and Farming in the Eastern Woodlands*. University Press of Florida, Gainesville.

Scarry, C. M., and V. P. Steponaitis
1997 Between Farmstead and Center: The Natural and Social Landscape of Moundville. In Gremillion, ed., *People, Plants, and Landscapes*, pp. 107–122.

Scarry, J. F.
1984 *Fort Walton Development: Mississippian Chiefdoms in the Lower Southeast.* Ph.D. dissertation, Case Western Reserve University. University Microfilms, Ann Arbor.
1990a The Rise, Transformation, and Fall of the Apalachee. In M. Williams and Shapiro, *Lamar Archaeology*, pp. 175–186.
1990b Mississippian Emergence in the Fort Walton Area: The Evolution of the Cayson and Lake Jackson Phases. In B. D. Smith, ed., *Mississippian Emergence*, pp. 227–250.
1991 The Apalachee and Mississippian Exchange: Speculations on the Impact of Geographic Location. Paper presented in the symposium "Mississippian Economies" at the 56th Annual Meeting of the Society for American Archaeology, New Orleans.
1992 Political Offices and Political Structure: Ethnohistoric and Archaeological Perspectives on the Native Lords of Apalachee. In Barker and Pauketat, eds., *Lords of the Southeast*, pp. 163–183.
1994a The Apalachee Chiefdom: A Mississippian Society on the Fringe of the Mississippian World. In C. Hudson and Tesser, eds., *Forgotten Centuries*, pp. 156–178.
1994b The Late Prehistoric Southeast. In C. Hudson and Tesser, eds., *Forgotten Centuries*, pp. 17–35.
1996a The Nature of Mississippian Societies. In J. F. Scarry, ed., *Political Structure and Change*, pp. 12–24.
1996b Looking for and at Mississippian Political Change. In J. F. Scarry, ed., *Political Structure and Change*, pp. 3–11.
1996c Stability and Change in the Apalachee Chiefdom. In J. F. Scarry, ed., *Political Structure and Change*, pp. 192–227.
1999 Elite Identities in Apalachee Province: The Construction of Identity and Cultural Change in a Mississippian Society. In *Material Symbols: Culture and Economy in Prehistory*, edited by J. Robb, pp. 342–361. Occasional Paper 26. Center for Archaeological Investigations, Southern Illinois University, Carbondale.

Scarry, J. F. (editor)
1996d *Political Structure and Change in the Prehistoric Southeastern United States.* University Press of Florida, Gainesville.

Schambach, F. F.
1970 Pre-Caddoan Cultures in the Trans-Mississippi South: A Beginning Sequence. Unpublished Ph.D. dissertation, Department of Anthropology, Harvard University, Cambridge.
1982 An Outline of Fourche Maline Culture in Southwest Arkansas. In *Arkansas Archeology in Review,* edited by N. L. Trubowitz and M. D. Jeter, pp. 132–197. Arkansas Archeological Survey *Research Series* No. 15, Fayetteville.
1983 The Archeology of the Great Bend Region in Arkansas. In *Contributions to the Archeology of the Great Bend Region,* edited by F. F. Schambach and F. Rackerby, pp. 1–11. Arkansas Archeological Survey *Research Series* No. 22, Fayetteville.
1996 Mounds, Embankments, and Ceremonialism in the Trans-Mississippi South. In *Mounds, Embankments, and Ceremonialism in the Midsouth,* edited by R. C. Mainfort and R. Walling, pp. 36–43. Arkansas Archeological Survey *Research Series* No. 46, Fayetteville.

Schambach, F. F., N. L. Trubowitz, F. Rackerby, E. T. Hemmings, W. F. Limp, and J. E. Miller
1983 Test Excavations at the Cedar Grove Site (3LA97): A Late Caddo Farmstead in the Great Bend Region, Southwest Arkansas. In *Contributions to the Archeology of the Great Bend Region,* edited by F. F. Schambach and F. Rackerby, pp. 90–129. Arkansas Archeological Survey *Research Series* No. 22, Fayetteville.

Schneider, M.
1928 Brother Martin Schneider's report of his journey to the upper Cherokee Towns. In S. C. Williams, ed., *Early Travels,* pp. 245–265.

Schoeninger, M. J., N. J. van der Merwe, K. Moore, J. Lee-Thorp, and C. S. Larsen
1989 Decrease in Diet Quality between the Prehistoric and Contact Periods. In *The Archaeology of Mission Santa Catalina de Guale: 2. Biocultural Interpretations of a Population in Transition,* edited by C. S. Larsen, pp. 78–93. Anthropological Papers No. 68. American Museum of Natural History, New York.

Schoolcraft, H. R.
1851– *Historic and Statistical Information Respecting the History, Condition, and Pros-*
1857 *pects of the Indian Tribes of the United States.* Lippincott, Philadelphia.

Schortman, E. M.
1989 Interregional Interaction in Prehistory: The Need for a New Perspective. *American Antiquity* 54:52–65.

Schroedl, G. F.
1978 Louis-Phillipe's Journal and Archaeological Investigations at the Overhill Town of Toqua. *Journal of Cherokee Studies* 3:206–220.
1980 Structure and Village Pattern at the Historic Overhill Cherokee Towns of Chota and Tanasee. Paper presented at the 37th Annual Meeting of the Southeastern Archaeological Conference, New Orleans.
1983 Eighteenth-Century Overhill Cherokee Domestic Structures. Paper presented at the 40th Annual Meeting of the Southeastern Archaeological Conference, Columbia.
1986a Overhill Cherokee Archaeology from the Perspective of Chota-Tanasee. In *Overhill Cherokee Archaeology at Chota-Tanasee,* edited by G. F. Schroedl,

pp. 531–551. Department of Anthropology, University of Tennessee, Report of Investigations 38, Knoxville.
1986b Structures. In *Overhill Cherokee Archaeology at Chota-Tanasee*, edited by G. F. Schroedl, pp. 217–272. University of Tennessee, Department of Anthropology Report of Investigations 38, Knoxville.
1989 Overhill Cherokee Household and Village Patterns in the Eighteenth Century. In MacEachern et al., eds., *Households and Communities*, pp. 350–360.
1991 Cherokee Public Architecture and Culture Change in the Eighteenth and Nineteenth Centuries. Paper presented at the 39th Annual Meeting of the American Society for Ethnohistory, Tulsa.
1998 Mississippian Towns in the Eastern Tennessee Valley. In Lewis and Stout, eds., *Mississippian Towns*, pp. 64–93.

Schroedl, G. F., and B. H. Riggs
1989 Cherokee Lower Town Archaeology at the Chatooga Site. Paper presented at the 46th Annual Meeting of the Southeastern Archaeological Conference, Tampa.
1990 Investigations of Cherokee Village Patterning and Public Architecture at the Chattooga Site. Paper presented at the 47th Annual Meeting of the Southeastern Archaeological Conference, Mobile.
1992 Cherokee Village Patterning at the Chattooga Site. Paper presented at the 57th Annual Meeting of the Society for American Archaeology, Pittsburgh.

Schultz, M., and C. W. Larsen
1997 Porotic Hyperostosis in Spanish Florida: Nature and Etiology of a Frequently Observed Phenomenon. *American Journal of Physical Anthropology* Supplement 24:206.

de Schwienitz, F.
1928 Journey of the Moravians to the Cherokee and Cumberland Countries. In S. C. Williams, ed., *Early Travels*, pp. 445–525.

Scott, J. C.
1985 *Weapons of the Weak: Everyday Forms of Peasant Resistance*. Yale University Press, New Haven.

Scott, S. L.
1982 Yarborough Site Faunal Remains. In *Archaeological Investigations at the Yarborough Site (22C1814) Clay County, Mississippi*, edited by C. Solis and R. Walling, pp. 140–152. Office of Archaeological Research, Report of Investigations No. 30. University of Alabama, Tuscaloosa.
1983 Analysis, Synthesis and Interpretation of Faunal Remains from the Lubbub Creek Archaeological Locality. In *Prehistoric Agricultural Communities in West Central Alabama*, edited by C. S. Peebles, pp. 272–390. U.S. Army Corps of Engineers, Mobile District. National Technical Information Services, Springfield, Virginia.

Sears, W. H.
1958 *The Wilbanks Site (9CK-5), Georgia*. Bureau of American Ethnology, Bulletin 169, pp. 131–194. Smithsonian Institution, Washington, D.C.

Service, E. R.
1962 *Primitive Social Organization*. Random House, New York.
1975 *The Origins of the State and Civilization: The Process of Cultural Evolution*. W. W. Norton, New York.

Setzler, F. M. and J. D. Jennings
1941   Peachtree Mound and Village Site, Cherokee County, North Carolina. Smithsonian Institution, Bureau of American Ethnology Bulletin 131, Washington, D.C.

Shea, J. G. (editor and translator)
1853   Discovery and Exploration of the Mississippi Valley. J. S. Redfield, New York.

Sheldon, C. T., Jr.,
1974   The Mississippian-Historic Transition in Central Alabama. Unpublished Ph.D. dissertation, Department of Anthropology, University of Oregon, Eugene.
1997   Historic Creek "Summer" Houses of Central Alabama. Paper presented at the 62nd Annual Meeting of the Society for American Archaeology, Nashville.

Sheldon, E. S.
1978   Childersburg: Evidence of European Contact Demonstrated by Archaeological Plant Remains. Southeastern Archaeological Conference Special Publication 5:28–29.

Sierzchula, M. C., M. J. Guccione, R. H. Lafferty III, and M. T. Oates
1995   Archeological Investigations in the Great Bend Region, Miller County, Arkansas, Levee Items 2 and 3. Report 94-5. Mid-Continental Research Associates, Inc., Lowell, Arkansas.

Silver, T. A.
1990   A New Face on the Countryside: Indians, Colonists, and Slaves in South Atlantic Forests, 1500–1800. Cambridge University Press, Cambridge.

Simmons, W. S.
1988   Culture Theory in Contemporary Ethnohistory. Ethnohistory 35:1–14.

Skiles, B. D., and T. K. Perttula
1998   The Sacred Landscape of the Caddo: Aboriginal Trails and Mound Centers in East Texas. Paper presented at the 6th Annual East Texas Archeological Conference, Tyler.

Smart, T., and E. S. Hoffman
1988   Environmental Interpretation of Archaeological Charcoal. In Current Paleoethnobotany, edited by C. Hastorf and V. S. Popper, pp. 167–205. University of Chicago Press, Chicago.

Smith, B. A.
1979   Distribution of Eighteenth-Century Cherokee Settlements. In B. D. Smith, ed., Cherokee Indian Nation, pp. 46–60.

Smith, B. D.
1975   Middle Mississippi Exploitation of Animal Populations. Anthropological Papers No. 57. Museum of Anthropology, University of Michigan, Ann Arbor.
1978b Prehistoric Patterns of Human Behavior: A Case Study in the Mississippi Valley. Academic Press, New York.
1978c Variation in Mississippian Settlement Patterns. In B. D. Smith, ed., Mississippian Settlement Patterns, pp. 479–503.
1985   Mississippian Patterns of Subsistence and Settlement. In Badger and Clayton, eds., Alabama and the Borderlands, pp. 64–80.
1986   The Archaeology of the Southeastern United States: From Dalton to de Soto, 10,500–500 B.P. Advances in World Archaeology 5:1–92.
1992   Mississippian Elites and Solar Alignments: A Reflection of Managerial Necessity, or Levers of Social Inequality? In Barker and Pauketat, eds., Lords of the Southeast, pp. 11–30.

1996   Agricultural Chiefdoms of the Eastern Woodlands. In Trigger and Washburn, eds., *Cambridge History of the Native Peoples*, pp. 267–323.

Smith, B. D. (editor)
1978a   *Mississippian Settlement Patterns*. Academic Press, New York.
1979   *The Cherokee Indian Nation: A Troubled History*. University of Tennessee Press, Knoxville.
1990   *The Mississippian Emergence*. Smithsonian Institution Press, Washington, D.C.

Smith, F. T.
1995   *The Caddo Indians: Tribes at the Convergence of Empires, 1542–1854*. Texas A&M University Press, College Station.
1996   *The Wichita and Caddo Indians: Relations with the U.S. 1846–1901*. Texas A&M University Press, College Station.

Smith, H. G.
1973   *Analysis of the Lamar Site (9BI7) Materials at the Southeastern Archaeological Center*. A Report prepared for the National Park Service. Copies available from the Department of Anthropology, Florida State University, Tallahassee.

Smith, J. R.
1986a   [1608] A True Relation. In *The Complete Works of Captain John Smith (1580–1631)*, Vol. 1, edited by P. L. Barbour, pp. 3–118. Originally published in 1608. University of North Carolina Press, Chapel Hill.
1986b   [1624] The General Historie of Virginia, New England, and the Summer Isles, 1624. In *The Complete Works of Captain John Smith (1580–1631)*, Vol. 2, edited by P. L. Barbour, pp. 25–488. Originally published in 1624. University of North Carolina Press, Chapel Hill.

Smith, M. T.
1987   *Archaeology of Aboriginal Culture Change in the Interior Southeast: Depopulation and the Early Historic Period*. University of Florida Press, Gainesville.
1989a   Aboriginal Population Movements in the Early Historic Period Interior Southeast. In P. H. Wood et al., *Powhatan's Mantle*, pp. 21–34.
1989b   Early Historic Period Vestiges of the Southern Cult. In *The Southeastern Ceremonial Complex: Artifacts and Analysis*, edited by P. Galloway, pp. 142–146. University of Nebraska Press, Lincoln.
1991   Indians of Mississippi: 1540–1700. In *Native, European, and African Cultures in Mississippi, 1500–1800*, edited by P. K. Galloway, pp. 31–41. Mississippi Department of Archives and History, Jackson.
1992   *Historic Period Indian Archaeology of Northern Georgia*. University of Georgia, Laboratory of Archaeology, Report 30, Athens.
1994a   *Archaeological Investigations at the Dyar Site, 9GE5*. University of Georgia, Laboratory of Archaeology Series, Report Number 32, Athens.
1994b   Aboriginal Depopulation in the Postcontact Southeast. In C. Hudson and Tesser, eds., *Forgotten Centuries*, pp. 257–275.

Smith, M. T., and D. J. Hally
1992   Chiefly Behavior: Evidence from Sixteenth-Century Spanish Accounts. In Barker and Pauketat, eds., *Lords of the Southeast*, pp. 99–109.

Smith, M. T., and S. Williams
1994   Mississippian Mound Refuse Disposal Patterns and Implications for Archaeological Research. *Southeastern Archaeology* 13:27–35.

Solis, C., and R. Walling (editors)
1982   *Archaeological Investigations at the Yarborough Site (22CL814) Clay County, Mis-

250 / References

  sissippi. Office of Archaeological Research, Report of Investigations No. 30. University of Alabama, Tuscaloosa.

Spencer, C. S.
1987 Rethinking the Chiefdom. In *Chiefdoms in the Americas*, edited by R. Drennan and C. A. Uribe, pp. 369–389. University Press of America, Lanham, Maryland.
1994 Factional Ascendance, Dimensions of Leadership, and the Development of Centralized Authority. In Brumfiel and Fox, eds., *Factional Competition*, pp. 31–43.
1997 Evolutionary Approaches in Archaeology. *Journal of Archaeological Research* 5:209–264.

Spencer, H.
1862 *First Principles*. Williams and Norgate, London.
1967 [1898] *The Principles of Sociology*, edited by R. L. Carneiro. University of Chicago Press, Chicago.

Spicer, E. H.
1962 Types of Contact and Processes of Change. In *Perspectives in American Indian Culture Change*, edited by E. H. Spicer, pp. 517–544. University of Chicago Press, Chicago.

Stahl, A. B.
1993 Concepts of Time and Approaches to Analogical Reasoning in Historical Perspective. *American Antiquity* 58:235–260.

Stahle, D. W., M. K. Cleaveland, D. B. Blanton, M. D. Therill, and D. A. Gay
1998 The Lost Colony and Jamestown Droughts. *Science* 280:564–567.

Stein, G. J.
1998 Heterogeneity, Power, and Political Economy: Some Current Issues in the Archaeology of Old World Complex Societies. *Journal of Archaeological Research* 6:1–44.

Steinen, K. T.
1992 Ambushes, Raids, and Palisades: Mississippian Warfare in the Interior Southeast. *Southeastern Archaeology* 11:132–139.

Steinen, K. T., and R. Ritson
1996 In Defense of the Frontier: Considerations of Apalache Warfare during the Mississippian Period. *Florida Anthropologist* 49:111–120.

Steiner, A., and F. de Schwienitz
1928 Journey of the Moravians to the Cherokee and Cumberland Countries. In S. C. Williams, *Early Travels*, pp. 445–525.

Steponaitis, V. P.
1978 Location Theory and Complex Chiefdoms: A Mississippian Example. In B. D. Smith, ed., *Mississippian Settlement Patterns*, pp. 417–453.
1983 *Ceramics, Chronology, and Community Patterns: An Archaeological Study at Moundville*. Academic Press, New York.
1986 Prehistoric Archaeology in the Southeastern United States, 1970–1985. *Annual Review of Anthropology* 15:363–404.
1991 Contrasting Patterns of Mississippian Development. In Earle, ed., *Chiefdoms*, pp. 193–228.

Steward, J. H.
1940 Native Cultures of the Intermontane Area. In *Essays in Historical Anthropology*

  of North America. Smithsonian Miscellaneous Collections, Vol. 100, pp. 479–498. Washington, D.C.
1942 The Direct Historical Approach to Archaeology. *American Antiquity* 7:337–433.
1955 *Theory of Culture Change: The Methodology of Multilinear Evolution.* University of Illinois Press, Urbana.

Storey, R.
1991 Bioanthropological Studies of the Lake Jackson Elite. Paper presented at the 48th Annual Meeting of the Southeastern Archaeological Conference, Jackson.

Story, D. A. (editor)
1982 *The Deshazo Site, Nacogdoches County, Texas,* Vol. 1: *The Site, Its Setting, Investigation, Cultural Features, Artifacts of Non-Native Manufacture, and Subsistence Remains.* Texas Antiquities Permit Series No. 7. Texas Antiquities Committee, Austin.
1995 *The Deshazo Site, Nacogdoches County, Texas,* Vol. 2: *Artifacts of Native Manufacture.* Studies in Archeology 21. Texas Archeological Research Laboratory, University of Texas at Austin.

Strachey, W.
1953 [1612] *The Historie of Travell into Virginia Britania.* Edited by L. B. Wright and V. Freund. Series 2, Number 103. Hakluyt Society, London.

Strausbaugh, P. D., and E. L. Core
1978 *Flora of West Virginia.* Seneca Books, Grantsville, West Virginia.

Strong, W. D.
1935 *An Introduction to Nebraska Archaeology.* Smithsonian Miscellanous Collections Vol. 93, no. 10, Washington, D.C.
1940 From History to Prehistory in the Northern Great Plains. In *Essays in Historical Anthropology of North America.* Smithsonian Miscellaneous Collections Vol. 100, pp. 353–394. Washington, D.C.

Sturtevant, W. C.
1966 Anthropology, History, and Ethnohistory. *Ethnohistory* 13:1–51.
1977 The Ethnological Evaluation of the Le Moyne-De Bry Illustrations. In *The Work of Jacques Le Moyne de Morgues, a Huguenot Artist in France, Florida and England,* edited by P. Hulton, pp. 69–74. British Museum Publications, London.
1978 Louis-Phillipe on Cherokee Architecture and Clothing in 1797. *Journal of Cherokee Studies* 3:198–205.

Styles, B. W., and J. R. Purdue
1984 Faunal Exploitation at the Cedar Grove Site. In *Cedar Grove, An Interdisciplinary Investigation of a Late Caddo Farmstead in the Red River Valley,* edited by N. L. Trubowitz, pp. 211–226. Arkansas Archeological Survey *Research Series* 23, Fayetteville.

Sullivan, L. P.
1987 The Mouse Creek Phase Household. *Southeastern Archaeology* 6:16–29.
1989 Household, Community, and Society: An Analysis of Mouse Creek Settlements. In MacEachern et al., eds., *Households and Communities,* pp. 317–327.
1995 Mississippian Community and Household Organization in Eastern Tennessee. In Rogers and Smith, eds., *Mississippian Communities and Households,* pp. 99–123.

Swan, C.
1855 Position and State of Manners and Arts in the Creek, or Muscogee Nation in

1791. In *Indian Tribes*, edited by H. R. Schoolcraft, Vol. 5, pp. 251–283. Lippincott, Philadelphia.

Swanton, J. R.

1911   *Indian Tribes of the Lower Mississippi Valley and Adjacent Coast of the Gulf of Mexico.* Bureau of American Ethnology, Bulletin 43. Smithsonian Institution, Washington, D.C.

1922   *Early History of the Creek Indians and Their Neighbors.* United States Bureau of American Ethnology, Bulletin 73. Bureau of American Ethnology, Washington, D.C.

1928   Social Organization and Social Usages of the Indians of the Creek Confederacy. In *42nd Annual Report of the Bureau of American Ethnology*, Vol. 42, pp. 31–726. Bureau of American Ethnology, Washington, D.C.

1942   *Source Material on the History and Ethnology of the Caddo Indians.* Bulletin 132. Bureau of American Ethnology, Smithsonian Institution, Washington, D.C.

1946   *Indians of the Southeastern United States.* Bulletin 137. Bureau of American Ethnology, Smithsonian Institution, Washington, D.C.

1952   *The Indian Tribes of North America.* Bulletin 145. Bureau of American Ethnology, Smithsonian Institution, Washington, D.C.

1985   [1939] *Final Report of the United States De Soto Expedition Commission.* United States House of Representatives Document no. 71, 76th Congress, 1st Session. Reprint, Smithsonian Institution Press, Washington, D.C.

Tainter, J. A.

1975   Social Inference and Mortuary Practices: An Experiment in Numerical Classification. *World Archaeology* 7:2–15.

Tanner, H. H.

1989   The Land and Water Communication Systems of the Southeastern Indians. In P. H. Wood et al., *Powhatan's Mantle*, pp. 6–20.

1993   The Caddos in the Era of the Republic of Texas. 3 Parts. *Caddo Nation News* 2 (Nos. 2–4).

1996   Foreword. In *Source Material on the History and Ethnology of the Caddo Indians*, by J. R. Swanton, pp. ix–xii. University of Oklahoma Press, Norman.

Taylor, W.

1983   [1948] *A Study of Archaeology.* Southern Illinois University, Center for Archaeological Investigations, Vol. 69. Southern Illinois University, Carbondale.

Teltser, P. A. (editor)

1995   *Evolutionary Archaeology: Methodological Issues.* University of Arizona Press, Tucson.

Thomas, C.

1894   *Report on the Mound Explorations of the Bureau of American Ethnology.* Smithsonian Institution, Bureau of American Ethnology Report 12:3–742, Washington, D.C.

Thomas, D. H.

1993a *Historic Indian Period Archaeology of the Georgia Coastal Zone.* Georgia Archaeological Research Design Paper No. 8. University of Georgia Laboratory of Archaeology Series Report No. 13. Athens.

Thomas, D. H. (editor)

1990a *Columbian Consequences*, Vol. 1: *Archaeological and Historical Perspectives on the Spanish Borderlands East.* Smithsonian Institution Press, Washington, D.C.

1990b   *Columbian Consequences*, Vol. 2: *Archaeological and Historical Perspectives on the Spanish Borderlands East*. Smithsonian Institution Press, Washington, D.C.
1991   *Columbian Consequences*, Vol. 3: *The Spanish Borderlands in Pan-American Perspective*. Smithsonian Institution Press, Washington, D.C.

Thomas, K.
1983   *Man and the Natural World: Changing Attitudes in England 1500–1800*. Oxford University Press, Oxford.

Thoms, A. V. (editor)
1997   *The Upper Keechi Creek Archaeological Project: Survey and Test Excavations at the Keechi Creek Wildlife Management Area, Leon County, Texas*. Technical Report No. 3. Center for Environmental Archaeology, Texas A&M University, College Station.

Timberlake, H.
1927   *Memoirs of Lieutenant Henry Timberlake*, edited by Samuel Cole Williams. Watauga Press, Johnson City, Tennessee.

Tregle, J. G., Jr.
1975   Introduction, In *The History of Louisiana*, by Antoine Simone Le Page du Pratz, edited by J. J. G. Tregle. Facsimile edition of the 1774 English translation. Originally published in French in 1758. Louisiana State University Press, Baton Rouge.

Trigger, B.
1978   *Time and Traditions: Essays in Archaeological Interpretation*. Columbia University Press, New York.
1980   Archaeology and the Image of the American Indian. *American Antiquity* 45:662–676.
1982   Ethnohistory: Problems and Prospects. *Ethnohistory* 29:1–19.
1983   American Archaeology as Native History: A Review Essay. *William and Mary Quarterly* 40:413–452.
1984   Archaeology at the Crossroads: What's New? *Annual Review of Anthropology* 13:275–300.
1985   *Natives and Newcomers*. McGill-Queens University Press, Montreal.
1986   Ethnohistory: The Unfinished Edifice. *Ethnohistory* 33:253–267.
1989a   *A History of Archaeological Thought*. Cambridge University Press, Cambridge.
1989b   History and Contemporary American Archaeology: A Critical Analysis. In Lamberg-Karlovsky, ed., *Archaeological Thought*, pp. 19–34.
1991   Distinguished Lecture in Archaeology: Constraint and Freedom—A New Synthesis for Archaeological Explanation. *American Anthropologist* 93:551–569.

Trigger, B. G., and W. R. Swagerty
1996   Entertaining Strangers: North America in the Sixteenth Century. In Trigger and Washburn, eds., *Cambridge History of the Native Peoples*, pp. 325–398.

Trigger, B. G., and W. E. Washburn (editors)
1996   *The Cambridge History of the Native Peoples of the Americas*, Vol. 1: *North America, Part 1*. Cambridge University Press, Cambridge.

Turnbaugh, W. A.
1993   Assessing the Significance of European Goods in Seventeenth-Century Narragansett Society. In Rogers and Wilson, eds., *Ethnohistory and Archaeology*, pp. 133–160.

Turner, E. R., III
1976   An Archaeological and Ethnohistorical Study on the Evolution of Rank So-

cieties in the Virginia Coastal Plain. Unpublished Ph.D. dissertation, Department of Anthropology, Pennsylvania State University, University Park.

1992 The Virginia Coastal Plain during the Late Woodland Period. In *Middle and Late Woodland Research in Virginia: A Synthesis*, edited by T. R. Reinhart and M. E. Hodges, pp. 97–136. Special Publication 29. Archaeological Society of Virginia, Richmond.

1993 Protohistorical Native American Interactions in the Powhatan Core Area. In Rountree, ed., *Powhatan Foreign Relations*, pp. 76–93.

Turner, R. L., Jr.

1992 *Prehistoric Mortuary Remains at the Tuck Carpenter Site, Camp County, Texas*. Studies in Archeology 10. Texas Archeological Research Laboratory, University of Texas at Austin.

Ubelaker, D. H.

1974 *A Reconstruction of Demographic Profiles from Ossuary Skeletal Samples: A Case Study from the Tidewater Potomac*. Smithsonian Contributions to Anthropology Number 18. Smithsonian Institution Press, Washington, D.C.

USDA (United States Department of Agriculture)

1998 www.ars-grin.gov/npgs/tax/index.html. Genetic Resources Information System of the National Plant Germplasm System. GRIN Taxonomy web page. Agricultural Research Service, United States Department of Agriculture. Accessed 2/13/98.

Usner, D. H., Jr.

1992 *Indians, Settlers, and Slaves in a Frontier Exchange Economy: The Lower Mississippi Valley before 1783*. University of North Carolina Press, Chapel Hill.

VanDerwarker, A. M.

1998 Qualla Phase Cherokee Foodways at the Coweeta Creek Site. Paper presented at the 55th Annual Meeting of the Southeastern Archaeological Conference, Greenville, South Carolina.

VanDerwarker, A. M., and K. R. Detwiler

1999 Gender, Feasting, and the Consumption of Plant Foods at Coweeta Creek. Paper presented at the 56th Annual Meeting of the Southeastern Archaeological Conference, Pensacola.

Van Horne, W. W.

1993 The Warclub: Weapon and Symbol in Southeastern Indian Societies. Unpublished Ph.D. dissertation, Department of Anthropology, University of Georgia, Athens.

VanStone, J. W.

1970 Ethnohistorical Research in Southwestern Alaska: A Methodological Perspective. In *Ethnohistory in Southwestern Alaska and the Southern Yukon: Method and Content*, edited by M. Lantis, pp. 49–69. University Press of Kentucky, Lexington.

Vaughn, J. G., and C. A. Geissler

1997 *The New Oxford Book of Food Plants*. Oxford University Press, Oxford.

de la Vega, G.

1993 [1605] *La Florida*. Translated by C. Shelby, edited by D. Bost, footnotes by V. J. Knight, Jr. In Clayton et al., eds., *De Soto Chronicles*, Vol. 2, pp. 25–561.

Vehik, S. C., and T. G. Baugh

1994 Prehistoric Plains Trade. In *Prehistoric Exchange Systems in North America*, edited by T. G. Baugh and J. E. Ericson, pp. 249–274. Plenum Press, New York.

Vennum, T. R.
1994 *American Indian Lacrosse: Little Brother to War.* Smithsonian Institution Press, Washington, D.C.

Vogel, J. O., and J. Allan
1985 Mississippian Fortifications at Moundville. *Archaeology* 38:62–63.

Ward, H. T., and R. P. S. Davis, Jr.
1999 *Time before History: The Archaeology of North Carolina.* University of North Carolina Press, Chapel Hill.

Ward, H. T., and C. B. Rodning
1997 Reconsidering the Relationship between Pisgah and Qualla Phases of the Appalachian Summit. Paper presented at the 54th Annual Meeting of the Southeastern Archaeological Conference, Baton Rouge.

Waselkov, G. A.
1985 *Culture Change on the Creek Indian Frontier.* Final Report to the National Science Foundation (Grant No. BNS-8305437). Manuscript on file, Department of Sociology/Anthropology, University of South Alabama, Mobile.
1988 Historic Creek Architectural Adaptations to the Deerskin Trade. Paper presented at the 45th Annual Meeting of the Southeastern Archaeological Conference, New Orleans.
1989a Seventeenth Century Trade in the Colonial Southeast. *Southeastern Archaeology* 8:117–133.
1989b Indian Maps of the Colonial Southeast. In P. H. Wood et al., *Powhatan's Mantle,* pp. 292–343.
1993 Historic Creek Indian Responses to European Trade and the Rise of Political Factions. In Rogers and Wilson, eds., *Ethnohistory and Archaeology,* pp. 123–131.
1997 Changing Strategies of Indian Field Location in the Early Historic Southeast. In Gremillion, ed., *People, Plants, and Landscapes,* pp. 179–194.

Waselkov, G. A. (editor)
1988 *Culture Change on the Creek Frontier.* Final Report to the National Science Foundation (Grant No. BNS-8305437). Manuscript on file, Department of Sociology and Anthropology, University of South Alabama.

Waselkov, G. A., and K. E. H. Braund
1995 *William Bartram on the Southeastern Indians.* University of Nebraska Press, Lincoln.

Waselkov, G. A., J. W. Cottier, and C. T. Sheldon Jr.
1990 *Archaeological Investigations at the Early Historic Creek Indian Town of Fusihatchee* (Phase I, 1988–1989). Report to the National Science Foundation (Grant No. BNS-8718934). Manuscript on file, Department of Sociology and Anthropology, Auburn University, Montgomery.

Watson, P. J.
1990 Trend and Tradition in Southeastern Archaeology. *Southeastern Archaeology* 9:43–55.

Watson, P. J., S. A. LeBlanc, and C. L. Redman
1971 *Explanation in Archaeology: An Explicitly Scientific Approach.* Columbia University Press, New York.

Watt, B. K., and A. Merrill
1975 *Handbook of the Nutritional Contents of Foods.* Dover, New York.

Webb, C. H.
1959   The Belcher Mound, a Stratified Caddoan Site in Caddo Parish, Louisiana. Memoir No. 16. Society for American Archaeology, Salt Lake City.

Weddle, R. S.
1987   The Talon Interrogations: A Rare Perspective. In *La Salle, the Mississippi, and the Gulf: Three Primary Documents*, edited by R. S. Weddle, pp. 209–224. Texas A&M University Press, College Station.

Wedel, M. M.
1978   *La Harpe's 1719 Post on Red River and Nearby Caddo Settlements*. Bulletin 30. Texas Memorial Museum, University of Texas at Austin.

Wedel, W. R.
1938   *The Direct Historical Approach in Pawnee Archaeology*. Smithsonian Miscellaneous Collections Vol. 97, no. 7. Washington, D.C.
1940   Culture Sequence in the Central Great Plains. In *Essays in Historical Anthropology of North America*. Smithsonian Miscellaneous Collections Vol. 100, pp. 291–352. Washington, D.C.

Weinstein, R. A.
1985   Some New Thoughts on the De Soto Expedition through Western Mississippi. *Mississippi Archaeology* 20:2–24.

Weisman, B., and J. T. Milanich
1976   Dietary Scarcity: A Stimulus for Warfare among Southeastern United States Horticulturalists during the Historic Period. *Florida Journal of Anthropology* 1:31–37.

Welch, P. D.
1991   *Moundville's Economy*. University of Alabama Press, Tuscaloosa.
1996   Control over Goods and the Political Stability of the Moundville Chiefdom. In J. F. Scarry, ed., *Political Structure and Change*, pp. 69–91.

Welch, P. D., and C. M. Scarry
1995   Status Related Variation in Foodways in the Moundville Chiefdom. *American Antiquity* 60:397–419.

Wesson, C. B.
1997   *Households and Hegemony: An Analysis of Historic Creek Culture Change*. Ph.D. dissertation, University of Illinois. University Microfilms, Ann Arbor.
1998   Mississippian Sacred Landscapes: The View from Alabama. In Lewis and Stout, eds., *Mississippian Towns*, pp. 93–122.
1999   Chiefly Power, Household Production, and Food Storage in Southeastern North America. *World Archaeology* 31:145–164.

Wetmore, R. Y.
1983   Green Corn Ceremony of the Eastern Cherokees. *Journal of Cherokee Studies* 8:46–57.

White, L.
1959   *The Evolution of Culture: The Development of Civilization to the Fall of Rome*. McGraw-Hill, New York.

White, R.
1983   *The Roots of Dependency*. University of Nebraska Press, Lincoln.

Whitley, D. S.
1992   Prehistory and Post-Positivist Science: A Prolegomenon to Cognitive Archaeology. In *Archaeological Method and Theory*, Vol. 4, edited by M. B. Schiffer, pp. 57–100. University of Arizona Press, Tucson.

Widmer, R. J.
1994 The Structure of Southeastern Chiefdoms. In C. Hudson and Tesser, eds., *Forgotten Centuries*, pp. 125–155.

Wilcox, D. R., and W. B. Massey
1981 *The Protohistoric Period in the North American Southwest, A.D. 1450–1700*. Anthropological Research Paper No. 24. Arizona State University Press, Tempe.

Willey, G. R.
1985 Some Continuing Problems in New World Culture History. *American Antiquity* 50:351–363.

Willey, G. R., and P. Phillips
1958 *Method and Theory in American Archaeology*. University of Chicago Press, Chicago.

Willey, G., and J. Sabloff
1993 *A History of American Archeology*, third edition. W. H. Freeman, New York.

Williams, L.
1925– Colonel Joseph Williams' Battalion in Christian's Campaign. *Tennessee Histori-*
1926   *cal Magazine* 9:102–116.

Williams, M.
1993 Archaeological Excavations at the Bullard Landing Site (9TW1). Lamar Institute Publication 24, Watkinsville, Georgia.
1994 Growth and Decline of the Oconee Province. In C. Hudson and Tesser, eds., *Forgotten Centuries*, pp. 179–196.

Williams, M., and D. T. Elliot
1998 Swift Creek Research: History and Observations. In *A World Engraved: Archaeology of the Swift Creek Culture*, edited by M. Williams and D. T. Elliot, pp. 1–11. University of Alabama Press, Tuscaloosa.

Williams, M., and J. F. Harris
1998 Shrines of the Prehistoric South: Patterning in Middle Woodland Mound Distributions. In *A World Engraved: Archaeology of the Swift Creek Culture*, edited by M. Williams and D. T. Elliot, pp. 36–47. University of Alabama Press, Tuscaloosa.

Williams, M., and G. Shapiro
1996 Mississippian Political Dynamics in the Oconee Valley, Georgia. In J. F. Scarry, ed., *Political Structure and Change*, pp. 92–127.

Williams, M., and G. Shapiro (editors)
1990 *Lamar Archaeology: Mississippian Chiefdoms in the Deep South*. University of Alabama Press, Tuscaloosa.

Williams, R.
1977 *Marxism and Literature*. Oxford University Press, Oxford.

Williams, S.
1990 The Vacant Quarter and Other Late Events in the Lower Valley. In Dye and Cox, eds., *Towns and Temples*, pp. 170–180.

Williams, S. C. (editor)
1927 *Lieut. Henry Timberlake's Memoirs, 1756–1765*. Watauga Press, Johnson City, Tennessee.
1928 *Early Travels in the Tennessee Country, 1540–1800*. Watauga Press, Johnson City, Tennessee.
1930 *Adair's History of the American Indians*. Watauga Press, Johnson City, Tennessee.

Willis, P.
1981 Cultural Production Is Different from Cultural Reproduction Is Different from Social Reproduction Is Different from Reproduction. *Interchange* 12:48–67.

Wilms, D. C.
1974 Cherokee Settlement Patterns in Nineteenth-century Georgia. *Southeastern Geographer* 14:46–53.
1991 Cherokee Land Use in Georgia before Removal. In *Cherokee Removal, Before and After*, edited by W. L. Anderson, pp. 1–28. University of Georgia Press, Athens.

Wilson, D.
1997 Dental Paleopathology in the Sanders (41LR2) and Mitchell (41BW4) Populations from the Red River Valley, Northeast Texas. *Bulletin of the Texas Archeological Society* 68:147–159.

Wilson, D., and S. M. Derrick
1997 An Examination of Caddoan Responses to Recurring Epidemic Disease in the Protohistoric and Historic Periods. Paper presented in symposium "Conflict, Migration, and Coalescence, Native American Groups in Texas A.D. 1530–1878," Society for Historical Archaeology, Corpus Christi.

Wilson, G. D., A. VanDerwarker, K. R. Detwiler, and C. B. Rodning
1999 Boiling, Baking, and Pottery Breaking: Seventeenth-Century Foodways at the Coweeta Creek Site. Paper presented at the 56th Annual Meeting of the Southeastern Archaeological Conference, Pensacola.

Wilson, R. W.
1992 *Compliance Ideologies: Rethinking Political Culture.* Cambridge University Press, Cambridge.

Wilson, S. M.
1993 Structure and History: Combining Archaeology and Ethnohistory in the Contact Period Caribbean. In Rogers and Wilson, eds., *Ethnohistory and Archaeology*, pp. 19–30.

Wilson, S. M., and J. D. Rogers
1993 Historical Dynamics in the Contact Era. In Rogers and Wilson, eds., *Ethnohistory and Archaeology*, pp. 3–18.

Winterhalder, B., and C. Goland
1997 An Evolutionary Ecology Perspective on Diet Choice, Risk, and Plant Domestication. In Gremillion, ed., *People, Plants, and Landscapes*, pp. 123–160.

Wolf, E.
1974 *Anthropology.* W. W. Norton, New York.
1982 *Europe and the People without History.* University of California Press, Berkeley.

Wood, A.
1990 The Travels of James Needham and Gabriel Arthur through Virginia, North Carolina, and Beyond, 1673–1674. *Southern Indian Studies* 39:31–55.

Wood, J. W., G. R. Milner, H. C. Harpending, and K. M. Weiss
1992 The Osteological Paradox: Problems of Inferring Prehistoric Health from Skeletal Samples. *Current Anthropology* 33:343–370.

Wood, P. H.
1989 The Changing Population of the Colonial South: An Overview by Race and Region, 1685–1790. In P. H. Wood et al., eds., *Powhatan's Mantle*, pp. 35–103.

Wood, P. H., G. A. Waselkov, and M. T. Hatley (editors)
1989 *Powhatan's Mantle: Indians in the Colonial Southeast.* University of Nebraska Press, Lincoln.

Wood, W. R.
1990   Ethnohistory and Historical Method. *Archaeological Method and Theory* 2: 81–109.
Worth, J. E.
1998   *The Timucuan Chiefdoms of Spanish Florida.* University Press of Florida, Gainesville.
Wright, H. T.
1984   Prestate Political Formations. In *On the Evolution of Complex Societies: Essays in Honor of Harry Hoijer,* edited by T. K. Earle, pp. 43–77. Udena Publications, Malibu.
Wright, J. L., Jr.
1986   *Creeks and Seminoles: The Destruction and Regeneration of the Muscogulge People.* University of Nebraska Press, Lincoln.
Wynn, J. T.
1990   *The Mississippi Period Archaeology of the Georgia Blue Ridge.* Laboratory of Archaeology Report 27. University of Georgia, Athens.
Yarnell, R. A.
1982   Problems of Interpretation of Archaeological Plant Remains of the Eastern Woodlands. *Southeastern Archaeology* 1:1–7.
Yarnell, R. A., and M. J. Black
1985   Temporal Trends Indicated by a Survey of Archaic and Woodland Plant Food Remains from Southeastern North America. *Southeastern Archaeology* 4:93–106.
Yelton, J. K.
1995   Vertebrate Remains. In *Woodland and Mississippian Occupations at the Hayti Bypass Site, Pemiscot County, Missouri,* edited by M. D. Conner, pp. 263–289. Center for Archaeological Research, Special Publication No. 1. Southwest Missouri State University, Springfield.
Yoffee, N.
1993   Too Many Chiefs? (or, Safe Texts for the '90s). In *Archaeological Theory: Who Sets the Agenda?* edited by N. Yoffee and A. Sherratt, pp. 60–78. Cambridge University Press, Cambridge.
Young, G. A., and M. P. Hoffman (editors)
1993   *The Expedition of Hernando de Soto West of the Mississippi, 1541–1543: Proceedings of the DeSoto Symposia, 1988 and 1990.* University of Arkansas Press, Fayetteville.
Young, T. C., Jr.
1988   Since Herodotus, Has History Been a Valid Concept? *American Antiquity* 53:7–12.
Zimmerman, L. J.
1989   Made Radical by My Own: an Archaeologist Learns to Accept Reburial. In *Conflict in the Archaeology of Living Traditions,* edited by R. Layton, pp. 60–67. Routledge, London.
Zubillaga, F.
1946   *Monumenta Historica Societatis Iesu,* Vol. 69. Monumenta Missionum Societatis Iesu, Vol. 3. Rome.

Contributors

David H. Dye is associate professor and chair of anthropology at the University of Memphis. He received his Ph.D. in anthropology from Washington University. His research interests include ethnographic, ethnohistoric, and archaeological research in the Mid-South. His current research involves the analysis of artifacts from public and private collections in the Memphis area and an examination of iconography and warfare in the Southeast.

Kristen J. Gremillion is an associate professor of anthropology at the Ohio State University. She received her Ph.D. from the University of North Carolina-Chapel Hill. Her research interests include the origins of agriculture, human evolutionary ecology, and paleoethnobotany in eastern North America. She is currently investigating the ecology of early food production in the plateau country of eastern Kentucky.

David J. Hally is an associate professor of anthropology at the University of Georgia in Athens. He received his Ph.D. from Harvard University in 1972. His research interests include the nature of Mississippian households and settlement systems, the analysis of archaeological ceramics, and the anthropology of southeastern food habits. He has directed site surveys and excavations at a number of locations across the state of Georgia.

Mintcy D. Maxham is a doctoral candidate in the Department of Anthropology at the University of North Carolina-Chapel Hill. Her research interests include sociopolitical developments in Mississippian societies. Her current research focuses on rural settlement in the Moundville chiefdom, on which she has contributed a recent article to *American Antiquity*.

Timothy K. Perttula received his Ph.D. from the University of Washington and has been conducting archaeological and ethnohistorical research on the Caddo since the mid-1970s, focusing on the period immediately before and after contact with Europeans. He is a principal in Archeological and Environmental Consultants in Austin, Texas, and the Caddo Tribe's archaeological consultant.

Mark A. Rees is an assistant professor at the University of Louisiana, Lafayette. He received his Ph.D. in anthropology from the University of Oklahoma and has been involved with archaeological research throughout the eastern and midwestern United States. His research interests include historical anthropology and political culture. His dissertation research focused on the Moundville polity of west-central Alabama, and he is currently investigating mound sites in southern Louisiana.

Christopher B. Rodning graduated from Harvard University in 1994 with an A.B. magna cum laude in anthropology and is currently a Ph.D. candidate in anthropology at the University of North Carolina-Chapel Hill. His primary interests are the landscapes and lifeways of late prehistoric and protohistoric native peoples of eastern North America. His dissertation addresses the archaeology and ethnohistory of seventeenth- and early eighteenth-century native communities in western North Carolina.

Rebecca Saunders is an associate curator of the Museum of Natural Science at Louisiana State University. She received her Ph.D. from the University of Florida. Her research interests include contact period studies, southeastern United States prehistory, and pottery analysis.

John F. Scarry is a research associate professor of anthropology at the University of North Carolina-Chapel Hill. He received his doctorate in anthropology from Case Western Reserve University. His dissertation research focused on the development of Mississippian chiefdoms in northwestern Florida. Since that time, his primary research efforts have dealt with the late prehistoric and historic period Apalachee chiefdom and the Spanish missions to the Apalachee. His current research focuses on the articulation of households into larger social formations in West Jefferson and Moundville phases of Alabama and how that affected the development of the Moundville chiefdom.

Cameron B. Wesson is assistant professor of anthropology at the University of Illinois at Chicago. He holds degrees in anthropology and architecture from Auburn University and received his Ph.D. in anthropology from the University of Illinois at Urbana-Champaign. His research interests include household archaeology, architecture, and political economy. His current research addresses the sociopolitical dynamics of Late Woodland and Early Mississippian communities in central Alabama.

Index

Accomacs, 154, 161–62
acculturation, 2–3, 4–5, 24, 27, 52. *See also* culture contact
acorns, 24, 36. *See also* subsistence
Adair, James, 107
agency, 4, 7–8, 111–14, 143–44, 166–69, 195–96
agriculture: English descriptions, 16–17; European introduced plants 13; gardens and fields 24; maize, 12, 36, 194; Native American practices, 7, 16, 24, 29–30, 39–40, 42–43, 49, 52, 59. *See also* plants; subsistence
Alabama, 22, 70, 84, 90, 92, 96, 99, 103, 110–11, 117–18, 187
Algonkians, 16–17, 153
Amelia Island, 47
American Bottom, 174
Aminoya, 134
Angelina River, 53, 59
Annales school, 32
Anunciacion, Fray Domingo de la, 91–92
Apache, 63, 65
Apalachee, 28, 46, 135, 139, 142–53; ballgame, 148–50, 152; burials 147–49; compared to the Powhatan 163–69; decline in elite power 152; elites 149–51; elite political strategies 150–51; legitimacy of elites 150, 151; location 145; material symbols of elites 149, 150; Missionization 145, 147, 152; Mississippian traits 145, 163; sociopolitical organization 147–48, 151; warfare 148
Apalachicola River, 147

Appalachian region, 18, 67–68, 70–76, 78, 85–87, 90, 92, 95, 100–101, 107, 175
archaeobotany, 22–26
archaeological record, 35, 48, 60, 143, 171; biases 33, 44–45; inadequacies, 1, 33
archaeology 13, 31–33; ecological questions 14–15; historical archaeology, 1–6, 32; historical-processual perspective, 174, 184, 196; post-processualism, 7, 8, 32; prehistoric archaeology, 1–6, 13; problems of interpretation 14; processualism, 6, 8, 11, 32, 171; southeastern archaeology, 6, 7, 8, 11, 175; theory, 1–2, 5–6, 170
Archaic period, 43
architecture: domestic, 10, 70, 72, 157; public, 54, 145, 175. *See also* houses; households
Arkansas, 50, 60, 171, 190
Arkansas River, 50, 52
arthritis, 61. *See also* disease
Atasi phase, 96, 119, 120
Atlantic Coast, 26, 32–33, 35, 38–39, 41–43, 45–46, 157, 163
Ayllón, Lucas Vasquez de, 39, 40, 46; Ayllon colony 41, 46; expedition 45

ballgame, 148–50, 152
Bartram, William, 9, 10, 21, 83–85; comments on architecture 76–77, 103; comments on Creek architecture 101, 103; comments on trade 81–82; contributions to Appalachian summit archae-

ology 85–87; journal 73–75, 86–87; travels 67–73
Beverley, Robert, 29
Biedema, J., 45, 91, 92
Big Cypress Bayou, 54, 59
bioarchaeology, 60–61. *See also* disease; epidemic disease bison, 49, 63
Bland, Edward, 19
Blue Ridge Mountains, 155
Broad River, 70, 73
Bry, Theodore de, 16
Byrd, William, 17, 25–26

Caddo, 49–66, 192; burials 54, 58–59; burial goods 57–58; ceramics 59; culture change 9; disease 60–61, 65; Guasco province 59, 63; Hasinai 53, 59, 62–63; health 61; households 81; Kadohadacho 54, 62; mortuary practices 57; mounds 62–63; Nabedache 62, 65; Naguatex province 49, 63; rituals 86; religion 58, 61–62, 65; settlements 50–51, 53; sociopolitics 61–62, 65; trade 59–60, 63–65; trails 62–63; Upper Nasoni 57
Cahokia, 192, 195
Canadian River, 60
caries, 44. *See also* disease
Carolina Piedmont, 17
Casqui, 171, 175–76, 182, 186
Catawba, 92
Catawba River, 18
Catesby, Mark, 17
Catholicism, 27. *See also* missionization
Charlesfort, 40, 42
Charlestown, 17, 70
Chattahoochee River, 73, 80, 129, 147
Chattooga River, 70
Chattooga site, 85
Cherokee, 21, 67, 70–87, 92, 107, 180; architecture, 72, 73. 76–78, 79–80, 85–86, 90, 103, 105, 107, 108; ballgame, 78; comparisons with the Creek, 84, 124; Echoe, 74; Lower towns, 86; Middle towns, 75, 82, 86; mounds, 78; movements, 75–76; Nequassee, 74; Nucasse, 74; Overhill towns, 72–73,

79, 82, 86, 105; relations with French, 83; rituals, 77–79, 82–83; town names, 74; trade, 80–82, 86; Valley towns, 82; warriors, 139–40; Whatoga 74
Chesapeake Bay, 153, 163
Chesapeake Indians, 155, 156
Chickahominys, 155, 163
Chickasaw, 63, 107; war camp description 140
Chicken, George, 79, 81
Chicora, 39, 40
chiefdoms, 38, 40, 49–50, 51, 64, 67, 114, 126, 129, 140, 153, 156
chiefs, 36, 123–24; burials, 157; competition among, 126, 129; decline in power, 135, 152; houses, 85, 156–57; inheritance of social position, 129; power strategies, 129–31, 140; roles in warfare, 128, 130, 135–36, 140–41
Choctaws, 137
Chota, 85, 103, 107
Cofitachequi, 45–46
colonialism, 7, 35
colonization, 10, 15, 18, 40–41, 52; English colonies, 18; French colonies, 19
Columbus, Christopher, 2, 27
Comanche, 65
Coosa, 46, 175, 187
Coosa River, 70, 129
Coosawattee River, 187
copper, 147, 149–50, 155, 158–59, 161–63. *See also* trade
council houses, 85, 86. *See also* architecture
Couper Field site, 43
Cowee, 70–73, 75–76, 79–80, 82
Cowee Mountains, 71, 76
Coweeta Creek site, 74–75, 77–78, 80, 84–86, 92, 99
cowpeas, 27, 29. *See also* agriculture; plants
Creek, 21, 25, 27, 37, 67, 70, 73, 75–76, 84, 92, 107, 117, 118, 121, 123; architecture, 90, 101, 103, 108, 111, 117; burials, 118–19; comparison with Cherokee, 84; households, 117–18, 120, 122; warriors, 139
Crenshaw site, 192
Crook, R., 36–39, 41

Crowley's Ridge, 181
cucurbits, 24, 27. *See also* plants; subsistence
cultural anthropology, 6
cultural chronology, 6, 7
culture: production of 143
culture contact 2–3, 9–12, 47, 52, 61; archaeological study of, 5; impacts on Native Americans, 1–3, 7–8, 11, 110, 113–14, 142, 144, 170
culture history, 2, 4–8, 11, 170, 172–74; criticisms of, 6, 170
culture process, 6
Cuming, Alexander, 79

Dallas phase, 100
Dartmouth, 73
DeBrahm, 103
de Luna, Tristan expedition, 15, 38, 91
Deshazo site, 53
de Soto, Hernando, 16, 134; chronicles, 16, 49, 86–87, 91, 130, 176; expedition 12, 15, 45–46, 62–64, 145, 152, 175–77, 182
deer, 24, 36, 45, 179, 181, 186–87, 194
deerskin trade, 76, 80–81, 108, 138. *See also* trade
Deetz, James, 6
depopulation, 35, 45–46, 60, 112, 114, 123–24, 136, 138, 171
diet, 44
Direct Historical Approach, 4, 6, 7, 33
disease, 33–34, 39, 45–47, 52, 60–61, 65, 76, 111, 121, 123, 128–29, 137, 171. *See also* epidemic disease
Dobyns, Henry, 45
documentary record. *See* historical documents
domestic architecture. *See* houses
drought, 42–43
du Pratz, Le Page, 19, 24, 27–28

Echoee, 81
ecology, 12, 18–20, 26, 28, 30–31; adaptability of introduced species, 28–29; data 13, 23; descriptions, 17–20, 25–26; landscape modification through fire, 17, 24; pollen and phytoliths, 22–23; protohistoric change, 9, 12, 15, 18–19, 24–31, 85; terminology 20–21; weeds, 25–26
elites: architecture, 157; burials, 147, 157; food storage 121–22, 186; legitimacy 150–51; material symbols 149, 150; political strategies 150–51; social roles 10, 41, 57, 110–11, 115, 122–23, 126, 145
Elvas, Gentleman of, 16, 45, 49, 176–77
endemic treponematosis 61. *See also* disease; endemic disease
English: documents, 16–18, 82–83, 101; exploration, 40; propaganda, 18; settlement, 68
epidemic disease, 12–13, 33–34, 45–47, 60–61, 65, 76, 112, 121, 128, 137, 171; mortuary evidence, 46–47. *See also* disease
Estatoe phase, 75
estuaries, 41
ethnic Identity, 1, 7. *See also* social identity
ethnographic analogy: uses in archaeology, 6, 7
ethnohistory, 5, 14, 32–33, 36–37, 42, 52, 68, 75, 83; definition, 174–75
ethnohistoric sources. *See* historical documents
ethnobotany, 42–44. *See also* plants
Etowah, 149, 151
European trade goods, 47, 74. *See also* trade
evolutionism, 8, 32, 171–72, 173; criticisms, 172–73
exploration, 10; English exploration 16–19; French exploration 19–20; Spanish exploration, 15–16

famine, 39, 40. *See also* plants; subsistence
farming, 25, 60. *See also* plants; subsistence
fauna, 22, 186–87, 190, 192
fine-screening, 44. *See also* ethnobotany
fire, 17, 24
fish, 36, 38–39, 42, 176, 179–80, 187, 190, 192, 195; use in mortuary rituals, 180
Florida, 17, 33, 40, 42, 70
Flotation, 43–45, 192

266 / Index

Fort Caroline, 33, 36–37, 40
fortification, 63
Fort James, 73
Franciscans, 34, 145, 152. See also missionization
Fredricks site, 27
French: colonization, 33, 40–42; documents, 19, 37, 38–39, 40–41, 63, 132; exploration, 32, 40, 128, 130; food stress, 38
fruit, 24. See also plants
Fusihatchee site, 22, 25, 27, 92, 95, 100, 103

Galloway, Patricia, 38, 45–46
Georgia, 27, 33, 42, 70–71, 79, 84, 90, 92, 187
Giddens, Anthony, 113
gift-giving, 171, 175–81
Graham-White site, 22, 25
Great Lakes region, 155
Guale, 33, 35–40, 42–44
Gulf Coast region, 19, 26, 36, 38, 135, 145
guns, 63, 137, 138. See also trade; warfare

Harriot, Thomas, 16–17
Harris Neck site, 42
Hawkins, John, 40–41
Hayti Bypass site, 190
hegemony, 130–31, 173
Henige, David, 112
herbs, 26
Hickory Ground site, 103
hickory nuts, 24, 36
historical anthropology, 7, 175
historical documents, 1–5, 13–16, 35, 48, 52, 86, 110; analysis, 3–4; archaeological uses, 4; biases, 4, 9, 33, 41; ecological implications, 15–20, 24; interpretation, 1, 14, 15, 16–17, 33, 45–46, 83
historiography, 7, 14, 35, 41
history, 6, 8–9, 14, 31, 32–33, 39, 62
Hiwassee River, 80, 99
Hoffman, Paul, 39, 41, 46
Hoithlewalli site, 103
horses, 63
households, 53, 81, 117, 118, 119–20;

food storage, 121–22; social competition, 123–24
houses, 91, 111; burials, 98, 100, 107; changes, 107–09; circular structures, 92–93; descriptions, 90; "hot" houses, 103–04; seasonally-specific structures, 91, 95–96, 98, 100, 103, 107, 120; square structures, 92, 95–96; subterranean structures, 91, 95–96
Hudson, Charles, 79
Hunting, 24, 59, 63

Iberville, Pierre Le Moyne d', 19–20, 21, 28
identity. See social identity
ideology, 8, 124–25, 128, 134, 136, 171, 194
Indian Field site, 43
Indian Point site, 158
infant mortality, 61. See also disease; epidemic disease
Irene site 35, 42–44, 47, 159
iron deficiency anemia 61. See also disease; epidemic disease

James River, 153, 155
Jamestown, 153
Jesuits, 33, 35–39, 42. See also missionization
Joe Clark site, 53
Jones, G. D., 37–38
Josselyn, John, 26

Kadohadacho, 54, 62
Kalm, Peter, 29
Keowee, 73, 79
Keowee River, 70, 75–76, 86
Kings Bay, 42
King site, 91, 95, 99, 107–08
Knappenberger site, 190
Knight, Vernon James, Jr., 112
Koasati, 92

Lake Jackson site, 145, 147–52
Lamar, 91
Larson, Lewis, 35–36
La Salle expedition, 52
Laudonnière, René, 35–37, 40–41, 45
Lawson, John, 17–18, 21, 26, 28–29

Leak site, 91
Lederer, John, 18–19
Legumes, 22, 24, 27, 30
Le Moyne, Jacques, 40
Leon, Alonso de, 53–54
Levaseur, Charles, 137
Lightfoot, Kent, 143
Lilbourn site, 190
linguistics, 84–85
Little Egypt site, 91, 187
Little River, 57
Little Tennessee River, 22, 71, 73–76, 79–81, 86, 99
Longe, Alexander, 78
Louisiana, 27, 50, 70
Lubbub Creek site, 187

maize, 18, 24, 35, 39, 43–44, 52, 61, 163, 179, 181, 185–86. See also agriculture; plants; subsistence
marine resources, 43
Marquette and Joliet, 138
Martyr, Peter, 39, 40
McLelland site, 53
Meeting House Fields site, 42
Mialoquo, 85
Middle Nodena site, 183
missionaries, 83
missions, 27, 28, 34–35, 145, 147, 152
missionization, 7, 15, 33–34, 35, 37, 65
Mississippi, 70, 187
Mississippian culture, 51–52, 61, 67, 85; architecture, 92; definition, 174. See also warfare.
Mississippian polities: competition among, 129; development and decline, 12, 67; politics, 195–96; towns, 85
Mississippi River, 174, 190, 192
Mississippi Valley, 19, 59, 70, 129, 134, 138, 170–71, 174, 175, 179, 181–82, 187, 190, 194–95
Mobile, 20, 70
mobility, 37
Monacans, 155, 161–63
Moscoso expedition, 62, 64
mounds, 54, 57, 62–63, 70, 73. See also architecture

Moundville, 129, 151, 195
Mouse Creek phase, 100, 107
mulluscs, 36, 42, 44

Nacoochee, 80
Nairne, Thomas, 135, 137, 139–40
Nansemond, 156
Narvaez, Panfilo de, 145
Natchez, 19, 180, 139
Native American Graves Protection and Repatriation Act (NAGPRA), 8, 61
Neches River, 53, 59, 63
Nequassee, 74, 79, 80
New France, 40
New Orleans, 19
North Carolina, 17, 22, 24, 27, 29, 67, 70–71, 73, 75–76, 79, 81–82, 84, 86, 90, 92, 99

Oachita River, 57, 59, 60
Oak forests, 36
Occohannocks, 154, 161–62
Oconee, 70
Oconee River, 92, 95, 99
Oklahoma, 50, 54, 60
Old Estatoe, 71, 76
Opechancanough, 160
Orista, 36, 40
Osage, 59, 63
ossuaries, 158
Oviedo, Gonzalo Fernández de, 39–40
oyster, 36, 42, 44. See also marine resources

Pacaha, 171, 176–77, 182, 186
Paiva, Juan, 150
paleopathology, 44. See also bioarchaology; disease; epidemic disease
Pardo, Juan expedition, 79, 91
Parkin site, 171
Paspahegh, 163
Patawomeck, 156, 159
peach, 21, 27, 28–29, 30, 76. See also agriculture; plants
Peachtree site, 80
Phillips, Phillip, 170, 181
phytoliths, 22–23
Pine Harbor site, 35–36, 47

Piscataway, 1
Plains, 59, 53
plants: economic uses, 23–24; 26–30; European introduced plants, 27–30; food uses, 26; medicinal uses, 25–26; nomenclature, 20–21; storage, 24, 36
political culture, 126, 171, 173, 175, 181, 194–96
political economy, 7, 124, 128, 136, 171–74, 177, 180–81, 194
pollen, 22–23, 44
population nucleation, 127
porotic hyperostosis, 44. See also disease; epidemic disease
Potomac River, 153–54
Potts Tract site, 91
Powhatan, 142–43, 144–45, 153–63; agricultural control by chiefs, 157; burial goods, 158–59; burials, 156, 159, 162; Chief Powhatan, 153, 156, 160–62; chiefdom development, 153–56; comparisons with the Apalachee, 163–69; elites, 153, 156–57; historical documents concerning, 158; houses 156, 157; material symbols of status, 160–62; military roles of elites, 160; mortuary treatment of elites, 157, 159, 162; ossuaries, 158; political legitimization, 155, 160–61; relations with the English, 162–63; relations with the Spanish, 153; religious beliefs, 157–58, 160; social competition, 163; social identity, 160; social organization, 156–57
Prestige goods 114–16, 119, 123, 128, 134, 145, 151–52, 156–59, 177, 180–81, 186
Protohistory: definition, 1, 142; interdisciplinary approaches, 5, 12; previous studies, 2–4; research difficulties, 1, 13–14; theoretical approaches, 8

Rangel, R., 45
Rappahannock River, 153, 154
Red River, 49–50, 52–54, 57, 59, 60–61, 63, 190, 193
Reitz, Elizabeth, 41–42
relocation, 65

Ribault, Jean, 35, 37–38, 40, 41, 45
Rios, Don Domingo Teran de la, 54
Roanoke colony, 16
Rogers, J. Daniel, 113
Romans, Bernard, 21
Ruckers Bottom site, 95, 100

San Augustín, 145
San Luis phase, 147–48, 149–50
San Miguel de Gualdape, 39
San Pedro Creek, 54
Santa Elena, 33–34
Sapelo Sound, 39, 46
Savannah phase, 43–44, 47
Savannah River, 70, 73, 92, 159
seasonality, 24, 32, 43. See also settlement
sedentism, 27, 32, 35–36, 38–39, 42–43. See also settlement
Sedeño, Antonio, 36
Seneca, 70
settlement: Crook's model of settlement movement, 36–37, 43; impacts of European settlements, 25–27; Native American, 18, 33–34, 36, 41–43, 45, 156
Shell 154, 158–59, 161–62; gorgets, 159
Shenandoah Valley, 18
Shine II phase, 119
slavery, 40, 63, 76, 137–39
Smith, John, 18, 156
Smith, Marvin, 111
social complexity, 7, 10, 39, 45, 61, 63, 114, 116, 123, 129, 148, 153–54, 156
social identity, 143–44; agency, 166–69; Apalachee elite, 148–50; European effects upon, 168–69; importance of discourse in the development of, 144, 161; material goods, 161; Powhatan, 157–61
sociopolitics 4–7, 10–11, 16, 110–11, 127, 135, 171–72, 177; chiefly cycling, 126–27; decline, 111–12, 123–25, 135–36, 151–52, 178; rebellion, 130, 151
Soule, William Stinson, 54
South Carolina, 17, 18, 70, 75, 81, 90, 92
South Edisto River, 40
Southeastern Ceremonial Complex, 47, 52
South Santee River, 46
Spanish: colonization, 33, 39–40, 46, 152;

documents, 15, 17, 37, 39–41, 63, 132; exploration, 32, 40, 49, 59, 68, 129, 130, 145, 153; food, 16; impacts on Native Americans, 177; missions, 27, 28, 33–34, 35–36, 52, 65, 145, 147; political relations with the Cherokee, 83
stable isotope analysis, 43–45
St. Augustine, 33–34, 152
St. Catherines Island, 43, 47
St. Domingue, 20
St. Francis River, 181
St. Johns phase, 47
St. Johns River, 36, 40, 43
St. Marys region, 42
St. Simon Island, 43
strawberries 24
subsistence, 13, 21–23, 26, 28, 32–35, 41–43, 45, 171; economy, 173, 175, 190, 192, 196; effects of exchange and trade, 13; importance of Southeastern data, 23; protohistoric change, 13, 42; stresses, 36
Swan, Caleb 103
Swanton, John R., 62
Swift Creek culture, 78
symbolic capital, 115–16, 177–81

Talbot, William, 18
Tallahassee, 147
Tallapoosa phase, 119, 120
Tallapoosa River, 70, 73, 92, 103, 121, 129
Tanasee site, 79, 103, 107
Taylor, Walter, 6
taxonomy, 20–21
Tennessee, 79, 82, 86, 90, 92, 99
Tennesse River Valley, 70
Texas, 50
Timberlake, Henry, 79, 103
Timucua, 33, 35–37, 39–40, 42, 44
Titus Phase, 54, 57–59
Tombigbee River, 187
Tonti, 139
Toqua site, 85–86, 98, 100
Townson site, 83
Trade, 17, 18. 20, 27–28, 38, 59–60, 63–65, 79–80, 82, 86, 124; deerskin trade, 70, 80–81, 108, 138; Native American culture change, 112–13, 123, 136; trade goods, 17, 27, 47, 74, 111, 114–15, 122, 136, 138, 158, 182
transhumance, 42–43
Trobriand Islands, 179
Tuckasegee River, 71, 80
Tuckasegee site, 83
Tugalo phase, 75
Tugalo River, 80
Tukabatchee site, 96
turkey 45

Upper Nodena site, 171, 182, 183–86, 187, 190, 194–95
Upper Saratown site, 27

Vega, Garcilaso de la, 45
Virginia, 17–19, 22, 24, 26, 29, 33, 42, 153, 155–56, 159, 166–67

warfare, 10, 126, 186; Apalachee, 148; architectural evidence, 127, 131–32; between Native Americans and Europeans, 134; bow and arrow, 127, 132; captives 137–38; coordination by chiefs, 129–30, 132–33, 134; defensive tactics, 130; demographic changes resulting from warfare, 138–39; effects of European contacts 127, 134–39, 141; European descriptions, 130, 132–33; factors leading to warfare, 135; guns, 137; hegemonic psychological tactics, 130–31; means of chiefly competition, 128–31; means of social advancement, 136, 138–40; militias, 133; Mississippian warfare, 126–29, 134, 141; mortality rates, 128; offensive tactics, 127, 129–30, 131–32, 136; protohistoric warfare, 129–41; raiding, 127; rituals, 138; war chiefs, 135–36; war clubs, 128, 132; war councils, 133–34, 140–41; warfare cults, 133–34, 140
Warren Wilson site, 80, 100
Washita River, 60
watermelon, 21, 27, 29, 30. *See also* agriculture; plants
weeds, 24–26. *See also* plants

Werowocomoco, 155
Westos, 138
Whatoga, 74, 77
White, John, 16
White River, 181
Wichita, 59, 65
Winyah Bay, 46

Woodland period, 147, 156, 158–60, 163, 190, 192

Yarborough site, 187
York River, 155, 163

zooarchaeology, 41–44